COAST TO COAST

BY AUTOMOBILE

COAST TO COAST

For ourselves, give us a good horse.

—*Wyoming Press* of Evanston (1906)

Your true motorist likes to settle down behind the wheel, knowing that his motor is running smoothly, and head away over new roads amid new surroundings, away from every-day places and things that have grown hum-drum through constant association.

—*The Complete Official Road Guide of the Lincoln Highway* (1916)

BY AUTOMOBILE

The Pioneering Trips, 1899–1908

Curt McConnell

STANFORD UNIVERSITY PRESS

Stanford, California 2000

Stanford University Press
Stanford, California

© 2000 by the Board of Trustees of the
Leland Stanford Junior University

Printed in the United States of America on acid-free, archival-quality paper

Original printing 2000

Last figure below indicates year of this printing:
09   08   07   06   05   04   03   02   01   00

Designed by Mark Ong
Typeset by Side By Side Studios and James P. Brommer
in 12/16 Granjon with Fenice display

This book is dedicated to my father,

Campbell R. McConnell,

and my mother,

Marilyn Knight McConnell,

who gave me the road map

for the journeys I've taken.

CONTENTS

ACKNOWLEDGMENTS

THOUGH I CONDUCTED the bulk of the research for this book, a great many others assisted. Specifically, I wrote hundreds of letters asking questions large and small, and seeking photographs, biographical information, and other details.

Besides reference librarians—who fielded a great many of my questions—others who assisted me included archivists, curators, historians, college and university alumni officers, and experts in a particular make of auto. Many of these people were helpful far above and beyond the call of duty. I wish I had room here to thank each person by name.

In other instances, my debt of gratitude is so great that I must name names. For their help in editing drafts, I'd like to thank my father, Campbell R. McConnell, and my sisters, Lauren McConnell Davis and Beth McConnell. My special thanks go to Marilyn McConnell, Aiyana and Mariah McConnell-Beepath, Ben and Holly Davis, Stephen and Audrey Broll, and Bonnie Helmink.

For general research assistance or help with specific questions on a number of chapters, I gratefully acknowledge the contributions of David L. Cole, Ralph Dunwoodie, Beverly Rae Kimes, David Smith, and Karl S. Zahm, as well as Kim Miller of the Antique Automobile Club of America's Library & Research Center, Hershey, Pennsylvania; Peggy Dusman, Dan Kirchner, and Karen Prymak of the American Automobile Manufacturers Association, Detroit; Louis G. Helverson, Stuart McDougall, and Bob Rubenstein of the Automobile Reference Collection, Free Library of Philadelphia; Serena Gomez and Mark Patrick of the National Automotive History Collection, Detroit Public Library, and Tom Sherry, the collection's contract photographer; Roger White of the Transportation Division, Smithsonian Institution, Washington, D.C.; and the staffs of Bennett Martin Public Library, Lincoln, Nebraska, and Love Library, University of Nebraska–Lincoln.

Though I reviewed my letters and notes to prepare the following list, I'm sure I'm overlooking someone. So let me say only that *among* those who made vital contributions to specific chapters are these helpful souls:

Chapter 1, 1899 National Duryea and 1901 Winton: Roger Allison, David L. Cole, Carl F. W. Larson, Terry Martin, Richard P. Scharchburg, Marilyn Vogt, and Jim Winton.

Chapter 2, 1903 Winton: Marilyn Vogt and Jim Winton.

Chapter 3, 1903 Packard: Terry Martin.

Chapter 4, 1903 Oldsmobile: Helen J. Earley and James R. Walkinshaw, Oldsmobile History Center, Lansing, Michigan; and Bette Roberts, Mattapoisett (Mass.) Historical Society.

Chapter 5, 1904 Franklin: Peter Kunan, William Lewis, and Sinclair Powell.

Chapter 6, 1906 Franklin: Peter Kunan, William Lewis, Sinclair Powell, and George Tuck.

Finally, I would like to thank the people who assisted me in my seemingly never-ending search for photos. A full list of photo sources appears in the Illustration Credits section, page 343, since abbreviations are used in captions throughout this book to avoid unnecessary clutter.

C.M.

PREFACE

As I compiled a war chest of articles, ads, and other material for each chapter of *Coast to Coast by Automobile*, I discovered many factual errors in the available sources, as well as conflicting versions of specific events. As a case in point, when a Franklin auto crashed one night in eastern Ohio while setting a 1906 speed record, press accounts clashed on all of the basic details: the cause, the location, the driver, the passengers, the injuries, and the damage to the car. Thus, as I researched and wrote this book, I assumed the wary posture of a detective sifting through evidence. I have used my best judgment in deciding what to keep and what to throw away, preferring to point out discrepancies rather than ignore them.

I have consulted many city directories and local "who's who" books so as to provide correct spellings and biographical details for drivers and other important participants. Motorists who traveled without maps frequently misspelled town names. In addition, transcontinental drivers frequently referred to towns or sites that have since disappeared—if not in reality, then at least from modern road maps. To correctly spell and place such landmarks, I collected road maps dating from 1910 to the 1940s. Numerous state libraries and historical societies have helped me in this task.

Some trip accounts have come directly from articles written by the drivers themselves or from factory advertising, in-house magazines, or special booklets that were written to herald yet another transcontinental conquest. Although incomplete, Carey S. Bliss's *Autos Across America: A Bibliography of Transcontinental Automobile Travel, 1903–1940* (Austin, Texas: Jenkins & Reese, 1982), helped me identify some of these books and booklets. To write brief histories of the automakers that sponsored many of the transcontinental treks detailed in this book, I often consulted Beverly Rae Kimes and Henry Austin Clark, Jr., *Standard Catalog of American Cars, 1805–1942*, 2d ed. (Iola, Wis.: Krause Publications, 1989).

A few writers before me have attempted to describe some of the journeys documented in *Coast to Coast by Automobile*. These have often appeared as articles in old-car magazines. With rare exceptions, these writers have picked up and repeated flawed information, either by relying on a single, suspect source—such as a factory publicity booklet that is short on facts but long on hyperbole—or by relying on a handful of auto-journal articles that are likewise full of errors and omissions.

I have tried to avoid such pitfalls by unearthing as much new information as possible. I began my task with a thorough scouring of the automobile journals. I also searched general-circulation magazines, large national newspapers published in New York, San Francisco, and Los Angeles (where the transcontinental trips invariably began or ended), and smaller daily and weekly newspapers all along the routes the drivers followed.

For the chapter about the first family transcontinental trip, I discovered long-forgotten letters that Jacob M. Murdock had written to his hometown paper, the *Johnstown (Pa.) Daily Tribune*, letters that shed new light on old events. Similarly, the articles Charles B. Shanks wrote for the *Cleveland Plain Dealer* about the coast-to-coast trip he attempted with Alexander Winton in 1901 are much more detailed than the abbreviated auto-journal accounts.

In short, I have found a wealth of new information, corrected errors made by earlier writers, meticulously created itineraries where none previously existed, located rare and revealing photographs, and in every way possible sought to flesh out events of long ago, all to answer the basic and neglected question: "What was it like to drive across the continent when such a trip bore an unmistakable resemblance to an expedition?"

What follows is a brief explanation of the various styles and conventions I have adopted in this book:

Elapsed time, running time, and calendar days: Elapsed time is the total length of time it took to travel between coasts. Running time is the actual time spent driving, and excludes stops for sleep, repairs, and the like. In reality, few drivers kept detailed records of their daily running time in hours and minutes. And, as transcontinentalist Lester L. Whitman so aptly warned, "Nothing but the actual performance—the elapsed time from start to finish—should be considered." All the same, some drivers and more automakers liked to boast about achieving low running times, which were customarily expressed in hours instead of days.

As a check against such unsubstantiated figures, when I had enough information to do so, I calculated running times based on calendar days. I have counted every day in which a car made forward progress—whether towed by horses or under its own power—as one day of its total running time. Thus, if a coast-to-coast trip took ten calendar days, and if during this time the car was idle for two entire days, its elapsed time would be ten days and its running time would be eight days. Be aware that "calendar days" do not always equal "elapsed days"! Dr. H. Nelson Jackson's elapsed time of 63 days, 12 hours, 30 minutes, for example, actually represents 65 calendar days.

Mileage: If you scoff in disbelief when reading that a pioneer motorist traveled 69 miles between two cities that you know are only 51 miles apart, consider this: old mileages are not the same as new mileages. Early roads often zigzagged along section lines. New highways follow diagonals. As roadbuilders found more direct paths over, around, or through obstacles, mileages declined. Thus, the Lincoln Highway spanned 3,389 miles in 1913 but only 3,142 miles in 1924. Where reported mileages sounded extreme, I have checked them against old highway maps and commented on any discrepancies.

Newspaper names: I have faithfully reproduced the names of newspapers as they were used at the time. For example, in the early 1900s it *was* the *Chicago Daily Tribune* (now simply the *Chicago Tribune*). Following the lead of the Associated Press, I have used newspaper style when necessary to clearly identify the newspaper in question, particularly in endnotes: *Albany (N.Y.) Times-Herald* and *Laramie (Wyo.) Boomerang*.

Place names: A surprising number of changes have occurred in place names or spellings since the first autos crossed America. Since very few people own 1915 road maps, I have tended to use the newer names, except in direct quotations. Thus, it's not Boise City but Boise, Idaho; not Edwards Post Office but Edwards, Colorado; not Pittsburg (the old spelling) but Pittsburgh.

For this book, which is filled with place names, I have decided that many larger U.S. cities are familiar enough to stand alone without a state reference. These cities include Boston, Chicago, Cincinnati, Cleveland, Denver, Detroit, Indianapolis, Los Angeles, New York City, Philadelphia, Pittsburgh, St. Louis, Salt Lake City, San Diego, San Francisco, and Seattle.

Quotations: Spellings and terminology were in flux when the automobile was new. Reporters had their choice of "gasolene" or "gasoline," "mechanician" or "mechanic," "carburettor" or "carburetor." Fenders were often "mud guards," and transmissions "change-speed gears." No one referred to a head-on collision: it was a head-end collision.

At the turn of the twentieth century, newspapers also followed their own distinct styles of spelling and punctuating. Many journalists disdained using the lowly hyphen, even in compound modifiers, writing "coast to coast trip" when they surely meant "coast-to-coast trip." Others championed shortened versions of such words as "though" ("tho") and "through" ("thru"). Another journalistic convention was to use lowercase letters for generic words in proper nouns: Missouri river, New York city, Elm street, and so on. The same was true with many trade names: instead of "Kodak cameras," it was often just "kodaks."

Today, some standard spellings have evolved, but in the early 1900s it was evidently a toss-up between "enquire" and "inquire," "trans-continental" and "transcontinental," "bowlder" and "boulder." Other spellings have changed completely: "broncho" has become "bronco," while "cañon" has become "canyon." Handling such idiosyncrasies as I might a fragile, yellowed newspaper clipping, I have decided that any attempt to standardize this colorful mix of spellings and punctuation would only interpose a filter between the past and present. Within quotations, therefore, you will see the same words, expressions, and spellings that newspaper and auto-journal readers of the day encountered.

Time zones: In 1883, U.S. railroads, which a decade earlier had been using more than fifty different times, settled upon the four standard time zones we know today as Pacific, Mountain, Central, and Eastern. The exact boundaries for each of these time zones have changed often since 1883, but this is largely irrelevant for our purposes. What *is* important is that record-setting drivers compensated for the changes in local time by adding or subtracting three hours from their coast-to-coast elapsed times. Where they have neglected to do so, I have adjusted the time for them.

Finally, a word about citations. Some readers like lots of footnotes; other readers decry "footnote clutter." As a compromise, I have often cited the general source in the text itself, providing notes in the back of the book in the case of direct quotations and for more extensive information. With rare exceptions, newspaper citations include both page and column numbers.

COAST TO COAST
BY AUTOMOBILE

INTRODUCTION

*C*oast to Coast by Automobile explores the pioneer period of record-setting, coast-to-coast automobile trips. This period began in 1899 with the first attempt to cross the continent, and ended in 1908 when the first family motored across America. Occurring over a ten-year span, these trips both reflected and spurred the development of the American automobile.

The first serious, though unsuccessful, attempts to cross the continent by auto occurred in 1899 and 1901. Then, in 1903, driving a Winton, Dr. H. Nelson Jackson and Sewall K. Crocker became the first persons to drive across the country. Two other cars repeated the feat a few weeks later. Although these and the coast-to-coast trips that followed were primarily advertising stunts, they were widely reported and offered valuable data about automobiles and roads. As the deluge of articles in the popular press indicates, Americans closely followed such exploits and thereby soon came to appreciate the automobile's utility.

The crude automobiles of the early pioneer period were as novel as the very idea of traveling long distances in one. Drivers were mainly mechanics, professional chauffeurs, or others connected with the auto industry. The cars broke down often, as reflected in the 1903 transcontinental crossing times (rounded to the nearest day) of sixty-four days, sixty-two days, and seventy-three days.

Two spectacular coast-to-coast speed runs convincingly proved the automobile's superiority to the horse and hinted at greater speeds to come. First, Lester L. Whitman

1

and C. S. Carris cut the transcontinental speed record to thirty-three days in 1904. Joined by other drivers in 1906, they more than halved their previous record by driving coast to coast in fifteen days. (By 1916, autos were zooming across the continent in just five days, rivaling railroad time.)

The 1904 and 1906 record-setting trips prompted a flurry of editorials hailing the arrival of a new era in transportation. According to *Motor World*, Whitman's fifteen-day speed run did for motoring what the 1869 completion of the transcontinental railroad did for railroading. Whereas the first tentative transcontinental autos had traveled no faster than a bicycle, "successive trials have cut days at a time off the record, finally culminating in Whitman's marvellous dash," observed *Motor World*. "Nothing demonstrates so strikingly the phenomenal development of the automobile as his reduction of the performance of three years ago by more than two thirds. It is indeed a far cry from the 64-day trip of Dr. Jackson in 1903."[1]

A crossing time of little more than two weeks was particularly impressive given the primitive trails that served as highways in the United States. By 1907, highway mapper A. L. Westgard had observed firsthand what he called

> the real nature of the country west of Chicago—a land of floods at all seasons of the year, of deserts and sagebrush plains, and deep prairie roads. The vast stretch of country between the Rocky mountains and the Sierra Nevadas is a country with stiff climbs and steep descents in succession. Quicksands seem to be one of the terrors of the routes. . . . The majority of roads in the Middle and Eastern States, especially in wet weather, are a difficult problem to tackle and are apt to be quite as serious a bar to comfort, speed and time-records as any physical difficulties encountered in the West.[2]

Despite such roads, the transcontinental trips made from 1903 to 1908 forcefully demonstrated that the automobile had produced what Ralph C. Epstein termed "An Epoch in Transportation." Epstein was one of the first researchers to assess the economic impact of the auto industry. Writing in 1928, he observed: "The motor car satisfies the desire not merely for transportation, but for transportation that is both *swift* and *individualized*. . . . It gives 'a quick, immediate, individual transportation service' with sufficient speed to reduce distances amazingly and to make possible a great multitude of activities which could not otherwise readily take place."[3]

Seeing is believing, and because of the early coast-to-coast trips, many Americans saw an automobile for the first time. News of Jackson's approach to Lakeview, Oregon, in 1903, had "every man, woman and child in Lakeview on the keen edge of expectancy," according to the *Lakeview Herald*. "The town had the gala appearance of a holiday as the streets were thronged with crowds of eager people, all craning their necks for the first sign of the first automobile ever seen in this part of the State."[4]

Within a few years, however, the popular press began referring to the automobile not as a novelty but as a necessity. Thus, James J. Flink, author of *America Adopts the Automobile, 1895–1910*, could claim that "the period of trial was definitely over for the motor vehicle in the United States by 1906."[5] Nevertheless, long-distance auto trips remained the purview of expert drivers until 1908, when Jacob M. Murdock became the first person to drive coast to coast with his family on board. This trip also represented the first automobile crossing by women and children. Just as Murdock's trip ended the Pioneer Period of transcontinental motoring, so this book concludes with a chapter about Murdock.

Curiously, historians have largely ignored the transcontinental trips, preferring instead to look at how racing, the Glidden Tour reliability runs, hill climbs, economy contests, and other highly regulated events stirred public interest in the automobile. But if historians have been reluctant to explore the notion that coast-to-coast trips helped sell Americans on the automobile, they have at least acknowledged the truth of the argument. For instance, Flink declares that "it was the long-distance reliability run that most excited the average person's imagination about the romance of motoring."[6] What were transcontinental crossings but long-distance reliability runs on a grand scale? Likewise, in his *American Automobile: A Brief History*, John B. Rae contends that, even more than racing, "of greater importance in getting the motor vehicle accepted were demonstrations of ability to cover long distances."[7]

The journal *Automobile*, which covered contests of all varieties, even suggested that no test of an auto surpassed the transcontinental journey: "That these tests provide a magnificent demonstration of the strength of a car is undeniable. It would be hard to find any possible test in the world that means more."[8]

Even during the period from 1899 to 1908, many automakers discounted the value of track racing. *Motor Age* expressed this sentiment as early as 1903: "In an industry whose greatest success is founded upon reliability in hard, useful road service, a transcontinental trip over the kind of routes that grace the western section of our country, is of more real value than the winning of a half-dozen pure speed races."[9] Except in the earliest years, race cars were highly modified versions of the automobiles sold to the public. Spectators found racing entertaining, but, as Flink put it, the emphasis on speed made races "more important for their contributions to automotive technology as tests for weaknesses in design than as publicity for the motorcar."[10]

The annual Glidden Tours, organized by the American Automobile Association beginning in 1905, "were intended to demonstrate the reliability of the automobile as a means of travel," according to Rae. Drivers scored well by traveling a route within a specified time limit, but lost points for making repairs. Rules limited entrants to owners driving only stock autos. But such rules were easy enough to circumvent, and the Glidden Tours were soon dominated by professional drivers, including C. S. "Clean Score" Carris, who helped set transcontinental speed records in 1904 and 1906. Furthermore, winning the Glidden "came to carry so much prestige that automobile firms took to entering specially built cars, so that the tours lost their real purpose and were finally discontinued in 1914."[11]

Winning a hill climb depended more upon gear ratios and driving skill than upon an automobile's design, construction, and reliability. Lax rules in most economy contests rendered the results meaningless to ordinary drivers. For instance, until 1924 the Yosemite Economy Run—the best-known annual economy contest of the era—allowed entrants to overinflate their tires and coast with their engines shut off.[12] In short, the results of regulated events—racing, Glidden Tours, hill climbs, and economy contests—could not and did not suggest what automobile ownership would mean to the ordinary Americans who constituted the mass market.

Why have historians failed to examine the impact of transcontinental trips in demonstrating the practicality and usefulness of the automobile? The main reason is the great time and effort that is required to compile accurate accounts of these coast-to-coast trips. The work is daunting for even a single trip, much less several. One must collect and study accounts in automobile journals, but one must also seek the reflections of a more accurate mirror of public opinion—daily and weekly newspapers. Although such digging yields rich treasures, it is extremely time-consuming.

Thus, historians, if they have considered transcontinental runs at all, typically have done so only in passing, and they often have erred in reporting even the most basic factual details. In *The American Automobile: A Centenary, 1893–1993*, Nick Georgano's brief sketch of several transcontinental treks contains numerous factual errors of this sort. For example, in discussing the 1909 New York–Seattle race (a crossing that falls outside the scope of this book), he names the wrong contestant as the winner![13] And so it goes.

In those rare instances when writers have attempted to examine the lessons or implications of such journeys, they have drawn inaccurate conclusions based on faulty or insufficient information. Flink, for example, briefly mentions the first three successful coast-to-coast crossings, which all took place in 1903. In the first of these, Dr. H. Nelson Jackson and Sewall K. Crocker "traveled from San Francisco to New York City in a new Winton in sixty-three days." A Packard and an Oldsmobile duplicated the Winton's feat later that summer. Thus, Flink concludes, "the reliability of the moderately priced light car was now established in the mind of the public."[14] Actually, Jackson had purchased a secondhand Winton for his expedition with Crocker. And press coverage of the three coast-to-coast trips of 1903 clearly indicates the opposite of what Flink concludes: that in traveling on America's frightfully bad roads, early automobiles were notoriously *un*reliable. The automobile had quickly proven its utility, as W. E. Scarritt, president of the Automobile Club of America, declared in 1904, but "the question of reliability is the one remaining factor that disturbs us all."[15] Crocker and Jackson, for instance, spent nineteen days of their sixty-three-day journey either repairing their Winton or waiting for parts to arrive. Both connecting rods in their 2-cylinder engine came apart: one punched a hole in the crankcase; the other wrapped itself around the crankshaft.

The second transcontinental car, a Packard driven by Tom Fetch, exhibited weaknesses in such critical parts as axles, springs, and steering linkages. Fortunately, the drivers of the third car to cross America were employed as mechanics. During twelve full days lost to breakdowns and repairs, Eugene I. Hammond and Lester L. Whitman replaced fifty parts or sets of parts to keep their Oldsmobile mobile.

The three 1903 crossings hinted at possibilities. They demonstrated what an automobile *could* do if money and time were limitless, and if the driver-mechanics were resourceful, patient, determined, and brutishly strong. As for reliability, early transcontinental trips suggested that driving an automobile over long distances was out of the question for ordinary motorists.

The three 1903 coast-to-coast trips did little to induce the average motorist to drive long distances. That inspiration came later, thanks largely to Murdock's 1908 crossing with his family. "Transcontinental automobile travel, not for records, but for the pure enjoyment of touring, is growing in popularity," the *New York Morning Telegraph* could report in 1910, outlining five such journeys.[16]

Arriving with his family in New York City to end his 1908 crossing, Murdock predicted that coast-to-coast pleasure trips would soon become everyday occurrences "scarcely worthy of mention." As he wrote in 1911: "Just how true this prophecy was is shown by the fact that in one day last summer [1910] no fewer than six cars passed through Evanston, Wyo., all transcontinental bound."[17] By 1910, then, transcontinental motoring—still fraught with peril—was hardly the extraordinary undertaking of days gone by.

At the dawn of the nineteenth century, Meriwether Lewis and William Clark led an expedition from St. Louis through the American West to the Pacific Ocean. Americans today revere the names of Lewis and Clark. Yet little is remembered of a handful of explorers who at the turn of the twentieth century pioneered long-distance motoring in coast-to-coast crossings of the American continent. All but forgotten are the names and exploits of John D. and Louise Hitchcock Davis, Dr. H. Nelson Jackson, Tom Fetch, Marius C. Krarup, Eugene I. Hammond, Lester L. Whitman, Jacob M. Murdock, and others who blazed the trails that millions of motorists follow today. Here, then, is the long overdue story of the auto-borne explorers, resourceful and determined, who changed America forever by courageously driving into the yawning maw of the unknown.

THE TRAILBLAZERS

1

"One thing that I have learned about automobile touring is that a man must have plenty of pluck, patience and profanity."

—John D. Davis, 1899

"Our machine is in perfect order, our spirits good and our nerve with us."

—Charles Shanks, leaving San Francisco, 1901

Humans have a curious tendency to remember the winner of a race and forget the runners who place second or third or last. So it is that most historians have overlooked two pairs of automotive pioneers, idealists who set out to become the first persons to cross America by automobile—and failed.

In 1899 John D. Davis and his wife, Louise Hitchcock Davis, of New York City, undertook the first serious attempt to cross the continent by auto. They achieved what was, in its day, quite likely a world's distance record for an automobile. But their flimsy machine—little more than a motorized carriage—broke down repeatedly, which ultimately forced a halt to their journey.

Two years later, in 1901, automaker Alexander Winton and his publicity agent, Charles B. Shanks, began a much more promising coast-to-coast auto trek. Because their automobile performed so admirably, it appeared that the two men would become the first motorists to cross America. Instead, an impatient Winton, discouraged by a stretch of deep sand in Nevada and unwilling to explore alternate routes, abruptly ended the trek.

While it is true that both teams fell short of their goals in two very public undertakings, their failures nevertheless provided valuable lessons for those who would follow. Moreover, their efforts were achievements in and of themselves. For they were the first to act on a dream held by many at the dawn of the twentieth century—that somehow, someday, it would be possible to cross the country in a self-propelled machine that ran not on rails but over the road.

FROM HERALD SQUARE, I SALLY

American inventors began tinkering with steam-powered self-propelled road vehicles in the early 1800s. By the end of the same century, a variety of automobiles—powered by steam, electricity, and gasoline—were in production in the United States. Newspapers and magazines sought to capitalize on the widespread interest in this new mode of transport. Some newspapers exploited the mechanical marvel as a way to boost circulation; many automobile producers were eager to demonstrate what their newfangled machines could do.

Thus, in 1899 a Connecticut automaker provided a 2-cylinder Duryea machine and newspapers in California and New York generated the publicity for the first recorded attempt to cross America by auto (see Fig. 1). U.S. automakers hoped the 3,700-mile stunt would prove that American autos, not their European rivals, were best suited for American roads.

Davis, an inexperienced but well-prepared driver under doctor's orders to seek healthy western air, hoped he and his wife would reach San Francisco in little more than a month. Cities as far west as Omaha, Nebraska—home to the Union Pacific, the first transcontinental railroad—planned brass-band receptions for the Davises.

THE Sunday Edition CALL

SAN FRANCISCO SUNDAY, JULY 2, 1899

ACROSS THE CONTINENT IN AN AUTOMOBILE

San Francisco to Be the Objective Point of a Race That Fills With Wonder the Eyes of the Civilized Nations.

LEAVING THE NEW YORK HERALD.

MRS. JOHN D. DAVIS OUTLINES HER WORK FOR THE SUNDAY CALL.

I AM ready for my journey—my long and perhaps perilous journey from ocean to ocean across the broad bosom of our country of immense distances. The nearly 4000 miles over which I am to travel stretch before me a long vista of possibilities. The probabilities I know; the possibilities I guess; but neither daunts me. With supreme confidence in the invisible steed which is to bear me swiftly over roads and plains and mountain passes to my journey's end, and in the driver whose skilled hand and cool judgment will be our safeguard in time of danger, I look forward to my trip with an enthusiastic impatience which I cannot express.

To be the first woman to cross the continent in an automobile! That is in itself reward enough for whatever of personal discomfort may fall to my lot on the way.

To be, the two of us, alone in the pathless silence of untrodden wilds; to see the sun rise and set unobscured by the lowering smoke of civilization; to pitch our tent in the mountain fastnesses and be face to face with Nature in her wildest moods, and through it all to be going onward and ever onward—swiftly, silently, surely—toward our haven in the city of the Golden Gate! This is the prospect that allures me and beckons me irresistibly on.

True, there may be perils in the way, but they have no terrors for me. The glory of effort, the pride of accomplishment is to be mine. The knowledge that I have done what no woman before me has even dreamed of doing will always be a source of gratification; but better still will be the knowledge that I have, through real difficulties and—I am sure—imagined dangers led in the way along which other women may follow in peace and pleasantness.

The trip having been proven by us to be possible in spite of the obstacles which we shall unavoidably meet, the chief of which will no doubt be the bad roads about which every one tries to discourage us, may be an incentive to the building of a great national boulevard stretching its smooth length from east to west, and binding them together in closer unity. Along such a road automobiles—distance-de-

A DANGEROUS CROSSING

Most Remarkable Trip the World Has Known. It May Revolutionize the Entire System of Locomotion.

Their trip had at least four purposes, according to the *New York Herald* and *San Francisco Call*, which sponsored the journey. First, according to the *Herald*, the Davises would demonstrate the excellence of American vehicles: "French and English makers have persistently asserted the superiority of their carriages. . . . Mr. Davis hopes to change all this by a simple run across the continent. He will take a camera with him to get snap shots of his carriage in climbing mountains, fording rivers and doing other feats."[1] Second, by such a journey, "the usefulness of the automobile will be subjected to a severe and thorough test," as the *Call* put it. "The trip is therefore one which will mark the opening of a new epoch in the history of transportation." After all, a *Leslie's Weekly* article asserted, "No new motive agency for travel by land or water can consider its reputation firmly established until a test has been made of its powers in a tour across country from New York Bay to the Golden Gate." Third, the Davises would be the first to chart the cost of a transcontinental auto trip, and, fourth, they would "collect data as to the condition of the roads," also a pioneering enterprise.[2]

The *Herald* and *Call* professed to sponsor the trip so as to test the automobile "for general use in all parts of the United States and on roads of all kinds. It is, therefore, an experiment in the interests of the public and will be so treated from start to finish."[3] Ignoring this grand declaration, the *Call*'s own cartoonists would later gleefully poke

Fig. 1. The *San Francisco Call* joined the *New York Herald* in sponsoring the Davis trek. Both papers abruptly ended their coverage when the trip evolved into "the bust of the century" (*San Francisco Call*, July 2, 1899).

WE WERE PACED
SEVEN MILES BY A
NERVOUS COW".-DAVIS.

Fig. 2. The Davis trip became cartoon fodder (*San Francisco Call*, Aug. 3, 1899).

fun at the Davises' tribulations, often stretching the truth in the process (see Fig. 2).

Other newspapers, such as the *Chicago Times-Herald*, held out little hope for the "courageous adventurers": "The difficulties of nature will be but slightly diminished in many places by paths that are a mockery." Still, the Davis trip would "perform a public service in giving a new impulse to the agitation for better roads." Yet, surprisingly, given the newness of the automobile, other newspaper editors saw in the Davis trip the dawning of a new era. "Alas, poor horse!" cried the editor of the *Santa Monica (Calif.) Outlook*.[4]

Though incorrectly asserting that electric automobiles would become "the motive power of the future," the *San Francisco Call* nevertheless made an otherwise accurate prediction: "The long stretch of 3700 miles has been covered by men on foot, on horseback, in wheelbarrows and on bicycles, but none of these trips meant anything special to the world in general. . . . The undertaking of Mr. and Mrs. Davis means . . . a revolution in our entire system of locomotion and burden-bearing—a changing of Things as They Are into Things as They Ought to Be."[5]

The Davises drove an auto manufactured by the National Motor Carriage Company, which was making Duryeas, under license, in Stamford, Connecticut. They began their trek on July 13. More than two and one-half months and some twenty-five breakdowns later, the Davises' motor buggy finally limped into Chicago. Legal troubles, which halted the car temporarily in Toledo, Ohio, further hindered their progress. So slow was their pace that a transcontinental bicycle rider had easily overtaken the car en route. After the Davises' first month out, and responding to the cat-calls of the automotive journals ("Ring the curtain down on this farce!" snarled one *Horseless Age* editorial[6]), embarrassed *New York Herald* and *San Francisco Call* editors quietly dropped their daily trip coverage.

Soon after reaching Chicago, the Davises ended the spectacle once and for all. Though they failed in their grand scheme of driving an automobile across the continent, their contribution to the development of the automobile industry was greater than many of their critics realized at the time.

"Not an Experiment"

At the close of the nineteenth century, Duryea autos were "Not an Experiment," at least according to the advertising claims of the National Motor Carriage Company. In fact, brothers Charles E. and J. Frank Duryea had begun building their first auto in Chicopee, Massachusetts, in 1893.[7] Contrary to its claims, National was experimenting, as it looked for ways to strengthen or otherwise improve the engine, transmission, brakes, and other parts of the car. If the Duryea itself was "not an experiment" in 1899, a coast-to-coast crossing in one certainly was.

From press accounts, it is unclear whether it was Davis's or National's idea to cross the continent. According to *Autocar* magazine, Davis, a former *New York Herald* reporter, had been advised to "try the climate of the Pacific coast for his health." The *Erie (Pa.) Morning Dispatch* also reported that Davis's physician had ordered him to "keep out of doors a year or more."[8] So it seems likely that Davis approached National, which then supplied him with the $1,250 Duryea "touring cart" in exchange for the publicity that his trip would generate.

Davis carefully studied a road map published by the League of American Wheelmen, a bicycling group. The map, which the *New York Herald* published for its readers, contained a warning from the Wheelmen's group: "The L.A.W. has no official information whatever about roads between Denver and San Francisco."[9]

According to published reports (see Fig. 3), the Davises planned to follow a route from New York City to Chicago that would later become a favorite of transcontinentalists. From Chicago, they planned to drive through Davenport, Des Moines, and Council Bluffs, Iowa, and Omaha, North Platte, and Ogallala, Nebraska. Press accounts often conflicted on the tentative route westward from Ogallala, but it appeared

Fig. 3. The Davises' proposed route to Chicago (*New York Herald*, July 13, 1899).

the Davises would reach California by traversing either Colorado or Wyoming, and continuing through Utah and Nevada.

John Davis's methodical preparations for the trip included packing "a supply of arnica [a tincture applied to sprains and bruises] for people who get in the way of the machine," according to *Leslie's Weekly*. In a disclaimer of sorts, the *New York Herald* noted that, because he would be driving an untested car fresh from the factory, it would "not be at all surprising" if Davis had breakdowns on the road.[10] Davis himself held no illusions about the likelihood of mechanical problems:

> I look for all kinds of mishaps, from punctured tires to breaks in parts of the machinery due to rapid running on rough roads. I shall carry such duplicate parts as are not too heavy, and will have a kit of tools to tighten up nuts that rack loose or to make any other repairs that are necessary. Every part of the motor is easily accessible, and I have watched the workmen put the machine together, so that I think I can adjust anything that gets out of order and overcome any ordinary difficulty. Of course if we meet with a serious accident we will depend upon the nearest machine shop to fix up things.[11]

Two Resourceful Writers

Davis described himself as a capable mechanic, and his resourceful wife assisted in her own way. While waiting for repairs south of Albany at Stuyvesant, New York, for example, Louise Hitchcock Davis (as she signed her newspaper articles) happened upon a nickel slot machine in the local hotel. "They finally had to drag me away from it," she told the *Albany Times-Union*, "but not until I had won enough money to pay our expenses for the day and come out ninety cents on top."[12]

Little is known about John Davis's background, although the *Herald* reported that Buffalo was "the old home of Mr. Davis," and that he had "spent several years on the plains, and is more or less familiar with the country between Denver and San Francisco." The *Albany Times-Union* could only add that John Dyre Davis "has a collection of good stories, having been in the army, and being a brother of Col. Davis of the commissory [*sic*] department of the army."[13]

According to the *Cleveland Plain Dealer*, "the talented young newspaper writer" Louise Hitchcock Davis, unlike her husband, had "never laid eyes on the bounding prairies." The *Albany Times-Union* reported, "Before she married Mr. Davis she was Miss Louise Hitchcock of New Haven, Conn., and for four years wrote for the *New Haven Palladium*. She has also done work for nearly all of the big New York papers and magazines. She has been engaged by six magazines to write of her travels, and for better remembering the names of the places she stops at, Mrs. Davis keeps a journal."[14] The articles Louise Hitchcock Davis agreed to write for the six magazines could contain new insights into the Davises' trip; press accounts, unfortunately, neglected to name the six magazines in which she would write of her adventures. Mrs. Davis was about 24 years old, according to the *Cleveland Plain Dealer*, which declined to estimate her husband's age. The automobile industry expressed particular interest in Mrs. Davis's journal. "Several manufacturers have asked me to keep them advised regarding the behavior of the machine on this trip with a view to helping them in their future designing," she wrote. Because she did not name these automakers, it is difficult to know how—or if—they improved their designs based on her observations.[15]

Accidents and problems in the preparation of the transcontinental Duryea postponed the original scheduled start of the run. Probably anticipating the difficulties of driving in the Rockies, National workmen added to the Duryea's standard brakes "a plain old fashioned hand brake that would clutch the tires and assure safety going down any hill." Workers thus copied the hand brakes used on horse-drawn wagons (see Fig. 4). In addition, one day before the planned start date, during a test near the National factory in Stamford, "the steel rod snapped and injured the pneumatic tires." The start had to be rescheduled from July 1 to July 3. But then the automaker asked for more time to install "a much stronger brake than was first provided and to strengthen several of the working parts of the motor." The National Duryea touring cart that finally reached the starting line on Thursday, July 13, also carried a non-stock "roadometer"—a combination speedometer and odometer—and "special gears which will enable it to climb mountains of quite a steep grade."[16]

In its final configuration, this National Duryea weighed about 850 pounds unloaded. Fully loaded, however, with 10 gallons of gasoline and 8 gallons of cooling water, two adults, and the Davises' small trunk and suitcase strapped on behind, the chain-driven car weighed about 1,200 pounds. With a bore and stroke of 4½ inches, the opposed 2-cylinder engine reportedly developed from 5 to 7 horsepower.[17] In addition, the touring cart had a 3-speed transmission and used 2½-inch-diameter Diamond pneumatics on 32-inch front wheels and 36-inch rear wheels.[18]

'Frisco or Bust

With the car finally ready on Wednesday, July 12, the Davises drove the 25 miles from Stamford, Connecticut, to the offices of the *New York Herald* at Broadway and 35th

Fig. 4. Louise Hitchcock Davis, *left*, and husband John in the National Duryea. Poised in front of each rear tire is "a plain old fashioned hand brake" (*Scientific American*, July 29, 1899).

Street. There, they announced their intention of starting for San Francisco the following day. According to the *New York Herald*'s account, on July 13 an enthusiastic crowd (see Figs. 5 and 6) sent the overland voyagers on their way West:

> Herald square was densely packed when Mr. and Mrs. Davis in their touring cart arrived at five minutes before eleven o'clock.... When the touring cart stopped in front of the *Herald* building, hundreds rushed forward to get a good look at the machine and its occupants ... and for a few moments there was danger of the carriage being overwhelmed. The police eventually succeeded in clearing a small space.[19]

The Davises' light auto "would have passed for a physician's gig" except for the control levers and the missing horse, the *Herald* noted. "The back is built high for comfort and well cushioned, and a buggy top, which may be lowered at will, covers the vehicle. The driver sits on the left side, with his right hand on a nickel plated steering lever. Two shorter levers are within reach of his left hand. These control the speed gears. One of them moved forward gives a speed up to ten miles, a second increases the speed to twenty miles, and thrown back to thirty-five miles an hour." The gas engine "is concealed in the box beneath the seat" (see Fig. 7).[20]

START FROM NEW YORK FOR SAN FRANCISCO.

START ACROSS THE CONTINENT

Mr. and Mrs. John D. Davis will leave in their automobile at 11 o'clock this morning from Herald square, New York, for The Call building, San Francisco.

Fig. 5 (above). An artist's depiction of a Herald Square throng encircling the coast-to-coast auto (*San Francisco Call*, July 14, 1899).

Fig. 6 (below). A *San Francisco Call* artist mistakenly depicted the car leaving New York City with its top down and Louise Hitchcock Davis in the driver's seat (*San Francisco Call*, July 13, 1899).

Fig. 7. At the controls of the National Duryea outside the *New York Herald* building, John D. Davis grips the steering tiller in his right hand and a gearshift lever in his left. Two horseshoes adorn the headlamp as tokens of good luck (*Harper's Weekly*, July 22, 1899).

According to the *Herald*, the small car allowed Louise Hitchcock Davis, "an attractive young woman," to carry just one outfit in addition to her daily attire—described as "a short skirt, bicycle boots, shirt waist and a soft gray felt hat adorned with an eagle's feather." The hat had "a very wide brim," and was known in the shops as "an 'automobile.'" Mrs. Davis's skirt was "of the length approved by the Rainy Day Club—six inches clear of the ground." Describing John Davis's attire, the *New York Tribune* was somewhat less voluble: "Mr. Davis was dressed in ordinary costume."[21]

When Davis began moving, at 11:02 AM, the *Herald* reported, "There was a lusty cheer from a thousand throats." Many in the crowd were women, the newspaper claimed. The *New York Times*, however, recorded a crowd "composed mostly of small boys." Regardless, the cheering throng included Frank Duryea, in a new Duryea surrey, and Arthur S. Winslow, National Motor Carriage Company secretary, in one of National's Duryea traps. The Davis auto led a virtual parade of automobiles and bicyclists along Fifth Avenue (see Fig. 8). "Regardless of clashing business interests, the makers of these machines sent them to accompany the tourists from the Herald Building to the Harlem River." Reaching Central Bridge at 11:46 AM, the Davises spent an hour or more saying good-bye to their friends and escorts. "When a parting toast was offered, Mr. Davis replied:—'This is to 'Frisco or Bust!'"—a prophecy.[22]

Taunts and Tributes

The Davises' departure presented "an animated and really dramatic picture," gushed the *San Francisco Call*,[23] which also printed H. F. Rodney's poetic tribute to the two overland explorers:

> I take my argonautic spree,
>   From Herald square, I sally,
> By Riverside and Tappan Zee,
>   And through the Mohawk Valley,
> With here and there a little stop
>   To tinker up a puncture,
> And here and there a little flop
>   At some unlucky juncture.
> Yet in my epoch-making race,
>   With gusto and devotion,
> I'm out to make the record pace
>   To the Pacific Ocean.[24]

Fig. 8. The Davises, *far left*, and their entourage in New York City, shortly after leaving the *Herald* building (AAMA).

With his announcement that the National Duryea could outperform foreign automobiles, Davis ensured that the trip would receive international attention. When the pair reached Wappingers Falls, New York, on Day 2, the Reverend Michael Powers, "stepped up to the automobile and gave Mr. and Mrs. Davis his blessing, adding, 'Now go in and beat the French!'"[25]

But the French came to regard the American transcontinental trip as a bad joke. Two weeks into the trip, the *San Francisco Call* ran a dispatch from Paris: "The American colony here is constantly twitted by French automobilists on the grotesque picture of Mr. and Mrs. Davis crawling wearily from village to village in the Empire State, not conspicuous for bad roads." Even the editors of *Automobile* magazine joined in: "The Frenchman evidently knew what he was talking about who, in speaking of Davis' proposed transcontinental trip, said: In planning a trip here we look out for a place for a good dinner. In the United States you seem to have to look out for a place where you can get your automobile repaired."[26]

Trouble on the Trail

"There is no more delightful way of seeing the country than to view it from the comfortably cushioned seats of an automobile vehicle, which is never tired, and knows neither hunger nor thirst," *Scientific American* observed early in the Davis trip.[27] But it became evident almost immediately that breakdowns would become an everyday feature of the Davis expedition.

Besides being nearly two weeks late in starting, Davis was never able to keep to his daily schedule. He had hoped to cover the 175 miles to Albany during the first day, for instance, but did not arrive there till nearly midnight on Day 4. Between the July 13 start and August 8, when the *New York Herald* ran its last trip article, the Davis car broke down or

Fig. 9. Reporters documented every misadventure as the Davises crept westward toward the *San Francisco Call* building.

received repairs at least twenty times, according to reports. The number of break-downs soon rose to twenty-five, *Scientific American* reported (see Fig. 9).

The most serious breakdowns during the early going occurred on the sixth, ninth, eighteenth and twentieth days. Davis had hired a "Mr. Fisher" as a mechanic to accompany him westward from Peekskill, New York. Mr. Fisher may have done as much harm as good, since the weight of an extra passenger undoubtedly strained the car's engine and suspension. On July 18, Day 6, the metal-spoked right rear wheel collapsed at Little Falls, New York, "due to the overheating of the steel rim in welding."[28] Davis spent three days at nearby Utica, home of the Weston-Mott Company, which made him a new set of heavier rear wheels on which tires of 3 inches replaced the original 2½-inch tires.

Davis left Utica on July 21, Day 9, and after a 54-mile run had just reached Syracuse, some 350 miles northwest of New York City, when "the bolt connecting the piston between the two cylinders snapped and the forward piston tore a big hole in the casing of the cylinder and bent the cam shaft." It took five days for a new cylinder to reach Syracuse and three days to rebuild and test the engine. "Truly, it is ''Frisco or bust,' but so far there has been more 'bust' than we like," John Davis conceded.[29]

The Davises left Syracuse on July 29, Day 17, but the following day an engine valve broke, costing them an afternoon spent at a repair shop. Later, in Rochester, Davis had stronger valves made. On Day 20, August 1, Davis hit a "stone flagging over the gutter" in Bergen, New York, and bent the front axle, which a blacksmith repaired.[30]

Davis replaced the car's springs in Syracuse and also struggled with a twice-broken cylinder petcock, chronic valve trouble, an overheating engine, bad wheel spokes, disabled transmission gear, broken warning bell, and at least three instances of spectator-inflicted damage. "We have found it impossible to keep crowds away from the carriage, and while we are watching one part curious and mischievous persons toy with whatever is in sight," Davis fumed.[31]

So excited about the trip were rural New Yorkers that Davis "found it unsafe to leave the automobile beside the road for a few minutes even, without an attendant, because people would steal the nuts and bolts as souvenirs," one newspaper said. The very sound of the National Duryea's "gong" had the power to empty a country church in an instant, Davis related:

People would go to church under protest, fearing they would miss the machine while at their devotions and the moment its approach was heralded they were ready to leave the minister at any stage of his prayer. The countrymen work queer games on us for rides. Many times we are compelled to ask the way and a farmer will say: "Well, I can't tell you exactly, but if you can find room for a feller in there for a piece, I guess I can show you." And perhaps it's a straight road to the place we are looking for.[32]

Pettycock? Poppycock!

Davis called the cylinder petcock a "pettycock" and often used convoluted terms to describe other broken parts, remarked U.S. correspondent Hugh Dolnar, writing for the London-based magazine *Autocar*: "Evidently Mr. Davis has not yet learned the names of the parts of his waggon motor, but he will probably become quite familiar with the appearance of his machine elements before he reaches San Francisco."[33]

Yet Davis proved an astute mechanic in troubleshooting the car. Complaining of broken intake, or inlet, valves, he described to an *Erie Morning Dispatch* reporter how he had parked the auto, started the engine, and spent two hours listening and watching as the engine ran at a constant speed. It performed flawlessly. "Then I put it going in rough fashion, just as on roadways met often, and in throttling it found that the [valve] nut struck on the side of the controller and snapped the spindle [valve stem]. By means of an angle iron I secured an equal distribution in working the inlet valve. Since then I have had no trouble whatever."[34]

On August 2, three weeks into the trip, Davis was finally able to report from Buffalo that "the motor has worked perfectly all day, and not a hitch has occurred. This is the first day without some trouble since leaving New York, and from now on I think everything will work satisfactorily." One item on the car that seemed to hold up well was the tires: Davis drove from New York City to Cleveland without tire troubles of any kind, "outside of a knife slash," added the *New York Herald*, without elaborating.[35]

Writing from Erie, Pennsylvania, out of New York state at last, Davis remained doggedly optimistic about the trip's prospects for success. "The accidents we have had are of a minor kind. They were not great or disabling, but simply annoying—what might be expected, in fact, when new machinery is used."[36]

The many difficulties led Louise Hitchcock Davis to conclude that the automobile "is a treacherous animal for a long trip." She continued: "Our particular vehicle, for example, has an antipathy for cities. As soon as one looms up before us, and we shake off the dust, straighten ourselves and try to make a fine appearance, then snap, some part of the mechanism divorces itself from the whole and we are stranded on the busiest corner until some friendly truck hauls the vehicle away to the nearest machine shop for repairs."[37]

Tie Distance Record

By reaching Cleveland on August 6, the Davises tied a Winton automobile's Cleveland–New York City distance record but not its speed, as Davis acknowledged to the *Cleveland Plain Dealer*. "Mr. Davis paid a high compliment to Mr. Alexander Winton of Cleveland, who made a trip to New York for the *Plain Dealer* to establish a record in the early part of the summer. He said: 'Mr. Winton performed a wonderful feat and deserves great credit. No other man in the world could beat his record.'"[38] Winton, president of the Winton Motor Carriage Company, covered the distance in a running time of 47 hours, 34 minutes, over a period of five days beginning on May 22, 1899.

Troubles continued to impede the Davises. During the twenty-five days from July 13 through August 6, their car was laid up for ten days—though half that time was spent awaiting the arrival of a new cylinder. Accidents and breakdowns during the remaining fifteen travel days meant that the car was often driveable only between three and four hours a day. Through August 5, according to daily distance figures published in the *New York Herald*, the Davises drove from 32 to 65 miles on travel days. On their best days, they averaged 18 miles per hour, and on their worst days, a mere 10 mph. From those rare instances when press accounts gave enough information to calculate gas mileage, it appears that 18 miles per gallon was high and 11 mpg was low. Davis himself reported that he averaged about 14 mpg in covering the 486½ miles from New York City to Buffalo, and that he paid between 4 cents and 22 cents per gallon of gasoline. That would place his average speed from New York to Buffalo at 9.9 mph.[39]

"Too Exhilarating for Words"

Louise Hitchcock Davis had her own reactions to the unfolding adventure, as she revealed in a dispatch from Buffalo that was published in the *Cleveland Plain Dealer*. "I am beginning to enjoy this trip," she wrote.

> It would be monotonous to go speeding across the continent without accident or mishap of any kind. One might as well fall back in the cushioned chair of a [railroad] Pullman car. But the joy of being thrown into a ditch, of having cylinders break while the motor

is running at top speed, of having a wheel come off [collapse], letting you gently down to earth, and of all sorts and conditions of mishaps, is something too exhilarating for words.

You will bear in mind, gentle reader, that this trip is largely in the nature of an experiment. It might have been made in less time had we waited for the manufacturers of horseless carriages to get the machine down so fine that it would be unbreakable, but that would have withheld from you the pleasure of reading about this trip for so long that it would have lost its charm. Besides, there would be no special credit in a trip in a carriage that was guaranteed not to break, not to buck or behave itself unseemly or give any more trouble than a docile donkey.[40]

For the Davises, perhaps the ultimate humiliation occurred when a one-armed, cross-country bicyclist who had departed from New York City ten days after the Davises' much-ballyhooed departure passed them at Syracuse on his fifth day of pedaling. Albert V. Roe, 19, whose left arm had been severed at the shoulder, the result of a train-switching accident, stated that he hoped to pedal 60–75 miles daily in his transcontinental bicycling attempt.[41]

Louise Hitchcock Davis described herself as having a "constitution of iron and nerves of steel," important attributes for any early female motorist. Yet, despite her own strong performance, she concluded that it would be "thoroughly impracticable" for even the healthiest of women to attempt such a long-distance drive alone. "The automobile is as yet imperfect in many ways," she observed. "Few women have the strength to manage one over the wretched country roads. Still fewer have the mechanical knowledge necessary to care for one, even exclusive of accidents."[42]

"The Coming Automobile" or "Bust of the Century"?

Meanwhile, press coverage of the trip was waning. Editors looking for tales of adventure and romance were forced instead to run a dull series of articles describing breakdowns and repairs. The *New York Herald*'s last trip dispatch, on August 8, reported that the transcontinental Duryea on the previous day had reached Cleveland, where it had its front axle strengthened. At that point, the *Herald* and *Call* abruptly ended their coverage, without explanation. In an August 14 editorial titled "The Coming Automobile," the *San Francisco Call* blamed its lapse on San Francisco's primary elections:

In the uproar of that great [political] event the machine was lost sight of, but Ohio remains on the map, and through the dawn's early light it can be seen the machine is still there. . . . In one respect the undertaking has been successful. It has verified the predictions of *The Call*. When the automobile started *The Call* said the experiment would test the mechanism and show where it is defective, and the results have been even so. There has been revealed every defect in the machine from the cylinders to the nut washers.

It was said the trip would test the country roads, and it has shown that some roads are rough, some are muddy, and some have ditches, and that the machine can break on the rough places, stick in the muddy places and run into the ditches with the greatest facility.

It was pointed out that the appearance of the vehicle on rural roads would prove whether people took an interest in it and whether cattle were scared of it, and so it did. It was an object of more popular interest than a circus; it was as startling to animals as a yellow journal freak to humanity, and it once chased a cow for half a mile and would have caught her if a valve hadn't broken.

The automobile is coming. . . . If the one now waiting for the election processions in Ohio to pass do[es] not reach here in time for exhibition as a specimen of successful mechanism at the Mechanic's Institute Fair, it will still serve an exposition purpose. It will be hauled to Chicago and placed on a monument in front of the Art Gallery of that city as the bust of the century.[43]

Living on Toledo Time

The newspaper, however, was too quick to write off the machine, which "had been overhauled at Cleveland" and continued west to Toledo, according to *Horseless Age*. The National Duryea had traveled 857 miles in 80½ hours of actual running time in reaching Toledo on the evening of Thursday, August 17, as John Davis told the *Toledo Blade* (see also Table 1). Thus, the auto's average speed from New York City to Toledo had been 10.6 miles per hour. Searching for superlatives, the *Blade* reported that the distance was "the greatest ever accomplished by any woman in an automobile."[44]

"One thing that I have learned about automobile touring," John Davis commented, "is that a man must have plenty of pluck, patience and profanity, and I think that I am becoming proficient." Because repairs had strengthened the automobile after accidents during the first leg of the journey, the Davises believed the worst was over, and they expected to "make good time for the remainder of the way." Evidently, "Mr. Fisher," or some other helper, was still attending to the auto: "Mr. and Mrs. Davis are accompanied by a man who is a machinist, and who acts as footman and hostler for the machine. Part of the time he rides with them in the carriage, and part of the time by their side on a bicycle."[45]

At 4:00 PM on Friday, August 18, one day after arriving in Toledo, the Davises headed west through the city, bound for Bryan, Ohio, at a "lively speed" of 8 miles per

TABLE 1. Davis Itinerary from New York City to Toledo, Ohio, 1899

Day / Date	City–City	Distance (daily / cumulative)
1 / July 13 Thu	New York City–Tarrytown, N.Y.	37 / 37
2 / July 14 Fri	Tarrytown, N.Y.–Poughkeepsie, N.Y.	53 / 90
3 / July 15 Sat	Poughkeepsie, N.Y.–Hudson, N.Y.	57 / 147
4 / July 16 Sun	Hudson, N.Y.–Albany, N.Y.	37 / 184
5 / July 17 Mon	Albany, N.Y.–Amsterdam, N.Y.	33 / 217
6 / July 18 Tue	Amsterdam, N.Y.–Utica, N.Y.	42 / 259
7 / July 19 Wed	*repairs in Utica, N.Y.*	– / 259
8 / July 20 Thu	*repairs in Utica, N.Y.*	– / 259
9 / July 21 Fri	Utica, N.Y.–Syracuse, N.Y.	54 / 313
10 / July 22 Sat	*waiting for parts in Syracuse, N.Y.*	– / 313
11 / July 23 Sun	*waiting for parts in Syracuse, N.Y.*	– / 313
12 / July 24 Mon	*waiting for parts in Syracuse, N.Y.*	– / 313
13 / July 25 Tue	*waiting for parts in Syracuse, N.Y.*	– / 313
14 / July 26 Wed	*install new cylinder, Syracuse, N.Y.*	– / 313
15 / July 27 Thu	*modify, test cylinder, Syracuse, N.Y.*	– / 313
16 / July 28 Fri	*test new cylinder, Syracuse, N.Y.*	– / 313
17 / July 29 Sat	Syracuse, N.Y.–Auburn, N.Y.	32 / 345
18 / July 30 Sun	Auburn, N.Y.–Newark, N.Y.	35 / 380
19 / July 31 Mon	Newark, N.Y.–Rochester, N.Y.	– / –
20 / Aug. 1 Tue	Rochester, N.Y.–Bergen, N.Y.	– / –
21 / Aug. 2 Wed	Bergen, N.Y.–Buffalo, N.Y.	56 / 486
22 / Aug. 3 Thu	*rest day in Buffalo, N.Y.*	– / 486
23 / Aug. 4 Fri	Buffalo, N.Y.–Fredonia, N.Y.	65 / 551
24 / Aug. 5 Sat	Fredonia, N.Y.–Erie, Pa.	49 / 600
25 / Aug. 6 Sun	Erie, Pa.–Cleveland	96 / 696
26 / Aug. 7 Mon	*repairs in Cleveland*	– / 696
27 / Aug. 8 Tue	Cleveland–?[a]	– / –
36 / Aug. 17 Thu	Milan, Ohio–Toledo, Ohio	– / 857

SOURCES: *New York Herald*, *San Francisco Call*, and local newspapers.

[a] The *San Francisco Call* ended its trip coverage on August 7, followed a day later by the *New York Herald*. Last reports said the Davises would leave Cleveland on August 8.

hour. But they did not get very far. "On Newberry street, near South, the rear axle broke squarely in two, the accident being caused by a flaw in the steel."[46] The Toledo Foundry and Machine Company set to work making a new axle, and the Davises settled in for at least a two-day wait.

But the next morning, Saturday, August 19, the Davises "had their trip unceremoniously interrupted by an attachment warrant on the vehicle, which was served . . . at the instigation of C. A. Thatcher, as agent of the Edward Malley Company, a dry goods firm doing business at Sta[m]ford, Conn." The attachment was for $60.52 worth of "furniture and furnishings," although it was unclear from the newspaper account what "furnishings" were at issue.[47] No matter, rear-axle repairs had to be postponed until after a court hearing, which was set for two weeks away, on August 30. A report in *Motor Vehicle Review* suggested that the legal proceedings against the Davises in Toledo stemmed from the factory's financial problems:

> STAMFORD, Ct., Aug. 28 [1899]—The stock here of the National [Motor] Carriage Company, in one of whose automobiles John D. Davis and wife recently began a trip across the continent, was attached today by various creditors, including a number of the employees. The exact amount of the claims against the company are not known, but they are believed to aggregate about $10,000. Supt. T. G. Graham stated this afternoon that the difficulties were due to a reorganization of the company and that all claims will soon be paid.[48]

On to Chicago

A search of newspapers and auto journals uncovered no information on precisely how or exactly when the Davises resolved the legal and mechanical problems they encountered in Toledo. Resolve them they did, evidently, for various terse reports tell of their departure from Toledo on an unspecified date. *Scientific American* covered the Davis trip in the magazine's occasional "Automobile News" column, using dispatches borrowed from auto journals or taken from the wire services. Unaccountably, the September 2, 1899, edition reported, "On August 19, Mr. and Mrs. John B. [*sic*] Davis reached Detroit . . . and the trip has been abandoned."[49]

It is possible that the Davises were heading for Detroit, 50 miles north of Toledo. But the credible, first-person report in the *Toledo Blade* said August 19 was the day a lawsuit delayed the trip for at least two weeks in Toledo. Furthermore, a page-by-page search of the *Detroit Free Press* from mid-August through the end of October 1899 uncovered no mention of the Davises having arrived there. In fact, the couple's stay in

Toledo stretched to a full month, according to *Motor Age*. In an article from Toledo datelined September 30, 1899, *Motor Age* reported that the Davises had left Ohio and entered Michigan, but the article did not mention Detroit as the couple's destination. Curiously, the auto journal also failed to mention the Davises' legal problems:

> The trans-continental automobile trip of Mr. and Mrs. John Davis has not proven a great success up to date. For nearly a month the Davises have been trying to get out of Toledo, but without success. Repair work on their machine kept them here for three weeks. A week ago Sunday [September 24] they broke away from the city, but their tour was short-lived for in Michigan, less than a score of miles from here, they broke down again and are stalled. [50]

Truly, the best indications are that the Davises reached Chicago (although one automotive-history book stated flatly—and misleadingly—that, after leaving Detroit, "neither the Davises nor their machine were ever seen again"![51]). And while they may have had their fill of transcontinental auto travel and thus dropped out of the news columns, it was not because they vanished without a trace. (*That* would have been front-page news!)

The Davises reached Chicago in October, having traveled 1,030 miles from New York City, according to estimates made by the *Herald*. Strangely, neither *Automobile Review*, *Horseless Age*, nor *Motor Age* specified the actual date of arrival.[52] From late September through mid-October, the *Chicago Times-Herald* makes no mention of the coast-to-coast auto. Nor does the *Chicago Daily Tribune* mention the trip from late September through late October 1899. But according to *Automobile Review*, the intrepid couple was still planning to reach Denver by the end of October. Earlier press accounts had reported that the Davises had a new part made when their rear axle broke in Toledo. Seemingly unaware of this, the October 17, 1899, issue of *Motor Age* reported:

Fig. 10. The Davises hoped to drive across the country in one month. This newspaper artist's rendering of their triumphal arrival at the *San Francisco Call* building, actually never occurred (*San Francisco Call*, July 2, 1899).

> Mr. and Mrs. John D. Davis have reached Chicago with their ill-fated motor carriage. Little of the original motor and running gear mechanism with which the couple started from New York under the auspices of the *New York Herald* was left, the principal remainder, it is said, being the rear axle; and that broke at the crossing of 71st street and Bond avenue in Chicago. When a new axle shall have been fitted it is the intention to proceed on the way to San Francisco.[53]

But the Davises' paper trail, and quite likely their overland trail, ended at Chicago (see Fig. 10). Presumably, the first two people to launch a coast-to-coast motor trip made it to San Francisco by some other means. Like all the other details surrounding the end of their trip, the fate of their 1899 National Duryea is lost to history. If the Davises made any further transcontinental attempts, they did so quietly.

Press Pooh-Poohs

While the trip dragged on, the trade journals, instead of evaluating the evident need for stronger autos and better roads, had merely voiced increasingly bitter opposition to the run: "The adventurous couple who are endeavoring to make 'San Francisco or bust' in a motor carriage have apparently taken the latter alternative. At the rate at which they are traveling they could not reach San Francisco in less than five months from the date of setting out, and at the rate at which they are 'busting' they would have an entirely different carriage if they ever reached the Pacific Coast," opined one *Horseless Age* writer. "An immediate termination of the journey would be welcome by the motor vehicle industry of the United States."[54]

Even the unflappable *Scientific American* had groused: "All value to the industry of a trip of this kind is taken out of it by the long delays and the many breakdowns." In a later issue it added: "Trips of this nature do more harm to the automobile industry than they do good."[55]

Early in the trip, the U.S. correspondent for *Autocar* had observed, "The record so far is full of small disasters and repairs at wayside smithies." But, he had conceded, "some of the worst stretches of road in America lie between New York and Albany . . . as these roads are very little used, because the two towns are connected by the finest railway and river steam boat lines possible." A writer for *Harper's Weekly*, a general-circulation magazine, had been more generous: "The real contest lies between the enduring quality of the American-built machinery and the destructive energy of the awful American highways. If Mr. Davis gets to San Francisco at all, that will be record enough in itself."[56]

The fanfare accompanying the start of the journey had so overexcited expectations that many disappointed trade-journal editors and, undoubtedly, industry leaders were later blinded to the Davises' accomplishments and the lessons of their trip. Though he failed to travel from coast to coast, John Davis quite possibly set a world distance record for a one-way trip.

The European distance record was reported variously as 621 miles ("over the most perfect roads") and between 750 and 800 miles.[57] Using modern roads, the New York–Chicago distance is 800 miles, but according to the calculations of the *New York Herald*, the Davises would have traveled 1,030 miles on their 1899 route. Detours and side trips actually ran the Davises' odometer well beyond that figure.

Before Davis reached Chicago, Elwood Haynes and E. L. Apperson had driven a Haynes-Apperson car on an estimated 1,050-mile route between Kokomo, Indiana, and New York City, at an average speed of 20 miles per hour. Their Kokomo–New York City mileage was questionable, however, because the auto's odometer had malfunctioned for a time.[58] The Davises, on the other hand, reported a distance of 857 miles between New York City and Toledo. Distance calculations from the mid-1920s tell us that the then-shortest route from Toledo to Chicago was about 275 miles.[59] This means that the Davises had to have traveled at least 1,132 miles to reach the Windy City, apparently outdistancing Haynes and Apperson handily. Had a driver in Europe or elsewhere in the world made a longer trip as of late 1899? Perhaps not, though the truth remains elusive.

The Value of a Lesson

The Davises' transcontinental attempt ultimately failed to achieve three of its four stated goals. First, rather than proving American autos were better than their European counterparts, the trip strongly hinted at the opposite. Second, instead of opening "a new epoch in the history of transportation," the Davis journey perhaps delayed the coming new epoch by discouraging similar trips. (By merely undertaking the daunting journey, however, the Davises demonstrated their early belief—shared by many other visionaries—in the possibilities of the automobile.) Third, the cost of a transcontinental auto trip was as much a guess after as before the Davises' trek. Davis did partially achieve his fourth goal by reporting on road conditions at least as far west as Toledo.

Yet the Davis journey yielded a wealth of information that proved to be highly useful in the years to come. For example, the Davises' experience demonstrated that early American cars were simple enough to be repaired in blacksmith shops; between breakdowns, they could travel 50 or 60 miles over frightfully bad roads, a good performance indeed for a fledgling automobile. The trip's greatest value was in demonstrating that, to prosper, American automakers would need to build more rugged, dependable autos, and they would have to support the building of better roads for their use.

"The trip has been not a particularly good brief for the American motor carriage," *Scientific American* concluded. "The natural inference is that our carriages are too light for the rough service which is entailed and the badness of many of our roads." Davis was vocal in condemning what passed for American roads in 1899. "He finds stretches of the finest that could be desired and then long reaches of the most execrable that could be imagined, turf and big stones being the materials used in the annual road making as conducted under existing laws," the *New York Herald* reported.[60]

Rural New York roads, as Davis described them, were "a disgrace to an unexplored region, let alone a thickly populated country. . . . Grades have never been cut, rocks are left to roll about under foot and wheel, ruts to run deeper, and things have been left generally to care for themselves." Ultimately, a *Chicago Times-Herald* editorial predicted (correctly, as it turned out), the Davises' trip would inspire a public demand for better roads by "jolting a complacent conservatism with facts, figures and humiliating comparisons."[61]

RIGHT HERE WE ARE MET BY THE IMPOSSIBLE

Nearly two years elapsed before anyone else attempted another coast-to-coast trip by automobile. Then, in early 1901, in search of a splashy publicity stunt, the *Cleveland Plain Dealer* made a pitch to pioneering U.S. automaker Alexander Winton of Cleveland: "Will you . . . dare to attempt the ride across the American continent, starting at San Francisco with New York city the objective point?" In May 1899, Winton and his factory publicity man, Charles B. Shanks, had set a speed and distance record by racing from Cleveland to New York City in a running time of 47 hours, 34 minutes during a five-day period. But that trek had offered them at least the semblance of roads. This was an entirely different proposition, an "exceedingly doubtful enterprise," replied the 40-year-old president of the Winton Motor Carriage Company, who nevertheless enjoyed a good challenge. He accepted the dare.[62]

Thus, Winton and Shanks, a former *Plain Dealer* reporter, left San Francisco on May 20, 1901, on the second serious attempt to conquer the continent by automobile. They were soon climbing California's snow-covered mountains and dreading the desert that lay beyond. "It is perhaps needless to say that if the feat can be done at all, these two gentlemen will accomplish it," *Automobile Review* blithely predicted.[63]

In the Sierra Nevada, steep, boulder-strewn trails and unbridged streams greeted the autoists. Rain, hail, and snow pummeled the open car and its occupants, who also suffered from the cold at high altitudes. A front axle broke while the car forded a rocky stream. Winton temporarily repaired the damage. Later, at a blacksmith's forge in a remote lumber camp, he spent a day welding a broken crankshaft. "That there is a whole piece left of the motor is not the fault of the rocks and snow covered roads and the elements with which we had to contend," Shanks telegraphed the *Plain Dealer*.[64]

At last, however, the transcontinental expedition rolled out of the mountains and into Reno, Nevada, where, according to the local newspaper, it awed humans and scared horses. Ahead of the two travel-hardened men lay the "soft, shifting, bottomless, rolling" sands of Nevada. It would make their mountain travel look like a picnic.

Winton: Man of Firsts

Alexander Winton was among the most prominent early U.S. automakers. "If any single individual can be credited with lighting the spark which set the automobile industry going in America, it would be Alexander Winton," declares automotive historian Beverly Rae Kimes.[65] Arriving from Scotland in about 1880,[66] he founded the Winton Bicycle Company of Cleveland in 1891, built an experimental auto in 1896, and on March 1, 1897, established the Winton Motor Carriage Company, which manufactured autos in Cleveland until 1924.

Early in 1898, Winton sold his first auto. He had sold twenty-one more by the close of 1898, and the next year he sold one hundred Wintons. One biographer writes, "Although Winton did not sell the first gasoline automobile in America, he was the first to set up the orderly production schedule that was requisite for moving the automobile from machine or bicycle shop into a proper industry." A lifetime of inventiveness earned Winton at least eighty-eight patents for bicycles, automobiles, and marine and diesel engines. Given his capacity for and devotion to work, Winton developed a bulldog-like personality. As his friend and associate, William S. McKinstry, described him, "He thought and lived in a mechanical world, a world of cogs and wheels, setting him apart, gruff and autocratic."[67]

Even at age 40, Winton—about 5 feet, 8 inches tall and 170 pounds—was still stocky and powerfully built from his days of promoting Winton bicycles by racing them. Undaunted by grand undertakings, Winton was just the man to pioneer an auto route across the United States.

Cleveland to New York in 1899

Fig. 11. Charles B. Shanks (*Automobile Trade Journal*, Dec. 1, 1924).

Shanks (see Fig. 11), who sent daily dispatches to the *Cleveland Plain Dealer*, his former employer, and wrote a follow-up article for the *Scientific American Supplement*, was "a gentleman of much experience in operating power vehicles."[68] But, as

during their 1899 run, he accompanied Winton only as a helper and observer. Winton did all the driving.

And Winton the driver, later famous as an automobile racer, had "a wonderful amount of grit," as Shanks wrote in an 1899 factory booklet, *Cleveland to New York in a Motor Carriage*. "His skill in handling the machine and piloting it successfully over rough roads while going at high speed was a beautiful exhibition." As with the 707.4-mile journey of 1899, the *Plain Dealer* suggested and sponsored the 1901 transcontinental trip. The 1899 trip had duplicated, with greater fanfare, an 1897 Cleveland–New York City drive that Winton and his shop superintendent, William A. Hatcher, made at a slower pace. In 1899, an impressed Mayor Robert A. Van Wyck had received the autoists in New York, exclaiming: "This trip has opened the eyes of Americans to the possibilities of the automobile as a practical power carriage for road work."[69]

It was Shanks's detailed dispatches from the road that opened their eyes. As *Automobile Trade Journal* reminisced years later, the 1899 journey "became one of absorbing interest to newspaper readers because of the victories won from roads by the automobile." Shanks's trip dispatches also popularized the American use of the French word "automobile," one historian claims. Winton was so pleased with Shanks that he lured him away from the *Plain Dealer* in 1899 to become "advertising manager, press agent and general boomer of the Winton company."[70]

Dear Sir: Will You Dare It?

The *Plain Dealer* announced the forthcoming transcontinental trip in a front-page story on March 17, 1901, referring to its earlier sponsorship of Winton's 1899 Cleveland–New York City trek. "Now, at the request of the *Plain Dealer*, Mr. Winton will undertake a trip of much greater hazard, surrounded by more difficulties than any ever attempted in this or any other part of the world. About May 1 Mr. Winton, accompanied by Mr. Charles B. Shanks, who will act as the *Plain Dealer*'s correspondent, will start from San Francisco to New York city on an automobile."[71] The newspaper made its original overture to Winton in this March 14 letter:

> Dear Sir:
>
> During the past two years, in fact ever since you made your first remarkable record run between Cleveland and New York, for the *Plain Dealer*, in May, 1899, some of the most enthusiastic automobilists have considered the trip overland from the Atlantic to the Pacific, but on account of the unknown hardships which will assuredly be encountered throughout that vast expanse of mountain and desert country in the west, every one has decided that the trip with an automobile would be utterly impossible. . . .
> If the *Plain Dealer* agrees to back the enterprise, will you in company with Mr. Charles B. Shanks . . . dare to attempt the ride across the American continent, starting at San Francisco with New York city the objective point?
>
> Two years ago, on the Cleveland–New York run, we backed our faith in you and your machine. Believing that it is in your power to overcome even the vastly greater difficulties of the trans-continental enterprise, the *Plain Dealer* herewith suggests that you undertake the latter and will gladly agree to back you in the enterprise if you will enter upon it. . . .
> Awaiting your answer, which we hope will be favorable, we remain,
> Very truly yours,
> THE PLAIN DEALER[72]

Winton quickly accepted the offer. But in his March 16 reply to *Plain Dealer* executives, he said: "I am disposed to question your wisdom in being willing to stand sponsor for such an elaborate and exceedingly doubtful enterprise. . . . I may not get through, but will do my best, and so hereby announce acceptance to your proposition."[73]

To the *Plain Dealer* reporter who interviewed him just after he accepted the challenge, Winton said he was still mulling over his route. He might drive through Nevada, Utah, Colorado, and Kansas; he was also contemplating a southern route from San Francisco to Los Angeles, and then eastward through Arizona, New Mexico, and Texas. "As far as I can gather any of them are bad enough," Winton explained. He also issued a disclaimer: "I don't want you to say that I am going to put the trip through to a successful finish. If you believe what people say about it being an absolute impossibility, and if such proves to be the case, you can but rest assured that I did my best. A Winton motor carriage cannot be expected to work a miracle."[74]

Pumas and Vultures and Bears (Oh, My!)

To build suspense and interest in its venture, the *Plain Dealer* played up the "Hardships for Automobilists," as the headline read over its next trip article. "Has Alexander Winton agreed to attempt the impossible?" began the article, which then went on to enumerate the "objects of fear" Wilton would encounter on his route through the Sierra Nevada and into the desert beyond. These included:

Rugged mountain trails "of doubtful nature . . . [that] have been considerably neglected since the railroad made its advent."

California's Mojave Desert and the deserts of Arizona and New Mexico, "strewn with the bones of animals which have died of thirst or hunger. No sooner do they drop in their tracks than a swarm of vultures descend and quickly reduce the carcasses to skeletons."

Rattlesnakes, "gigantic saguana scorpions," black and grizzly bears, jaguars, wildcats, pumas, ocelots and red and gray wolves.[75]

Ignoring such doom and gloom, the *Motor Vehicle Review* focused upon the rewards awaiting the daring driver:

Alexander Winton's motor vehicle trip from San Francisco to New York will demonstrate what a gasolene carriage can do under the severest test. . . . Mr. Winton is an old time athlete, whose friends say that he is daunted by nothing, and they add that if success in this endeavor is possible, Mr. Winton will surely achieve it.

Certainly the experiment could not be in better hands, for this pioneer in the manufacture and operation of American gasolene vehicles has already proved himself a tourist of genuine ability, and a speed performer of unblemished success.

Mr. Winton's progress on this trip will be watched by the public with considerable interest and his success will be one of the best possible advertisements for motor vehicles in general, gasolene carriages in particular and the Winton especially.[76]

By the end of March, Winton had abandoned the idea of traveling south through Arizona, New Mexico, and Texas. He instead chose a central route through twelve states, "thinking perhaps it will be better to put his machine to the mountain tests rather than to run what would be a splendid chance of perishing in the alkaline deserts of the south."[77]

Thus, Winton and Shanks, after traversing the Sierra Nevada in California, would head for Reno, Nevada; Ogden and Salt Lake City, Utah; Cheyenne, Wyoming; Denver and Julesburg, Colorado; Omaha, Nebraska; and Council Bluffs, Des Moines, and Clinton, Iowa. They would cross Illinois to Chicago; travel through Indiana and Ohio with a stop in Cleveland; and cross Pennsylvania to reach New York City by way of Buffalo and Albany.

In choosing the route, Winton professed to be "conscious of its terrible possibilities" and aware that the 20- or 30-foot snow cover in the High Sierras would not begin melting until June. Still, he refused to postpone his departure date, declaring: "I am going over these mountains during the early part of May if it is possible."[78]

But when the postmaster at Towle, California, warned that deep snow would remain at the summit through the first part of July, Winton finally agreed to postpone the trip. "Just as soon as it is possible to cover that trail over the mountains I am going over. When the stage coaches can do it I will make the attempt."[79]

Go West, Young Motorist

Shanks, the scout, left for the West by train on April 12, planning to stop "at perhaps twenty-five stations between Chicago and San Francisco to learn something about the best route, snow on the mountains, etc." Shanks told the *Ogden Standard* of Utah that he and Winton hoped to complete the trip in two months or less. That was their goal because "important business affairs require Mr. Winton's presence in New York during the middle of the season." Though he had remained in Cleveland, Winton would "hold himself in readiness to leave the factory as soon as he receives word that all the arrangements have been made and that the roads are in fit condition to travel on."[80]

Modern travel by automobile would represent an incalculable advance over the wagon trains that plied the same trails, mused the *Plain Dealer*:

> Imagine then the picture to be presented at this early day in the twentieth century. Two lone men, seated in a carriage, to which no horses, mules or oxen are attached. They start from the blue waters of the Pacific and head toward the other great ocean. . . . When night overtakes them and it is necessary to "go into camp" there is no killing of game or kindling of fires. . . .
>
> They simply jump out and down from a motor carriage, pull out a small gasoline stove, upon which coffee is made; a can of corned beef takes the place of buffalo meat and in a few minutes there is a meal of corned beef, canned baked beans, crackers and coffee, with sugar and condensed milk. They will have blankets [rather than buffalo robes] in which to roll for sleep, and instead of depending upon the early moving of horses to awaken them, chances are they will have an alarm clock to sound the signal for the beginning of another day.[81]

Army Chief to Meet Car

Before leaving Cleveland, the enterprising Shanks wrote to commanding General of the Army, Lieutenant General Nelson A. Miles in Washington, D.C., asking that he "sanction the proposed expedition and assist in the matter of giving it a semi-official character by authorizing the transportation of military documents from the Pacific to the Atlantic."[82]

Miles, who began his military career during the Civil War and later became "one of the Army's premier Indian-fighters,"[83] was nonetheless forward-looking. Like Winton, he belonged to the Automobile Club of America, and he appreciated the military value of the automobile. *Cycle and Automobile Trade Journal* reported that Miles had written to the War Office as early as 1903 to recommend "the use of motor cars and motor cycles in the army, declaring that the cavalry is obsolete, and that motor vehicles will take the place of horses in the next war."[84]

Miles replied to Shanks, saying, "I shall be pleased to receive you in New York personally, or through one of my staff officers, such message as you may bring by automobile from San Francisco." Further, he suggested that Shanks seek the message from "the officer commanding on the Pacific coast." Miles made no further commitment or endorsement. Yet the *Plain Dealer* printed his letter and a large lithograph of Miles under the front-page headline, "Miles to Receive the Automobilists/The Commander-in-Chief of the United States Army Interested in the Plain Dealer's Transcontinental Trip."[85]

Shanks garnered headlines of his own upon reaching San Francisco in early May—evidence that the newspaper stunt was attracting "no little attention," a satisfied *Plain Dealer* noted. The proposed trip would be a "hazardous journey," acknowledged the *San Francisco Bulletin*:

> That's a long trip ahead of Charles B. Shanks and Alexander Winton—over mountain and plain in an automobile from San Francisco to New York—but then the former gentleman is backed by the enterprise and progressive spirit of the *Cleveland Plain Dealer*, while the latter is known to cha[u]ffeurs the world over as president of the Winton Motor Carriage Co. . . . Mr. Shanks is here now, stopping at The Occidental [Hotel] and the automobile is somewhere between Cleveland and San Francisco. . . .
>
> Mr. Shanks is an enthusiastic little man, who is all wrapped up in the project outlined, and who does not look at the impossible side of the venture at all. . . . "The journey is full of difficulties, you know, but," he added with a merry little twinkle in his eye that bespoke the enthusiasm and confidence within him, "I think we will be able to make it."[86]

Stock Car Offers Best Test

For three reasons, the coast-to-coast Winton would be a stock car instead of a specially prepared vehicle, Shanks advised *Motor Age*:

> We at first thought of making the trip in a machine built for speed. This idea was abandoned, however, first because a machine of the standard pattern will render better service in fording streams and in rough use generally, second because duplicate parts, should any become necessary, are readily obtainable, and last, but by no means least, because the ride on a standard vehicle will be a better test of the real merits of an automobile. So we shall make the trip on a machine with no other special preparation than increased storage room for gasoline.[87]

Shanks said little about how the men prepared and equipped the car. But photographs reveal that it carried a large coil of rope, a bucket, and a pair of headlamps. Other equipment included a block and tackle, an ax, and a cyclometer—an early form of speedometer and odometer. "The party will be equipped with a Winchester repeating rifle and each will carry a new model regulation army revolver," the *Plain Dealer* reported.[88]

One valuable item aboard the transcontinental auto was a letter of introduction from a Southern Pacific official addressed to "Agents, Southern Pacific Company." It asked railroad agents to assist Winton and Shanks in any way possible to "further the success" of the overland trip.[89]

A day before departing, Shanks picked up a second letter when he visited Major General William R. Shafter, well known for leading the 1898 American attack on Cuba during the Spanish-American War. Shafter, as commanding general of the Department of California, gave Shanks "a packet of military documents" to deliver to Lieutenant General Miles. Winton, who arrived in San Francisco on May 17, spent the day before the start looking over the automobile.[90]

Off to New York

According to the *San Francisco Examiner*, Winton and Shanks climbed into their auto and left the Occidental Hotel at 6:30 AM on Monday, May 20, 1901, heading toward the harbor. Thus, the travelers reached their starting point bright and early. Shanks wired the *Plain Dealer*:

They're Off.

We are off to New York, across the continent by automobile, the longest and most arduous journey ever undertaken by a horseless carriage in this country. I drop this message at the last telegraph office on the outskirts of San Francisco.

As I wired the *Plain Dealer* last night Mr. Winton had completed all arrangements and the start was made this morning at 7:15, promptly on time, from the Ferrier [Ferry] building, at the foot of Market street.

The newspapers have paid much attention to the novel journey backed by the *Plain Dealer*, and in consequence a big crowd gathered to see us off and wish us good luck on the way [see Fig. 12]. We shot away from the cheering mass, and our journey was begun....

It is our intention to go at least as far as Sacramento today, but prophets are not lacking who say that on account of the low, swampy country ahead of us, we shall be forced to lay up over night before reaching that city. Our machine is in perfect order, our spirits good and our nerve with us.[91]

"A Guessing Contest Will Add Interest to the Trip,"[92] proclaimed the *Plain Dealer* as it began its daily coverage of the transcontinental trek. The newspaper offered $100 in prizes to readers who came closest to guessing the elapsed time of the journey (see Fig. 13).

If Winton and Shanks "shot away" from the cheering masses, it was only to drive aboard the steam-powered ferry that took them across San Francisco Bay to Oakland. According to Monday's *Oakland Enquirer*:

> At exactly two and one half minutes before 8 o'clock this morning and about thirty seconds after the creek boat, Garden City, had touched at Broadway slip an automobile shot up the apron, across the wharf and up Broadway. . . . [Winton and Shanks] lost no time in getting

Fig. 13. The *Cleveland Plain Dealer* invited readers to guess the car's elapsed time to New York City (*Cleveland Plain Dealer*, May 23, 1901).

started this morning and after hurried farewells to a number of automobilists who met them at the slip, they started at a high rate of speed for Port Costa, hoping to catch the train which leaves the Oakland mole connecting with the 8 o'clock ferry boat from San Francisco. This would give them about an hour and fifteen minutes in which to reach Port Costa. . . . The rate of speed at which they expect to travel [across the country] will be from 7 to 30 miles an hour and may exceed the latter rate on good roads.[93]

Road Hazard: Adobe Mud

In his rush to reach Port Costa, Winton made a wrong turn that added 12 miles to the 32-mile drive. Thus, the autoists missed the 9:15 AM ferry boat that carried South Pacific Express No. 4 across the mile-wide Carquinez Strait. They crossed on the 11:17 AM railroad ferry instead. As their boat neared the east bank, a sudden downpour ended a three-week dry spell and produced roads so muddy that the Winton drivers wrapped rope around their tires for extra traction—but got stuck anyway. The men traveled 60 miles in the rain, which began about noon and continued all day, soaking the occupants of the topless Winton.

Rain soaked them on five of the run's ten days, Shanks would report. On Day 1, extricating the car from the "adobe mud" (see Fig. 14) with a block and tackle became a formidable chore, as Shanks describes in clipped prose:

> Pull out block and tackle, wade around in the mud, get soaked to the skin and chilled from the effects of the deluge, make fastenings to the fence or telephone post and pull. Pull hard, dig your heels into the mud and exert every effort at command. The machine

Fig. 14. "One must get deep into adobe mud to fully appreciate it," the cutline read (*Scientific American Supplement*, Aug. 3, 1901).

moves, your feet slip and down in the mud you go full length. Repeat the dose and continue the operation until the machine is free from the ditch and again upon the road.[94]

Winton and Shanks stopped for the night at A. W. Butler's ranch, about 10 miles west of the town of Rio Vista, ending what had been a twelve-hour travel day. "The machine is run in his barn, we eat supper with intense relish, go to bed and get up early to find more rain, but a breaking up of the clouds with prospect of sunshine later," Shanks wrote.[95]

The Climb Commences

Leaving Butler's ranch shortly after 7:00 AM on Day 2, Tuesday, May 21, the motorists drove through heavy mud and crossed the Sacramento River on a ferry near Rio Vista. They bought gas in Sacramento at 1:15 PM, and then drove on eastward and upward into the Sierra Nevada, through Roseville, Rocklin, Loomis, Penryn, and Newcastle to Auburn.

"From Auburn the climb commenced, and when Colfax was reached and passed Mr. Winton was busy with his skillful knowledge in crowding the machine up steep mountain grades, along dangerous shelf roads from which one might look deep into canons and listen to the distant roaring of rushing waters below," Shanks wrote.[96] Fortunately, the sun was out and drying the roads.

The car chugged higher and higher as it traveled east from Colfax to Cape Horn Mills and Gold Run, a gold-mining camp where the transcontinentalists stopped for the night at 7:40 PM, as darkness fell. The car had traveled 123 miles and climbed to an altitude 3,200 feet higher than the Sacramento River in an elapsed time of twelve hours—a fast 10.25-mph pace considering the hills.

Fig. 15 (opposite). One source identified this scene as the "Yuba Valley"—that is, the South Yuba River, which Winton (*pictured*) and Shanks followed eastward from Cisco, California (JW).

Winton and Shanks left Gold Run at 6:45 AM on Day 3, Wednesday, May 22. Negotiating progressively more rugged mountain roads, they climbed through the northern California towns of Dutch Flat, Towle, Blue Canyon, Emigrant Gap, Cisco, and Cascade. About 3 miles northwest of Cisco, the South Yuba River joined the trail. The

Fig. 16. "Up and up we went," Shanks wrote. This snapshot, taken at an unidentified point in the Sierras, illustrates his point (*Auto Era*, Sept. 1901).

travelers would run alongside the South Yuba (see Fig. 15) until they neared the Sierra Nevada summit.

Between Gold Run and Cascade, the car forded several streams. To stay dry, Winton and Shanks occasionally had to lift their feet from the floorboards. "Up and up we went, winding around and turning in many directions—but always up," Shanks wrote (see Fig. 16).[97] Reaching Emigrant Gap at mid-morning, Shanks wired the *Plain Dealer*:

Grades from Gold Run to this place were so bad that it has taken more than two hours to cover the twenty miles. . . . Monday there was a three-inch snowfall preceded by a half-inch rainfall. As a consequence the trails are heavy and dangerously slippery.

Mr. Winton has to operate with great care to prevent going off the narrow trails into deep canons. Ours is the first automobile ever to reach this altitude in the high Sierras. People here in Emigrant Gap . . . express grave doubts as to our ability to get through the snow up the several grades necessary to climb but we are going against it nevertheless.[98]

A Wheel Falls Off

More specifically, the residents warned Winton and Shanks that the worst roads of their transcontinental journey would be from Emigrant Gap east to Donner Lake. Indeed, the rocks in the road got larger as Winton approached a natural formation called New Hampshire Rocks, where a jolt pitched Shanks into the air. "I was not thrown from the machine, however, and thereafter busied myself hanging on with hands and bracing with feet."[99]

Would Winton tackle New Hampshire Rocks and thus "put the machine to what appeared to me the supreme and awful test"? Shanks wondered. "Of course I will," was Winton's short and meaningful answer, and on he went (see Fig. 17).[100]

Safely beyond the Rocks and topping an elevation of 6,300 feet, the car forded Cascade Creek—clear, rocky, and swollen from melting snow. As it edged toward the east bank, the car hit an obstruction that pitched the front end into the air. When it landed, "the right front wheel with a wet tire struck a wet slanting rock. . . . The front axle on the right side sustained an injury, and after a lurch ahead the machine came to a sudden standstill."[101] Shanks walked a mile to a railroad telegraph station, where he wired the Cleveland factory for a new part. He also summoned help from Emigrant Gap.

Shanks's *Plain Dealer* dispatch, "Lost a Wheel in the Mountains," was more dramatic and immediate, yet differed slightly from the article he wrote two months later for the *Scientific American Supplement*:

> When nearly across and things looked lovely there came a sudden stop like running against a stone. The wheels were wedged and the momentum of the machine caused such pressure that something had to give way, and off came the right front wheel.
>
> When the wheel came off the power pushing the machine, together with the axle bounding on the bowlder, caused the front end of the carriage to shoot up and, as good luck had it, the front went up on the last bank and free of the water. . . .
>
> The accident occurred at 12:30, and after an hour's wait L. S. Kelley of Emigrant Gap came driving along with an ax. We cut a sapling, Mr. Winton got in the machine, and when Mr. Kelley and I lifted the front end to relieve the pressure from the ground, he applied the power, straddled the bowlder which caused the trouble and got the machine up from the water at the side of the road.[102]

"The Wildest Adventures"

Winton and Shanks left the car and returned with Kelley to Emigrant Gap, 14 miles away. The new part would arrive in about four days, Shanks predicted. "In the meantime we will have opportunity to enjoy some good hunting and fishing."[103]

Too impatient to wait for replacement parts, Winton set out the next morning, Thursday, May 23, and spent the day making temporary repairs to the axle. Later, at a railroad station farther east, Winton planned to pick up and install the replacement part sent from Cleveland. The two men set off from Cascade Creek in the repaired Winton at 7:00 AM on Friday, May 24. "From that hour until 1:40 this afternoon our experience has been nothing short of the wildest adventures," Shanks telegraphed from the train dispatcher's office in Summit, California, which he also called Summit Station:

> Twice we slid off the snowbank into the ditches and at other times it was necessary to use the ropes to get the machine up to the snow level again. On the last slide the machine narrowly escaped being overturned because the rear wheel came in contact with a bowlder during its course downward.
>
> To make the situation all the more trying, it was raining hard when we rode from Cascade creek at 7 o'clock and as we approached the higher altitude hail and snow were encountered. Both of us are wet to the skin, but before leaving here we shall take time to dry out and straighten up a bit.
>
> Of Mr. Winton's heroic work in getting the machine this far along, too much cannot be said. That there is a whole piece left of the motor is not the fault of the rocks and snow covered roads and the elements with which we had to contend [see Fig. 18].[104]

Stalled in a Snowdrift

The weather remained poor and Summit residents warned of "a fearfully steep hill," slushy and slippery, 4 miles to the east. Regardless, Winton and Shanks left Summit that afternoon to attempt the drive to Truckee. "As they have not arrived here yet," reported a later wire-service dispatch from Truckee, "it is supposed they are stalled in the huge snow drifts above Donner Lake."[105]

That, in fact, is exactly what happened. According to Shanks's later account, they had been aided by "a small crew with shovels" (see Fig. 19), after which the car safely

Fig. 18. "That there is a whole piece left of the motor is not the fault of the rocks and snow covered roads," wrote Shanks, who snapped these photos at unidentified locations in the Sierra Nevada (*Auto Era*, Sept. 1901).

descended the hill that Summit residents had warned them about. But at the bottom, when "the last important snow deposit was reached . . . the machine sank through so deep that it could not be extricated with ease by ropes or shoveling."[106] The snowbank was just 17 miles from the Cascade Creek ford where Winton and Shanks had started that morning.

Abandoning their car for the second time in three days, the men walked back to spend the night at the Summit hotel. On Saturday, May 25, Day 6, aided by "some kindly disposed railroad men who could handle shovels most effectively," Winton and Shanks freed the car from the snowbank. The adventurers had set out from San Francisco believing they could drive on top of the snow. "I had made a special advance trip up to the summit and my investigation bore out that belief," Shanks recalled. But several days of rain "had rotted the snowdrifts to such an extent that the crusts were not sufficiently strong to support the weight of the machine and it was necessary to fight it through bad places."[107]

Once free, the travelers forged ahead through smaller drifts to at last reach Truckee, a gas stop. Continuing east at about noon, the men traveled just 7 miles to arrive during a "terrific downpour" at the town of Hobart Mills, California, owned by the Sierra Nevada Wood and Lumber Company. Winton, who hoped to find the new part waiting in Wadsworth, Nevada, wanted to again strengthen the car's front axle. Thus, the men spent Saturday afternoon and evening at Hobart Mills, and remained over on Sunday, May 26, to rest and dry their clothes, Shanks wrote in his 1901 accounts.[108]

Fig. 19. Volunteers help Shanks and Winton free the car from a deep snowdrift east of Summit, California. Shanks took this photo on either May 24 or May 25 (*Auto Era*, Nov. 1901).

"The Crankshaft Is Busted"

Thirty years would elapse before Shanks finally revealed (for an article in *MoTor* magazine) what *really* happened in Hobart Mills:

> Just as we were approaching the Nevada line and had pulled up to the summit of a sand hill that permitted a view into the beautiful valley in which nestled Hobart Mills—a little lumber mill town—something went wrong with the motor. It began to "race" at a terrific speed. Mr. Winton switched off the ignition and took advantage of our momentum to coast down the grade and, providentially, came to a stop right in front of the lumber camp's blacksmith shop.
>
> "What's the matter?" I asked the skipper. "Oh! nothing much," he answered. "The crankshaft is busted and there isn't another like it in the whole world."
>
> So there we were—off the line of [the] railroad and as completely out of touch with civilization as one could wish to be.
>
> But we were on our way again next morning. Mr. Winton dismantled the motor, welded the shaft at the blacksmith's forge and reassembled the job between sundown and sunup. Which was certainly going some.
>
> The reason there wasn't a duplicate of the broken shaft was because the motor was "hand made." Pioneer experiences such as that emphasized the need of standardization in parts.[109]

Despite Shanks's later assertion, in his *MoTor* article, that he and Winton were back on the road by the following morning, the two men actually spent all day Sunday at Hobart Mills. It represented "the only really comfortable twenty-four hours we have had since we left San Francisco last Monday morning," Shanks wrote in his *Plain Dealer* dispatch from the lumber camp:

> We have kept both warm and dry. . . . The machine is clean, and, as far as the power is concerned, in perfect order. The front axle, broken in fording the chilly waters of Cascade creek, has been once more strengthened until Mr. Winton believes it will stand the trip on to Wadsworth tomorrow morning. There we touch the railroad again and expect to receive the extra parts necessary to replace the broken axle.[110]

Fear and Admiration in Reno

Leaving Hobart Mills at 6:00 AM on Monday, May 27, Day 8, Winton and Shanks continued east across the Nevada border to Reno. "Never before had an automobile crossed the Sierras," Reno's *Daily Nevada State Journal* declared, "and the two voyagers will be many years older before they again essay the trip. . . . This auto is the first that has ever invaded the State and was respectively admired and feared by people and horses."[111]

The men ate breakfast at the Riverside Hotel and left for Wadsworth at 9:40 AM. But they "had scarcely cleared the boundaries of Reno before the clouds opened and such a spill of moisture as followed would be hard to imagine."[112]

Shanks telegraphed Monday afternoon from Wadsworth, some 35 miles east of Reno and 385 miles beyond San Francisco: "At noon we were in the midst of a terrific thunderstorm. Lightning flashed in all quarters. Fear was felt lest the steel construction of the machine would attract a bolt, but it escaped. We continued in the rain, however, and at 3 o'clock reached Wadsworth." They were "splashed and covered with mud, wet through and hungry."[113] They were also disappointed because the parts for repairing the Winton's damaged axle had not yet arrived.

Shanks had no illusions about the next stage of the journey, as he wrote in his daily *Plain Dealer* dispatch:

> From Wadsworth east our troubles are expected to begin afresh. The dreaded desert sand and alkali will envelop us. The towns and ranches occur at very remote periods. If from this time on you do not get a report from us each evening you may know that we are out of telegraph office range and in camp somewhere in the sand and alkali. From this time on we will carry rations and water for drinking [see Fig. 20].[114]

According to Tuesday's *Wadsworth Semi-Weekly Dispatch*:

> The automobile that is making a transcontinental trip arrived Monday afternoon. It was repaired here and started east this morning. It was Wadsworth's first sight of such a machine and attracted much attention. . . . [Winton and Shanks] carried a letter addressed to "General Nelson A. Miles, Commanding [the] Army, Washington, D.C. Transmitted by the first automobile to cross the Continent of North America," from General Shafter.[115]

Rough Going "Cannot Be Described"

Wadsworth residents had warned Winton and Shanks about a sandhill 2 miles to the east. Leaving town at about 7:00 AM on Tuesday, May 28, the autoists had "ascended part of the stiff sand grade when Mr. Winton decided to change to a lower gear so as to ease the machine over the sands, in which we were deeply imbedded when half way to the summit."[116] Making the change took about six hours; they left Wadsworth a second time at 2:30 PM. Even with the lower gear, the men had to cut sagebrush to

Fig. 20. Somewhere in northwestern Nevada, Shanks photographed his employer during "a halt for 'dinner' in the desert" (*Scientific American Supplement*, Aug. 3, 1901).

feed under the Winton's wheels so the auto could climb the steep sandhill. Shanks wrote at the end of the day's difficult 9-mile run:

> What has been experienced by the "Plain Dealer Overland Limited" during this day cannot be described so that our good friends in the east would understand. . . . From [Wadsworth] to Desert Station, where I am now writing, the country through which we passed was something terrible.
>
> Although we had tied ropes around the driving wheels, they slipped, slid and cut around in the sand in a terrible manner. That we got this far is a wonder. The hard rainstorm which swept over us during the several hours did good in the way of preventing a sandstorm. It lowered the temperature, but made the sand none the less hard to pull through. . . .
>
> It was hard, slow work, but we pulled through on our own power. We reached Desert Station at 5:45 p.m.—three hours and fifteen minutes to cover nine miles. So it can be imagined what work we had.[117]

Desert Station was not actually a town, but rather "a box car which had been set out on a short siding."[118] Its inhabitants were D. H. Gates, the Southern Pacific section boss, and his wife; telegraph operator J. O. Howard; and nine Japanese laborers. Gates fed them and Howard "has given us the use of his bunk tonight," Shanks advised the *Plain Dealer*. He concluded his dispatch from Desert Station on a sober note: "We are in the depth of the desert. Our progress must necessarily be slow. A schedule is impossible, but Mr. Winton will certainly get this automobile through if it is within the range of possibility."[119]

Soft, Shifting Quicksand

A clear day greeted the travelers when they left Desert Station at 6:00 AM on Wednesday, May 29, Day 10 of their transcontinental trek. Traveling northeasterly, over better roads, they forded four streams and used spare railroad ties to fill and cross a washout.

South of Lovelock, the auto crossed the Humboldt Sink, an area where the Humboldt River disappears into the sand (see Fig. 21). Arriving at noon, the first automobile ever seen in Lovelock "attracted considerable attention," according to the *Lovelock Argus*. Added the *Lovelock Tribune*: "The automobile went through Wednesday and drew quite a crowd. Mr. Winton and Mr. Shanks took lunch here and took on

Fig. 21. "Ploughing through Humbol[d]t Sink, in the Nevada sand desert, on a Winton" (*Auto Era*, Nov. 1901).

board twenty gallons of gasoline. Only a mile below town they stuck fast in a mudhole and Mr. Stoker had to pull them out. That mud hole should be fixed."[120]

Just before 5:00 PM, Winton and Shanks reached Mill City, Nevada, 136 miles from Desert Station—their best day's travel since leaving San Francisco. Shanks said the men received a warning about the trip to Winnemucca:

> The Southern Pacific agent there said we could never get to Winnemucca (thirty miles to the east) that night because of the sand hills; the quicksand would bury us, he said. Another man who came up discussed the sand proposition with Mr. Winton and told him that there would be only one way in which "that there thing" could get through this thirty miles' stretch of quicksand. "How?" asked Mr. Winton. "Load her on a flat car and be pulled to Winnemucca."
>
> "Not on your life," retorted the plucky automobilist; into the carriage I jumped, he pulled the lever and off we went. The course led up a hill, but there was enough bottom to the sand to give the wheels a purchase and from the hill summit we forged down into the valley where the country was comparatively level. Nothing in sight but sage brush and sand, sand and sage brush.
>
> Two miles of it were covered. Progress was slow, the sand became deeper and deeper as we progressed. At last the carriage stopped, the driving wheels sped on and cut deep into the bottomless sand. We used block and tackle, got the machine from its hole and tried again. Same result. Tied more ropes around [the] wheels with the hope that the corrugation would give them sufficient purchase in the sand. Result: Wheels cut deeper in less time than before.
>
> It was a condition never encountered by an automobilist in the history of the industry. We were in soft, shifting quicksand where power counted as nothing. We were face to face with a condition the like of which cannot be imagined—one must be in it, fight with it, be conquered by it, before a full and complete realization of what it actually is will dawn upon the mind.
>
> Mr. Winton said to me: "Do you know what we are up against here? I told the *Plain Dealer* I would put this enterprise through if it were possible. Right here we are met by the impossible. Under present conditions no automobile can go through this quicksand." I suggested loading the machine and sending it by freight to Winnemucca. "No, sir," he flashed back emphatically. "If we can't do it on our own power this expedition ends right here, and I go back with a knowledge of conditions and an experience such as no automobilist in this or any other country has gained."[121]

Help from Husky Horses

In marked contrast to his *Scientific American Supplement* account, written two months after the fact, Shanks wrote in his *Plain Dealer* dispatches that he and Winton used a block and tackle to free the auto not once but three times, each time progressing a few feet. "Then we were hailed by a man who had come out from Mill City on the railroad track to see what progress we had made. He said the sand was as bad, and in many sections worse, all the way to Winnemucca."[122]

At that point, 530 miles from San Francisco by the car's cyclometer, the autoists gave up and walked back to Mill City, where they hired a rancher and "a husky team of horses" to recover the car. The horses pulled out the auto and, "aided by the motor's power and the laying of planks here and there, Mill City was finally reached." Winton arranged to ship the car by rail from Mill City back to Cleveland. The men then "jumped"—apparently literally—onto the caboose of a freight train as it rolled through the town, finally arriving in Winnemucca about midnight.[123] From Winnemucca the next day, Thursday, May 30, Winton and Shanks boarded the 2:40 PM eastbound Southern Pacific passenger train, arriving home in Cleveland at 7:35 PM on June 2.

Because Shanks had been unable to wire any news on Wednesday, Thursday's *Plain Dealer* could only speculate in its headline that the travelers were "Probably Camping in the Desert." The word finally came via press dispatch on Thursday: "The automobile transcontinental trip is off and the adventurous tourists will finish their trip in a Pullman car."[124] It was only on Friday that the Cleveland paper could report the travelers' "Hopeless Fight with Desert Sand" (see Figs. 22 and 23) to its readers.

Shanks later reflected on the lessons of the trip:

> That the expedition failed is no fault of the machine Mr. Winton used, nor was it due to absence of grit or determination on the part of the operator. Neither was the failure due to roads. The utter absence of roads was the direct and only cause. . . . It was the soft, shifting, bottomless, rolling sand—not so bad to look upon from [train] car windows, but terrible when actually encountered—that caused the abandonment of the enterprise.[125]

Next Time, a Portable Bridge

Both men arrived home "brown as berries" from the desert sun. Winton appeared in good health, though he walked "with a decided limp, produced by injuries to his knee received in jumping a freight train in the desert after his machine had got stuck," the *Cleveland Plain Dealer* reported.[126] Because there had been no roads or trails to follow on their route through Nevada, the men never lost sight of the railroad, Winton explained:

Fig. 22 (above). Winton called off the trek when his car stalled in deep sand 2 miles east of Mill City, Nevada. Does this photo show that point? The cutline said merely: "Quick-sand in Nevada desert, where machine would sink to the axles, rendering progress impossible" (*Scientific American Supplement*, Aug. 3, 1901).

Fig. 23 (right). Headlines tell of the hardships that ended in "a Hopeless Fight with Desert Sand."

There being no roads, there were of course no bridges. We could not go over the railroad bridges, and were forced to ford the majority of the streams and ravines.

Those which were too deep, or where the bottom appeared impracticable, we had to cross by means of bridges built by ourselves. All along the line of the railroad were piles of ties, and we utilized these on more than one occasion for bridge building purposes.

If I ever attempt the trip again I shall certainly carry a bridge along with me. This is not a joke, but very serious. I do intend to make another attempt at the transcontinental trip, and I intend to have a portable bridge constructed. . . . I surely intend to try it over again. I hate to give up anything which I have started to do.[127]

Though disappointed with the results, Winton nonetheless regarded the transcontinental attempt as a valuable test of his automobile:

I started at the Pacific because of the greater hardships to be met at this side of the continent and wishing to finish the worst end if possible before getting into the east, where there are roadways. I have put the machine over the high Sierras, I have run over the rockiest road in America, have driven through snow and we have pulled and shoveled her from snowdrifts into which she has fallen. Streams without number have been forded; in short, this automobile has taken more abuse and hard service than any machine ever stood. But with all her power it is utterly impossible to drive through this sand.[128]

A Success as Far as It Went

In a face-saving editorial, "A Success as Far as It Went," the *Plain Dealer* echoed the sentiments of Winton and Shanks:

> Through the plucky persistency of Mr. Winton, the inventor and manufacturer of the Winton automobile, and of the *Plain Dealer* representative, Mr. Shanks, who accompanied him on his daring and perilous journey, a record has been made beyond anything ever attempted in automobile history. . . .
>
> Mr. Winton has effectively demonstrated that his automobile will do what had never before been done by an automobile. He has found that not even his machine can traverse the loose sand and alkali of the desert, where there is no hold for the wheels and where their revolutions only cut the way downward instead of forward.
>
> The *Plain Dealer* automobile expedition has attracted widespread attention and there was a general hope that the plucky automobilists would succeed in the adventure, although they had from the beginning expressed doubts of getting through. It has shown that more can be accomplished than was before regarded possible. It has also made evident the limitations of automobile possibilities.[129]

In generally praising the attempt, automobile journals treated Winton more favorably than they had John D. and Louise Hitchcock Davis two years previously. It helped, of course, that the Winton–Shanks attempt had engaged the public's interest for just ten days (see Table 2), instead of dragging on for weeks. Likewise, the automobile journals—which had been kept in the dark about the auto's broken crankshaft—evidently believed that the Winton performed more reliably than had the Davises' National Duryea.

"The failure of the transcontinental run of Winton and Shanks calls attention to the terrible condition of the desert trails in the Western part of the United States," *Horseless Age* declared. The trip's lesson "seems to be that the automobile is not a sand plow, and that efforts in the direction of its improvement can find a more promising field than the desert lands of . . . North America."[130]

Motor Vehicle Review predicted that the Winton company would "secure considerable advertising out of the unsuccessful yet remarkable trip recently made by Messrs.

TABLE 2. Winton and Shanks's Daily Progress, 1901

Day / Date	City–City
1 / May 20 Mon	San Francisco, Calif.–east of Port Costa, Calif.
2 / May 21 Tue	East of Port Costa, Calif.–Gold Run, Calif.
3 / May 22 Wed	Gold Run, Calif.–east of Emigrant Gap, Calif.[a]
4 / May 23 Thu	*repair day*
5 / May 24 Fri	East of Emigrant Gap, Calif.–east of Summit, Calif.[b]
6 / May 25 Sat	Summit, Calif.–Hobart Mills, Calif.
7 / May 26 Sun	*repair day at Hobart Mills, Calif.*
8 / May 27 Mon	Hobart Mills, Calif.–Wadsworth, Nev.
9 / May 28 Tue	Wadsworth, Nev.–Desert Station, Nev.
10 / May 29 Wed	Desert Station, Nev.–2 miles east of Mill City, Nev.

SOURCES: Charles B. Shanks's *Cleveland Plain Dealer* dispatches and *Scientific American Supplement* summary; auto journals; local newspapers.

[a] When it broke a front-axle part, Shanks and Winton left the car overnight at Cascade Creek, 14 miles east of Emigrant Gap. They rode in a wagon back to Emigrant Gap.

[b] The men hiked to Summit for the night, leaving the car stuck in the snow 4 miles east.

Winton and Shanks." This was largely due to Shanks's photos, which were said to be "as thrilling as some of Kipling's sketches." The Winton company published Shanks's photos and account of the trip in a booklet. "From the photographs shown in this book," commented *Cycle and Automobile Trade Journal*, "the roads encountered are shown to be the worst conceivable."[131]

When the auto finally arrived by train in Cleveland, it was bought by Indianapolis Winton agent Carl G. Fisher—father of the Indianapolis Motor Speedway, the Lincoln Highway, and many other business ventures. "Carl geared it up and 'cleaned up' around the state fairs in Indiana during the latter part of 1901,"[132] Shanks related. The fate of this would-be first automobile to cross America is lost to history.

Winton and Shanks Move On

Following their failed attempt, Shanks continued working for Winton. In June 1908, however, he announced that he would leave Winton to run the Cleveland and northern Ohio agency for the Chalmers auto. Shanks held a succession of jobs in the ensuing years: he was sales and advertising manager for the makers of the Stearns auto in Cleveland and the Premier auto in Indianapolis; led his own real estate company in Spokane, Washington; helped produce the Commer and Kelly trucks and the Guy Vaughn car; and directed business affairs for the Class Journal Company, publishers of four auto journals.[133] In 1931 he was sales director for the McCandlish Lithographing Corporation of Philadelphia. Little is known of his later years. In a 1924 special edition on the history of the auto industry, *Automobile Trade Journal* recognized Shanks's years at Winton as "set[ting] the pace that publicity men have had as a mark since."[134]

Winton was too late in mounting another effort to drive the first automobile across America. The Cleveland automaker said in mid-1903 that he "expected eventually" to accomplish the feat. But his attention turned to racing, and he never made an attempt to repeat his undertaking.[135]

Though without a Winton at the wheel, a Winton car, at least—driven by Dr. H. Nelson Jackson—did make the first successful crossing that very year (see Chapter 2). After the last autos bearing his name appeared in 1924, Winton focused on building Winton diesel engines, until he largely retired from business in 1928. He died on June 21, 1932, one day after his seventy-second birthday.[136]

Not Beaten, Just Distracted

In a 1972 article, "Alexander Winton: An Unsung Genius," Winton biographer William S. McKinstry lamented that Winton's contributions to the U.S. auto industry had been widely overlooked. "How many remember him today as a wizard of mechanical and motive invention?" McKinstry asked. Instead, Winton's name is more often connected with automobile *sales*, for in 1898 Alexander Winton sold one of his cars to Robert Allison of Port Carbon, Pennsylvania. That car later found its way into the Smithsonian Institution, which displayed it as "The First Automobile of American Manufacture Sold in the United States."[137]

Had Winton in 1901 become the first person to drive across the country, he would have earned a more secure place in history than he perhaps now enjoys. Ironically, however, it would still have been for reasons other than his inventiveness.

One senses that Winton did not consider himself beaten by the Nevada sands. Rather, like a distracted bulldog, he lost interest in solving an old problem—that of crossing the continent as an automobile publicity stunt—and sank his jowls into a new challenge: automobile racing. Given the auto's general sturdiness and Winton's abilities as a mechanic and driver, it is likely that by persevering he would have finished his 1901 trip. His quick submission to the sand suggests he was both unprepared for it and unwilling to make the sacrifices necessary to continue.

Within five days after calling off the trip and declaring "we are met by the impossible," Winton had solved the problem: he told the *Plain Dealer* he would attempt another trip across Nevada in a car equipped with a portable bridge. Undoubtedly inspired by Winton's difficulties, other drivers would prove it a sound idea. For example, two years later, Tom Fetch, N. O. Allyn, and Marius C. Krarup drove through Nevada in the second car to span the continent, they crossed the deepest sand by spreading strips of canvas in front of the car—thereby using, in effect, a portable bridge (see Chapter 3). As late as 1908, the Thomas entry in the New York–Paris race traveled across parts of America with sturdy wooden planks—another portable bridge—strapped to its sides.

There were other ways to cross deep sand. During their 1903 crossing, for instance, Lester L. Whitman and Eugene Hammond wrapped the rear wheels of their Oldsmobile with "sand tires," cotton-stuffed canvas coverings that gave the tires a wide, flat point of contact with the sand (see Chapter 4). Regardless, had Winton stayed in Nevada to refine his idea for a portable bridge, he might have been able to resume the journey from Mill City after a few days, at most.

Winton also had other Nevada routes open to him, had he cared to consult with some Nevadans or even explore such routes personally. Faced by sandy or otherwise impassable roads, many later record-breaking drivers avoided these obstacles by driving over a railway roadbed for short distances or simply returning to a previous town to seek alternative routes. Two years after Winton bogged down nearby, Fetch's Packard arrived in Mill City. Duly warned by residents about the deep sand ahead, Fetch skirted the area by taking a steep mountain trail to Dun Glen, Nevada. Others, like Dr. H. Nelson Jackson in 1903, or Cannon Ball Baker years later, took northern or southern routes that avoided Nevada altogether.

Winton based his decision to quit the run partly on the opinion of a man who said "the sand was as bad, and in many sections worse, all the way to Winnemucca." Who was this man, and what made him such an authority on the motorists' projected route? Had Winton made other inquiries, he might have heard other opinions less dire. In 1903 Hammond and Whitman drove a route similar to Winton's. Their lightweight Oldsmobile would naturally have less trouble in the sand than the heavier Winton, yet Whitman reported that the only place he had to use his sand tires to any

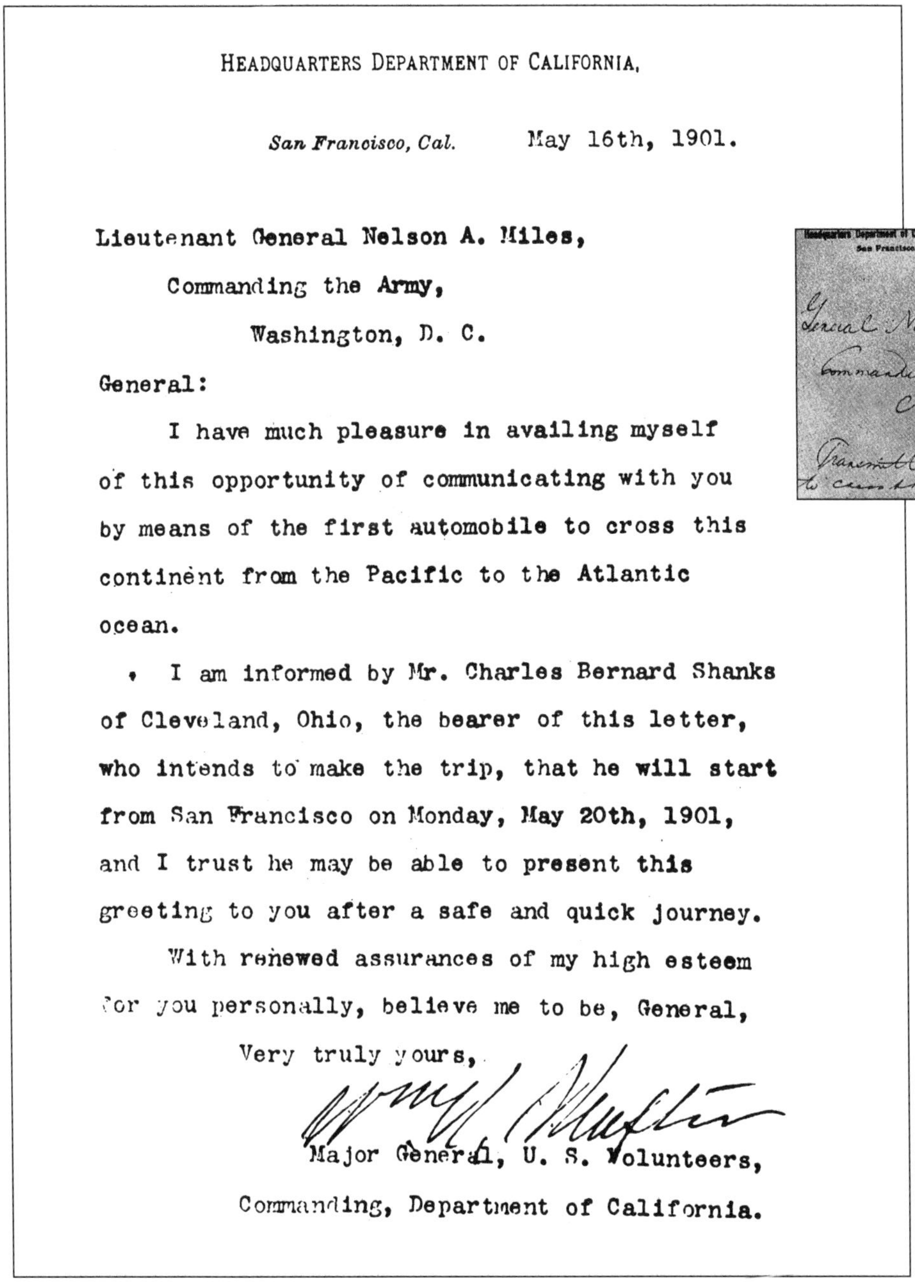

HEADQUARTERS DEPARTMENT OF CALIFORNIA,

San Francisco, Cal.   May 16th, 1901.

Lieutenant General Nelson A. Miles,

    Commanding the Army,

        Washington, D. C.

General:

    I have much pleasure in availing myself of this opportunity of communicating with you by means of the first automobile to cross this continent from the Pacific to the Atlantic ocean.

    I am informed by Mr. Charles Bernard Shanks of Cleveland, Ohio, the bearer of this letter, who intends to make the trip, that he will start from San Francisco on Monday, May 20th, 1901, and I trust he may be able to present this greeting to you after a safe and quick journey.

    With renewed assurances of my high esteem for you personally, believe me to be, General,

      Very truly yours,

      Major General, U. S. Volunteers,

    Commanding, Department of California.

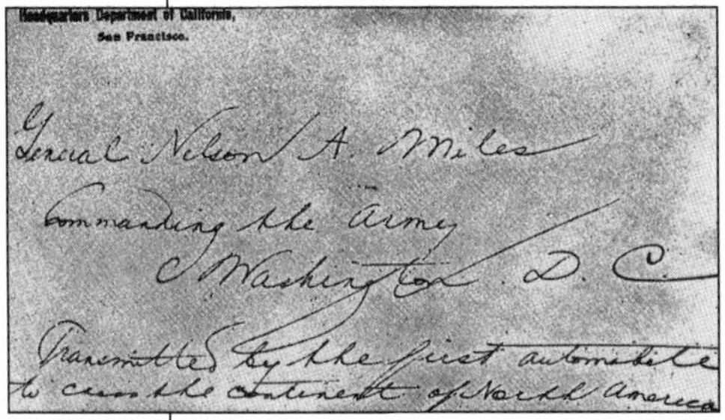

Fig. 24. This letter (and envelope) from Major General William R. Shafter gave the Winton expedition "a semi-official character." But Shafter's message never reached Washington, D.C. (MOT).

extent was "at Wadsworth and Winnemucca, where we encountered 6 to 8 miles of sand drifts 8 to 10 feet high."[138] Thus, at least part of the 30-mile stretch between Mill City and Winnemucca was evidently better than the section Winton and Shanks encountered directly east of the city.

Later drivers followed Winton's example by refusing to ship their autos by train for even short distances. Often, however, they freed themselves from sand or mud by hitching up behind horses—something Winton refused to do. Three cars drove across the country in 1903; each was pulled by horses at one time or another. Though admirable, Winton's rule against accepting help from horses was unrealistically strict. It was also arbitrary, considering he had received help from snow-shovelers earlier. By refusing to adapt to conditions, Winton ultimately doomed his trip. The inventor only added to the strain of a difficult undertaking by allowing himself just two months to complete it. Exploration on a tight deadline seldom produces results.

"Both Generals Shafter and Miles have long since passed from this world of toil and strife," Shanks wrote in 1931, a year before Winton's death. "The rock strewn roads over the High Sierras, the adobe roads of the California valleys, and the shifting sand trails through Nevada, have been replaced with macadam highways. Two, four, eight and sixteen cylinder cars have succeeded the puny single cylinder horseless carriages of those days."[139]

What became of the important-sounding "packet of military documents" that Winton and Shanks carried with them in 1901? It turned out to be merely a friendly note from one officer to another, Shanks revealed in his 1931 account of the trip. The letter, by then, had become "a treasured memento in the Shanks family" (see Fig. 24).[140]

A TRIUMPH TRULY
REMARKABLE

2

"We have come to the conclusion that we can run our car over any road that a man can take a team of horses and a wagon, providing we can get traction."

—Dr. H. Nelson Jackson

WITH NO HELP from the automaker and little preparation on their part, a young Vermont physician and an even younger Tacoma, Washington, mechanic left San Francisco on May 23, 1903, in a 2-cylinder Winton. Dr. H. Nelson Jackson and Sewall K. Crocker[1] drove upwards of 6,000 miles through parts of a dozen states in 63 days, 12 hours, 30 minutes. Their quiet arrival in New York City on July 26—at 4:30 AM, too early for crowds to gather—concluded the first auto trip across the United States.

During their trek, Jackson and Crocker spent nineteen days idle, primarily waiting for shipments of parts. Their 1903 Winton broke a front spring in northern California; lost its front-wheel ball bearings in Idaho; broke both connecting rods in Wyoming; and snapped a front axle near Omaha, Nebraska. By most accounts, including Jackson's, the car used a great many tires, though the exact number is unknown.

Imaginative and conflicting newspaper accounts make it especially difficult to piece together the events of the Jackson–Crocker trip. Jackson is partly to blame. Though the Winton company published Jackson's edited journal after the trip, Jackson himself waited until 1936 to publish the six-page magazine article that auto historians today often consult as a definitive source of the 1903 adventure.[2] Unfortunately, this piece contains some factual errors—in arrival and departure times, for instance, and in recalling where certain incidents occurred—and, given its brevity, many errors of omission. Jackson also embellished some of the already colorful incidents he had written about or described immediately following his 1903 adventure.

Moreover, by refusing to speak to reporters until he had reached the Midwest, Jackson made it difficult for historians to piece together a day-to-day record of his crossing. "After I started I made up my mind to avoid all newspaper men, and I did not talk to one until we reached Omaha. You see my purpose was to keep the trip quiet until I was sure of success. I made this trip without any notoriety," he told the *Cleveland Leader*.[3]

The *San Francisco Chronicle* did learn of the trip and ran a short preview article, without quoting Jackson. The local Winton agent, who knew about Jackson's plans, quite possibly tipped off the newspaper. According to Jackson, not even the Winton Motor Carriage Company factory in Cleveland had known about the trip until it was in progress.

But Jackson found it difficult to remain anonymous while driving through towns whose residents were seeing their first automobile. Thus, newspapers in Oregon, Idaho, Wyoming, and Nebraska generally learned enough to name the two drivers, report their plans, and relate an amusing incident or two. When Jackson and Crocker stopped for repairs or supplies, "most everyone in town took a look at the horseless carriage and asked all sorts of questions."[4] Enterprising reporters then got their stories by simply interviewing witnesses to the spectacle. For that matter, the autoists could have chatted with a crowd of onlookers without knowing that a reporter was among them.

So even without his cooperation, newspapers west of Omaha chronicled Jackson's passage and the commotion it caused. Still, this attempt at a news blackout helped spark rumors that the men either used two cars or shipped their automobile part way by rail. To quell such rumors, Jackson and the Winton company offered $25,000 to anyone who would come forward with evidence discrediting the trek. Apparently, no one did.

In the West, Jackson and Crocker often slept outside. Bystanders who had never before seen an automobile gaped in wonder, or sometimes took flight, at the approach of the coast-to-coast automobile. "Whenever possible, we took citizens for short rides," Jackson wrote. "In more remote places, where natives had never even seen a train, they mistook our machine for a railroad coach which somehow had got off the rails."[5]

Fig. 25. Crocker and car at a shallow ford in an unidentified mountain stream (*Auto Era*, July–Aug. 1903).

Like their failed predecessors, Winton and Shanks, Jackson and Crocker had to do without roads or even bridges in many spots (see Fig. 25). They were able to cross San Francisco Bay and the Snake River separating Oregon and Idaho by ferry boat. Otherwise, "we either bumped over ties on railroad trestles between train schedules, forded streams, or worked the machine across by block-and-tackle."[6] At times, the men winched their car up steep mountain trails and even built their own roads by rolling away boulders or cutting sagebrush for traction over sandy or muddy stretches. To avoid traveling east into the Mojave Desert and the sands of Nevada, where Alexander Winton's transcontinental attempt of 1901 had bogged down, Jackson and Crocker headed north through California's Sierra Nevada.

They crossed into southern Oregon, headed east over mountainous trails through Idaho and Wyoming, and dipped briefly south to Julesburg, Colorado, to reach the smoother, though often muddy, roads crossing the Great Plains of Nebraska into Omaha (see Table 3). At that point, the remaining trip across Iowa, Illinois, Indiana, Ohio, Pennsylvania, and New York notwithstanding, the hard part of the journey was over. The final obstacle was rain, not terrain: "With the exception of Saturday, the last day of our journey, it rained each day from Chicago to New York," Jackson wrote.[7]

Ex-Physician Finds Ingenious Mechanic

Poor health had forced Jackson, 31, to quit his Burlington, Vermont, physician's practice, leaving him free to travel to the West Coast in 1903. Although contemporary

TABLE 3. The Jackson–Crocker
Itinerary, 1903[a]

City	Date of Arrival
San Francisco	May 23 (start)
Tracy, Calif.	May 23
Sacramento, Calif.	May 24
Alturas, Calif.	May 30
Lakeview, Ore.	June 2 or June 4[b]
Chewaucan, Ore.	June 6
Burns, Ore.	June 8
Nampa, Idaho	June 12
Pocatello, Idaho	June 15
Montpelier, Idaho	June 17
Rock Springs, Wyo.	June 21
Rawlins, Wyo.	June 23
Cheyenne, Wyo.	July 2
Kearney, Neb.	July 11
Omaha, Neb.	July 12
Chicago	July 17
Toledo, Ohio	July 19
Cleveland	July 20
Buffalo, N.Y.	July 21
Syracuse, N.Y.	July 23
Schenectady, N.Y.	July 25
New York City	July 26 (finish)

SOURCES: Newspapers, auto journals, and Jackson's
1936 *American Legion Monthly* account.

[a] No attempt was made to search every newspaper
on the route, which partly accounts for the gaps in this
itinerary.

[b] The *Lake County Examiner* and *Lakeview Herald*
disagree on the car's arrival date.

press accounts fail to name Jackson's affliction, a retrospective piece refers to "a touch of tuberculosis." A 1929 biography described Jackson as an 1893 graduate of the University of Vermont medical school, who, "due to illness, was forced to abandon his profession" in 1900. Post-run Winton advertisements nevertheless heralded Jackson as "one of the best known surgeons in the country."[8]

According to *Smithsonian* magazine, Jackson could afford to retire from medicine at such an early age because he had "married the daughter of a Civil War general who made a fortune with Payne's Celery Compound, a patent medicine compounded of, among other things, 20-percent grain alcohol. Comfortably heeled, the Jacksons had gone to California for the winter of 1902–03."[9]

But Alaska and Mexico were also on the itinerary. Jackson and his wife, Bertha (Wells) Jackson, left home in late January 1903 for a business trip to Mexico, according to the *Burlington Daily Free Press*. "I'd gone west for my health," Jackson insisted in one account, but he also told *Motor World* that he was actually "combining business with pleasure."[10]

The business was mining. "We had come down [to California in 1903] from Alaska, where I had been prospecting for gold, and placer mining," Jackson recalled. He ultimately bought interests in several Mexican silver properties and organized a company to mine the silver, serving as the company's managing director from 1904 to 1910.[11]

Jackson's poor health was evidently cured by 1903. At least, no mention of ill health appears in the *New York Herald*'s report of the arrival by auto of the nearly 6-foot-tall Jackson, "a fine, stalwart, blond young giant" who weighed 225 pounds at the start of his trip. Likewise, *Motor World* described Jackson as "bronzed and vigorous, full of energy and vitality." Jackson shed 21 pounds between San Francisco and Cleveland, but said "he was more than thankful for that." By contrast, the trim Crocker weighed about 150 pounds.[12]

At the start of his transcontinental trek, Jackson was new to automobiles. "Until I had bought my first automobile a short time before I had been something of a horse-fancier, owning a small stable of thoroughbreds. But I had succumbed completely to a primary enthusiasm for the new-fangled horseless buggy." As recently as 1901, Jackson had "owned a string of fast horses, and was no friend of the automobile. When he got onto the Vermont boulevards, however, his fast horses were quite unable to keep pace with the iron horses [automobiles], and that discouraged him into buying one himself."[13]

In his 1936 retrospective account, Jackson did not say how he met Crocker, whom he called "an ingenious mechanic."[14] One account suggests that Crocker—who was somewhere between 19 and 22 years of age[15] and also "a professional chauffeur"—chanced to be visiting San Francisco while Jackson was there.[16] Another says Jackson first hired Crocker as his driving instructor.

Crocker "was a professional bicycle racer of repute on the Pacific coast and once drove a pacing machine for 'Dutch' Waller, of six day fame," said the *New York Herald*, referring to the once-popular six-day bicycle races. "As such and as a mechanic in a gasolene engine factory he got the experience which induced Dr. Jackson to choose him as his expert for the long journey." Despite Crocker's driving skills, both men drove the car on their transcontinental journey, according to press accounts and photos showing each man behind the wheel. The *Cleveland Plain Dealer* noted that the young Crocker, who died ten years after the 1903 transcontinental trip, was "not in the best of health" at the start.[17]

To Bet or Not to Bet?

In San Francisco, as Jackson tells it, "I purchased two motor cars, and thereby became very much interested in horseless machines. I was very fortunate in securing the services of Sewell [*sic*] K. Crocker of Tacoma, Wash., an experienced chauffeur." According to *Automobile*'s version of the conversation that inspired America's first coast-to-coast auto trip, during a May 19, 1903, visit to the University Club in San Francisco, "the Doctor overheard some young men . . . discussing automobiling, during the course of which it was asserted to be a practical impossibility to cross the continent in an automobile, and the different unsuccessful attempts that had been made were cited."[18]

Jackson later wrote: "This led me to seriously consider the question and I discussed the matter with Mrs. Jackson and Mr. Crocker. The outcome was that I decided to make the attempt with the assistance of Mr. Crocker."[19] By the time he left on his trek, Jackson had supposedly made a $50 bet—with whom, it is not clear—that he could drive across the country within ninety days.

Jackson's famous bet was never mentioned in interviews at the time. In fact, while discussing his purpose for the trip, Jackson pointedly told a *Cleveland Leader* reporter: "There is no side bet or wager on the result. I was positive that I could make the trip, and undertook it." In his 1936 article, however, he says: "Yes, I collected my fifty-dollar bet." Likewise, in a 1953 interview, Jackson acknowledged making the bet, but added: "The man never paid it. And I never asked him for it." The whole matter of Jackson's supposed bet, then is "subject to debate."[20]

Wanting a Winton

The make of Jackson's first two autos was long in question. One retrospective article, however, identifies his first motor vehicle as an Autocar and his second as a Stanley steamer. But according to a 1953 *Mechanix Illustrated* article, Jackson reportedly purchased a steam-powered Locomobile just a few weeks before the transcontinental journey and then hired Crocker to teach him to drive the car.[21]

Whichever brand of auto he already owned, Jackson evidently judged it inadequate for the transcontinental trip. "After considering various machines and at Mr. Crocker's suggestion, I decided that a 'Winton' was the one I would use," he wrote to the Winton factory three days after reaching New York City. "As there were no new machines in stock on the coast, and a delay would be entailed by waiting for the next shipment, I purchased a 'Winton' by giving a bonus to a private gentleman who had bought one several weeks before and had it in use."[22] The seller was said to be a friend of Jackson's, one "L. C. Rowell of the Wells, Fargo & Company."[23]

Years later, Jackson said he paid $3,000—or $500 over the factory retail price—for a "four-weeks-old stock 1903 Winton touring car, sport-model two-place." In his 1903 letter to the Winton factory, however, Jackson revealed that he actually made the car into a two-passenger sport model by removing the tonneau, or back seat, which allowed him to carry more luggage. He had bought the red car, serial number 1684, with 500 miles on it, and promptly nicknamed it "Vermont," in honor of his wife's native state, he said. Cowboys who traveled for miles to see the passing auto, however, dubbed it the "Go Like Hell Machine."[24]

With a carburetor for each of two opposed cylinders, the engine—mounted amidships, under the seats—developed 20 horsepower. According to the Smithsonian Institution, which today displays the historic Winton in its National Museum of American History, the car has a bore and stroke of 5¼ × 6 inches; a muffler cutout or bypass, to give the car extra power for climbing hills; an under-hood tank in two sections—one for cooling water, the other for 10 gallons of gas; a water pump and radiator; an air pump to supply compressed air for opening the carburetor intake valves; rod-operated petcocks to relieve some cylinder pressure for cranking the engine; a 1-quart sight-drip oiler mounted on the dashboard; an exposed differential gear but enclosed axle shafts; 32 × 4-inch wood-spoke wheels; 91-inch wheelbase; 56-inch tread (the distance between the left and right wheels); a body and four fenders of wood; and a removable hood of wood and metal.[25]

"I had an extra twelve-gallon gasoline tank underneath the front of my car, and only once on the whole trip did we run out of gasoline," Jackson later wrote in a letter to *Automobile* magazine.[26] Its gas supply would allow the car to travel between 200 and 250 miles. The two men left San Francisco carrying an extra 5 gallons of oil. Besides adding a gas tank, Jackson and Crocker further modified the car by removing its rear seat and roping their supplies in its place.

Their 2,500-pound car carried a "dead load" of luggage weighing 336 pounds. Adding Crocker (150 pounds) and Jackson (204 pounds, after losing weight on the trip) brought the car's weight up to about 3,190 pounds, according to Jackson's calculations. By way of preparation, Jackson and Crocker carefully studied the roads over which they expected to travel. They also depended on post office inspectors' records for information concerning roads and distances. Furthermore, Jackson visited the San Francisco Winton agent and arranged for him to send spare parts as the men progressed, just in case they might be needed.[27]

Pistols and Mackintoshes

Four days after Jackson is said to have made his bet, at 1:00 PM on Saturday, May 23, 1903, he and Crocker cranked up the Winton in San Francisco and headed for the Oakland ferry. Jackson's wife took the train back to Burlington, Vermont. There was no large farewell gathering. Jackson would later recall: "I must admit that not many paid much attention to me at the time."[28] That is hardly surprising considering that

Jackson had carefully avoided any pre-trip publicity and that he claimed to have spent only four days preparing for the trip. Indeed, the *San Francisco Chronicle*'s first article about the journey was published on the very day Jackson and Crocker left.

According to the June 4 *Lakeview County Examiner* of Lakeview, Oregon, however, Jackson actually began preparing for the coast-to-coast trek not days but weeks before his May 23 departure: "This trip was projected early in the spring, when Postmaster Wilcox was written to about the roads through here, and who assured them that via Lakeview lies the only feasible way to avoid the sandy deserts from San Francisco to New York."[29]

What might one take on a transcontinental auto trip in 1903? "Planning to sleep where night caught us, we started out with complete camping and cooking outfits, the single spare tire, extra spark plugs and a few tools," Jackson wrote. The spare was fastened to the front of the car (see Fig. 26).

> Taking the tonneau off I used the space for our equipment, which consisted of sleeping bags, rubber mackintoshes for the car and ourselves, leather coats, sweaters, canvass [*sic*] water bag, canteen, a cooking outfit, shot gun, rifle, pistols, ammunition, fishing tackle, a block and tackle with one hundred and fifty feet of rope, a firemans [*sic*] axe, a spade, two

Fig. 26. A coffee pot, canteen, and spare tire are among items lashed to the Winton, which here is stuck in an unidentified western stream (*Auto Era*, July–Aug. 1903).

Barrett jacks [a brand name], a vice, a set of machinists' tools and two telescope valises for clothing.[30]

Each sleeping bag had two blankets inside, of wool and rubber, and a waterproof flap to deflect rain from the sleeper's head. The travelers also packed a variety of canned foods. The only extra parts carried were "one chain, breaker box parts, a full set of engine screws and small parts and one tire shoe or casing and two inner tubes." Their supplies also included a medicine chest, a few books "and the most useful thing of all, as it afterward turned out—pneumatic mattresses of rubber."[31]

Onward to Oregon

Their first day out, Saturday, May 23, the men drove through Oakland and Hayward to reach Tracy, California, for the night. On their second day, they drove through Stockton to Sacramento. The Winton raised a choking cloud of dust as the men bounced over a rutted, bumpy section of road. "We never noticed as our cooking utensils jolted off one by one. When we discovered our loss we could not afford to turn back to seek them. Then and there we decided to live off the country," Jackson recounted.[32]

Thereafter the two subsisted on cold lunches, "or sometimes on the memories of lunches they had had the day before."[33] The losses continued to mount. "We were lucky not to have lost our block [and] tackle, for bit by bit our equipment was disappearing, including my own spectacles and fountain pen. It became necessary to have made a special leather bag so that our precious tools could not be scattered along our trail" (see Fig. 27).[34]

The autoists reached Sacramento at 2:30 PM on Sunday, May 24, Day 2. "There we remained a day supplement-

Fig. 27. Hanging low on the rear of the Winton, the bag fastened by three heavy straps is likely the one Jackson and Crocker had made for their tools (*Auto Era*, July–Aug. 1903).

ing our equipment, notably adding a special headlight in preparation for night driving. Our flickering side-lanterns were useless to illuminate the road" (see Fig. 28).[35] From Sacramento, the travelers drove north through Marysville, Oroville, Chico, Anderson, and Redding in northern California. Near Sacramento, "a woman misdirected them 54 miles in order that her family might have the opportunity of seeing them."[36] In 1953, Jackson would write:

> North of Sacramento we were lost. We met a red-haired young woman riding along on a white horse. "Which way to Marysville?" I asked her. "Right down that road," she said

Fig. 28. A prominent cyclops headlamp made night driving safer. Here, Jackson tends to the auto at an unspecified location (*Auto Era*, July–Aug. 1903).

> and pointed. We took that road for about 50 miles and then it came to a dead end at an isolated farmhouse. The family all turned out to stare at us, and told us we would have to go back. We went back and met the red-haired young woman again. "Why did you send us 'way down there?" I asked her. "I wanted paw and maw and my husband to see you," she said. "They've never seen an automobile."[37]

In his earlier 1936 article about the adventure, Jackson curiously failed to mention this incident; moreover, in that article he claimed that the only time he and Crocker had backtracked was in Idaho. At Nampa, Idaho, as he describes it in is 1903 letter to the Winton company: "We were directed to a wrong road, taking us to Swanton Falls, a distance of 38 miles, which road we had to retrace."[38] Many retrospective accounts have thus transplanted the red-haired-woman incident to Idaho. Jackson may well have freshened the story as he traveled east. A Rawlins, Wyoming, newspaper quotes him as saying that the incident occurred "shortly after leaving" Green River, Wyoming.[39]

A Bad Time with Tires

Crossing northern California, the motorists turned northeast at Redding to pass through Bella Vista, Adin, Canby, and Alturas, thus crossing the Sierra Nevada at a summit of little more than 5,000 feet. Still, the route was dangerous. As Jackson wrote in 1936:

Often the trail narrowed to ten feet, one-way thoroughfares established by nature. Sometimes it was necessary to remove boulder blockades by hand. Slipping on shale and loose rocks, weaving around mountain ledges, we staked our careers against none too reliable brakes on steep descents. It is still possible to raise goose-flesh after thirty-three years by recalling certain hair-pin turns where, jolting and skidding, we suddenly looked down unfenced sheer precipices.[40]

From Alturas, the men pushed their 2-cylinder Winton northward into south-central Oregon, from Lakeview to Burns, and then northeast to Vale and Ontario—neighboring east-central Oregon towns near the Idaho border. Jackson said the car was out of touch with the railroads from Anderson, California, to Ontario, Oregon. Jackson and Crocker followed the Oregon Short Line Railroad from Ontario to southwestern Wyoming. From Granger, Wyoming, they followed the Union Pacific tracks to Omaha and the Chicago & North Western route from Omaha to Chicago.

The Winton punctured and popped its tires early and often during the trip (see Fig. 29). The B. F. Goodrich Company insisted that Jackson "made the entire trip, a distance of 5,600 miles by cyclometer, on the Original Goodrich Tires, fitted in San Francisco."[41] This is obviously false. Just what the truth is, however, remains speculative. Several accounts say the car—or more precisely, the rough roads it traveled—chewed up one used tire and seven new tires on the trip.

Fig. 29. Jackson pumps up a tire at an unidentified desert location.

Unable to buy new spares, the men had begun the trip on worn tires, according to Jackson. Crocker reported blowing out a tire the first day, just beyond Oakland. The rocky road over the Sierra Nevada had so torn up the rear tires that the travelers had to stop in northern California and await replacements. "Not being able to secure any extra tires when we left the coast, although those on the rear wheels were in poor condition when we started, we were forced to remain at Alturas for several days in a vain effort to get them," Jackson wrote to the Winton factory. "Failing in this we patched them up with rope and journeyed directly north," to Lakeview, Oregon.[42]

In Lakeview, the men received two tires from San Francisco. They continued to have a "bad time" with tires until Jackson wired the Goodrich factory to send an entire set of new tires, "and thenceforth I had no trouble."[43] But further tire trouble apparently did occur.

"During the past few days, the Winton company has received successive telegrams from Dr. Jackson from points in Wyoming and from the character of his orders it appears that he is having much trouble with tires," reported a June 29 dispatch from Cleveland, home of the Winton factory.[44] "In all four 4-inch Goodrich tires were used on the rear wheels from Ontario, Ore., to New York City," according to another source.[45] Some accounts said the Winton received one or two new front tires west of Troy, New York.

"A Real Live Automobile"

The car also broke a spring in northern California:

> The first automobile to visit Lake County arrived in Lakeview Thursday afternoon [June 4] about 4 o'clock having spent six hours on the road from Alturas to this place, a distance of 60 miles. The wonderful machine would have made much better time had it not been for the accidental breaking of one of the main springs over the front axle a few miles this side of Alturas in consequence of which the machine had to be moved more slowly and with greater precaution than usual.
>
> An automobile is a novelty to most people of Lakeview, few of whom had ever seen one before. . . . This was enough to put every man, woman and child in Lakeview on the keen edge of expectancy. The town had the gala appearance of a holiday as the streets were thronged with crowds of eager people, all craning their necks for the first sign of the first automobile ever seen in this part of the State. After a long and patient wait they were finally rewarded and the sight of an automobile in Lakeview was a reality.[46]

Lakeview's *Lake County Examiner*, however, said that the Winton arrived on Tuesday, June 2—two days earlier than reported in the *Lakeview Herald*. Under a bold, front-page headline, "A Real Live Automobile," the *Examiner* printed its version of the Winton's arrival:

> The way the streets of Lakeview were lined with people Tuesday afternoon, one would think a circus was coming to town, or a 4th of July procession was about to pass. While it was neither, the people's curiosity had been aroused from a report that an automobile was coming this way, and that if they wished to see it pass it was necessary to have a seat in the front row, otherwise it might go through at the rate of 90 miles an hour, and would be out of sight before they could run a block.
>
> It hove in sight at just 4 o'clock and the crowds surged forward to get a first look at a real live auto, a machine that nine-tenths of the people of Lake county had never seen. The machine drove up in front of Hotel Lakeview and stopped. The Chauffeur enquired for a blacksmith shop, having had a mishap coming over the rough roads. A broken

spring and a badly worn tire caused a halt in Lakeview. The machine was taken to Arzner's shop where the necessary repairs were made.[47]

On Wednesday afternoon, June 3, Jackson and Crocker bade the citizens of Lakeview "a hearty farewell as they sailed away in their cushioned car," with hopes of covering the 170 miles to Burns that night. Moments later, the automobile's drivers bade a hearty greeting to the same citizens: "The machine broke down before it got out of town and will have to remain a day or two longer."[48]

Tires caused the delay. The *Examiner* buried this bit of news in the paper's "Additional Local" section on page 5—a reflection, perhaps, of the editor's obvious disenchantment with automobiles:

> The new tires for the automobile arrived last Friday evening on the southern stage, and bright and early Saturday morning, Dr. Jackson was on his way to Burns. They reached Chewaucan in good season and were scheduled to reach Burns that night, but another accident stopped them until 3 o'clock in the afternoon, when they again started on their long journey to New York. If they meet with as many accidents and are delayed as long as they were at Alturas and Lakeview . . . it will be winter before they see the Atlantic.[49]

29 Miles from Gas

The Winton's misadventures continued into central Oregon, where, near a place Jackson called "Silver Springs," the car ran out of gas for the only time during the journey. "Crocker had to walk twenty-nine miles to Burns for more. He returned in the morning with three gallons of benzine and two of gasoline."[50]

But the *Harney Valley Items* newspaper of Burns, more reliable than Jackson as a source of local place names, said the autoists ran out of gas "at Oakerman's on Silver Creek . . . and to replenish their supply a trip to Burns by other locomotion was necessary." Crocker, the former cyclist, somehow located a bicycle, but it "broke down on the way, and the remaining distance was made on foot and the return trip in a wagon" (see Fig. 30).[51]

Fig. 30. Crocker at one point searched for gasoline. Jackson, here, is evidently searching for water. Carrying two pails and a water bag, he wends his way through the sagebrush at an undisclosed location (*Auto Era*, July–Aug. 1903).

The refueled auto reached Burns at 2:00 PM on Monday, June 8, and stopped for an hour. Wrote the *Harney Valley Items*: "The sight of an automobile on our streets is not to be caught every day, so when it was announced Monday morning that such was to be a street attraction for the day a fair sized crowd gathered to witness the maneuvering of the horseless carriage when it should make its appearance."[52]

Gas was otherwise readily available, but from San Francisco to Omaha the price averaged 35 cents a gallon—expensive for the time. The highest price the men paid for gasoline was $1.05 a gallon, in Medicine Bow, Wyoming, where one storekeeper "became aware that we were without much gasolene and compelled me to pay him five dollars and a quarter for five gallons," according to Jackson. "Years later I learned that he was a native of my own home town."[53]

Western merchants often abused the motorists, Jackson complained to Cleveland reporters: "Apparently we had the sign 'We are easy, come and do us' placarded upon our machine. The way that we were held up in the western country was something frightful. . . . In all, however, we have met with most courteous treatment, although we did have to pay for it."[54]

This Bud's for You

The car's arrival in Vale during the week of June 11 (the local paper failed to specify the exact day of arrival) "furnished a novel sight for some of our citizens who had never seen such a machine before. . . . On rough mountain roads they make an average of about 12 miles per hour, but on good valley roads they travel a speed of from 20 to 25 miles per hour."[55]

After crossing the Snake River by ferry into southern Idaho during the third week of the trip, Jackson and Crocker drove eight hours in the rain to reach Caldwell at about midnight on June 12.[56] On the way, they used their block and tackle for the first time to extract the Winton from deep mud.

In Caldwell, they picked up an apparent stray dog, "a bull pup named Bud—the one member of the trio who used no profanity on the entire trip." In his 1936 article, Jackson affectionately remembered the dog:

> The intelligent pup soon learned to watch the road for obstructions with the same intentness as his companions. Intuitively learning to brace himself for shocks, Bud soon became an enthusiast for motoring. Alkali dust gave him some bother by getting in his eyes over the desert, but a pair of goggles soon provided the same protection enjoyed by his masters.[57]

The story about how Bud came to join the expedition had changed by the time Jackson wrote his 1953 *American Weekly* article. According to that later story, some Caldwell residents had "staged a dogfight for us, and one of the two bull terriers was Bud. 'You'll have to stop this!' I finally called out. 'It's savage.' 'All right, but take Bud with you as a gift,' one of the townsmen said. And so we acquired faithful, adventurous Bud. He could almost talk." Of course, it is hard to understand why the owner of a fighting dog would give the animal away—especially to someone who is breaking up a dogfight. In a 1903 account, the *New York American* wrote that, according to Jackson, Bud "insisted on joining them, running after the automobile for at least two miles and finally being taken aboard."[58]

Motor World offers what may be the most reasonable account. In a long interview after his trip, Jackson told the magazine that he simply bought the dog. "No, it did not run after us, as the papers say. I saw and liked him and struck a bargain for him without much trouble." Newspapers in Nampa and Pocatello, Idaho, described Bud at the time as "a recent purchase," tending to confirm this version. However Jackson may have acquired the dog, Bud was described by yet another newspaper as "so ugly that he is handsome."[59]

36 Hours Without Food

From Caldwell, the men traveled east through southern Idaho, passing through Nampa, Mountain Home, Hailey, Blackfoot, Pocatello, Soda Springs, and Montpelier. Jackson wrote: "Before arriving at Mountain Home, our machine was stalled in a stream where the wheels sank into the mud up to the body of the car. After vainly endeavoring to release ourselves by working four hours we, for the first time, secured a team [of horses] which dragged the car to the bank of the stream." It was from Hailey, he continued, that "I telegraphed to you [the Winton factory] for the first time, requesting you to send us a new air intake pipe, as we had dropped ours somewhere on the road."[60] The pipe, a "funnel-shaped air intake, with its gauze strainer, to the rear carburetor," had apparently been lost and "its absence was not noted until the valve began to stick from the sand that worked in."[61] As had happened elsewhere, Jackson and Crocker became the center of attention in Mountain Home. "Being the first horseless carriage seen in the village, it created quite a sensation and attracted crowds of curious who surrounded it as flies surround a keg of sorghum."[62]

According to Jackson, the team made good progress across Idaho. "If roads were rough and rocky they at least were free of sand. Ruts gave us trouble in places yet we navigated through trackless forests with great success, managing to maneuver true on our course by instinct among mighty trees."[63] The men pushed into extreme southeastern Idaho on Wednesday, June 17, where their auto became "the first machine of its kind to run the streets of Montpelier," according to Friday's *Montpelier Examiner*. "The tourists went on their way yesterday morning after having some work done here at the blacksmith shop."[64]

Once during the trip, Jackson and Crocker went one and one-half days without food. Many historians quote Jackson's 1936 *American Legion Monthly* assertion that the incident happened in the "Idaho wilderness." That fanciful account has a hungry Jackson and Crocker "stealing speculative glances at Bud as we tightened belts." But the more detailed account Jackson wrote immediately after the trip sounds more believable. It gives the setting as extreme southwestern Wyoming:

> At Granger we found that we were following in the wake of what they called a "cloud burst." The rain had continued for several days and we were told the roads were completely washed out. This was verified by our experiences soon after leaving Granger. Striking one of these washouts we were unable to ascend the opposite bank and had to follow the gully which led us in a northwest direction to the foot hills, bringing us back a little north of Cokeville [Wyoming], where we had been before.
>
> Frequently we were obliged to cut sage brush and place it in the mud in order to secure traction and from time to time we had to use our block and tackle. Coming to the bank of a river we judged from our maps and compass that it was Green river, and we resolved to follow its downward course. Having lost our cooking outfit and provisions, and being in an uninhabited region, we were obliged to go 36 hours without food.
>
> At last we came upon a lonely sheepherder, who after hearing our hard luck story cooked us a sumptuous dinner of mutton and canned corn. For this he would receive no money; so I presented him with my rifle, and had he asked for anything we had, with the exception of the car, I think we would have given it to him.[65]

Like a folktale, however, other accounts flourished. "Suddenly on the brow of a hill appeared a flock of sheep," the *New York American* related. "Dr. Jackson seized one of his rifles and was about to shoot when, just behind[,] the gaunt figure of the shepherd —an aged, white-bearded man—appeared. He had a little hut in the hills, and took them there. He gave them dinner." Jackson's 1953 *American Weekly* story confirms that the incident occurred "when we turned off a washed-out road north of Granger, Wyoming." But this latter-day account adds that the sheepherder, when he spied what appeared to be "a fantastic kind of locomotive . . . fell on his knees and prayed."[66]

Wyoming: Rains and Washouts

More breakdowns slowed the travelers in Idaho and Wyoming (see Fig. 31). At Montpelier, in eastern Idaho near the Wyoming border, the pair lost the ball bearings of a front wheel: "The ingenious Crocker borrowed bearings from a mowing machine which would not be used for several weeks and we induced the superintendent of the car-repair shop to build a cone for them." At Moyer, Wyoming, "we discovered that this cone had been made out of iron and had gone to pieces." But at Diamondville, "The machinist of the coal mine turned us a new cone from a piece of tool steel which Mr. Crocker tempered."[67]

On the trail again after their wet-weather detour from Granger back to Cokeville, the travelers picked up the Union Pacific Railroad, which they followed eastward across Wyoming through Green River, Rock Springs, Bitter Creek, Rawlins, Medicine Bow, Laramie, Cheyenne, and Archer. From Granger to near Chicago, the pioneer motorists followed what would become the Lincoln Highway.

The Winton reached Cheyenne on July 2. By all accounts, the Wyoming trails had been sandy, muddy, and steep. "This part of the trip was the hardest traveling because of the rains and washouts," according to the July 25, 1903, *Automobile*. "From Granger to Omaha, the block and tackle had to be used at least two or three times every day."[68]

Fig. 31. By all appearances, Crocker is repairing the Winton's engine. But the Winton company's magazine, which printed this photo, insisted that Crocker was "tak[ing] a final nap in the car" at a campsite in the desert West (*Auto Era*, July–Aug. 1903).

While Jackson's Winton was traversing the American continent, the Winton company had shipped two racing Wintons to near Dublin, Ireland, to take part in the July 2, 1903, running of the 370-mile Gordon Bennett International Cup Race. Race drivers Alexander Winton and Percy Owen were far off the pace (little more than two-thirds of the way through the course) when the winners of the Irish race crossed the finish line. Winton publicity man Charles B. Shanks blamed the poor showing on his company's experiment with a "much vaunted Russian gasoline." The gas contained paraffin, which had repeatedly clogged the carburetor inlet valves and stalled the engines of the Winton racers, he claimed.[69] Reminded of the story of the tortoise and the hare, *Motor Age* later contrasted the eventual triumph of the plodding Jackson–Crocker expedition with the tribulations of the Winton racing cars.

Careening Connecting Rods

Floods often prevented the men from using roads paralleling the Union Pacific tracks. "We made use of cross roads whenever any favoring us were to be found; and where they were not we took to the fields or prairie and zigzagged as best we could. . . . Where the railroad went one mile we would frequently go five. This was kept up nearly all the way across Wyoming; and when we crossed into Nebraska it became worse instead of better. Here it rained constantly."[70] The worst part of the trail, Jackson recalled, began at Bitter Creek, one-third of the distance in from Wyoming's western border.

The transcontinentalists arrived at Rawlins about 7:00 PM on Tuesday, June 23, one month to the day after leaving San Francisco. "While running our machine from the hotel to the livery stable at Rawlins, the stud bolts of one of the connecting rods broke, which caused it to pierce the cover of the crank [case] and it was five days before this could be replaced," Jackson wrote. East of Rawlins, crossing the North Platte River at Fort Steele, the Winton headed southeast for Elk Mountain, an 11,162-foot peak. There, the pair "met with the most difficult mountain climbing of the entire journey, due to a very steep grade over a rocky and sandy road." To climb the mountain, "not only was it necessary to use block and tackle to move forward . . . but frequently we had to jack up the car to get over boulder obstructions and out of deep ruts."[71]

By contrast, the trip from Laramie to Cheyenne was made over "our first good road since we left Sacramento valley." While stuck in a Wyoming stream at some unspecified point, "three Italians came tramping along with heavy packs on their shoulders. They were bound for a place twelve miles beyond, and I told them that if they would pull us out of the stream I would carry their packs to their destination for them. They gladly consented, and then I carried out my bargain, although their packs each contained more than 100 pounds" (see Fig. 32).[72]

East of Cheyenne near Archer, Wyoming, the engine virtually repeated its Rawlins breakdown. As a result, Jackson and Crocker spent "five days in a graders' camp waiting for stud bolts from the Winton factory," according to *Auto Era*, Winton's promotional magazine (see Fig. 33).[73] The car left Cheyenne in good shape, but Jackson later reported:

> After making good speed for about 18 miles there was a sudden crash and our car came to a dead stop. With great trepidation we unscrewed the cover to our crank case and to our horror discovered that the stud bolts of the other connecting rod had broken, and that the rod had literally tied itself in a knot around the main shaft. Our feelings may be more easily imagined than described. With great sadness, I telegraphed home, "delayed here for five days."[74]

Fig. 32 (above). Crocker, *left*, and the three Italian men who helped winch the stranded auto out of a Wyoming stream (*Auto Era*, July–Aug. 1903).

Fig. 33 (left). Waiting for parts on the Wyoming prairie, a forlorn-looking Bud and Jackson eye the stripped Winton, its disassembled engine covered with canvas (*Auto Era*, July–Aug. 1903).

An *Automobile* correspondent, mistakenly believing that the transcontinental car carried no extra oil, wrote that Jackson at one point had to melt axle grease to use in the engine. "At another time he melted paraffine for this purpose. But the paraffine gummed and refused to flow through the lubricating tubes, causing hot bearings in several places. Naturally something gave way, and it proved to be the stud bolts on one of the connecting rods, necessitating a lay-over until the new parts could be obtained."[75]

Untrue, Jackson wrote afterward:

I have read of many such statements that have been given out as coming from me. Not once in our whole trip did we run out of lubricating oil. We provided ourselves, before leaving San Francisco, with an extra five-gallon storage tank. Once in Oregon, near Vail [Vale], we ran a little low and as I didn't want to run any chances, we used axle grease in the gear box for a little while.

At Vail [Vale] we telephoned to a Mr. Fraser, at Ontario, who got us ten gallons. Of course we didn't always get a first-class variety, nevertheless, we always managed to get some kind of gas-engine lubricating oil that would do. . . . There is as much foundation to the report of my using melted paraffine in place of lubricating oil as there was in the report of my saying that our machine floated in crossing the streams and Mr. Crocker swimming ashore with a rope.[76]

Jackson's disavowal that the car floated across streams may have been a reference to a report in the *Cleveland Leader*, in which Jackson was said to have described to Thomas Henderson, vice-president of the Winton company, how the car forded streams: "When we came to a stream or creek we put on full force, and usually made it, the car going across like a launch. Sometimes we would be caught in midstream but Mr. Crocker would swim ashore with a rope, and I would start the engines, and the rest was easy."[77]

"We Don't Give No Hand-Outs Here"

Resuming their eastward trip after repairs to the engine, the autoists crossed into the panhandle of western Nebraska. They dipped south briefly to follow the established railroad route through Julesburg, Colorado, before resuming their journey across Nebraska to a mixed reception:

In contrast to the hospitality of the sheep-herder who saved us from hunger, I recall an attempt to buy food at a farmhouse along the way. Perhaps I did look trampish when I knocked at the housewife's door, but no sooner did I mention food than the door was slammed in my face with the admonition, "We don't give no hand-outs here."[78]

Elsewhere, the Winton terrified a Nebraska farmer, "who unhitched his team and let his horses run. With his wife he then crawled under his wagon and waited for the horseless machine to pass."[79]

Heavy rains left western and central Nebraska roads in "horrible condition," with mud deep enough to nearly cover the tops of the wheels. Compared to what he was expecting, crossing the Sierra Nevada "really proved easy, while through Wyoming the going was much worse; and as for Nebraska, that was where we nearly failed to get through," Jackson told *Motor World* afterward (see Fig. 34).[80] The men even veered north for a time to follow what Jackson called the "foot hills," presumably meaning the Nebraska Sandhills:

It was a most arduous task on account of the continued rain and the deep sloughs termed "buffalo wallows." Many times each day we had to make use of our block and tackle to

Fig. 34. A farmer and his mules prepare to pull the Winton from a mud-hole, possibly in Nebraska (*Auto Era*, July–Aug. 1903).

extricate our machine from these places. Fortunately we made the discovery that by planting our block and tackle we would attach the end of the rope around the brake drum of the wheel that slipped, which, when the engine was started, would act as a windlass and thus extricate the machine by its own power.

During one day [in Nebraska] we had to pull the car out no less than 17 times, after standing in mud and water reaching to our knees, and that day we only made 16 miles. Frequently we had to use the pick and shovel in digging the wheels out. On two of these occasions we had to call for the assistance of teams to release the machine.[81]

Easier Going East of Omaha

Crocker and Jackson had by then traveled 3,600 miles in seven weeks to reach Kearney, Nebraska, on Saturday, July 11. The *Kearney Daily Hub* reported: "These gentlemen are traveling across the country with an automobile and stopped in Kearney for repairs for their machine, which was given an overhauling by expert T. H. Bolte. . . . Their destination is New York City, which they expect to reach in about three weeks."[82] The newspaper failed to specify what repairs Bolte made, but in early usage the term "overhauling" often meant minor adjustments.

Despite a more accommodating roadbed, the pair's problems were not over: "The last 60 miles to Omaha were over the old military road which was a pleasing contrast to our previous experiences. In this latter run, however, we broke our front axle in the center, which we repaired by the use of a short piece of iron pipe from a farmer. Into this we shoved the broken ends of the axle, which we secured in place by using the tire iron as wedges. After running thus for about 20 miles we found a blacksmith who welded the axle."[83]

Jackson and Crocker arrived at the H. E. Fredrickson garage in Omaha on Sunday, July 12 (see Fig. 35). As *Motor World* would report, "It was not until the travellers reached Omaha . . . that they began to attract notice."[84] This undoubtedly was because of Jackson's earlier refusal to speak to reporters.

According to the *Omaha Daily News*: "The machine was in perfect condition when it arrived, save for a sprung front axle and a worn tire. It was covered with mud an inch thick, however, and looked decidedly 'trampish.'"[85]

Rain and repairs had delayed Jackson eighteen days, reported the *World-Herald*, another Omaha daily. "People have flocked to the small towns to see the machine, news of the coming having been telegraphed ahead." *Motor Age* added: "In many of

Fig. 35. Onlookers inspect the Winton—and Bud returns the stares—outside H. E. Fredrickson's automobile, bicycle, and carriage dealership in Omaha (UVSC).

the small towns where their coming had been announced by telephone the schools were closed and the people lined up along the roadside to see them go by."[86]

The high price of gasoline in the West "has been but an iota compared with the general expense of the trip, for the repair bills have been enormous, to say nothing of the other expenses," the *World-Herald* commented.[87] The men hoped to reach Chicago in three days. According to Jackson:

> When we reached Omaha our difficulties proved to be nearly over. The constant rains made the roads very bad, but after the buffalo wallows they were child's play. A few inches of mud made little difference to us then, and we seldom had to fall back on our faithful block and tackle.[88]

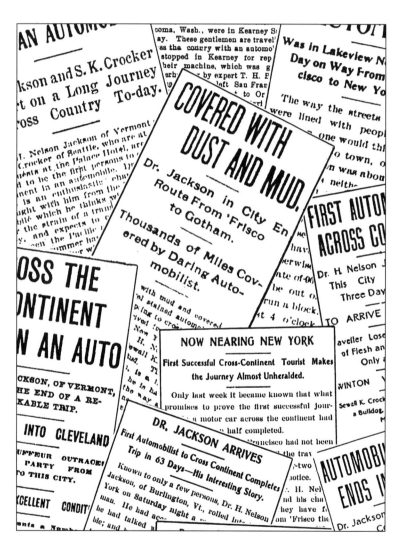

Fig. 36. In the news since leaving San Francisco, Crocker and Jackson garnered ever more headlines as they neared New York City.

Jackson Refuses Factory Aid

Jackson was full of confidence upon reaching Chicago on Friday, July 17, 1903, Day 56. "We have come to the conclusion that we can run our car over any road that a man can take a team of horses and a wagon, providing we can get traction.... We were unlucky in choosing this year to make the trip, as the heavy rains in the west made the roads the worst they have been for years.... The car is in first-class condition and I anticipate no trouble from Chicago on to my home in Vermont."[89]

When they reached Chicago, Jackson said, years later, "reports of our progress were gaining front pages of the nation's press as our goal appeared in sight" (see Fig. 36). A group of auto enthusiasts from Hammond, Indiana, drove to Chicago to escort the coast-to-coast machine out of the Windy City (see Fig. 37). Reporters "besieged" them in Cleveland, as did

Fig. 37. Seated in what appears to be a 1902 Winton (*background*), a group of autoists from Hammond, Indiana, bids farewell to Jackson (*driving*) and Crocker (*Motor Age*, July 23, 1903).

Winton officials, who offered to clean up and repair their car. "The Winton people were anxious to overhaul the car when it reached Cleveland, but Dr. Jackson would not even permit it to be examined . . . and [said] that he preferred to make the entire trip without aid from the factory."[90] Jackson evidently wanted the trip to remain untainted by even the appearance of factory sponsorship, especially coming so late in the journey.

Early on, the Winton company had recognized that a public-relations boon would undoubtedly follow the news that an ordinary Winton owner had crossed the United States unaided. The automaker had accordingly (and correctly) denied "that it had any connection with the project or that it is backing Mr. Jackson in the trip."[91] The manufacturer's resolve to remain in the background would weaken, however. Two Winton touring cars from the factory would meet Jackson and Crocker at Elyria, Ohio, to escort them into Cleveland. Officials wanted to replace the front axle and clean the car, presumably so it would look more presentable at the finish.

The Cleveland automaker's sales and advertising manager, Charles B. Shanks, who had accompanied Alexander Winton on his 1901 transcontinental attempt, "gathered together a party of Winton enthusiasts and met the continent-trotters at Elyria, 27 miles west of Cleveland" (see Fig. 38): "The Jackson party left Chicago at noon Saturday and arrived in Cleveland at 5 p.m. Monday, remarkably good time for notoriously bad roads which had been rendered worse by continued hard rains. . . . The party went to the Hollenden for a cleaning up and for supper while the faithful bull dog mascot remained in charge and fought flies and kept off inquisitive newsboys."[92]

That evening, according to *Motor Age*, the auto went into the Winton garage for cleaning, which conflicts with the *Automobile* account that Jackson refused any such assistance during the ocean-to-ocean run. Jackson apparently decided to accept the factory's offer of assistance, but only after he had completed the trek. From New York the car would be shipped to the Cleveland factory for refinishing, at the automaker's expense. Moreover, Jackson agreed to write a detailed description of his experiences on the tour, to be published as a booklet by the Winton Company.[93] The automaker designated its July–August 1903 edition of *Auto Era* as the "Transcontinental Number," fea-

Fig. 38. Jackson (*at wheel*), Bud, and Crocker at Elyria, Ohio (*Auto Era*, July–Aug. 1903).

COAST TO COAST BY AUTOMOBILE

turing "Dr. H. Nelson Jackson's Own Story" of the historic auto trip (see Fig. 39). The special edition contained thirty-seven of Jackson and Crocker's snapshots but identified the precise location for only five of them. Thus, little information is available about the surviving trip photos. Winton's ads also exulted over Jackson and Crocker's accomplishment: "It was not a specially constructed car with attachments designed for special service in the mountains and upon the deserts. The men who occupied the seats were not selected factory mechanics who had spent weeks and months in preparation."[94]

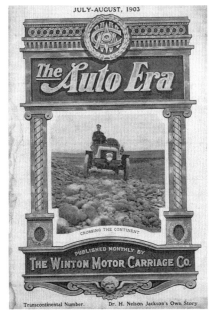

Fig. 39. Winton's in-house magazine played up the trek.

The Joke's on Alexander Winton

Two rain showers caught the autoists between Toledo, Ohio, and Cleveland, where their mud-covered Winton arrived at 5:00 PM on Monday, July 20. According to the *Cleveland Leader*, "Both men wore canvas suits and caps, and they were in anything but presentable shape when they arrived." Alexander Winton, president of the automobile company he founded in 1897, was in Europe and thus unable to greet the travelers personally. It was just as well, for he might have winced at the boastful edge to Jackson's remarks: "When we started on this trip my wife asked me how long it would take. I told her six weeks and possibly six months. I also told her that I would make the trip if it took a lifetime. I was positive that it could be done, and I have met with success where Winton and others failed."[95]

At least the *Leader* did not report, as did the *Omaha Daily News*, that Jackson and Crocker were "chuckling at the joke they have played on [Alexander Winton]."[96] The joke was that two young men, with little preparation—though perhaps more than the four days that Jackson claimed—had driven a stock car so much farther than Winton himself had done during his abortive 1901 transcontinental attempt.

By accident or design, the *Leader* was misinformed when it reported: "With but a single exception the automobile has not needed any repairs on the road. One trifling break was repaired without much trouble." The newspaper also reported that, according to Jackson, the Winton had scared just one horse, at an unspecified location between San Francisco and Cleveland, and that was the owner's fault: "We had stopped, but he waved for us to come along. A horse was hitched to the rear of the wagon. The horse reared as we passed, his front feet striking the wagon, but that was all the damage that was done." In his interview with the *Cleveland Plain Dealer*, Jackson credited Crocker with "much of the success of my trip."[97]

Quiet on the Eastern Front

The men selected a route through Cleveland and across northern Pennsylvania into New York to avoid the Allegheny Mountains. Yet on its detour around the mountains, the car had a potentially serious mishap east of Buffalo, New York. Jackson later reported that "traveling in high—at least twenty miles an hour—the machine struck a hidden obstruction in the road. Crocker, Bud and myself were thrown high in the air. Both mud-guards [fenders] were torn off and the machine otherwise damaged but fortunately none of us was hurt."[98] On the same page of this 1936 recounting, Jackson contradicts himself by saying the car arrived in New York City with one broken mud guard, a fact that is echoed by New York City newspapers. Photographs taken in New York City, however, appear to show undamaged fenders on both sides of the car, though the car may have been repaired before the photo session.

Jackson and Crocker finished their run as quietly as they began it. They reached the Holland House at Fifth Avenue and 30th Street in New York City at 4:30 AM on Sunday, July 26, by traveling 230 miles from Little Falls, New York, in twenty-four hours. It had taken them 63 days, 12 hours, 30 minutes to make the crossing from San Francisco. Throughout the day of its arrival, while housed in a garage at West 58th Street, the car "was visited by admiring automobilists, and curious passersby peeped in upon it. In honor of its achievement it was decorated with tiny flags and draped with national standards" (see Fig. 40).[99]

How far did Jackson and Crocker travel? The car's first cyclometer—an early speedometer and odometer—fell off in Idaho, and two more were lost. Press accounts generally give figures ranging from 5,000 to 6,000 miles. *Cycle and Automobile Trade Journal* played it safe in estimating the total distance at "over 5000 miles." Exactly how far Jackson traveled "is somewhat a matter of estimate," the *New York Herald* pointed out, just as carefully, "for he says three of his cyclometers were swept off by the sage brush. The Doctor estimates the distance up the Pacific coast and across to Ontario [Oregon], at 1,200 miles, and from this town to Omaha at 2,600 miles. The 700 miles to Chicago and 1,100 to this city complete the 5,600 miles."[100]

The same day that the *New York Herald* published Jackson's estimate of 5,600 miles, the *Burlington Daily Free Press* reported that Jackson claimed that he and

Fig. 40. The Winton in New York City (AAMA).

Crocker had traveled 6,000 miles. In Jackson's 1936 recounting of the trip, he asserts that the distance "could not have been less than 6000 miles." In burning "about 800 gallons of gasolene,"[101] the Winton thus would have averaged 6.25 miles per gallon if the trip had been 5,000 miles, 7.00 mpg for a 5,600-mile trip, or 7.50 mpg for a 6,000-mile trip.

For its elapsed time of just over 63½ days, the transcontinental car would have recorded a daily average driving distance of about 79 miles for a 5,000-mile trip, 88 miles for a 5,600-mile trip, or 94 miles for a 6,000-mile trip. By splitting the difference between extremes—5,000 and 6,000 miles—and assuming a trip of 5,500 miles, we may calculate that Jackson and Crocker traveled coast to coast at an average speed of

3.61 miles per hour. Their journey occupied sixty-five calendar days. On nineteen of those days, they did not travel at all, waiting instead for tires and parts to arrive at various locations—"a continuous aggravation."[102]

Trip to Burlington "Eventful"

Jackson and his wife left New York City on Thursday, July 30, in the coast-to-coast Winton for an eventful drive home to Burlington. "Dr. Jackson's chauffeur, Mr. Crocker, left him in New York, where he has taken a desirable position," the *Burlington Daily Free Press* reported, without elaborating.[103] The Jacksons spent a day in Hudson, New York, when the transmission's low-speed gear broke, and later had to return to Albany from 12 miles north of that city after the high-speed gear went out. Jackson telegraphed the Winton factory for new parts.

They left Albany in a "pouring rain" at noon on Wednesday, August 5. The car's breaker box failed near Middlebury, Vermont, on Friday, August 7, "and it was necessary to make a new one out of some old parts. Perhaps the most peculiar feature of the whole journey was the fact that the [drive] chain of the machine did not break or give way during the whole trip, until just as they were going into the stable [Friday] afternoon," shortly after the car's 5:00 PM arrival.[104]

Jackson's expenses far exceeded the $50 he may have bet on the outcome. According to *Smithsonian* magazine, "In the end the good doctor estimated that the whole trip cost him about $8,000 for everything—the price of the car, Crocker's salary, about 800 gallons of gasoline and two sets of tires." Only a little money went toward hiring horses, Jackson said. "With the exception of using horses simply to pull us out of a deep stream once, and three times out of deep mud holes (and the ferries to cross San Francisco Bay and Snake River), my Winton, No. 1684, came all the way with her own power, and I am prepared to stake any sum on the above assertions."[105]

Responding to Rumors—$25,000 Reward

Jackson had cause for sounding defiant. Rumors circulated that he had "used two automobiles instead of one on the long journey and that in some places he loaded the machine into a freight car for transportation across rough country." The source of these rumors, Jackson charged, was "a rival automobile manufacturer who shortly thereafter sponsored another transcontinental run which, carrying newspapermen and after careful advance preparations, lowered my record by a few days."[106] He was alluding to the Packard Motor Car Company's factory-sponsored transcontinental car that reached New York City on August 21, 1903, after a sixty-two-day crossing (see Chapter 3). The Winton company also blamed Packard, without specifically naming the other automaker:

> There are on file at the Winton office copies of interesting letters sent from the main office of an automobile manufacturing company which was directly interested in another transcontinental enterprise and while these letters, which were presumably sent to all their representatives and agencies, do not directly charge Dr. Jackson and Mr. Croker [sic] with misrepresentation and fake they give excuse sufficient to stir into activity an imagination that would not need to be more than fifty per cent. developed. This letter says that "if" Dr. Jackson did not so and so he did use two machines on the trip, using one until broken down, then placing the other one in commission, etc. It further says that, in the presence of some more "so and so" that the Doctor possibly railroaded his car over bad sections of the country. Further the letter goes on to say that according to the opinion of several experts the car used by Dr. Jackson, upon its passing through Cleveland, did not look as if it had been driven more than 500 miles. . . . When the letter above mentioned was sent forth it started, or at least is supposed to have started, the stories of alleged fake and misrepresentation which were freely circulated by agents and other representatives of the aforementioned automobile manufacturing company which had transcontinental interests of their own. The agents and other representatives omitted the "if" from all their stories and stated the slanders as alleged facts.[107]

Jackson argued that his route from northern California to eastern Oregon was nowhere near the railroads. Springing to Jackson's defense, *Automobile Topics* also argued that the Packard crossing was a factory publicity stunt. "That there was no such damning feature of the Jackson trip is beyond controversy. As Dr. Jackson dolefully observed, when relating his experience of communications with either the Winton or Goodrich firms, 'Every order I sent to them for the first 2,000 miles of the trip was shipped C.O.D., and express charges alone amounted to something in those places.' There is a touch of realism in that statement which no press agent could compete against."[108]

While Crocker and Jackson were still on the road, *Horseless Age* called it "rather peculiar that nothing was heard of this attempt to cross the continent until practically all the difficulties were behind and the plains States had been reached." But in its

Fig. 41. Winton ad in the Sept. 3, 1903, *Motor World*.

July 29, 1903, issue the journal ultimately sided with Jackson: "To prove that the trip was thus completed in a fair manner, Dr. Jackson shows indisputable evidence in the form of press clippings, letters, etc., dated at the various towns en route."[109]

The Winton company leaped into the fray by offering a $10,000 reward to anyone who could prove the charges. The automaker increased its reward and generally used the controversy to publicize its machines (see Fig. 41).

Crocker Plans World Tour

Crocker would probably settle in New York City, "so many flattering business offers having been received by him as the result of the fame and proven mechanical expertness the trip brought him," *Motor Age* speculated.[110] Two weeks later, however, *Automobile* reported that Crocker was in New York City "negotiating with one of the metropolitan daily newspapers." He was seeking a sponsor for a six-month, round-the-world journey "from the east coast of the Atlantic Ocean to the west coast of the Pacific in China or Japan."

> He thinks the country in the Western United States through which he and Dr. Jackson came on their recent trip is as nearly roadless as any territory he is likely to traverse, at least until he gets well into Central Asia. . . . Crocker is a well-built young man with an apparent large stock of stamina and perseverance though in manner quiet and unassuming. . . . The Winton car stood the long and severe journey remarkably well, he says, and he would like to use the same car or a duplicate in his further touring."[111]

The absence of any further coverage in the automobile journals of the day suggest this round-the-world trek never occurred.

Crocker, however, got his wish to explore foreign lands by auto, and was so doing when his father, Benjamin David Crocker, 55, died of Bright's disease on May 15, 1910. Sewall Crocker "is at present on a two years' automobile trip through Europe and it probably will be some days before he can be reached by cable and notified of his father's death," the *Tacoma (Wash.) Daily Tribune* reported.[112]

It was perhaps looking after family property in Mexico that brought on Sewall King Crocker's own death just three years later on April 22, 1913. He died "after a nervous breakdown, due largely to his strenuous exertions in protecting property interests in Mexico. He owned a tobacco plantation at Oaxico [Oaxaca] and was one of the last Americans to leave Mexico after the revolution got to the point when it was no longer safe for foreigners to remain. He went to Hawaii, where he was taken ill. His mother went after him, bringing him back to Tacoma about six weeks ago," the *Tacoma Daily Ledger* reported. Crocker's obituary failed to mention the transcontinental auto trip of 1903, but called him "an expert automobile mechanician, ranking with [Barney] Oldfield and men of that class."[113]

Jackson Pursues Diverse Interests

Jackson, just 31 years of age at the end of his historic journey, had a full and diverse life ahead of him. While Crocker sought someone to sponsor his own round-the-world trip, Jackson attempted to organize a cross-country race. Contestants would choose their own routes and vie for a $30,000 first-place prize in a race that Jackson said he would watch but not participate in. Jackson "declares that such an event would assist the industry prodigiously," *Automobile* editorialized. "For the present, however, we are going to keep our enthusiasm over the scheme carefully within bounds. There are much cheaper ways, and quite as effective, of spoiling automobiles; and what the public wants is not phenomenal machines but serviceable ones at the lowest consistent price."[114] Jackson's race never came about.

The decorated World War I veteran—often referred to as Colonel H. (for Horatio) Nelson Jackson—helped organize the American Legion and became "the father of the American Legion in Vermont."[115] In later years, Jackson published the *Burlington Daily News*, owned and operated WCAX radio and was president of the Burlington Trust Company. He once ran unsuccessfully as a Republican candidate for Vermont governor. He donated the transcontinental Winton to the Smithsonian Institution in 1944. At his death, in Burlington, on January 14, 1955, Jackson was 82.

"A Triumph Truly Remarkable"

The *New York American* called the 1903 run "a triumph truly remarkable when it is remembered that not more than three years ago long distance trips in automobiles that were attempted proved utter failures and brought only ridicule upon those who essayed them." This was an oblique reference to the transcontinental attempts of John D. and Louise Hitchcock Davis in 1899 ("Ring the curtain down on this farce!" *Horseless Age* had bellowed) and Alexander Winton and Charles Shanks in 1901.[116] Because Winton was a pioneer automaker and his trip mercifully short, the auto journals generally treated him more respectfully than they had the Davises.

It was fitting that a Winton became the first ocean-to-ocean auto, because the 1901 expedition had used a Winton, a *Motor Age* editorial writer pointed out:

> The other point is that while two Winton cars were running disappointing races in the great automobile Derby [the Gordon Bennett Cup race in Ireland], another Winton car was gamely plugging along over all kinds of roads and over places where roads that were not might have been—establishing a record of endurance and reliability never before made.
>
> To those across the waters who shrug their shoulders at the performance of American racing cars, the Jackson trip is an object lesson in the character of American cars. In an industry whose greatest success is founded upon reliability in hard, useful road service, a transcontinental trip over the kind of routes that grace the western section of our country, is of more real value than the winning of a half-dozen pure speed races.[117]

Thus, by 1903, the battle lines were drawn between auto enthusiasts who saw track racing as the ultimate challenge and those who believed that endurance or reliability contests were more revealing. Some observers argued that both racing and reliability contests pinpointed weaknesses in the American auto and stimulated improvements.

In completing a 5,000- or 6,000-mile endurance contest, Jackson and Crocker proved the usefulness of an emerging technology and simultaneously deflated its critics. After July 26, 1903, it was harder to argue that a horse could outperform a horseless carriage.

A generation later, a corps of barnstormers in war-surplus biplanes would provide thrilling five-minute demonstrations of the wonders of flight to anyone who could pay the fare. Jackson and Crocker introduced America to the automobile just as dramatically. For, as newspapers had reported, from small towns and cities throughout the West, the approach of the ocean-to-ocean motor car caused a sensation: daily commerce came to a standstill, teachers dismissed their pupils, and adults and children alike lined the streets, sometimes for hours, to catch a glimpse of the auto and the daring men operating it. By simply appearing on their hometown streets, the automobile became a reality for thousands of spectators (tens or hundreds of thousands, if one includes the readers of these local newspapers).

Such a powerful spectacle could incite as well as excite: dusty and worn as they doubtless looked, Jackson and Crocker were modern-day adventurers—men who had mastered a machine, traveled great distances, faced danger, and overcome it. Who among the crowds that lined the streets of small towns in Oregon, Idaho, Utah, or Wyoming could gaze upon a throbbing, smoking transcontinental automobile and not feel the lure of the open road? Or ignore the implications?: This could be *mine*. If *I* had such a mechanical marvel, I could explore the vastness of America, draw adoring gazes everywhere I went, the master of my own destiny!

But the first transcontinental trek by auto also taught some hard lessons about motor travel:

Motor cars could and would break down, usually far off the beaten path.

It was difficult to get new parts quickly.

Tools, food, and supplies could fall off a bounding auto.

Tires failed frequently, so it was necessary to carry plenty of spares.

Roads were unmarked and often bad.

Gasoline and oil were sometimes hard to find. Where available, they were expensive and of questionable quality.

Traveling by train was far cheaper, faster, and more comfortable than crossing the country by auto.

The Winton company paid nothing for the publicity it received from the Jackson-Crocker trip. Other automakers, seeing how such journeys excited the newspapers and auto journals, were willing to spend a bit of money to gain a lot of exposure. And, for their part, the many drivers who stepped forward to pilot other ocean-to-ocean autos hoped to steer their way to stardom. After all, Dr. H. Nelson Jackson did not earn his place in history for his doctoring skills, any more than Sewall K. Crocker earned his for his mechanical abilities.

The Winton Motor Carriage Company of Cleveland—later renamed the Winton Motor Car Company, and in 1915, simply, the Winton Company—produced its last autos in 1924. According to one automotive historian, the pioneer automaker ultimately failed because it continued to produce only high-priced cars even as cheaper, mass-produced autos flooded the market.[118] In 1912 Alexander Winton founded a subsidiary Winton Gas Engine & Manufacturing Company to make marine, stationary, and (beginning in 1913) diesel engines. After he closed his auto factory, Winton focused on building marine diesel engines. General Motors bought him out in 1930 and operated the engine plant as its Cleveland Diesel Division.[119]

Though neither of the two men to first cross the continent by auto ever attempted another coast-to-coast record-setting trip, they set the stage for the spate of records that followed. Lester L. Whitman, who also completed a transcontinental run in 1903, would halve Jackson and Crocker's time in 1904, and in 1906 he would cut the cross-country record even further, to just over fifteen days.

A DEMONSTRATION OF UNFAILING RELIABILITY

3

"The territory of unbridged ravines and washes was behind us; two ruts with unsubdued nature between them was no longer the only thoroughfare."
—Marius C. Krarup in Colorado, reflecting upon
the trip through Nevada and Utah

WHILE THE FIRST AUTOMOBILE to cross the country was still in motion, two more automobiles left San Francisco in the summer of 1903 to begin the long drive to the East Coast. Though following far different routes, both cars succeeded in duplicating the feat of Dr. H. Nelson Jackson and Sewall K. Crocker.

Tom Fetch and Marius C. Krarup, who occupied a Packard that became the second car to cross America, drove straight through the Rocky Mountains to Denver on the fastest of the three automobile treks. For two reasons—the support of the Packard Motor Car Company of Warren, Ohio, and the regular dispatches written by Krarup, a reporter—the Packard trip received more publicity than was accorded to the first car to cross the continent.

An Oldsmobile driven by Lester L. Whitman and Eugene I. Hammond became the third car to drive from ocean to ocean, establishing several records—becoming, for instance, the first low-priced, low-powered, mass-produced car to essay the journey. In addition, the Oldsmobile traveled between the farthest-removed points, starting in San Francisco and ending in Portland, Maine. Whitman and Hammond's machine was also the first automobile to carry the U.S. mail across the country.

American newspapers and auto journals followed the exploits of the second and third autos to cross America as closely as they did the first. Likewise, their crews became as famous as Jackson and Crocker. The second and third crossings are nearly as historically important as the first, for they served to underscore the emerging notion that the automobile, despite occasional breakdowns, could go virtually anywhere.

With an editor of *Automobile* magazine along to document the journey, E. Thomas Fetch drove a 1-cylinder Packard from San Francisco to New York in 1903 over a route that a "dumb fool" advertising man had chosen with an eye toward publicity, not practicality.

But with the assistance of Packard mechanic N. O. Allyn on the western half of the trip, Fetch and Marius C. "Chris" Krarup, the *Automobile* reporter, overcame all natural hazards, and two legal obstacles as well. They averaged 64 miles a day over sagebrush, mountain trails, deep ruts, and sand in the West, in addition to mud in the Midwest and in rural New York, to cover some 4,000 miles. Finishing on August 21, 1903, the second transcontinental car shaved nearly 1½ days from the record that Jackson and Crocker had established a month earlier.

The rough trails punished the axles, springs, and steering linkages of "Old Pacific," a nickname for the car that Krarup usually shortened to "Pac." or "Pac" in his writings. Nevertheless, asserted Krarup, "interruptions due to failure of the motor or driving mechanisms were unimportant and brief."[1] This was a slight exaggeration, for to complete the trip the car needed frequent adjustments and an infusion of 28 new parts, plus new batteries and tires.

Though slightly modified for the trip, the 12-horsepower Packard, weighing 2,200 pounds empty and 3,000 pounds loaded,[2] was too low for the rocky trails of Nevada, Utah, and Colorado, and often boiled away its cooling water. "A greater surplus of power than we had and a motor fan—now so commonly used—would have been of advantage," Krarup wrote in a May 1904 illustrated feature for *World's Work* magazine.[3] Nevada's deep sands had ended Alexander Winton's 1901 coast-to-coast attempt, but Fetch and Krarup had a secret weapon: they used two wide sheets of canvas, placing one before the other as necessary, to bridge such soft sands, an idea other transcontinentalists eagerly copied.

Excising Prejudice Against Autos

The Packard company sponsored the trip "with the purpose of demonstrating the ability of the American moderate powered automobile to negotiate the all but impassable mountain and desert roads and trails of the Far West." As with John D. Davis's 1899 attempt, the Packard trip also hoped to show that the American auto was "quite distinct from the one which has come to us from the French racing car as a model for imitation."[4]

In an advertisement after the run, Packard stated that its purpose had been only partly to show what its own product could accomplish:

> We wanted to demonstrate its unfailing reliability under the most severe test that could possibly be conceived of, and to keep a complete record of every repair made on this fearful undertaking . . . [so] that we might add our mite to the ever increasing volume of evidence of the complete practicability of the motor car and in that way help in the removal of the last traces of prejudice against it as an experiment.[5]

During the journey, Krarup became an automobile explorer of sorts, carrying "a surveyor's aneroid barometer, a compass and clinometer, a thermometer," a logbook, and a camera.[6] He took an estimated 750 photos on the trip and freely peppered his reports with the barometer readings, from which he calculated altitude, and with precise distances, temperatures and grades.[7]

In the finest tradition of the auto industry, however, James Ward Packard and company advertising man Sidney D. Waldon were actually doing nothing more than staging a stunt, as Waldon revealed years later:

> I realized that we had to attract public attention with a spectacle, but it had to be a useful spectacle. So I sent a man named Tom Fetch and a mechanic named Allen [*sic*], a great, big, six-footer . . . and a photographer named Krarup, out to San Francisco and arranged for them to make a San Francisco–New York trip in "Old Pacific," a car which later became famous.

I didn't understand the difficulties and consequently selected the wrong route—from San Francisco to . . . Reno, Lovelock, Winnemucca, around the north end of Great Salt Lake, and from Salt Lake City told them to go right through the center of Colorado. Like a dumb fool, I was thinking from the standpoint of publicity, with pictures of the mountains and canyons, but what I sent them into was something terrific.[8]

Our Little Party

After a five-day train trip from the East Coast, "our little party" arrived in San Francisco on June 7 to spend two weeks preparing the car, Krarup wrote in the first installment of his trip report. By contrast, the drivers of the Winton that had departed San Francisco on May 23 claimed to have spent just four days preparing. Krarup was not originally scheduled to travel with the car. Newspapers in Salt Lake City and Ogden, Utah, later revealed that the Packard company had contracted with an Ogden man to guide the car but had fired him before the start. Krarup became his substitute; he "wasn't much of a guide, but he was ideal for publicity."[9]

Krarup described Fetch (born Elmer Thomas Fetch), of Warren, Ohio (but originally from nearby Jefferson), as a "capable operator and mechanic" for Packard in Warren (see Fig. 42). According to other accounts, Fetch had been a Packard "demonstrator," or test driver, and a plant foreman. The *Denver Post* described Fetch as "a man of small stature" who referred a reporter's inquiries to Mr. Krarup. The *Chicago Inter Ocean* reported that Krarup was "a Dane by birth." In fact, Krarup—"a man of medium height with a stubby beard and mustache"—may have been an immigrant, since he supposedly spoke "with a somewhat foreign accent." The Packard company described Krarup as "an engineer and writer of considerable note, but whose principal recommendation lay in the fact that he stood for truth."[10]

A third team member, N. O. Allyn, described as "an expert machinist from the factory at Warren," originally followed the car by train from San Francisco. "The inactivity being irksome, he asked the privilege of going with the car to see the scenery. He continued with the party from Reno to Colorado Springs, seated on the baggage when the car was in motion."[11] Editors often misspelled the surnames of all three men: Allyn would appear as Allen; Fetch as Fetsch, Fitch, and even Tetch; and Krarup, the most creatively and consistently misspelled last name, appeared as Krarrup, Krasup, and Krareep.

Fig. 42 (opposite). Tom Fetch in "Old Pacific" (NAHC).

Modifying Old Pacific

The Packard company shipped to San Francisco a 1903 Model F touring car—"taken at random from stock"—with the rear tonneau removed, exposing a sloping rear deck on which the travelers strapped their gear.[12] Displacing 184 cubic inches with a bore and stroke of $6 \times 6\frac{1}{2}$ inches, the 1-cylinder engine developed 12 horsepower at 850 rpm. Normally geared, a 1903 Packard could hit 20 mph in third speed at 650 rpm, with an even higher top speed. Old Pacific, serial no. 322, had an 88-inch wheelbase, a tread (the distance between the left and right wheels) of $56\frac{1}{2}$ inches, a 3-speed sliding-gear transmission, and 34×4–inch Diamond detachable tires on wood-spoke rims. At Cliff House, where the $2,300 Packard started its trip, the odometer showed 68 miles (see Fig. 43).[13]

As modified, the car could carry 10 gallons of gas in its main tank, 6 gallons in a reserve tank that was separate from the fuel-feed system, and 1 gallon in a tank mounted near the carburetor. The small tank could supply the carburetor on steep hills, when the gas level in the standard tank was often too low to flow by gravity to the engine. Adding a special nine-tooth forward drive sprocket—the standard sprocket had ten teeth—gave the car a lower gearing for steep mountain grades.

By installing special metal blocks, or shims, Fetch had the option of boosting the engine's compression and pulling power "by lengthening the connecting rod a trifle— so as to offset the power loss due to high altitude." Because the car's power loss in the mountains was "imperceptible," Fetch never used this option.[14]

The travelers further modified the car by adding a cyclometer to measure distance and speed. A single kerosene headlamp supplemented the two dash-mounted carriage lamps that came with the car. The transcontinental crew rigged a canvas undercarriage shield that the sagebrush quickly shredded. In Wadsworth, Nevada, on Day 7, the crewmen made a canvas awning to both shade and direct cooling air through the radiator coils.

Pack a Pick and Pistol

The car carried two 6-foot-wide strips of canvas 20 or 24 feet long for crossing loose sand.[15] "The principal difficulties which we anticipate are the sand in Nevada and the drivers of mule teams on the mountain roads," Krarup explained. Tire chains, "an

Fig. 43. Fetch takes a break from driving in what is perhaps Krarup's most famous 1903 trip photo. It shows Old Pacific in detail (NAHC).

extra axle" strapped to the rear deck, and an unspecified toolkit were among the other items they packed for the long trip.[16] There was more:

> Some repair material stowed away in the front hood, two valises of small size containing personal belongings, one pair of rubber boots, a portable camera . . . and one 38-caliber revolver in a holster on the dashboard, completed the baggage piled behind the seats. An axe was strapped on top of a three-gallon tank intended to contain drinking water and located over the right rear axle bearings. A camping outfit it was decided should be procured at Sacramento, but a stout shovel was carried along from the beginning.[17]

Fetch and Krarup also carried a pick, the automaker revealed. Later, the men added a large parasol to the car. Perhaps Allyn also brought a gun with him, for Krarup reported that "bullets from two revolvers missed the mark" when the motorists spotted a coyote in Nevada.[18] Curiously, the car lacked a block and tackle, an item that Dr. H. Nelson Jackson had found indispensable on his earlier trip in a Winton.

The men shipped extra items ahead by rail, including most of their personal luggage. Krarup confirmed the success of this arrangement: "We had no difficulty whatever with our supplies, always sending a quantity ahead to stations where we knew we would stop."[19]

Traveling in "Complete Ignorance"

From Sacramento, on Day 3, the Packard's trail would follow an old stage trail and the Southern Pacific Company's rails nearly due east into the Sierra Nevada. Passing south of Lake Tahoe to reach Carson City, Nevada, the team would turn north to Reno; work their way north and east across the desert state to Utah; cross the north side of the Great Salt Lake; and then head sharply south and gently east into Colorado's Rocky Mountains, following the route of the Denver & Rio Grande Western Railway through Utah, and the companion Denver & Rio Grande Railway to Denver. At the start of the trip, no route had yet been selected for the trek eastward from Denver.[20]

Krarup would later reveal: "We traveled in almost complete ignorance of what the next turn of the road would bring forth, depending upon information picked up at our nightly lodgings for finding the road or trail that would take us with least inconvenience to another stopping place."[21] Crew members learned of their route east of Denver only when the Packard company informed them at the last moment.[22] Krarup soon learned how to interpret the directions he received from other travelers:

As a rule, every bit of advice had to be translated, as it were, from the natural mental bias of one who speaks from experiences with horses and stages. . . . Almost invariably rough road surface was represented as a more serious hindrance than it proved to be, and, on the other hand, troubles arising from deep and loose sand were underestimated, as we found afterwards. Yet at this writing none of the troubles predicted for us have proved formidable enough to stall the car at any time, though at times we have stopped for awhile to consider the best way of proceeding and to give the faithful hard-working engine a cooling-down spell.[23]

The crew did carry maps. Krarup's familiarity with U.S. Geological Survey maps—"which give the altitudes at the various points, though not the names under which the points are now generally known"—suggests that these maps were in his collection.[24]

The Packard crewmen timed their June 20 departure so as to reach Salt Lake City in two weeks, on July 4, at about the same time Americans would hear results of the July 2 Gordon Bennett International Cup Race in Ireland (see Table 4). "This probable coincidence of dates might lead to a comparison of the relative importance of two events—one a race at breakneck speed over a smooth course, and the other only steady plugging over rough and almost untrodden ground, yet each in its way intended to demonstrate what this product of modern ingenuity and patience, the automobile, may be trusted to do," Krarup wrote.[25] Unfortunately for the Packard plan, all three American Gordon Bennett entries—a Peerless and two Wintons—failed to finish the 370-mile race.

What Happened Surfside?

Conflicting press accounts make it difficult to reconstruct the events of the starting day. Krarup, the trip's chronicler, compounds the confusion due to discrepancies between his *Automobile* dispatches and his later summary of events for *World's Work*. Two facts are in question: First, did Fetch become the first transcontinentalist to back his car into the surf of the Pacific Ocean, as some claimed? And, second, when did Old Pacific leave San Francisco?

Some contemporary accounts maintained that Fetch backed into the Pacific surf to wet the car's rear wheels. Krarup's first *Automobile* dispatch, curiously, mentions only that he and Fetch drove to Cliff House, an oceanfront landmark, "to depart with a few whiffs of salt breeze to cheer our memory on the long land-bound

TABLE 4. Old Pacific's Daily City-to-City Progress, 1903

Day / Date	City–City
1 / June 20 Sat	San Francisco–Port Costa, Calif.
2 / June 21 Sun	Port Costa, Calif.–Sacramento, Calif.
3 / June 22 Mon	Sacramento, Calif.–Placerville, Calif.
4 / June 23 Tue	Placerville, Calif.–Sugar Loaf, Calif.
5 / June 24 Wed	Sugar Loaf, Calif.–Carson City, Nev.
6 / June 25 Thu	Carson City, Nev.–Wadsworth, Nev.
7 / June 26 Fri	*idle day in Wadsworth, Nev.*
8 / June 27 Sat	Wadsworth, Nev.–Lovelock, Nev.
9 / June 28 Sun	Lovelock, Nev.–Winnemucca, Nev.
10 / June 29 Mon	Winnemucca, Nev.–Battle Mountain, Nev.
11 / June 30 Tue	Battle Mountain, Nev.–Elko, Nev.
12 / July 1 Wed	Elko, Nev.–Wells, Nev.
13 / July 2 Thu	Wells, Nev.–Tecoma, Nev.
14 / July 3 Fri	Tecoma, Nev.–Promontory, Utah
15 / July 4 Sat	Promontory, Utah–Salt Lake City
16 / July 5 Sun	*sheriff holds car in Salt Lake City*
17 / July 6 Mon	*sheriff holds car in Salt Lake City*
18 / July 7 Tue	Salt Lake City–Tucker, Utah
19 / July 8 Wed	Tucker, Utah–Price, Utah
20 / July 9 Thu	*idle day in Price, Utah*
21 / July 10 Fri	Price, Utah–Green River, Utah
22 / July 11 Sat	Green River, Utah–east of Thompsons, Utah[a]
23 / July 12 Sun	East of Thompsons, Utah–Grand Junction, Colo.[a]
24 / July 13 Mon	Grand Junction, Colo.–Rifle, Colo.
25 / July 14 Tue	Rifle, Colo.–Glenwood Springs, Colo.
26 / July 15 Wed	Glenwood Springs, Colo.–Gypsum, Colo.
27 / July 16 Thu	Gypsum, Colo.–Redcliff, Colo.
28 / July 17 Fri	Redcliff, Colo.–Buena Vista, Colo.
29 / July 18 Sat	Buena Vista, Colo.–Florissant, Colo.
30 / July 19 Sun	Florissant, Colo.–Colorado Springs, Colo.
31 / July 20 Mon	Colorado Springs, Colo.–Denver
32 / July 21 Tue	*idle day in Denver*

33 / July 22 Wed	*idle day in Denver*
34 / July 23 Thu	*idle day in Denver*
35 / July 24 Fri	*idle day in Denver*
36 / July 25 Sat	Denver–Fort Morgan, Colo.
37 / July 26 Sun	Fort Morgan, Colo.–Sterling, Colo.
38 / July 27 Mon	Sterling, Colo.–North Platte, Neb.
39 / July 28 Tue	North Platte, Neb.–Kearney, Neb.
40 / July 29 Wed	Kearney, Neb.–Grand Island, Neb.
41 / July 30 Thu	Grand Island, Neb.–Fremont, Neb.
42 / July 31 Fri	Fremont, Neb.–Omaha, Neb.
43 / Aug. 1 Sat	*rain day in Omaha, Neb.*
44 / Aug. 2 Sun	*rain day in Omaha, Neb.*
45 / Aug. 3 Mon	Omaha, Neb.–Adair, Iowa
46 / Aug. 4 Tue	Adair, Iowa–Des Moines, Iowa
47 / Aug. 5 Wed	*rain day in Des Moines, Iowa*
48 / Aug. 6 Thu	Des Moines, Iowa–Marengo, Iowa
49 / Aug. 7 Fri	Marengo, Iowa–Wheatland, Iowa
50 / Aug. 8 Sat	Wheatland, Iowa–Dixon, Ill.[b]
51 / Aug. 9 Sun	Dixon, Ill.–St. Charles, Ill.
52 / Aug. 10 Mon	St. Charles, Ill.–Chicago
53 / Aug. 11 Tue	Chicago–South Bend, Ind.
54 / Aug. 12 Wed	South Bend, Ind.–Bryan, Ohio
55 / Aug. 13 Thu	Bryan, Ohio–Norwalk, Ohio
56 / Aug. 14 Fri	Norwalk, Ohio–Cleveland
57 / Aug. 15 Sat	Cleveland–Jefferson, Ohio
58 / Aug. 16 Sun	Jefferson, Ohio–Fredonia, N.Y.
59 / Aug. 17 Mon	Fredonia, N.Y.–Batavia, N.Y.
60 / Aug. 18 Tue	Batavia, N.Y.–Syracuse, N.Y.
61 / Aug. 19 Wed	Syracuse, N.Y.–Herkimer, N.Y.
62 / Aug. 20 Thu	Herkimer, N.Y.–Hudson, N.Y.
63 / Aug. 21 Fri	Hudson, N.Y.–New York City

SOURCES: Marius C. Krarup's accounts in *Automobile* and *World's Work*; other auto journals; the Packard Motor Car Company's post-run ads; and local and national newspapers.

[a] To avoid the heat, Old Pacific's crew left Thompsons at 8:00 PM on July 11 and drove all night. The car's exact position at midnight on July 11 is therefore unrecorded.

[b] This is the Packard company's version of Old Pacific's itinerary through eastern Iowa. Crewman Marius C. Krarup's dispatches include gaps for this section; auto journals offer conflicting accounts.

expedition." The following day's *San Francisco Chronicle* carried an article about the trip to Cliff House, but made no mention of the transcontinental car backing into the surf.[26]

Krarup surely would have photographed an immersion ceremony, if one had taken place. None of his starting photos survive, however, because a Sacramento photographer ruined the dozen negatives that Krarup took on the first two days of the trip. Upon reaching Denver, Krarup pointedly told the *Rocky Mountain News*: "No, we did not put the hind wheels of the car into the Pacific; no theatrical play about it. We are making an endurance trip."[27]

The *Denver Post* and *Denver Times*, however, both mentioned a wheel-wetting ceremony. The *Denver Times* even quoted Krarup as saying, "We have come a distance of 2,000 miles since June 20, when we left San Francisco with our hind wheels in the Pacific ocean."[28] Subsequently, newspapers frequently mentioned that the autoists were making a coast-to-coast trip, literally—having started in the Pacific surf and planning to end in the Atlantic. Whether or not the story is true, later cross-country drivers continued the wheel-wetting "tradition."

Krarup's *World's Work* article gives a starting time of "June 20th, in the evening." Old Pacific actually began its trip hours earlier, according to Krarup's *Automobile* dispatches, other press reports, and the Packard company, which reported that at 2:00 PM on Saturday, June 20, the crewmen drove out of "the garage of Harold W. Larzalere, the Packard Company's Pacific Coast agent, 1814 Market street."[29]

From the Larzalere garage, Fetch and Krarup drove to Cliff House. Krarup's *Automobile* account says they left the shore at 3:05 PM—which becomes the official starting time of their eastward trek—and, "after driving the six to seven miles from the ocean to the Oakland Ferry there was nothing to do but await the departure of the ferryboat which took place at 5:15 o'clock with that irregularity for which ferries on the Coast are noted, the schedule time being 5 sharp."[30]

Factory Foists "First" Fiction

Packard officials, who had been planning their transcontinental trip for at least three months, were undoubtedly frustrated when they learned that Old Pacific would not be the first coast-to-coast car. It is hard to know if, at their June 20 start, Fetch and Krarup were aware of Dr. H. Nelson Jackson's attempt, under way, in a Winton, since in the early stages Jackson received little national press coverage. If Fetch and Krarup didn't know, they learned about Jackson soon enough: Krarup's own journal, *Automobile*, published the first of several articles about Jackson's adventures on June 27.[31]

But neither Packard Motors nor the Packard crew informed local editors of Old Pacific's second-place position behind Jackson's Winton. By this omission, both parties promoted the persistent belief that Fetch was the first to drive across the country. Some newspaper editors allowed this manipulation. The *Cleveland Plain Dealer* should have known better, because it published a July 21 article about Jackson reaching Cleveland. Still, when the Packard arrived the following month, on August 14, the *Plain Dealer* unquestioningly swallowed Packard's claim that Old Pacific was making "the first official transcontinental run ever accomplished."[32]

Off to Placerville

Dropped by ferry on the east side of San Francisco Bay, Fetch and Krarup left Oakland about 6:00 PM and promptly got lost. Finally, with the brakes working "sweetly and noiselessly," they descended a steep, 2-mile canyon road to reach Port Costa at 8:15 PM, 38 miles from San Francisco and their destination for Day 1. The car's single crank bearing had run hotter than normal; otherwise, the car had performed well.[33]

The next morning, Fetch discovered that the crank bearing had run hot because its oil valve was "mutilated at the point with a pair of nippers, and its seat was filled with waste and soap." The damage was "plainly the work of one who did not wish us success," Krarup concluded. Curiously, the Packard company reported no such suspicions, saying only that the bearing had run hot because "the point of the lubricating needle valve had been broken off and the packing of the valve had got in under the broken point. The needle valve was filed to its proper shape and the bearing worked itself into order during the second day's drive."[34] The repairs delayed the team's start until 9:00 AM.

Arriving at Dixon, California, that afternoon, Krarup discovered his bag of maps, negatives, and instruments had fallen from its resting place within the "ring of the spare tires over the tailboard."[35] This loss cost the men two hours and 26 miles to retrace their route and retrieve the items. They reached their destination, Sacramento, at about 8:00 PM after a 109-mile day.

Cresting the Summit

Leaving Placerville at 9:00 AM on Day 4, Tuesday, June 23, the motorists headed east on "stony, sandy and unkempt roads" along the American River. But the trail evolved into a better state road that, though ungraded, had a "well kept surface." The first auto travelers in the region took their meals at stage company way stations, which were situated every dozen or so miles.[36]

Fetch and Krarup left Sugar Loaf, California, at 5:00 AM on Day 5, Wednesday, June 24, for the difficult 56-mile trek to Carson City, Nevada. Their transcontinental car soon tackled Slippery Ford, "a tortuous grade of 13 to 17 per cent., sandy and strewn with loose stones." Twice they pulled aside for oncoming stage coaches. Just after 10:00 AM, they reached the Sierra Nevada summit, on the California side, at an altitude of 7,300 feet, and ate lunch at Lakeside Hotel on Lake Tahoe at Stateline, California (see Fig. 44).[37]

Afterward, the pair encountered a mile-long sandy grade of 10 to 12 percent. In 70 minutes' time, by 3:30 PM, the car had climbed 1,000 feet to top the Nevada summit of the mountain range, also at 7,300 feet. Then, in 37 minutes, they descended 2,400 feet in 6 miles to enter the Carson Valley of Nevada through Daggett's Pass. "The roadbed was deeply sandy and the front wheels slewed somewhat at the sharp turns. It was necessary to watch closely and not go too fast." Roadbuilders of the 1850s and 1860s had leveled the natural 45-percent grade to between 12 and 20 percent, according to Krarup's gradometer, which he also called a clinometer. Still, "over the last, the Kingsbury Grade, the brake-rings became so heated that we stopped three times to cool them."[38]

Fig. 44. "A rest before reaching a steep and tortuous grade near Lake Tahoe" (*World's Work*, May 1904).

Desert Driving, Drear Waiting

Leaving Carson City at about 7 o'clock the next morning, Thursday, June 25, the duo traveled north for 2½ hours over a rough road of sand and stone to Reno. There, N. O. Allyn, the Packard company's "skillful machinist," left the train to take a place on the back of the two-passenger car, where he would ride for the next month or more.[39]

East of Reno, bound for Wadsworth, the three auto travelers took a canyon road that meandered across the Southern Pacific tracks ten times "and finally emerged onto an old neglected stretch of macadamized road, full of holes but affording fairly good driving." This 7- or 8-mile stretch of macadam was the first rural road surfacing they had discovered to that point. Their 70.5-mile sixth day put the trio 362.5 miles out of San Francisco.[40]

Sandy roads were the norm during the next five days as the three men traveled northeast and east through the Humboldt River Valley from near Lovelock to Deeth, Nevada. "The road consists of two ruts inclosing a ridge overgrown with stout sagebrush. Frequently the ridge is so high that the low-built car cannot be driven ahead," Krarup wrote. "Then we drove many miles beside the trail, where the old sage bushes grow as thick as an arm and up to man's height" (see Fig. 45).[41]

The three-man crew reluctantly spent all of Day 7, Friday, June 26, in Wadsworth, a "little railroad division town," waiting for film and freight bills to arrive. But they used an hour of their "drear waiting" building and mounting a canvas sun shield over the radiator coils. "The purpose of getting more air into the coils by this device was thwarted, however, for all the way through the sand what little air was stirring was with us and there was no possibility of progressing fast enough to create a current by speed." On Saturday, as they prepared for a 7:00 AM departure into the desert, "a genial soul who had known thirst on these plains, presented us with a case of twelve bottles of Milwaukee beer packed in ice and wrapped in wet gunnysacks."[42]

Climbing with Canvas

Meantime, a crowd of thrill-seekers had gathered at a steep sandy hill outside Wadsworth, where they expected the automobile to bog down. The spectators showed "boundless surprise," however, when the transcontinentalists mastered the hill by using the two long canvas strips they carried for just such a contingency:

Fig. 45. Fetch (*driving*), Allyn, and Old Pacific on the sagebrush trail (NAHC).

One was placed between rear and front wheels, crosswise, and the other lengthwise before the front wheels extending up the hill. Though the rear canvas was much crumpled by the process, enough traction was left to get the car entirely onto the front canvas, and then it rolled easily upward, as the weight on the front wheels prevented the rear wheels from pulling the canvas backward. Three times each strip of canvas was laid before the other, and then the top was reached, the entire climb being only about 120 feet in length.[43]

The men used the canvas twice more that morning (see Fig. 46). "The nature of the sand may be imagined from the fact that on downgrades of 10 per cent. in one place and 14 per cent. in another, the car not only did not coast down but required the use of the low gear to reach the foot of the incline." It took the motorists 3 hours, 40 minutes to travel 12 miles through the desert heat—94 degrees Fahrenheit in the shade and 125 degrees on the sand. As the car's water steadily boiled away, Krarup found himself wishing his car had an engine fan or "a largely increased radiation surface." Shortly after reaching the firmer footing of the glittering white "alkali plains,"

Fig. 46. A slightly retouched photo shows Allyn, *left*, and Fetch spreading canvas in the desert (NAHC).

Fetch turned the car around to make a 52-minute, 10-mile round-trip detour to recover a canvas strip that had fallen from the car unnoticed.[44]

Typically, Nevada rivers "disappear in the ground when evaporation and irrigation have exhausted their resources," as was the case for the Humboldt River in a "sink" southwest of Lovelock, Krarup reported. Though the Humboldt Sink's smooth, white alkali surface appeared ideal for driving, "only when it has been dry for some time will it support the load of a car, and after any little rain it becomes so treacherous and slippery that it is better to pass around it when at all possible." Nonetheless, the Packard transcontinental crew crossed sections of the Humboldt Sink to reach Lovelock at 7:12 PM, ending a 77-mile day. The trail alongside the Southern Pacific tracks was hazardous for automobile tires, strewn as it was with "the relics and debris which denote where a gang of men had recently been working." The result: the men spent 20 minutes late in the afternoon patching an inner tube after the left front tire picked up a nail (see Fig. 47).[45]

Fig. 47. Allyn, *left*, and Fetch repair a tire near Lovelock, Nevada. The discarded bottle symbolizes the "relics and debris" of a passing railroad crew (NAHC).

COAST TO COAST BY AUTOMOBILE

Curious Cattle Bar Car

The greatest obstacles to their 78-mile drive along the Humboldt River from Lovelock to Winnemucca on Sunday, June 28, Day 9, were the deep ravines, called arroyos, Krarup wrote. Allyn, Fetch, and Krarup drove 25 miles to Rye Patch, Nevada, in 80 minutes, stopped for 8 gallons of gas, then continued through Humboldt House to Mill City. When Mill City residents warned them of deeper sand ahead, they abandoned their route along the Humboldt River lowlands and instead climbed a mountain trail to Dun Glen (see Fig. 48), northeast of and some 1,500 feet higher than Mill City. The Dun Glen trail was steep but good all the way to the mining town at the summit, where "a few old men still dig away for treasure, while the more enterprising young men have left for better fields."[46] On his 1901 transcontinental attempt, a stubborn Alexander Winton, despite similar warnings, had driven due east from Mill City, directly into the deep sand, thereby ending his trip.

Fig. 48. Dun Glen, Nevada (NAHC).

Fig. 49. A curious cow approaches Old Pacific (*World's Work*, May 1904).

Understandably, many animals took flight at the approach of the noisy motor car. Through Dun Glen Pass, however, the transcontinental Packard "met roaming flocks of cattle and horses, which all but barred the way by their curiosity" (see Fig. 49). Coyotes and badgers showed the same "manifest curiosity."[47]

At 2:25 PM, the motorists started down the mountain from Dun Glen along a trail "steep and winding with many abrupt turns and curves and plenty of places where a car not conducted with caution might fall down some 400 or 500 feet onto the rocks." At 5:20 PM, Old Pacific again reached the sandy lowland trail, still several miles from Winnemucca. The last 4 miles through deepening sand "would have required about two hours of hard pulling" if not for road improvements. Winnemucca residents "had cut down the sage brush on both sides of the track and spread it over the sand, turning it into what is locally called a 'brushed road.'"[48]

Trapped in Deep Ruts

Rain the next morning, Monday, June 29, delayed until 1:20 PM the men's start from Winnemucca. Fetch used the extra time to tighten the Packard's drive chain, clean its spark plug, and oil various moving parts. "With the cooling water nearly boiling, for the day was sultry and calm," the 1-cylinder auto chugged to the summit of Battle Mountain, a 4½-mile climb. Because slightly richer, firmer soil prevailed east of Golconda, Nevada, the wheel ruts grew deeper and sagebrush grew rank on the ridge between them. Fetch drove carefully, "lest the car should get hung up on the [differential] gear casing with the drivers [rear wheels] lifted from the ground." Having crossed the mountain of the same name, the travelers reached the north-central Nevada town of Battle Mountain at 6:17 PM to end their tenth day, 577 miles from San Francisco.[49]

The travelers' 90-mile trip from Battle Mountain to Elko, Nevada, on Day 11, Tuesday, June 30, took them over a trail slippery from rain. The Humboldt River had also overflowed in places. At a ford across swollen Rock Creek, Fetch operated the controls from outside as he helped push the car across. At 2:40 PM, shortly after lunch at a ranch house near Dunphy, the car hung up on the trail's center ridge:

> The cause was the usual one; the ridge was higher than it looked, caught the rear axle brace under the differential gear case and turned it around the axle until the upper cross-piece of the case frame bore down upon the sprocket chain. In twenty minutes it was all twisted back to its place and the set screws tightened, but the chain had been weakened by the irregular strain and at 4:15 o'clock it came nearly apart at another similar ridge, and four links had to be replaced with new ones.[50]

Eerie Experience Entering Elko

Repairs took 20 minutes after the first accident, 45 minutes after the second. The next day, after damaging the rear-axle brace a third time, the men discovered they could straighten it quickly by jacking up under it against the weight of the car. Because of delays crossing the creek and repairing the car, including replacing an inner tube that morning, it was 7:30 PM when the coast-to-coast Packard reached Carlin, still 28 miles from Elko. The first 14 miles of the road ahead lay through a darkening elevated canyon:

> We took the chance of getting through the hills during daylight and making the last fourteen miles by lamps, and in this we barely succeeded. The last two miles of the mountain seemed a trifle uncanny, being rough and steep and appearing more so in the darkness which was fast settling around us. Almost we overlooked a little stack of cut-off sagebrush which had been placed at one side of the forking trail, and which Carlin people had told us meant that here we had better turn off onto a hogback slope which would be safer for a night descent into the valley than the lower pass.

We found the hogback was pitched just about right for a gentle coasting, though its width was hardly more than fifteen yards and sufficiently irregular in outline and surface to call for sharp attention to the steering. If we had lighted the lamps in this place, the shadows would probably have been more confusing than the light could have been helpful. Finally we arrived on the good road, however, and here the headlight, when lighted, showed a plain course.[51]

"The motor car arrived in Elko about 9 o'clock Tuesday evening," according to the local *Free Press*, whose editor evidently saw the futility of specifying which motor car. Fetch's Packard was the *only* automobile to pass through town. "While in Elko it attracted a great deal of attention," concluded the economical three-sentence report.[52]

Trainman Terrified

The next morning, Wednesday, July 1, Day 12, the Packard crew "heard of a brakeman who had wanted to jump from the train which we met on the last part of the journey. Seeing our headlight coming toward his train rapidly—perhaps there was a curve in the road—his vision depicted a head-end collision, and only his fellow-brakeman— who told us the story—averted the leap by assuring him it was the light from a limekiln located in that vicinity."[53]

On Wednesday's drive to Wells, Nevada, the widely spaced trail ruts—deeply worn by wagons with a tread of 60 inches, compared to the Packard's 56½ inches— spelled trouble for Old Pacific's tires. If Fetch drove with one wheel squarely in a rut, "the other tire would drag against the raised inner edge of the other rut, and . . . the grinding action was rapid and severe. And the car would naturally wabble from one rut to the other according to the slope of the surface, so that both front tires were ground about evenly. The rear tires, being more rigid in relation to the body and weight of the car, escaped some of this action."[54]

While crossing a snow-fed rivulet across the road through the Star Valley east of Deeth, the Packard "was unexpectedly mired so deeply that it required a half-hour of hard work with the jack, the shovel and some fence posts to get under way again."[55]

On July 2, the trio was hoping to travel through Fenelon and Toana to Tecoma— all railroad towns or outposts in northeastern Nevada (see Fig. 50). Krarup and later transcontinentalists often cited railroad outposts that do not appear on road maps of the period. But that was because "many of the railroad stations consisted of a signboard and footprints outward bound."[56]

Fig. 50. Old Pacific followed the railroad, literally, sometimes just a few feet from the crossties, as in this unidentified view (NAHC).

"A Hill That Stunned Us"

At a railroad section house near Fenelon, the motorists "were confronted with a hill that stunned us." Fetch tackled the hill by a method that punished Old Pacific but worked. Krarup wrote:

> To go up on the lowest gear steadily was out of the question. It was a case of jumping the car by fly-wheel momentum, stopping on the brakes when the momentum gave out—and jumping again. The chain had its four new links in, but it was not quite certain that other links had not been weakened. However, the attempt had to be made.
>
> Allyn and self secured stones to place behind the drivers (the rear wheels) at critical moments, and proceeded to help by pushing. Pac was jumped probably five or six feet. Quick brake action and equally quick stone action had the desired effect, though it trembled in the balance.[57]

They repeated the jumping a full dozen times on the grade, which averaged 40 percent. "After this we ceased to fear grades, figuring that Pac had about 30 horsepower on the jumping plan."[58]

Old Pacific ground and spun its way through 11 miles of deep sand between Tecoma and Lucin, Utah, after a 5:45 AM start on Friday, July 3, Day 14. The three men covered 114 miles to Promontory, arriving at 8:00 . It was at Promontory, on May 10, 1869, that the Union Pacific Railroad's westward construction had met the Central Pacific's eastward construction to complete America's first transcontinental railroad. Since that date, transcontinental trains had been passing north of the Great Salt Lake to rumble through Promontory—the same route Old Pacific followed.

Gullies Every 100 Feet

The trail had grades twice as steep as any in the Sierra Nevada or Rocky Mountains:

> Any one who may try in the future to drive an automobile from Lucin to Terrace . . . will remember the trip afterwards. Gullies cross the trail about every 100 feet. . . . The front wheels must be lowered into each of these gullies cautiously, with danger of driving the headlight against the opposite bank. Then the rear wheels must be nursed down into the ditch, and, if the latter is not very broad, that means that the front end of the car must simultaneously be nursed up on the other side.
>
> Then when the rear wheels are safely down, the whole car must be shot up by flywheel momentum, and if the two banks don't happen to be parallel this means a very energetic use of the steering gear, too, so as to have both front wheels in contact with the ground, and not one of them lifted into the air while the other is twisted around scraping against the paint of the boot.
>
> This series of operations repeated about 50 times per mile for 23 miles, leaves an indelible impression on the memory, sore spots in the driver's hands, and a very lively realization of the fact that a car to go across such country must have a highly flexible running gear and several other qualities, that would tempt the most modest manufacturer to do a little pardonable bragging.[59]

Because of such obstacles, the Packard company estimated that in Utah "the clutch and gears were operated 2,000 times in a single day's run." Yet, during the entire 62-day trek, the clutch would require "only five adjustments."[60]

Car Inspires "Opened-Mouthed Wonder"

Despite the difficulties, the car reached Terrace at 11:30 AM and traveled over a level road to reach Kelton at 1:30 PM. Farther east at Lake Station, the Packard climbed a hill that, while not as steep as the one at Fenelon, Nevada, was longer and littered with loose stones. As at Fenelon, the car climbed the hill in violent, gear-wrenching spurts. "It was scaled in full view of a number of railroad men, who cheered the performance from a distance by a chorus of locomotive whistles," Krarup wrote. "Their professional sympathy was with the motor."[61]

Two days of hard wear and tear on the car were evident the next day, Day 15 of the trip, as Fetch drove the 106 miles from Promontory to Salt Lake City on Saturday, July 4. "It was plain that the car had suffered somewhat from its ordeals. The front spring, inverted elliptic, sagged after the inordinate abuse to which it had been subjected in the gullies and 'twisters' (twister is a gully with converging banks or crossing the trail at an acute angle); the lug holding the rear axle brace rod on the right was broken, nobody knew where; the chain's pitch was irregular—yet everything functioned well enough to run over 100 miles in 8½ hours."[62] To reach Salt Lake City at all, however, Old Pacific had required frequent adjustments and repairs since leaving San Francisco (see Table 5).

Salt Lake City residents displayed "considerable opened-mouthed wonder . . . [at] the arrival at the Cullen hotel of three dusty, sun-browned men in a big twelve-horse-power touring car, showing evident signs of a long day's travel over dry roads." The car, capable of 20 miles per gallon, was averaging 12 mpg "on the kind of roads so far encountered," a Salt Lake City newspaper reported.[63]

A Little Piece of Paper

Undoubtedly, the men displayed their own open-mouthed wonder when, soon after their 4:35 PM arrival, the sheriff seized the car as security in a damage claim filed against the Packard Motor Car Company. Seeking $5,000 in damages, Charles D. Roberts of Ogden had filed the attachment in a breach-of-contract suit against the automaker, who had fired him as a guide for the transcontinental trip. "He was to receive $2,000 for his services and get a job with the company at the end of the journey," the *Salt Lake Herald* reported.[64] As Roberts stated his case in the *Ogden Standard*:

> The trip was my idea. I arranged it and had a contract with the company. Just before we started from San Francisco, Krarup, who represents a trade publication, came out. He was to follow on a train and we were to give him a ride now and then when convenient. Before we started he demanded a seat in the automobile the entire distance. There is room for only two, and one of us would have had to ride on the step. I offered to take turns with him riding on the step, but he said the dignity of his paper would not permit it. He wired them about it and they backed him up. The company left the dispute in the hands of its agent in San Francisco, and he discharged me without warning. They claim I

TABLE 5. Old Pacific's Reported Breakdowns and Repairs, San Francisco to Salt Lake City, 1903[a]

Day / Date	Location	Description of Breakdown or Repair
Day 2 / June 21	Port Costa, Calif.	Fetch repairs a broken needle valve that was preventing oil from reaching the crankshaft bearings.
Day 2 / June 21	Between Fairfield and Vacaville, Calif.	Fetch spends 10 or 15 minutes temporarily securing "the copper boat or chute along the connecting rod which catches the lubricating oil for the crank. It had worked loose of its hinge, probably during the hurried work on the needle valve early in the morning."
Day 3 / June 22	Sacramento, Calif.	Fetch permanently attaches the copper boat that worked loose a day earlier.
Day 3 / June 22	Between Sacramento and Placerville, Calif.	"The adjusting screw on the spark cam worked loose." Fetch adjusts it.
Day 4 / June 23	Riverton, Calif.	Fetch discovers the engine is running hot because of a wire he connected to the dash for making remote adjustments to an oil-control stopcock. "It was found that this wire when pulled out completely turned the cock too far and almost shut off the supply when it was supposed to be wide open." He fixes the problem.
Day 6 / June 25	Carson City, Nev.	When the engine begins missing, Fetch adjusts "the screw regulating the points on the induction coil."
Day 10 / June 29	Winnemucca, Nev.	Fetch cleans the spark plug for the first time and tightens the drive chain to take up wear in the links.
Day 11 / June 30	Battle Mountain, Nev.	Fetch tightens the clutch and cleans the gear box "of its old lubricant with the little detrition from the new gears which had accumulated since the beginning of the trip."
Day 11 / June 30	Near Carlin, Nev.	Fetch twice straightens a rear-axle brace after the car hangs up twice on the ridge between ruts. He also replaces four damaged drive-chain links.
Day 12 / July 1	East of Elko, Nev.	Fetch again straightens a bent rear-axle brace.
Day 12 / July 1	Near Deeth, Nev.	Krarup discovers the cyclometer (speedometer and odometer) is broken.
Day 13 / July 2	Wells, Nev.	Fetch adjusts the ignition cam, which was "found to have been worn slow."
Days 14–15 / July 3–4	From Tecoma, Nev., to Salt Lake City	"The front spring, inverted elliptic, sagged after the inordinate abuse" of crossing many deep gullies. The chain was stretched and a lug holding the right rear-axle brace rod was broken. Fetch oils the clutch. In Salt Lake City, a blacksmith replaces the lug.

SOURCES: *Automobile* (Days 2, 3, 4, 6, 11, 12, 13, 14–15); *Horseless Age* (Days 10, 11).

[a] Repairs exclude tire troubles. Where unspecified, it is assumed that Tom Fetch made the repairs. He may, however, have been helped by N. O. Allyn and Marius C. Krarup or by mechanics at Packard garages.

was not familiar with the route. I have been over the entire distance between San Francisco and Salt Lake on a bicycle.[65]

But the Packard company's contract "was worded so that Roberts could be discharged at any time the company thought it advisable to dispense with his services," reported the *Salt Lake Herald*, paraphrasing Krarup. According to Krarup:

> So far as I have been able to learn, Roberts has had an ambition to travel across the country in an automobile. He corresponded with various firms, and represented to the Packards that he was thoroughly familiar with the country. It was learned that his knowledge was second-handed; that is, it was not the result of personal travel over the country that would have to be traversed, and he was also regarded as uncongenial company, and I was substituted for him. I know nothing about the trip, but the company believed that a man would be safer who had no pretensions of knowledge to defend. We have got along famously.[66]

The Packard Motor Car Company on Monday would furnish a $5,000 bond to release the auto, the newspapers predicted. This is apparently what happened, as the sheriff held the car from late Saturday until Monday afternoon. "We expected to stay over Sunday so . . . the delay is not a serious one and means little inconvenience to us," Krarup told the *Salt Lake Herald*. The transcontinental crew spent the rest of Monday arranging gas supplies ahead. Before leaving Salt Lake City, "the rear brace lug had been replaced by the assistance of a blacksmith, and all machinery had been inspected, cleaned and oiled, with the exception that the motor proper was not touched."[67]

Utah: A Reputation of Rough Roads

During a twelve-hour, 95-mile day starting at 7:20 AM on Tuesday, July 7, Day 18, the crew headed southeast past the mining and smelting plants of Murray and Lehi to reach Provo for lunch. Following bad directions, they left Provo on the wrong road; in cutting back to the right road near Spanish Fork, the men spent 30 minutes stuck in the mud near an overflowing irrigation ditch. Later, beyond Thistle, Utah, the car hit a large hidden stone that "turned the rear axle with springs and braces, all together." The axle had to be "turned back," Krarup reported, without further explanation. The men spent the night at a hotel in Tucker.[68]

The ride from Tucker, over the summit of the Wasatch Range (see Fig. 51) to Price, Utah, on Day 19, Wednesday, July 8, unexpectedly became the most difficult of the journey. At 7:45 AM, the men left for Colton, where they learned that a washed-

Fig. 51. Old Pacific arriving at Soldier Summit in
Utah's Wasatch Range,
according to the Sept.
30, 1903, *Horseless Age*
(NAHC).

out wagon road to Castlegate would force them "to follow a devious course skirting the Uintah Indian Reservation and then to tack back to Price through Soldiers' Canyon, a piece of road which has a national reputation for roughness. It turned out to be the most difficult piece of ground, for an automobile, between San Francisco and New York."[69] Krarup recalled the difficulty of that day's 64½-mile trip:

> The very exit from Colton was so steep that the entire village population turned out to see the machine scale the height, and this was followed immediately by a succession of hills ranging up to 40 per cent., both up and down. The first 5 miles were said to be the worst. . . . The rest of the way had no such grades, but it was unceasingly rough. . . .
>
> Washouts across the track and the now familiar high ridge between the ruts became very numerous and annoying. . . . During the afternoon and evening perhaps twenty-five freighters were met, mostly with four horse teams and heavy loads, all hauling goods from Price to the mining camps up north. This traffic day after day had worn the ruts very deep, but had not touched the boulders in the middle, and unfortunately there was usually no room on either side of the track, which necessitated staying in it and overcoming the ridge and stones in the best way possible. . . .
>
> When freighters were sighted it was a question of reaching a turn out place before they passed it, or else of backing out a considerable distance. Luckily most of them were met farther down the canyon, when the passable area broadened more frequently. After sev-

eral unpleasant experiences with the boulders, resulting in stops to turn the rear axle back to its correct position, and also in a very slow pace so as to minimize the danger of breaking the chain or something else if the height of a ridge or stone were miscalculated, smaller stones were piled in the ruts on both sides of the obstruction in the middle and the car thus bodily lifted over the obstructions. Three miles negotiated in this manner consumed two hours, although the road was downhill nearly all the time.[70]

Fig. 52. Fetch, *driving*, and Allyn coax Old Pacific up a steep hill in central Utah's Castle Valley (NAHC).

Stuck at Price River

"Utterly astonished" Price residents who observed the car's 8:15 PM arrival begged for rides.[71] The next day, finally locating 10 gallons of gasoline at 10:00 AM, the transcontinentalists complied by giving rides for two hours. Because it was already noon, the men decided to spend the remainder of the day resting in Price, and started for Green River at 6:00 AM on Friday, July 10, Day 21. The travelers ate breakfast at Wellington, 6 miles down the Price River Valley. Between Wellington and Woodside, Old Pacific left the river trail to run through the broad Castle Valley (see Fig. 52).

Their new route forced them to run across arroyos that were as numerous but deeper and steeper than the ones they had encountered near Lucin, Utah, a week earlier. Krarup wrote:

> A long suffering front axle radius rod—the lower left one—was fractured at the ball joint, and nothing could be done except to strap it to the rod above it so as to prevent further damage and rattling. The incident did not seem to affect the car then, though it was suspected it would in course of time, since the two braces on each side certainly were not placed there without distinct purpose, and the fracture proved a high stress which now would have to be absorbed in some other portion of the car's anatomy, probably the front axle and spring and the steering rods and knuckles.[72]

The autoists would travel 300 miles before they had an opportunity to repair the radius rod. The front spring, which Krarup surmised would bear an unusual strain due to the broken radius rod, eventually broke east of Denver.

It took three hours to cross the Price River's shallow, sandy ford at Woodside (see Fig. 53). "The car was driven across the watercourse without trouble, although the first attempt was unsuccessful, and brush and jacks were needed to back it for a new start. The work with jacks and brush would have to be done over a second time; time was precious if Green River was to be reached that evening, and so, as a team of horses happened to be at work close by, the team was engaged to drag the car back from its false start. . . . The car then shot forth unassisted along the proper course, crossed the river again and made for the brink without further difficulties."[73]

Trail Becomes a Road

Near Desert Station that night, while chugging alongside the railroad tracks by the light of its single kerosene headlamp, Old Pacific met an oncoming train. Mistaking the auto's light for that of an approaching train, the engineer threw on his brakes and the train screeched to a halt. On it was James W. Abbott, special agent for the Rocky Mountains and Pacific Coast in the U.S. Department of Agriculture's Office of Public Road Inquiry. He "had specially gone to Green River to meet the transcontinental tourists, his interest in the expedition being due to the bearing it might have on the good roads movement in the West." The agent "proceeded to Price, took a return train to Green River, and saw the tourists the next morning."[74]

Flanked by State Senator Ed T. Taylor of Glenwood Springs, Colorado, Abbott was later photographed meeting with the transcontinentalists in Glenwood Springs. Abbott and Taylor were described as the "foremost representatives of [the] National Highway movement west of the Rockies."[75]

Leaving Green River at 9:00 AM on Saturday, July 11, Day 22, the car crossed the Green River on a cable ferry and drove through Solitude to reach Thompsons, Utah, at 3:15 PM. Because of the heat, "it was decided to wait till after sundown before continuing the journey toward Grand Junction, Col., 78 miles."[76] Accordingly, the men left Thompsons at 8:00 PM on Saturday for an all-night drive through Colorado's Grand Canyon, reaching Grand Junction, Colorado, at 2:00 PM on Sunday, July 12. From there, the Packard's route eastward would take the car to Rifle, Glenwood Springs, Leadville, Buena Vista, Colorado Springs, and Denver. Krarup sounded happy to leave Utah:

A change for the better came with our entrance into Colorado. The trail became a road— the beginning of a State highway which was continued thence to Denver; not a broad,

Fig. 53. Stuck beside the Price River at Woodside, Utah. *Above*, Allyn lifts the car with a makeshift lever while Fetch shoves tree branches under the wheel. The unidentified man at left perhaps owned the horses that eventually freed the car. *Below*, still stuck (NAHC).

macadamized avenue by any means, but a narrow strip of ground blasted out of rock for mile after mile, where necessary, and following the streams—first the Grand, then the Eagle, then the Homestake rivers—to the continental watershed at Tennessee Pass.

The territory of unbridged ravines and washes was behind us; two ruts with unsubdued nature between them was no longer the only thoroughfare. Nevertheless, the first few miles of the Grand Canyon road did more damage to the pneumatic tires than all of the desert and plains. Sharp ledges on the stiff grades gouged chunks of rubber from the casings, and at Grand Junction it was considered best to put the new unused reserve tires on the rear wheels.[77]

Rain Pursues Old Pacific

The *Daily Sun* recorded the automobile's July 12, 1903, arrival in Grand Junction:

> Shortly after noon yesterday a horseless carriage buzzed into this city. The car and the men on it looked like one mass of gray dust. The quality of determination, grim and stolid, which showed on the faces of the drivers was just as visible on the machine, too. On arriving in the city, they asked for hotel and livery accommodations. These were pointed out to them.
>
> Their first consideration was not for themselves. No, their car had to be put in order; the rear tires which had suffered some bad rock cuts had to be removed and replaced by others. Then the men with parched throats, tired and perspiring bodies, went to the hotel to get relief for which they had waited so long.[78]

Fig. 54. A muddy mountain trail near Rifle, Colorado (NAHC).

On July 14, the travelers reached Glenwood Springs, which Krarup remembered chiefly because "here we were treated to a bath and I will tell you it was a treat." Rain, which seemed to pursue Old Pacific across western Colorado, forced the travelers to install tire chains "before descending [a] steep and slippery hill" near Rifle (see Fig. 54).[79] On another day, muddy roads held the car to just 20 miles between Edwards (or Edwards Post-Office, as Krarup called it) and Redcliff (see Fig. 55).[80] As Krarup later wrote, "We had chains around the tires all the time, but they soon wore through at the most exposed links. They were pieced together with leather straps, and other

Fig. 55. Fetch poses beside a muddy Old Pacific, its tires chained, during a stop at Beck's Ranch in Edwards, Colorado. His hosts are unidentified (NAHC).

links were exposed thereafter."[81] A potentially fatal accident occurred between Leadville and Buena Vista:

> When going on a cliff road along [the] Arkansas River . . . the inner front wheel struck a stone which had tumbled down from above and the resilience of the tire caused the whole front portion of the car to bound to the right. An inch farther would have meant something serious for which not even the gorgeous aspect of the multi-colored cliff at that point could have compensated.[82]

On Sunday, July 19, the coast-to-coast tourists drove the 35 miles from Florissant through Crystola and Manitou to reach Colorado Springs (see Fig. 56). The transcontinental auto traveled from Colorado Springs to Denver on Monday, July 20, Day 31. Fifteen autos drove south from Denver to wait for Old Pacific at Littleton, according to the *Denver Post*. But George B. Gorton, "the automobile expert of the Packard people," drove one of two Packards that continued past Littleton to meet Fetch and Krarup about 5 miles south of the city. "The travelers were tanned a dark brown with

Fig. 56. Spying the auto and its dashing crew (*Fetch at the wheel, Allyn partly obscured behind him*), the women of Crystola, Colorado, "came forth like bees to blossoms," the *Denver Post* opined (NAHC).

the exposure of the trip, but seemed none the worse otherwise," the *Denver Times* reported.[83] The transcontinental crew was now down to two. At Colorado Springs, Allyn had boarded a train for his home in Warren, Ohio, according to the *Post*, though other sources reported that Allyn stayed with the car through Nebraska.[84]

"There They Are!"

The *Post* described Gorton's reaction upon seeing the coast-to-coast auto:

"There they are!" cried George B. Gorton, as he espied "Old Pacific" at the top of a hill, nearly a mile distant. At the same time the driver of "Old Pacific" saw the automobile coming to meet them, and both rushed on at top speed to meet the other. Such a tooting of horns and yelling of men as there was! . . .

Before Gorton's machine had come to a full stop, he leaped to the ground, and running to the mud-besplattered machine, he climbed up into it, and taking Fetch in his arms he gave three cheers for him, and then all gave three cheers for "Old Pacific."

The three machines then started to Littleton with "Old Pacific" in front, setting the pace with which it had crossed the mountains and deserts between here and San Francisco. When the town of Littleton was reached an enthusiastic reception was given the car and its occupants by the members of the Denver Automobile club. After lining up and having several photographs taken, the start was made for Denver.[85]

The *Denver Republican* picked up the narrative:

The ride into Denver was a corker. One of the local machines dropped in ahead of the transcontinental machine, but the driver of the latter was not satisfied with the pace kept up. He therefore pushed on ahead and showed the party how to approach a city. As the roads were rather dusty, the appearance was of a drove of cattle hustling along the highway. When the procession reached the edge of the city many of those having a wholesome fear of the city ordinance made for such cases, slowed their machines and dropped out of the rush. The others charged on downtown with horns sounding. A local car took the lead for the passage through the city, having a man standing up and shouting "There they are—the across the continent wagon."[86]

Automobile magazine reported: "A bouquet was thrown to Mr. Fetch en route by an enthusiastic woman, but it fell by the roadside and only the shouts of the cavalcade rewarded the pretty donor. Arrived in Denver, a circuitous route was followed to the Packard agency, giving all of Denver an opportunity to realize that 'Old Pacific' had finished the most difficult and, in places, perilous portion of its itinerary." When the visitors pulled up to the curb at the local Packard agency, the *Rocky Mountain News* related, "Instantly they were the targets for a dozen kodaks. Snap, snap, snap, and they were allowed to alight from their car."[87]

Schedule? What Schedule?

The autoists were "intending to run somewhere near a schedule prepared by the company," the *Salt Lake Tribune* had said. Krarup himself wrote that the crew timed its departure from San Francisco to reach Salt Lake City on July 4. Old Pacific reached Denver on July 20 "with a punctuality that will go down into history . . . on the day appointed," Packard advertised. Moreover, the northeastern Ohio city of Ashtabula—apparently with the Warren factory's blessings—was preparing a "celebration of the arrival of E. Tom Fetch August 10."[88] It looked for all the world as if Old Pacific was running on a schedule.

Not so, Krarup insisted from Denver: "We have not had any schedule to run by and many false stories have been published as to when we expect to arrive at New York. Now as we will have a good road, I can safely say that we will reach our destination in five weeks."[89] The car, in fact, would reach New York City 4½ weeks later.

Krarup told the same war stories to reporters in each new town. Perhaps most of all, he liked describing how the Packard's flickering headlamp scared the brakeman of the freight train that the car met west of Elko, Nevada, on June 30. As has been noted, a companion had barely prevented the train's brakeman from jumping from the train. But the story grew in the telling, undoubtedly with help from imaginative listeners, including a *Denver Times* reporter:

> It is doubtful if a phantom ship upon the ocean ever caused more consternation than this automobile turned loose by moonlight along the high places of Nevada, Utah and Colorado. Coming toward Elko, Nev., the auto drivers were going like the wind. At a certain point the road turned sharply and ran along a railroad track. A short distance ahead was a freight train running at full speed coming toward the auto.
>
> The latter carried all kinds of blazing headlights and was quickly eating up distance. The auto was racing along the road close to the railroad track so that to the men on the freight train the machine looked for all the world to them like a locomotive. . . . Expect-

ing a headend collision, the entire crew of brakemen jumped off the train, only to learn afterward that it was but an automobile.[90]

Nebraska Travel Amphibious

In Denver, the tourists took four days to rest and make "necessary repairs," including transmission modifications. "The machine is low geared, for mountain climbing, but will be changed at Denver, when the start is made across the plains," explained the *Colorado Springs Gazette*. Perhaps worn out from the hard driving, Fetch wrote that in Denver he "was laid up . . . with nervous trouble."[91]

The motorists found fences troublesome east of Denver: "Cattlemen had fenced in large blocks of land, without regard to the section-line roads, and the opening of gates became irritating, not only on account of their number, but particularly because they were nearly all fastened with barb-wire rings pulled very taut over the posts. These resulted in lacerated gloves and scratched hands."[92]

Also irritating were the muddy roads of Nebraska (see Figs. 57 and 58), where the Packard traveled from Ogallala in the west, through North Platte, Kearney, Grand Island, Central City, Clarks, Columbus, and Fremont to Omaha on the eastern border. According to Krarup, on the North Platte–Columbus stretch,

> Our travel was amphibious. Stretches of excellent road alternated with temporary lakes and mudholes, in which the car was swamped, the wheels spinning around in the sticky mud with no propulsive power. We had to use boards, fence-posts, brushwood, chains, the shovel, the jack, and strong pulls on the front wheels to get out of these predicaments. Only once—near Clark[s], Nebraska [see Fig. 59]—was the motor disabled. The water had entered the carbureter, and we had to employ horses to drag the car out.
>
> Fast in the mire seven times in one day was the record for that disagreeable trip along the Platte River, but the mudholes which were successfully rushed or laboriously traversed on the low gear ran into the hundreds. The front wheels were very useful as feelers in those days. With the rear wheels on terra firma we drove the front wheels cautiously into the water or mudhole, in confidence that we could always back out so long as the rear wheels had a firm hold.[93]

The Packard company would later claim that Clarks represented "the only instance on the entire trip when the motor was unable to meet the emergency." Though a team of horses hauled Old Pacific out of the Price River near Woodside, Utah, on Day 21, the automaker—like Krarup—dismissed the assistance as time-saving but unnecessary. In addition to the mud, it was also reported that "a pair of Nebraska

Fig. 57 (left). Fetch takes to the fields to avoid a flooded Nebraska road (NAHC).

Fig. 58 (below). Fetch, *left*, and Allyn survey Old Pacific's predicament in this unidentified photo, evidently taken in the Midwest (NAHC).

Fig. 59. Near Clarks, Nebraska (NAHC).

farmers threatened to take out the family shotgun in defense of the asserted rights to highway."[94] No further details about this incident were ever reported, and Krarup never mentioned the incident in his dispatches.

Ruddy and Muddy in Omaha

From Grand Island on Wednesday, July 29, Day 40, Fetch sent a telegram to the Packard company: "Start delayed till noon by fresh rains. Many detours to avoid miring. All Platte valley roads in abnormal condition." As he later described Nebraska, "It was simply a succession of mud-holes."[95]

However slowly, the car progressed eastward. At Columbus on Thursday, July 30, "A pair of alleged gentlemen riding an automobile . . . stopped long enough to load up with gasoline and other things," according to the *Columbus Telegram*. "They left no names nor information regarding the nature of their errand, although a large delegation of citizens assembled for the interview."[96]

The next morning, Fetch, Krarup, and Allyn rolled up to the Paxton Hotel in Omaha in "an auto whose red body was splashed with mud until it was the color of clay. One ruddy man got out and engaged rooms, baths and dinner, while the others

Fig. 60. Fetch and the
Packard near Grinnell,
Iowa (NAHC).

explained what they were doing, before they whizzed away to get the machine
cleaned."[97] Upon hearing reports of deep mud in Iowa, the travelers remained in
Omaha Saturday and Sunday, August 1 and 2.

As far east as Des Moines, the roads in Iowa were as muddy as those in Nebraska,
Krarup reported, "and the farmers were not always cordial. In two or three instances
they responded with much rudeness to our greetings." On Thursday, August 6, Fetch
and Krarup ran 97 miles to Marengo over roads described as "soft but . . . drying
up."[98] At Grinnell, the midway point of Thursday's drive, Old Pacific drove over a
pair of narrow planks in crossing a washed-out bridge approach (see Fig. 60). The
men stopped near Marengo to grind an exhaust valve.

Arrested on "Trumped-Up Charge"

On Friday, August 7, Fetch and Krarup drove from Marengo to Wheatland via Mechanicsville. There, they sent "a laconic telegram," which related "a little difficulty

with the upholders of the law at Mechanicsville, Iowa." To wit: "'Arrested Mechanicsville. Trumped-up charge. Settled rather than wait.'"[99]

Motor Age published a fuller explanation:

One uncomfortable incident occurred to the travelers in Iowa. They were driving along a country road when they met a man in a buggy leading a colt by a rope. The colt shied at the car, jumping into the buggy and damaging it. Fetch immediately slowed up to enable him to get by, but instead of driving past, the man jumped out of the buggy and rushed forward with his whip, demanding satisfaction for his wrecked vehicle. He was very obstreperous in his remarks and threatened to do all sorts of things if the tourists did not at once hand over a sum sufficient to pay for repairs.

When he had concluded his volley of vituperative language he found himself looking into the barrel of Krarup's revolver, and he was curtly informed that no hold-up was going to happen just then. The fight was all gone as soon as he saw the glistening gun barrel, and he listened respectfully while being told who the travelers were, and that they could be found at the next town, Mechanicsville, that evening, if he desired to bring legal action against them.

The man went on to Marion and telephoned to Mechanicsville, where Fetch and Krarup found the sheriff awaiting them. They told their story to the court, and a fine of $10 and costs was assessed. Krarup wanted to contest as he thought the fine unjust under the circumstances, and his temper was aroused because of the highwayman-like manner in which they had been accosted. Fetch, being mild-mannered and realizing that they would be delayed perhaps for several days, and would in the end pay more than that amount in standing the expense of a trial, argued that the best method would be to submit and pay the fine.

A compromise was finally suggested by which it was agreed that they pay $10 with the understanding that the money be applied to the costs of prosecution and that none of it go to the man who made the complaint. The judge saw this was the sensible way out of the difficulty, especially as the complainant lived in another county, and couldn't vote for him at the next election any way.[100]

Eastward Drive "Devoid of Interest"

The drive from eastern Iowa to New York State was routine, as Krarup summarized it: "The traveling, as such, was devoid of all incident and interest from Wheatland, Iowa, far into New York State, where the tires began to give out, and where heavy rains had drenched the roads, especially through the Mohawk Valley." On Monday morning, August 10, Day 52, members of the Chicago Automobile Club welcomed "two tanned and weather beaten travelers" who hoped to reach New York in six days (see Fig. 61).[101] The last part of their journey would actually take twice that long.

"The Packard machine was covered with mud many inches thick, but was in a remarkably good condition after the rough journey," the *Chicago Inter Ocean* reported. Dr. H. Nelson Jackson's transcontinental car, the first, had reached Chicago 3½ weeks earlier, with a pet bulldog on board. Though Fetch and Krarup "brought no mascots with them, they were well and happy."[102]

Arriving in Cleveland at 1:30 PM on August 14, Krarup told the *Cleveland Plain Dealer* about sand, high-center roads, and arroyos in Nevada and Utah. Krarup was perhaps too generous in his implied praise for Ohio's roads. As he later wrote, "Sandy or hilly roads in Indiana, Ohio, and Pennsylvania which had been looked upon as 'bad' seemed very acceptable highways after the roadless sections in the West" (see Fig. 62).[103]

Nighttime Drive "Intolerable"

On Sunday, August 16, the tourists drove from Jefferson, Ohio, to Fredonia, New York, making hurried stops in Conneaut, Ohio, and Erie, Pennsylvania. According to the *Conneaut News*:

Fig. 62. After conquering the Rockies and Sierra Nevada, this Pennsylvania hill seemed easy, Krarup said (*World's Work*, May 1904).

Messrs. Fetch and Krarrup [sic] stopped in Conneaut about fifteen minutes, during which time the former washed up, bought some cigars of the hotel clerk, and purchased a quantity of gasoline for his machine, familiarly known as "Old Pacific." The auto evidently had not been cleaned up since it presented a very hard and travel worn appearance. It can go some yet, however; and it is hinted that when the travelers entered town they did so at a clip that was hardly in keeping with the speed ordinance. They drew up at the hotel with a flourish, and in about three seconds they were surrounded by a group of awe-struck residenters who would have asked a great many questions had they dared.[104]

The men pulled into Erie at 1:30 PM and ate lunch "in a great hurry."[105] Despite frequent night driving, it took Fetch six days—from August 16 to August 21—to traverse New York State's wet roads. He slid through mud 10 inches deep to reach Albany, New York, on Thursday, August 20, Day 62, after a long day behind the wheel, as Krarup recalled:

> When we attempted, however, to drive from Albany to Poughkeepsie the same night we undertook too much. The night was very dark and the post-road was very muddy and very crooked. The oil lamps were in bad order and went out periodically. At every cross-road there is a quadruple guideboard. These had to be examined by matchlight. The slush, the darkness of all but the first ten feet in front of the car, lack of sleep, and nervous strain in general, produced a sense of insecurity that became quite intolerable on some of the steep hills. Part of the time it seemed impossible to determine whether we were in the road or beside it.[106]

Consequently, when the men reached Hudson at 2:00 AM, they stayed there to sleep and did not reach Poughkeepsie until early the following afternoon. By that time, Colonel K. C. Pardee, the New York City Packard agent, already had a half-dozen of his "large cars"—filled with reporters and others—heading west to meet Old Pacific. Joining these autos were "as many more driven by private owners."[107] By one count, fourteen cars of various makes were included in the welcoming escort. At one point, the enthusiasts waited on a hotel veranda for the transcontinental car to appear.

Auto "No Longer a Plaything"

Pardee, "after modestly declining many calls for a speech," finally relented. Deftly avoiding any mention of the transcontinental Winton's finish in New York City a month earlier, Pardee told of his pleasure at seeing so many agents for other autos among the entourage:

> The achievement which we have met to finish with our congratulations is of course particularly gratifying to my company, but it is more than that, which fact the presence of you gentlemen indicates is appreciated. The success of this trip is gratifying to the trade at large, and of marked interest to the sport of automobiling, and it cannot fail to benefit us all, because it has attracted the attention of the whole world, and has proven that the automobile is a reliable means of locomotion and no longer a plaything of the rich; that it is a factor of modern life, and must be considered in the light of a necessity and not as a luxury.[108]

The greeting committee motored westward to Sleepy Hollow Cemetery, outside Tarrytown. There, at 6:00 PM, the transcontinental Packard "hove in sight like a huge mud pile on wheels, stopped and was congratulated and photographed" (see Fig. 63). In returning to the New York City Packard agency, escorting drivers received "an

Fig. 63. Fetch and Old Pacific (*foreground, second car from left*) surrounded by escorting autos (*World's Work*, May 1904).

opportunity for seeing the little car reel off the twelve miles between Tarrytown and Yonkers at an eighteen mile an hour clip, on top of the long endurance run."[109]

In July 1899, Arthur S. Winslow, secretary of the National Motor Carriage Company, had watched John D. and Louise Hitchcock Davis chug out of New York City, intent on reaching San Francisco in one of his company's National Duryea autos. Now Winslow was among the autoists who escorted Fetch and Krarup to New York, driving a Cadillac "with a party of friends."[110]

"Thank the Lord, It's Over"

According to the *New York Times*'s account of the conclusion of the run on the evening of Friday, August 21, 1903:

> A mud-coated automobile, containing two very tired and dusty men, raced down Eighth Avenue . . . and rounded into West Fifty-ninth Street from the Circle at just 8:40 o'clock. The crowd which had awaited its coming sent up a rousing cheer, and half a dozen escorting machines tooted their whistles to the top of their ability. Finally the muddy automobile stopped, and the two tired men separated themselves from the dirt cake that seemed almost to mold them and their vehicle into a solid mass. On[e] of them said: "Thank the Lord, it's over."[111]

As Old Pacific pulled up, "hearty cheers from several hundred admirers in waiting greeted the plucky tourists."[112] Fetch and Krarup were apparently too tired to go ahead with plans to dip the car's front wheels in the Atlantic Ocean.

"We have suffered some on account of the almost total absence of reasonably good accommodations in many of the little settlements through which we have passed," Fetch commented, "but altogether the trip has been mighty enjoyable, and Krarup and I know more about the geography of the United States than lots of people who have spent more time studying it."[113] Where was the worst stretch of road? Fetch was asked. He had trouble making up his mind:

> The worst of it was from Tucker to Price, in Utah, although we found the roughest going in Colorado, between Grand Junction and Glenwood Springs. But neither Utah desert nor Colorado mountains could bother me half as much as common ordinary mud, which we found in all sorts of places. In Iowa we were obliged to put chains on the wheels to try to conjure up a little friction, and even this did not work very well.[114]

In their reporting, the *New York Times*, *New York Herald*, and *New York Tribune* all noted Jackson's earlier transcontinental run in a Winton. The Packard company overlooked it.

Repair Cost—1½ Cents per Mile

To its credit, however, the Packard Motor Car Company afterward ran a series of ads in the auto journals listing Old Pacific's itinerary and detailing repairs to the auto's carburetor, ignition system, engine, transmission, brakes, and running gear. The list included breakdowns and repairs that even the conscientious Krarup had failed to mention. In a final "Summary of Replacements" ad, Packard itemized the cost of repairs to the automobile, excluding tires and labor. The total bill came to $61.45, or about 1½ cents per mile (see Fig. 64). The ad also boasted: "It may safely be said that these same replacements would not be required in 10,000 miles of ordinary usage."[115]

For all its candor, the Packard company engaged in at least one sleight of hand. A photo Krarup used in his 1904 *World's Work* article shows Fetch observing as Allyn, lying on his back in the sand, repairs the car. "An uncommon experience—the only time this happened," read the photo caption. Packard, which copied and used Krarup's photos for its own publicity purposes, regretted that the experience occurred at all, and evidently said as much to a touch-up artist. Thus, the automaker's version of the photo transformed Allyn into a rock (see Fig. 65).[116]

How far did Old Pacific travel? "From San Francisco to Denver we kept account of the number of miles traversed, which was 1,783, but east of that point we lost all track of our mileage, owing to inability to keep a chronometer [cyclometer] on the machine," Krarup said.[117] From Atlantic, Iowa, the transcontinental crew reported breaking its fourth cyclometer of the trip. The car's actual coast-to-coast mileage is

---

In the preceding four issues we have given a detailed account of all the replacements upon the standard single cylinder Packard car, which made the overland journey from San Francisco to New York in the record time of 61¼ days time elapsed. Herewith is a summary with the same prices extended at which such parts are billed to our customers:

CARBURETOR—		TRANSMISSION—	
1 Nozzle	$2.00	4 Bushings	$8.00
		1 Sprocket (not on account of	
ELECTRICAL—		wear)	.00
20 Columbia Dry Cells	12.00	1 Chain	12.00
1 Pair Platinum Points	1.00	5 Chain Links	.75
2 Spark Plugs	3.00	1 Gear Box Lug	.25
MOTOR—		RUNNING GEAR—	
1 Fibre Washer	.05	1½ Front Spring	3.90
1 Exhaust Valve	6.00	4 Front Wheel Cones	2.00
1 Exhaust Valve Roller	1.00	1 Front Brace Rod	2.50
1 Exhaust Valve Sleeve	.75	1 Brace Rod for Rear Axle	.75
1 Connecting Rod Oil Boat	.50	1 Side Brake Band	5.00
		Total	$61.45

Fig. 64. Detail of Packard's *Horseless Age* ad, Sept. 30, 1903.

therefore guesswork. In his May 1904 *World's Work* article, Krarup neglected to even venture a guess, but the *New York Times*, *New York Herald*, and most other contemporary accounts accepted the figure given by *Automobile* magazine, which estimated 4,000 miles.

Comparative Performances

Fetch and Krarup left Cliff House near San Francisco at 3:05 PM on June 20 and reached New York City at 8:40 PM on August 21. Subtracting three hours for the time difference between coasts, that represents an elapsed time of 62 days, 2 hours, 35 minutes. They thus trimmed 34 hours, 5 minutes from Jackson and Crocker's time of 63 days, 12 hours, 30 minutes, set July 26, 1903.

Fetch and Krarup were on the road for sixty-three calendar days. Because they did not travel at all on eleven days—spending those days repairing the car, resting, or waiting for better weather—the Packard's running time was fifty-two days. On its 4,000-mile trip, then, Old Pacific averaged 64 miles per day for its elapsed time, and 77 miles per day for its fifty-two-day running time.

Like the Packard, Jackson's Winton, the first auto to cross the country, traveled an uncertain distance that most press accounts estimated at between 5,000 and 6,000 miles. Jackson's running time was forty-six calendar days. Depending on whether his distance is figured at 5,000 or 6,000 miles, the Winton thereby averaged somewhere between 79 and 94 miles daily for its elapsed time, and between 109 and 130 miles daily for its forty-six-day running time. For their respective elapsed times, the Winton averaged 3.61 mph (figuring 5,500 miles) and the Packard 2.68 mph. At this level of analysis, Jackson's Winton handily outperformed Old Pacific. Whether the two cars had faced the same obstacles is something their drivers could have argued.

Neither did Krarup provide figures for gas consumption and overall cost of the trip. The car averaged 12 miles per gallon over the 978 miles between San Francisco and Salt Lake City, according to the *Salt Lake Tribune*. For 4,000 miles, the Packard would have used 400 gallons at 10 mpg, or 333 gallons at 12 mpg. The *Warren Tribune*, in the Packard Motor Car Company's Ohio hometown, had at least an inkling of what the trip had cost the automaker. The *Tribune* reported that the public-relations coup would be "worth all the thousands of dollars it has cost the company."[118]

Tom Fetch and Old Pacific

Later in 1903, Fetch drove Old Pacific in the National Association of Automobile Manufacturers' eight-day, 793-mile endurance run from New York City, through Cleveland, to Pittsburgh, where the race ended on October 15. Heavy rains, muddy roads, and washed-out bridges sidelined many cars. After a grueling Day 2 run to Binghampton, New York, even Fetch "asserted without reservation that to-day's run was far worse than anything he had experienced on his long trip in the same machine from San Francisco to New York." On the last day of the contest, "Fetch and the Packard plunged into a mudhole and bent the front axle and broke a steering knuckle, but got in at night." In fact, of thirty-four starters, Fetch was one of just eight cars and drivers to win gold medals for arriving on time at each night control.[119]

Fetch drove another Packard, a 24-horsepower, 4-cylinder automobile, in a summer 1904 New York–St. Louis endurance run of 1,200 miles. And during the 1907 Glidden Tour, the American Automobile Association's annual endurance contest, Fetch drove a Packard press car. Outside Chicago, however, he gave the wheel to another driver and took a train into the city. It was explained, "Tom, who never could be accused of carelessness, had the misfortune to run down a man in the Windy City not long ago, and the police were looking for him. Tom was not conspicuous at any time during the stay in Chicago."[120]

Fetch worked for Packard into the second decade of the twentieth century. When he died in 1944, at age 72, the simmering dispute about who had been the first to cross America by auto—Jackson or Fetch—followed him to his grave. His obituary in *Automotive News* credited Fetch "with making the first transcontinental trip by motor car"—an honor that was not his to claim.[121]

The Packard Motor Car Company displayed the mud-covered Old Pacific at the 1904 St. Louis World's Fair, but thereafter largely neglected the automobile. A photo that accompanied a December 6, 1906, *Automobile* article showed the car, apparently stored outside, "in an obscure corner of the Packard factory yard," alongside James Ward Packard's first auto.[122] In 1935, the Packard factory replaced the car's radiator as part of a "superficial restoration" and gave Old Pacific to the Henry Ford Museum & Greenfield Village in Dearborn, Michigan.

In 1980 and 1981, Packard enthusiast Terry Martin of Warren, Ohio, authentically restored the machine for the museum.[123] Martin drove his own 1903 Packard over approximately the same coast-to-coast route in 1983 to celebrate the eightieth anniversary of the Fetch–Krarup run. Accompanying him was a modern-day Tom Fetch, Fetch's grandnephew.[124]

The Packard company's wistfulness lives on. Old Pacific, viewed at the Henry Ford Museum while this book was being written, was credited with being restored through the courtesy of the Packard Electric Division of General Motors Corporation. A plaque accompanying the exhibit identifies the car not as finishing second behind Dr. Jackson's Winton, for "second" is a word unknown in the Packard corporate vocabulary, at least relating to the 1903 coast-to-coast trek. Rather, Old Pacific is identified as "one of the first automobiles to drive across the country."

Strike the "Im" from "Impossible"

Twenty-seven months before Old Pacific rolled into New York City, a disheartened Alexander Winton, his automobile half-buried in the sand 2 miles east of Mill City, Nevada, had proclaimed: "Right here we are met by the impossible."[125] But Fetch had carefully avoided the epicenter of impossible by traveling northeast instead of east from Mill City. With a little help from a pair of canvas strips laid in front of the tires for traction, the 1903 Packard expedition thus proved that an automobile could cross Nevada's sandy desert wastes.

Old Pacific scored other firsts. As in a science lab, an experiment does more to prove a theory if it produces identical results a second or third time instead of merely once. By driving the second coast-to-coast automobile, Fetch, Krarup, and Allyn—those mad scientists of motoring—demonstrated that the earlier Jackson–Crocker transcontinental trip was no fluke. The Winton and Packard camps may have argued about the relative performance of their respective autos. The facts show, however, that the two autos achieved remarkably similar results: the Winton's longer trip consumed sixty-three days, the Packard's shorter trip consumed sixty-two days—a statistically insignificant difference.

Jackson and Crocker, however, labored in relative obscurity. By making a public spectacle out of its trip, the Packard Motor Car Company, admittedly furthering its own fortunes, was wildly successful in achieving its unstated purpose—publicizing its car. The company also dispelled some of the mystery surrounding the feat of driving from one shore of the continent to the other. Through photographs and articles, newspapers and auto journals alike showed all who cared to know exactly what obstacles Old Pacific faced and how it overcame them. A great many readers were afterward more comfortable with the idea that a motor car, still a mechanical wonder in 1903, could travel such long distances. So, as Packard officials had predicted, Old Pacific's record did help "in the removal of the last traces of prejudice against [the auto] as an experiment."

But the automaker's well-organized effort fell short of demonstrating the Packard's "unfailing reliability under the most severe test that could possibly be conceived of." The trip was a severe test, certainly, and a car that survived such a feat during the dawning of the American automobile industry deserves to be revered as a mechanical marvel. According to Packard's own accounting, Old Pacific received twenty-eight new parts, excluding dry-cell batteries and tires. Many of these parts—the drive chain and chain links, spark plugs, bearings and races, plus others—came not from the Packard factory but from suppliers. Nonetheless, they failed.

Krarup's articles and the automaker's ads reveal that Fetch made at least twenty-five roadside adjustments or emergency repairs—and probably many more minor adjustments that went unrecorded (see Table 6, which lists repairs and adjustments made from Salt Lake City to New York City). Thus, Old Pacific, on average, needed at least one new part or an adjustment—of its spark coil, clutch, brakes, carburetor, or some other part—each day, or about every 64 miles. The Packard was recognized as a well-designed car; other American makes might not have done so well. If product labeling had been in vogue at the time, American automakers might have affixed this notice to their 1903 offerings: "WARNING: Do not attempt a transcontinental journey in this automobile unless accompanied by an expert mechanic equipped with a full range of spare parts from the factory."

Even a driver capable of making his own repairs should travel with friends, Krarup had warned in Chicago: "One of the points brought out by this trip is that one man cannot run a machine for the distance, and if we had had two more men with us

TABLE 6. Old Pacific's Reported Breakdowns and Repairs, between Salt Lake City and New York City, 1903[a]

Day / Date	Location	Description of Breakdown or Repair
Day 18 / July 7	Near Thistle, Utah	The car "bumped against a big stone concealed in an innocent looking bush and turned the rear axle with springs and braces, all together." The men realign the parts.
Day 19 / July 8	Between Colton and Price, Utah	Fetch uses rubber tape to plug a leak in a hose connecting the water tank and radiator. The car strikes "several" boulders, "resulting in stops to turn the rear axle back to its correct position."
Day 20 / July 9	Price, Utah	Fetch uses a piece of bicycle tire to repair the leaky hose between the water tank and radiator.
Day 21 / July 10	Mounds, Utah	Crossing a ravine, the lower left front-axle radius rod breaks at the ball joint. The left front wheel remained out of alignment until repairs in Denver.
Day 28 / July 17	Buena Vista, Colo.	"A small fibre washer upon the inlet valve stem was renewed."
Day 30 / July 19	Colorado Springs, Colo.	"Two new [bearing] cones were placed on the right front axle."
Days 31–35 / July 20–24	Denver	Old Pacific receives new transmission shaft bushings, a new drive chain, and a "lower left hand brace rod to the front axle." Fetch adjusts the rear hub brakes and replaces the side brake band.
Day 37 / July 26	Sterling, Colo.	"A small lug on the gear box was found broken and replaced."
No date given	Near Sterling, Colo.	"One-half of the front spring" breaks and is replaced with a part sent from Denver.

Day 41 / July 30	Clarks, Neb.	Fetch replaces the spark plug when its porcelain cracks in a mudhole near Clarks. The new plug "acted indifferently and was changed after fifty miles."
Day 43 / Aug. 1	Omaha, Neb.	Fetch replaces all eight dry cells in the ignition system and installs a new pair of platinum points on the spark coil.
Day 45 / Aug. 3	En route to Atlantic, Iowa	"The breaking of the fourth cyclometer was the only incident reported."
Day 46 / Aug. 4	Des Moines, Iowa	Replace four of the eight "supposedly new" dry cells purchased in Omaha.
Day 49 / Aug. 7	Near Marengo, Iowa	"The only incident [was]… a stop to grind an exhaust valve as they neared Marengo. This was the first time that a valve had required grinding since leaving the Pacific Coast."
Day 52 / Aug. 10	Chicago	Replace the exhaust valve, valve roller, and valve sleeve, plus two bearing cones, or races, in the left front wheel.
Day 57 / Aug. 15	Jefferson, Ohio	"Some changes were made about the rear springs at the local shop" and the ignition system's eight dry cells were replaced.
Day 58 / Aug. 16	Erie, Pa.	Because dust had cut off oil flow to the crankshaft, Fetch grinds and files the crankshaft bearings. He also replaces the worn carburetor nozzle.
Day 59 / Aug. 17	Buffalo, N.Y.	"The copper oil boat for the oiling of the connecting rod had worked loose and was replaced."
Day 59 / Aug. 17	Batavia, N.Y.	Replace an "outer link" in the drive chain.

SOURCES: *Automobile* (Days 1, 45, 49); *Horseless Age* (Days 19, 20, 21); *Motor Age* (Day 58); various Packard ads (Days 21, 28, 30, 31–35, 37, no date given, 41, 43, 46, 52, 57, 59); and *World's Work* (Day 21).

[a] Repairs exclude tire troubles. Where unspecified, it is assumed that Tom Fetch made the repairs. He may, however, have been helped by N. O. Allyn (on the western half of the trek) and Marius C. Krarup, or by mechanics at Packard garages.

we could have used them at the wheel."[126] This remained the rule for many years to come: the first documented solo transcontinental auto trip would not occur until 1915, when silent-film actress Anita King drove a KisselKar from San Francisco to New York City.

Though perhaps a minor distinction, it is also worth noting that Packard set out to prove the ability of its "Standard Model F touring car," yet achieved its transcontinental success with a car that was no ordinary Packard.[127] Old Pacific was modified, albeit slightly, by the addition of an extra gas tank, removable shims to boost engine compression, and special mountain-climbing gearing. Thus, an ocean-to-ocean trip would have been even more harrowing in a stock Packard.

As a consolation, the second transcontinental crossing undoubtedly led to speedy improvements in standard models produced not only by Packard but by other American makers. Packard engineers, and their alert competitors, presumably used Old Pacific's experiences to design autos with better springs, rear-axle bracing, ignition systems, and engine oiling. Five years would pass before Jacob Murdock, also driving a Packard, proved that a coast-to-coast journey was practical for an average motorist in an ordinary car (see Chapter 7). And even he traveled with a mechanic, though this handyman had little to do but enjoy the scenery.

Old Pacific and other early transcontinental autos would eventually bear out the wisdom of Packard agent K. C. Pardee, who concluded that his company's 1903 trip "has proven that the automobile is a reliable means of locomotion and no longer a plaything of the rich . . . and must be considered in the light of a necessity and not as a luxury." True, Dr. H. Nelson Jackson and Sewall K. Crocker had proven this first in a Winton. But because its car generated more publicity from its later trip, the Packard company undoubtedly said it loudest.

COAST TO COAST
IN A MACHINE
OF THE MASSES

4

"No, sir. Had no trouble at all."
—Eugene Hammond to reporters, overlooking the
Oldsmobile's many breakdowns and repairs

Two california mechanics scored at least a half-dozen firsts in 1903 by driving an Oldsmobile runabout from San Francisco to New York City and on to Boston and Portland, Maine—the third automobile to cross America. Lester L. Whitman and Eugene I. Hammond started on July 6, well behind Dr. H. Nelson Jackson's Winton and Tom Fetch's Packard, so their third-place finish was no surprise. Instead, they and the sponsoring Olds Motor Works designed the trip to set several unique records.

For instance, the 800-pound car, about one-third the weight of the No. 1 Winton and No. 2 Packard touring cars, was the first light runabout to make a transcontinental trip. Priced at just $650—compared to the Winton's price of $2,500 and the Packard's of $2,300—the Oldsmobile became the first low-priced, low-powered (20 horsepower for the Winton, 12 for the Packard, and 4½ for the Olds), mass-produced car to do so. The runabout was also the first auto to deliver U.S. mail—one letter—coast to coast.

Such journals as *Automobile*, *Horseless Age*, and particularly *Motor Age* played up the photos and progress reports that Whitman mailed. This undoubtedly delighted automaker Ransom E. Olds, who filed away trip photos in his personal photo album, wired instructions and encouragement, and met with the drivers when they reached Detroit.

Afterward, the factory trumpeted the car's "perfection of mechanical construction," saying nothing about the frequent repairs that were necessary to keep its little coast-to-coast car running.[1] To be fair, the slightly modified transcontinental Oldsmobile suffered more abuse than would the average Olds in a lifetime. But like John D. Davis's 1899 experiences with a National Duryea, Whitman and Hammond faced nearly constant troubles. They were perhaps better prepared, more resourceful, and more determined than Davis, however, because they finished their trip. Having the automaker's eager backing helped in that regard.

Nevertheless, they lost twelve full days to breakdowns and repairs on their nearly seventy-nine-day trek from San Francisco to Maine. Alone or with assistance, they replaced some fifty parts or sets of parts to keep their runabout running about. Like the Winton and Packard autos before it, the Oldsmobile failed to cross the country entirely under its own power. Two horses towed it some 35 miles to a blacksmith's shop after a desert breakdown in Nevada. Halts of three days for repairs and eight days for muddy roads meant Whitman and Hammond spent more time—twenty full days—trying to cross Nebraska than they did crossing any of the sixteen states and one Canadian province they traversed.

Despite its flaws, the 1903 Olds runabout would travel miles without cooling water, run on stale gas, ford rivers, churn through mud, and bounce over the roughest roads. Whitman and Hammond slept in hotels and ate at restaurants where possible, sent spare parts ahead by train, and telegraphed ahead to shopkeepers to guarantee gas supplies. In pioneer fashion, they went days and weeks at a time without bathing. To save space and avoid waiting at laundries, they bought new clothes when their outfits became intolerably soiled.[2] Both men arrived in New York sunburned and slimmer.

During an average day they spent ten hours on the road, including food and fuel stops, and averaged 58 miles per day for their elapsed time and 77 miles per day for their running time. At their best, Whitman and Hammond traveled 170 miles a day (once in Iowa, once in Canada). They gained just 10 miles over wet roads on their worst day (in Nebraska). Roads were rocky, smooth, muddy, dry, marked, unmarked, and, in the West, frequently nonexistent. They asked directions of cowboys, townspeople, railroad crews, and teamsters. Whitman and Hammond had to push or pull the car through mud, across streams, or up steep grades during twenty-one of the thirty-eight running days between San Francisco and Omaha. But the runabout made the entire drive east of Omaha under its own power, according to logbooks Whitman and Hammond kept.[3]

Planning "A Pleasure Jaunt"

Both men had some experience in driving long distances. In June 1902, Whitman and a companion had driven Whitman's De Dion-Bouton Motorette from Pasadena on an eleven-day, 1,100-mile round trip to Yosemite National Park. Hammond's 36-mile round-trip drive in a 1-cylinder Packard on the winding dirt roads between Pasadena and Los Angeles was such a novelty that the *Los Angeles Times* gave him a half-page write-up.[4]

One night, riding the trolley home to Pasadena from their mechanics' jobs at Reuben and Leon T. Shettler's Los Angeles Olds agency, Whitman and Hammond discussed driving across the country. "Since no one had ever done it, though several had tried, the challenge of such an adventure became more exciting to us as we weighed the many hazards," Hammond recalled.[5] Whitman's Motorette was too low and the tread too narrow for country roads. An Olds runabout, however, appeared ideal for such roads, so Whitman mailed a proposal to Olds Motor Works.

Why did they undertake the journey? Hammond's son, John S. Hammond II, insists they "were one of three teams trying to set the first transcontinental record in an automobile." But they set out weeks after the two other cars and, as the younger Hammond later acknowledged, "their only chance of being first to arrive in New York would . . . hinge on the other two machines being forced out of the running for one reason or another."[6] The various auto journals of the day, with rare exceptions, covered the crossings not as a race but as three separate journeys.[7]

When Whitman and Hammond started on July 6, Fetch's Packard was in Salt Lake City and Jackson's Winton was in eastern Wyoming or western Nebraska. Whitman's own logbook repeatedly stressed that he and "Ham" (Whitman's nickname for his partner) were on a pleasure jaunt. *Automobile*, which ran Whitman's trip dispatches, said he and Hammond made the crossing "for the novelty of the experience." As Whitman told *Motor Age*, "We are not endeavoring to make a record run but are jogging along getting all the pleasure and photographs out of the trip we can—just going on and stopping when it suits our own will." Whitman and Hammond, transplanted Easterners, also wanted a chance to visit friends and family back home, they claimed.[8]

In Ogden, Utah, on July 28, the pair learned that Jackson's Winton had arrived in New York City two days previously. In an Omaha newspaper on August 22, Day 48, they read that Tom Fetch had reached New York in his Packard on August 21, thereby besting Jackson's time by nearly 1½ days. Upon reaching Denver, the Oldsmobile travelers had decided to continue their trip beyond New York City so as to become the first to drive from San Francisco to Portland, Maine.

Experienced with Gas Rigs

"I needed to look no further for a co-driver and mechanic than my fellow autoist and cheerful companion Eugene I. Hammond," Whitman wrote. "At 23 years of age, 180 pounds and 6 feet tall in his stockinged feet, he could lift any wheel of the Olds with one hand and was experienced with gasoline rigs" (see Fig. 66).[9]

Born May 3, 1880, in Mattapoisett, Massachusetts, Eugene Irish Hammond began racing bicycles at the age 16 and, as a professional rider, gained the sponsorship of the Columbia Bicycle Works. In the early 1900s he traveled to California as "a pacemaker for Frank Waller on the cycle track," and had stayed in Pasadena when "Dutch" Waller left for Australia.[10] (Curiously, the press reported that Sewall K. Crocker, who accompanied Dr. H. Nelson Jackson on the earlier Winton transcontinental crossing, had also ridden a pacing bicycle for Waller.) With a partner, Hammond opened an automobile-repair garage. Next, he worked as a mechanic for the Shettlers' Los Angeles Olds and Winton agency, where he met Whitman, who soon thereafter began working as a mechanic.

Equipping the Model R

According to Whitman, Ransom E. Olds himself offered to lend a car for the transcontinental trip. But Olds stipulated that Whitman pay his own travel expenses, which would later be reimbursed "if I could get the Olds to New York City under its own power successfully." In addition, the factory would pay him $1,000 for reaching

New York, and he would receive his tires free from the Diamond Rubber Company of Akron, Ohio.

An Easterner, like Hammond, Lester Lee Whitman was born in Turner, or nearby South Paris, Maine, on July 16, 1861.[11] He thus celebrated his forty-third birthday on the cross-country trip. As a young man, Whitman worked on a ranch, and, at New Gloucester, Maine, made sleds and sleighs. A 1903 *Automobile* article reported that he relocated to California in 1900. Whitman reportedly sold or repaired autos on his own before joining the Shettler agency. This may explain why the 1903–1904 Pasadena city directory lists him as foreman of the "Pasadena Automobile Stables." In a book about the 1903 coast-to-coast trip, Hammond's son called Whitman "a jovial, adventure seeking, strong-minded, competitive individual with considerable business acumen, a natural born craftsman, and a great story teller."[12]

Ransom Olds was a pioneer automaker. In 1885 he purchased a half-interest in his father's Lansing, Michigan, machine shop, which first made steam engines but introduced an Olds stationary gasoline engine in 1892. The younger Olds finished a steam auto in 1887 and another in about 1892. He built his first gas-powered car in the mid-1890s. Impressed, a group of Lansing investors on August 21, 1897, helped Olds incorporate the Olds Motor Vehicle Company, which evolved into the Olds Motor Works. The company was building ten cars per day in Lansing in 1902. By 1904, there were more Oldsmobiles in the United States than all other makes combined.[13]

Whitman and Hammond's Olds Model R runabout arrived in California on June 27, and for three days thereafter both men tested the car on the hills in and around Los Angeles and Pasadena. The car differed from a stock runabout in that behind the seat the factory had fit a special wooden luggage box, the sides and back of which announced: "Oldsmobile Enroute From San Francisco To New York." The box had to be removed in order to fill the car with gas, oil, or water. The transcontinental Olds, stripped of its fenders, also had a larger-than-normal "cooler"—radiator—for desert and mountain driving.

The two men weighed 350 pounds and carried 300 pounds of baggage and provisions in the 800-pound runabout. They believed the light machine "would be an advantage as they can push it along if it breaks down or the supply of gasoline fails." With a bore and stroke of $4\frac{1}{2} \times 6$ inches, the 1-cylinder engine developed $4\frac{1}{2}$ horsepower, giving the car—which lacked a speedometer—a top speed of from 25 to 30 miles per hour. The car came from Olds's Lansing, Michigan, factory equipped with pneumatic tires on 28-inch wire-spoke wheels, a 4-gallon gas tank, and a tiller instead of a steering wheel. Power was transferred through a single chain between the 2-speed planetary transmission and rear axle. The driver could apply mechanical brakes to the differential or transmission. "We most often referred to the machine as either 'the little Olds' or 'the little scout,'" Whitman said.[14]

To avoid a difficult 500-mile drive north to San Francisco, the men loaded themselves and the car onto the lumber schooner *Coronado* at Redondo, California, on July 1, bound for the Golden Gate, where they arrived on July 3 weak with seasickness. They stored their car at the Pioneer Automobile Company, the city's Olds agency.[15]

"We're Off!"

"In Pasadena we had previously bought khaki suits, leather coats, visored 'chauffeur's' caps and canvas leggings," Whitman recalled.

> In San Francisco we put into the baggage box one spare tire, a tire pump, a bag of tools, some small repair parts including a steering spindle, gaskets, nuts and bolts, extra spark coil and plugs, and a grip (valise). This last was not to contain tuxedos or stovepipe hats, but was to hold our film rolls, writing materials, our crude maps, such as they were, and the letter which we hoped to receive and deliver between the two mayors. We carried our complete wardrobe on our backs.[16]

They also carried such other supplies as a 5-gallon gas can, a 1-gallon can of cylinder oil, a small can of grease, a hatchet, compass, pistol, extra batteries, rope, two wool blankets, goggles, and a first-aid kit.

On Sunday morning, July 5, the day before leaving, Whitman and Hammond drove the runabout to Cliff House on the Pacific Ocean near San Francisco. Mounting his camera on a tripod, Whitman used a remote shutter release to photograph himself and Hammond beside the car, a practice he would repeat throughout the journey. On Monday, July 6, 1903, at an 11:00 AM City Hall ceremony, they received from Mayor Eugene E. Schmitz a letter for New York Mayor Seth Low (see Fig. 67).

According to Monday's *San Francisco Bulletin*:

> As the clock struck the hour of 11 this morning E. I. Hammond and L. L. Whitman, two enthusiastic automobilists, began what they hope will prove a successful attempt to cross the United States in an automobile. The two enthusiasts came here from Pasadena, having shipped their machine by steamer.

Upon arriving in town they were taken charge of by E. P. Brinegar [of the Pioneer Automobile Company], the local representative of the machine, who arranged what details the daring men had not attended to. . . .

This morning the machine and its occupants were photographed at the City Hall, with Mayor Schmitz in the act of handing them a letter, which is to be given to Mayor Low upon their arrival in Gotham. . . . The time necessary to make the journey, it is stated, will occupy about sixty days.[17]

Whitman recorded this conversation between the two adventurers: "'We're off!' said Hammond, with a brave attempt at a nonchalant smile. 'We're off!' I said, 'but not mentally, I hope.'"[18] Whitman and Hammond had the letter from Mayor Schmitz postmarked at the San Francisco post office before leaving on the 3:00 PM ferry for Oakland, where they had the letter postmarked a second time.

During their west-to-east crossing, the pair spent four full days in California; fifteen in Nevada; five in Utah; seven in Wyoming; five in Colorado; twenty in Nebraska; three in Iowa; two in Illinois; one apiece in Indiana and Ohio; two in Michigan; four in Ontario, Canada; six in New York; one in Connecticut; two in Massachusetts; one day crossing northern Massachusetts, New Hampshire, and southern Maine; and one full day in Maine. Uncertain western roads prompted them to follow the Southern Pacific tracks to Ogden, Utah, and the Union Pacific route from Ogden across much of Wyoming until their detour to Denver. Farther east, there existed a more dependable system of mapped roads.

Railroad telegraph operators, section bosses, and other employees, as well as the rails themselves, were an incalculable aid to Whitman and Hammond, as they were to other early transcontinental drivers. Fast rail deliveries made it possible for the factory or Olds agencies to send parts to the stranded travelers. As Whitman wrote from Utah after a fast express train delivered a new crankshaft, "What would we have done without the railroad?"[19]

Renewed Piece by Piece

Indeed, the Olds runabout that left San Francisco on July 6 was renewed piece by piece during its journey. After some 4,600 miles and eleven weeks of hard driving, a very different car reached Portland, Maine. Whitman and Hammond's logbooks show that they, or Olds mechanics along their route, replaced some fifty parts or sets of parts. A few were replaced in routine maintenance, but many more parts—including engine vitals—wore out or broke, often repeatedly. Upon reaching Detroit, Whitman and Hammond met for nearly two hours with R. E. Olds and his top engineers to discuss the car's weaknesses. Consulting his list of broken parts (see Table 7), Hammond recommended better piston wrist pins and rings, a heavier crankshaft, and brake improvements.

All the while, in their letters and articles to the auto journals and in interviews, the men downplayed their troubles. According to a badly deceived *Motor Age* reporter writing from Detroit, "The machine was in excellent shape when it reached here, the replacing of an occasional tire and spoke being practically all that had been necessary in the way of repairs en route." Upon reaching New York City, "Reporters dogged our heels asking many questions," Whitman wrote in his logbook. "They filled Ham's pockets with cigars and he in turn filled up the reporters. 'No sir,' Ham avowed, 'Had no trouble at all. . . .' Ham knew his onions, our troubles to be kept under our hats."[20]

Predictably, Whitman's chronicle put the Olds runabout in the best possible light by mentioning no breakdowns specifically, saying only:

TABLE 7. New Parts Installed on the Oldsmobile, 1903[a]

Day / Date	Location	Description of Repair / Replacement Part
Day 4 / July 9	Placerville, Calif.	Installed an exhaust cutout to quiet the engine, and "a new connection pipe between the gas tank and vaporizer."
Days 15–17 / July 20–22	Elko, Nev.	Replaced "a new set of fiber pads on the brake and replaced three on the low speed band"; a broken ball in a front wheel bearing; "the cap to the vaporizer lift pin"; piston wrist pin.
Days 22–23 / July 27–28	Ogden, Utah	Replaced flywheel, shaft, and transmission; front steering spring; drive chain; chain boot on the differential; rear truss rod; connecting rod; piston wrist pin. Repiped "all the rubber hose connections."
Day 25 / July 30	Evanston, Wyo.	Replaced head gasket.
Day 34 / Aug. 8	Denver	Installed oversize engine valves and a high-lift exhaust cam.
Day 36 / Aug. 10	Between Orchard and Julesburg, Colo.	Replaced the "gasoline pipe connection to the mixer"; installed a new rubber "body hanger."
Days 50–51 / Aug. 24–25	Omaha, Neb.	Replaced piston; piston wrist pin; cylinder; front steering spring; many wheel spokes; rear axle truss rod; dry-cell batteries.
Day 57 / Aug. 31	East of Council Bluffs, Iowa	Installed two new lower leaf springs and a drive chain.
Day 61 / Sept. 4	Between Rochelle, Ill., and Chicago	Replaced spark plug.
Days 62–63 / Sept. 5–6	Chicago	Replaced acetylene headlamp, front steering spring, and "a few loose and chattering spokes."
Day 65 / Sept. 8	Belle Island, Mich.—near Detroit	Replaced the four wheels; flywheel, shaft, and transmission; rear axles and differential (so the car could use a new roller-style drive chain); hand-crank starting chain; acetylene headlamp.
Day 75 / Sept. 18	New York City	Installed new piston rings.
Day 76 / Sept. 19	Between New York City and Hartford, Conn.	Replaced lost intake-valve pin.
Day 79 / Sept. 22	Boston	Installed "a new cam."

SOURCES: Lester L. Whitman's accounts in auto journals and his logbooks, reprinted in John S. Hammond II, *From Sea to Sea in 1903 in a Curved Dash Oldsmobile.*

[a] The table excludes approximately thirty reported repairs and adjustments that did not require new parts.

We had a few delays of that character where you perspire and fume, and say with your self-control working overtime, "I can't make the thing go." We had to put new leathers on the brakes, replace the rivets, and put in new clutch-bands and wiring. We had no trouble whatever with the spark—let that be writ large and impressive.[21]

Anticipating mechanical problems from the start, Whitman and Hammond sent a boxful of parts ahead to Winnemucca, Nevada. They also left two spare tires with the Pioneer Automobile Company, intending to send for them later, if necessary.

From Sacramento, the second day out, Whitman and Hammond shipped a 5-gallon can of gasoline 50 miles ahead by stagecoach. On Day 3, residents of Placerville, California, told the runabout drivers that three weeks previously a car that "was a 'whale' alongside our machine" had torn through town—it was Tom Fetch in his Packard.[22] The pair was more surprised, however, to find that no gasoline was available in Placerville. Finally, a mine superintendent directed them to a gas supply at his stamp mill 5 miles from town.

They reached the summit of the Sierra Nevada on Friday, July 10, Day 5, and descended 4,000 feet in less than 7 miles down the Genoa Grade to Carson City, Nevada. "Failure of the brakes or a broken chain could mean a dangerous runaway for our machine, so we stopped, chopped down a small pine tree and tied it onto the rear axle to be used as a drag," Whitman wrote.[23]

Ahead—Sand, Sun, and Thirst

The next day at Reno, Whitman and Hammond "set about to fortify ourselves against the demons of sand, sun and thirst," as Whitman put it. They equipped themselves for crossing the Nevada desert by buying an ax, shovel, canteens, and broad-brimmed pith helmets to deflect the desert sun (see Fig. 68). "We secured a capacious and practical sort of canteen to carry our drinking water." This may be the canteen that Whitman used on later trips, as was reported in 1905, when Whitman set off

Fig. 68. With pith helmets on their heads and a 5-gallon gas can at their feet, Whitman, *left*, and Hammond set out across the desert. Draped behind the seat is a pair of canvas tire wrappings for traction in the sand (*Motor Age*, Aug. 13, 1903).

to break the Los Angeles–San Francisco record in a Franklin auto: "[He] carries the same good luck canteen that he had when he crossed the country in a little Oldsmobile on his first trip."[24]

Heralding their 1903 arrival in Reno, the local *Daily Nevada State Journal* remarked that "both of these gentlemen are camera fiends and they have already taken over two hundred pictures of the scenery along the route."[25] Unfortunately, the automobile journals that published these photos rarely received—or at least rarely used—specific information about the scenes. It is thus difficult today to identify the exact locations depicted in many of the trip photos.

Many Reno onlookers, who were seeing their first automobile, surrounded the car, thereby preventing the men from departing. "Ham said there is only one way we can get away. Start the engine, race it, then shut off the ignition for a few seconds, turn it back on and let the engine backfire," Whitman said. "The loud explosion, which nearly split our muffler, did its work! Our frightened audience was scattering in all directions as we took the first opening to make our escape!"[26]

Upon reaching Wadsworth late in the day, their hotel proprietor "pointed out a shed to house the Olds for the night," Whitman recalled. "Here we found hanging on a wall one of Alexander Winton's tires removed from the car he was driving in an attempt to cross the continent." More frequently, the Olds team spotted signs of the passing of the 1903 Packard transcontinental car. "We ran across the trail of the Packard machine and saw on many a brush stump or hump in the road where Messrs. Fetch and Krarup left their mark as they hit the high spots with their axles," Whitman wrote from Ogden. The Oldsmobile left its own marks on the sagebrush in the trail (see Fig. 69).[27]

On Sunday, July 12, Day 7, Whitman and Hammond set off from Wadsworth, Nevada, in what soon became 115° heat. They were accompanied by the driver of a mule team for the first 15 miles of the 70-mile trip to Lovelock, Nevada. For the first time, the travelers installed the canvas "sand tires" they had shipped from Pasadena to Reno (see Figs. 70 and 71). Stuffed with cotton rags, the canvas tires were 7 feet long and 6 or 8 inches wide. "My wife Sophia and I had made them and I proposed to bind them around our rear rubber tires with rope to make a wide flat surface on which to ride over the deepest sand," Whitman said. Whitman originated this idea, according to many newspapers and journals, one of which reported: "In the extremely sandy roads this tire was found to pass smoothly, making but little impression in the sand."[28]

Fig. 69 (left). Whitman and the Oldsmobile in a sea of sagebrush at an unidentified location (OHC).

Fig. 70 (below, left). Whitman, *left*, and Hammond lash on sand tires (OHC).

Fig. 71. A rear view of the homemade tires (*Automobile*, Aug. 15, 1903).

Fig. 72. With a little
help, the Oldsmobile
climbs out of the Hum-
boldt River near Battle
Mountain, Nevada (JSH).

Nevertheless, the mule team had to rescue them from the deep sand several times on July 12, before the mule-team driver headed north and the 1-cylinder Oldsmobile drove east alone. The travelers received similar assistance later in the trip. On Saturday, July 18, between Battle Mountain and Dunphy, Nevada, two cowboys "lassoed our machine and helped us ford the main Humboldt River, at a cattle crossing where the banks were very steep," Whitman said (see Fig. 72).[29] According to Whitman's logbook entries, they were also pulled by horses on August 11, between Julesburg, Colorado, and Paxton, Nebraska, and on August 15, between Cozad and Elwood, Nebraska.

On Foot in the Desert

Climbing a hill in the Nevada desert late during the afternoon of their July 12 run from Wadsworth to Lovelock, the car sheared off the pins that held the drive-chain sprocket to the transmission—damage that Whitman and Hammond had neither the tools nor the parts to fix. They were midway between the two towns, or about 35 miles from each.[30] Thus, with a half-pint of water and some leftover sandwiches between them, they began hiking south toward the railroad tracks, which they reached at 8:00 PM. They then hiked east along the tracks, Whitman later recalled, and

> soon saw the light of a section house. We forgot our aching bodies and our parched throats at this—we even chatted gayly there in the dark and laughed a little. We said: "It

was a loud squeak, old man, but we're all right now." And then we reached the alleged section house and our cheery hail met with no hospitable response—our hearts sank— we hurried on, without speaking, to find no section house, but a blind siding—no human being, no water, no shelter, no food, no cheer, only a coldly blinking railroad lantern.

Had Hammond burst into tears I should have joined him with all my heart. May life hold no sorer disappointment for me, than the hopeless despair of that moment. We pulled our belts a notch tighter and trudged on along the ties. The second light came at last and with it, human beings. Two good fellows welcomed us with whole-souled hospitality and, what was more to the point, with water.[31]

Whitman's later recollection of events matched his logbook description, except for the cause of the late-night walk through the desert. In the logbook, Whitman described the breakdown; in his later chronicle, published in the sanitized Oldsmobile booklet, Whitman says the car stopped because "a brush had caught the petcock on the under side of the cooler . . . [and] the water had leaked away." Whitman's logbook did describe just such a situation, actually two similar situations, but neither happened on the evening of July 12. One occurred on July 17 between Golconda and Battle Mountain, Nevada, and the other on July 30 between Morgan, Utah, and Evanston, Wyoming.[32]

In any event, the travelers reached the second light at Brown's Station, a section house and telegraph office. They had walked for four hours along the tracks to reach it. The telegraph operator was forbidden to flag trains without telegraphed approval, so Whitman and Hammond waved burning sagebrush across the tracks to stop the 1:30 AM Overland Express. They reached Lovelock at 2:00 AM, wired the San Francisco Olds agency to send a new transmission, and then tumbled into bed.

After a few hours' sleep, they rented a two-horse spring wagon and at 7:15 AM left town, returning to Lovelock nearly twelve hours later with the runabout in tow (see Fig. 73). On the way back through the desert, Hammond killed a rattlesnake that had spooked the horses. The men spent the morning of the next day, Tuesday, July 14, removing the car's engine. The transmission that arrived on the noon express train was an earlier model and did not fit. Thus, they spent the rest of the day at a blacksmith's shop, removing the sheared pins with a hand drill and replacing them with homemade pins. The temporary repair enabled them to reach the Olds agency at Ogden.

Perhaps puzzled about how to cover the autoists' visit, the editor of the *Lovelock Argus* wrote a paragraph for the weekly oddities section, otherwise known as the local-news column. Thus, the following item appeared, flanked by news of an umbrella-

Fig. 73. Whitman, *left*, and Hammond hitched the Oldsmobile to a spring wagon, which towed the car to Love-lock, Nevada (JSH).

eating cow and a man who had endured six months with a 1½-inch-long glass shard in his foot: "A couple of automobilists arrived in Lovelock Monday evening and spent Tuesday in town making necessary repairs to their machine. . . . The gentlemen, whose names we did not learn, departed early Wednesday morning for their trip across the continent."[33] Whitman and Hammond arrived early Monday morning, of course; the editor evidently spotted them returning with their disabled car late in the day.

More Small Calamities

Whitman and Hammond lost the trail near Elko, Nevada, on Sunday, July 19, Day 14. While searching for the established route, the men carefully eased the car down and pushed it up a series of steep embankments. Despite their care, their piston wrist pin broke and they arrived in Elko with the engine pounding badly. There, they idled away July 20, July 21, and the morning of July 22, until a new pin arrived by mail. Later on July 22, the autoists resumed their trip, but two small calamities held their progress to the 33 miles between Elko and Deeth, Nevada.

First, they spent a half day with their shovel rebuilding a washed-out section of road. Then, two miles from Deeth, "without warning, the crankshaft broke in two at the hole drilled for the pin where the forward gear fastens to the shaft. The engine continued to run, but would not drive the forward gear," said Whitman. In reverse, however, the ends of the broken shaft meshed, so Whitman and Hammond slowly backed the car into Deeth. The next morning, Thursday, July 23, they pinned the broken shaft with 20-penny spikes, declining a blacksmith's offer to weld the break. "Perhaps he could have, but we doubted if the weld would have been smoothed up very well with only an axe and a horse rasp available for tools," Whitman said.[34]

The following day, between Wells and Tecoma, Nevada, the car stalled on the steepest hill it had encountered to that point. This was perhaps the hill at Fenelon that a "stunned" Tom Fetch and his Packard had climbed in spurts, while his two helpers blocked the rear wheels with stones. The Oldsmobile tourists drove up as far as their car would take them, stopped the car, and then carried their luggage to the top. Whitman and Hammond returned to the car and, each taking hold of a rear wheel, forced the runabout—its engine turned off—to the crest a few inches at a time, blocking the wheels for frequent rest breaks.

During the three days it took to travel from Wells, Nevada, to Ogden, Utah, the biggest worry was finding enough gasoline. A Tecoma, Nevada, grocery store had sold the 5-gallon tin of gas it had promised to hold for them. Fortunately, a local saloon-keeper's dugout cellar yielded "a 5-gallon can that Ham said smelled more of whiskey than gasoline. The barkeeper nearly lost the contents when a wandering stray pig dove between his legs. Down he fell, but triumphantly held the can upright, not spilling a drop while wasting some fluent language on the old sow!"[35]

A railroad storehouse was the only source of gasoline in Terrace, Utah, where the Olds runabout arrived at 2:00 PM on Saturday, July 25, Day 20. Rules prevented the sympathetic railway official from selling the gasoline, but he looked the other way while Whitman and Hammond helped themselves to what they needed. They had another close call the next day at Promontory, Utah, on the shores of the Great Salt Lake (see Fig. 74). Whitman had wired two weeks previously to have 5 gallons of gasoline shipped from Salt Lake City to a Promontory general store. But the storekeeper apologetically explained that he had given the gasoline to two other men driving the first automobile he had ever seen in Promontory. He had believed it was the Whitman expedition, he explained. Whitman wrote in his logbook that the car was presumably Tom Fetch's Packard. But Fetch reached Promontory on July 3, long before Whitman ordered the gasoline, and he was traveling through Utah with not one but two companions. Who received the gasoline remains a mystery. Fortunately for the Oldsmobile drivers, they had enough gas to reach Brigham City.

Baths and New Clothes

At 8:00 PM the next day, Sunday, July 26, with cracked lips and blistered faces, the men reached Ogden—and their first bath in eleven days. "The only thing fit to use in crossing from here to Reno is a flying machine," Whitman quipped in a letter. "No lonely mariner ever gazed upon land with more thankful hearts than [when] we saw the green grass, trees, and living water."[36] After they bought new clothes, local Olds agent L. H. Becraft displayed their discarded shoes and outfits in his store window (see Fig. 75).

From Morgan, Utah, the men reached Evanston in southwestern Wyoming at 5:30 PM on Thursday, July 30. A local newspaper reported, "Their machine on good roads will cover thirty miles an hour but in the mountainous country the speed is greatly reduced. They spent the night in town."[37] When Whitman and Hammond left Evanston the next morning, Friday, July 31, Day 26, they neglected their customary practice of asking for directions. By nightfall, they were lost in the sagebrush east of the crumbling log buildings of old Fort Bridger, where U.S. soldiers had been sta-

Fig. 75. Before discarding their soiled clothes, Whitman, at the tiller, and Hammond pose with Ogden Olds agent L. H. Becraft, *far right* (OHC).

tioned to prevent Indian attacks on Union Pacific construction crews in the 1860s. Unable to run by the weak light of their two kerosene carriage lamps, they started a sagebrush fire, dug out a sleeping pit, and spent a chilly night on the desert.

"To make it more pleasant, some twenty-five coyotes surrounded us in the near brush and howled by spells all night," Whitman said. "At times all seemed to join in the chorus." When some snarling coyotes approached within a few feet of the reluctant campers, "Ham scared them by firing his pistol in the air, but within an hour they were back again." To avoid getting stranded at night again, the men bought an acetylene headlamp for the front of the car.[38]

Weathering the Storm

The next day they found and passed through Granger, Wyoming. A day later, Sunday, August 2, near Rock Springs, they encountered the strong winds that some chroniclers—with Whitman's encouragement—have puffed up into a tornado. "A tornado of wind struck them near Rock Springs and they had to take refuge behind large rocks, as the wind almost blew both men and machine away."[39]

In a 1978 article, Hammond's son related a version he says is based on stories he heard the men tell in later years. As he tells it, Whitman and Hammond dashed behind a railroad station and fell upon the axles to hold the car. "When the dust cleared, the little machine had been bounced and turned almost 45 degrees by the wind."[40] In his account of the trip for the Oldsmobile booklet, *From Sea to Sea and Above the Clouds in an Oldsmobile*, Whitman presented a similarly exciting scenario:

> Just outside of Rock Springs, a tornado wind struck us. No doubt our progress would have been considerably accelerated had we yielded to the will of the wind, but feeling that the trip should be made without the kindly assistance of the strenuous element, we took refuge behind some friendly boulders. At that, machine, Hammond and I were nearly blown from our anchorage.[41]

But Whitman's logbook, written at the time, suggests nothing of the sort happened: "A windstorm mixed with a little rain chased us for the next 25 miles [east of Rock Springs] over some level alkaline country. The wind blew a gale, dust filled the air and we feared a tornado. Running the rig behind a section house, out of the wind, the sandwiches were unpacked and we sat down to eat our lunch. . . . By 2:00 PM the storm was over and we went back on the trail."[42] Another notable event occurred near Rock Springs when one of the rear tires picked up a nail, causing the first puncture of the trip.

Detour to Denver

Whitman and Hammond arrived in Laramie, Wyoming, on Wednesday evening, August 5. "They have had no trouble of any kind, have only slept out once and punctured one tire, the other three tires have not even been pumped up since they left San Francisco," the local newspaper declared. But this is scarcely believable, for an extant photo shows Hammond pumping up a tire "at a wayside stop in Nevada."[43]

The drivers further modified their auto after meeting with E. Linn Mathewson, the Denver Olds agency sales representative, in Laramie. Mathewson would later drive the winning Thomas car part-way across the United States during the 1908 New York–Paris race. In Laramie, he was demonstrating an Olds runabout equipped with oversize engine valves. The car "leaped around so friskily" that it was quickly sold, and Mathewson returned to Denver by train, Whitman related. Hammond and Whitman thus deviated 100 miles from their route to visit the Hannan Olds agency in Denver, which installed larger valves and a higher-lift exhaust-valve cam.[44]

To reach Denver, Whitman and Hammond left Laramie on Thursday, August 6, Day 32, for what became a two-day drive on muddy roads south to Denver through Fort Collins, Loveland, and Boulder, Colorado. On a downgrade south of Laramie, a front wheel came off as the car was "flying along at a pretty fast clip," pitching both men out onto soft ground. "Ham picked himself up and ran down the hill chasing our right front wheel as it rolled along. We knew at once that the front wheel spindle had crystallized and broken," Whitman said. Later, they also discovered a crack in the wooden body, presumably from the accident. Inexplicably, Whitman wrote a different account in a letter to *Horseless Age*: "As we were going slowly we were not thrown from our seats nor was any damage done." Both accounts say the tourists had a new spindle with them and quickly replaced the part.[45]

When the Oldsmobile reached Denver at 3:00 PM on Friday, August 7, "it looked as though it had spent several days in a quagmire, but it was still going and puffing along at a good rate. A trophy of the trip that was carried 1,000 miles into Denver is a broken shovel. This was picked up in Nevada. It was found very useful."[46]

"Didn't It Rain?"

On Sunday, August 9, Day 35, Whitman and Hammond left Denver and drove northeasterly for 92 miles to spend the night in Orchard, Colorado. The following day, they drove 141 miles to Julesburg, Colorado, and 50 miles from Julesburg into Nebraska on Tuesday, passing through Ogallala on the way to a night stop at Paxton. Ogallala's *Keith County News* noted that the Oldsmobile was "the third automobile" to reach town, behind Jackson's Winton and Fetch's Packard. "From the records reported by the several operators there seems to be but little difference in speed . . . but they [Whitman and Hammond] travel much cheaper," the paper reported.[47]

Only the tops of fence posts were visible along some water-covered roads in southwestern Nebraska near the swollen Platte River, Whitman said. The floods forced the transcontinental car to detour south from the Platte River Valley route that would later become the Lincoln Highway, the country's first transcontinental road. Thus,

from Ogallala, the pair traveled through North Platte, Cozad, Elwood, Minden, Hastings, Grafton, Fairmont, and Lincoln.

"In the country a few high hills showed above the water, and we took to these out of Cozad and along the Platte river going south and out through Lincoln," Whitman said (see Fig. 76).[48] "We put ropes on the rear wheels, took off our shoes and stockings and, half wading, half swimming, three-quarters cussing, pulled the machine through slimy, oozy lakes of mud. It rained six times in five days" (see Fig. 77).[49]

Even on this southern Nebraska route, rain and mud forced the men to lay over one day apiece in Cozad on August

Fig. 76 (above). The grass-lined road near Hastings, Nebraska, resembles a river (*Motor Age*, Aug. 27, 1903).

Fig. 77 (right). Hammond and the runabout wallow in mud near Minden, Nebraska (OHC).

14, in Elwood on August 16, and in Minden on August 19. When they could venture out on Nebraska's muddy roads, Whitman and Hammond frequently had to push the car and get help from passing horse teams. "Let me say of all mud this takes the cake," Whitman wrote to *Motor Age*. "It slips like lard. The rear wheels can spin for hours in a mud slough and there need be no fear of wearing the tires—or getting out of the hole, either." But "our machine is holding together well, being bound up in a cake of dried adobe—not a nut can jar off."[50]

East of Grafton, Nebraska, on Friday morning, August 21, a front tire blew out, destroying the casing, for which the men had no spare. They drove on the flat tire to Fairmont, where they packed it with cracked corn, plugged the hole with a rag, and secured the plug by wrapping the tire with another rag. During the next day's run, they repacked the tire with oats. Like the corn, the oats gradually trickled from the tire; the men then resorted to wrapping the tire with rope to reach Omaha.

Mud Center of the Universe

The "nervy pair" reached Omaha late Saturday afternoon, August 22, Day 48, with plans of "sojourning in the city for a few days to rest up."[51] In fact, a five-day weather delay followed three days of repairs in Omaha, a Missouri River port. "Had we been told that Omaha was really the mud center of the universe, we should have swallowed the assertion without a murmur," Whitman wrote. Observers routinely spotted houses floating down the river as the city and points east received daily showers, including 10 inches of rain in one twenty-four-hour period. Much of their planned route through Iowa was under water, too. "Bridges, all over the state of Iowa, we found washed away," Whitman would report. "Council Bluffs needed only a few mandolins and the imposing palace of the Doges to be a Venice."[52]

Leaving Omaha on Sunday, August 30, Whitman and Hammond drove across the Missouri River to inspect the roads east of Council Bluffs. "Before reaching there they found that the bridge [approach] at Main street was gone and that its replacement had proceeded only as far as the laying of stringers," one report stated. Another account specified that floodwaters spared the bridge but swept away its approach. The autoists "obtained permission from the superintendent to cross at their own risk, and did so amid the applause of a number of spectators. To them the feat was a trifle" (see Fig. 78).[53]

Fig. 78 (above). Whitman, *left*, and Hammond prepare to climb a pair of planks leading to the Missouri River bridge at Omaha (*Automobile*, Sept. 5, 1903).

Fig. 79 (right). Mechanics reattach the ejected rear axle east of Council Bluffs, Iowa (JSH).

The travelers finally resumed their journey from Omaha on Monday, August 31, Day 57, but "we had gone only 20 miles when, all at once, down dropped the rear end of our machine! The drive chain had come apart, catching in the transmission drive case on the rear axle," Whitman explained. "It twisted the axle housing so violently that it snapped off both main springs at the clips. The axle and wheels flew off into the ditch along the roadside while the engine kept merrily running!"[54] Two mechanics from the Olds Gasoline Engine Works in Omaha arrived with new parts to repair the car (see Fig. 79).

Ironically, given the wet roads, the worst tire wear of the trip occurred in Nebraska and Iowa, according to Whitman. As roads dried, the deep tire ruts hardened and chewed up their tire sidewalls; Whitman and Hammond would pick up two new Diamond tires in Chicago. Despite the ruts, on Wednesday, September 2, they tied for the longest run of their trip by driving 170 miles between Des Moines and Cedar Rapids, Iowa.

On to Chicago and Detroit

"Sheets of rain" discouraged two dozen carloads of greeters who had planned to escort the men to the Chicago Automobile Club upon their arrival Friday afternoon, September 4, Day 61. As *Motor Age* reported:

James Levy, of the Oldsmobile company, and the *Motor Age* representative, however, started forth and four cars from the club followed, so that five cars were present at the welcome extended under the boughs of a sheltering tree in Garfield park. As the reception committee rounded a sharp turn, Levy's car almost bumped into the tourist car, which was skipping along as friskily as a new car just out of the shop. Whitman threw on the reverse, Hammond pulled the tablecloth off his knee, thereby getting the one remaining dry spot wet. . . .

During the return journey to the club house many curious pedestrians paused and peered out from under their umbrellas at the procession, and when the legend "Oldsmobile, San Francisco to New York" was seen on the second car, the reason for the demonstration was plain. As the party turned into the driveway at the club house the sun came from behind the clouds and smiled a benediction, and soon the yard was filled with club members and their guests, all anxious to meet and greet the transcontinentalists.

Both Whitman and Hammond were liberally plastered with mud, and their first request was for water and plenty of it. A change of clothes was resurrected from the luggage box and a half hour later, "dressed and in their right minds," they were busy discussing a warm meal in the club dining room.[55]

Ransom E. Olds wired Chicago, asking the transcontinentalists to hurry to Detroit for a publicity appearance at the Grosse Pointe, Michigan, Labor Day auto races. Olds Motor Works sent factory advertising man Roy D. Chapin, future president of Hudson Motor Car Company, to Billy Rands's Olds agency to photograph Whitman and Hammond's September 7 Detroit arrival (see Fig. 80).

"There was an interesting event which was not down on the program," *Automobile* reported in its summary of the races. "A little Olds, looking much the worse for wear and containing two tanned and begrimed riders, came out on the track. . . . The little machine went around the track at a lively pace but the time was not announced."[56]

A sign on the car carried a message and an Olds sales slogan: "This is the First Runabout to Make a Record from San Francisco to Detroit. L. L. Whitman Left San Francisco July 6 and Arrived Detroit Sep. 7. Only 60 Days on the

Fig. 80. A crowd greets Whitman, holding tiller, and Hammond at the Detroit Oldsmobile agency (OHC).

Fig. 81. Whitman and the Olds at Grosse Pointe, Michigan (JSH).

THIS IS THE FIRST RUNABOUT TO MAKE A RECORD FROM SAN FRANCISCO TO DETROIT. L.L. WHITMAN LEFT SAN FRANCISCO JULY 6 AND ARRIVED DETROIT SEP. 7. ONLY 60 DAYS ON THE ROAD IT'S "MADE TO RUN AND DOES IT."

Road. It's 'Made to Run and Does It'" (see Fig. 81). The car was actually sixty-three days in reaching Detroit. Further, the claim of setting a San Francisco–Detroit runabout speed record had a hollow ring to it, considering the car was the first runabout to ever make the trip.

Broken Wheel "A Trifle"

At 3:00 PM on Wednesday, September 9, Day 66, the men drove their car onto the ferry between Detroit and Windsor, Ontario, resuming their journey with a variety of new parts, including tires and wire wheels. The car left Detroit wearing fenders, or "mud guards," which the autoists had done without on rough western roads. Their planned route across Canada to reach Niagara Falls was more direct than backtracking across Michigan, and then driving around the south end of Lake Erie through parts of Ohio and Pennsylvania to reach New York State. This route also gave Whitman and Hammond the distinction of being the first transcontinental motorists to use both U.S. and Canadian roads.

During the next day's drive eastward from Wheatley, Ontario, "as we were rounding a corner 3 miles from Shedden one of our brand new rear wheels caved in, busting the rim at the weld and it about collapsed," Whitman said. "We had to run very slowly in low speed for the last 3 miles into Shedden." The men wasted a day waiting for a new wheel—a factory shipping error sent it to the wrong town—until Whitman, in disgust, riveted a metal strap across the broken weld and Hammond trued the wheel. The wheel is "now as good, if not better, than a new one," Whitman remarked some days later, shrugging off the incident. "Transcontinental tourists must not be troubled with trifles like this."[57] Leaving Shedden at 11:00 AM on September 12, the pair drove 170 miles in fourteen hours to tie their Iowa one-day distance mark.

Asleep at the Tiller

After four full days in Ontario, the men spent the morning of Sunday, September 13, Day 70, touring the Canadian side of Niagara Falls. They then crossed to Buffalo, New York, and spent the night in Palmyra. On the following day's drive from Palmyra to Little Falls, New York, "our best road down the Mohawk Valley was on the towpath along the banks of the Erie Barge Canal," Whitman said. "Delays would occur about every hour, however, when mules were sighted up ahead pulling barges."[58] Each encounter with mules forced the men to pull off the road and kill the engine or risk scaring the animals. Sharing the public highways with horses was just as ticklish, Whitman said. "We find even in our travels across New York State many horses that look with critical eye on the automobile, and to avoid any possibility of accident the machine should be stopped at a reasonable distance."[59]

In their rush to reach New York City, they left Palmyra at 4:30 AM on Monday, September 14, Day 71, and reached Little Falls 18½ hours later. But it was slow going on rural New York roads. Whitman complained: "The roads down the Mohawk Valley to Albany are poor. Such roads are a disgrace to a State, especially through so wealthy and populous a district—large cities only a few miles apart and the most abominable road of cobble stones and mud thrown in 'most any old way.'"[60]

Weary from ten weeks of travel and nearing the end of a nineteen-hour travel day on Tuesday, September 15, Whitman dozed off on a bridge approaching Poughkeepsie, New York. "Ham was wide awake, fortunately, and grabbed the tiller, straightening her up before we hit anything!" he wrote.[61] The pair reached Peekskill about noon the next day and would likely have reached New York City that evening. But the strong winds and thunderstorms that moved through just as they reached Peekskill had flooded the roads ahead, forcing them to halt (see Fig. 82).

Fig. 82. Whitman, *fore-ground*, and Hammond enter Peekskill, New York, dressed for wet weather; flooded roads ahead would force them to halt for the day (MHS).

Bleary-Eyed Drivers Reach Gotham

In a rainstorm at about 3:30 PM the next day, Thursday, September 17, the men arrived at the New York City garage at 60th and Broadway where the car would be stored.[62] Whitman and Hammond "weigh normally about 180 pounds," the *New York Herald* related. "On the trip the former lost twenty pounds and the latter fifteen pounds."[63]

Cycle and Automobile Trade Journal reported:

As they finished, Messrs. Whitman and Hammond looked not unlike the old-time six-day [bicycle] riders at the completion of a record-smashing grind of the continuous order.

They were burned by sun and wind to the color of an Indian, bleary eyed and muddy as the result of the run from Yonkers in the rain.[64]

Another report noted, "Whitman says that he would not do it again for $100 a day, while Hammond, being young and robust, would start back to-morrow."[65]

Starting at 3:00 PM on July 6 and finishing at about 3:30 PM on September 17, 1903, and adjusting for the three-hour time difference, the trip's elapsed time was 72 days, 21 hours, 30 minutes. That compares to 63 days, 12 hours, 30 minutes for Dr. H. Nelson Jackson's Winton, and 62 days, 2 hours, 25 minutes for Tom Fetch's Packard. The Oldsmobile's trip to New York City actually consumed all or part of 74 calendar days. Whitman's logbook records delays to New York City totaling nineteen days—eleven days idle for repairs and eight days idle for muddy roads (see Table 8). Thus, the car's coast-to-coast running time was fifty-five days, compared to a running time of forty-six days for Jackson and fifty-two days for Fetch.

As with the earlier Winton and Packard crossings, the Oldsmobile's exact mileage will be forever open to speculation: Whitman and Hammond themselves did not know. The car's cyclometer—or odometer—reading was "approximately" 4,225 at New York City, Whitman wrote in his logbook. The reading was approximate because, as *Automobile* reported, the car lost three cyclometers on the trip. The Oldsmobile averaged 58 miles per day, or 2.41 mph for its elapsed time, making it the slowest of the three 1903 transcontinental autos (see Table 9).

Automobile contended that the Olds runabout set an Omaha–New York City speed record of 11½ days: 4 days to Chicago, 2 days to Detroit, and 5½ days to New York City. Whitman's logbook, however, shows the Omaha–New York City trip took 15 days' running time and 17 days' elapsed time. Jackson's elapsed time for the same trip was about 13 days; Fetch made it in about 19½ days.

At the conclusion of his run, Whitman sought to clear up all the rattlesnake rumors:

> The newspapers and magazines have written that Ham killed 20 rattlesnakes on the prairie and desert west of Omaha. Though he admits to having lost count he would put the figure at about 12 in number. We unavoidably ran over and killed two chickens, injured a farmer's pig, caused several horses to run away to say nothing of the Indians whom we scared out of their wits at the sight and sound of our "White Man's Thunder Wagon."[66]

In the Oldsmobile publicity booklet, however, Whitman—or, more likely, an advertising copywriter—asserted, "We killed rattlesnakes, scores of them, with the

Fig. 83. Hammond, *foreground*, and Whitman strain to hear as an unidentified city official greets them on the steps of New York's City Hall (MSU).

horsewhip" on the day Whitman and Hammond towed the disabled car into Lovelock, Nevada, behind a two-horse wagon.[67] If this was a "normal" day on the desert, the press had been far too conservative in estimating the total slaughter at just twenty snakes. Actually, Hammond had killed but one snake that day, Whitman noted in his logbook.

City Hall Ceremony

On Friday, September 18, the day after their arrival in New York City, Whitman and Hammond had the post office cancel the "water and grease-stained letter from the San Francisco mayor." Driving up City Hall's stone steps to the first landing in time for an 11:00 AM ceremony, they met a city official who escorted them inside (see Fig. 83). There, in a room crowded with reporters, New York City Mayor Seth Low read the July 6 letter aloud:

TABLE 8. Daily City-to-City Progress of the Oldsmobile, 1903

Day / Date	City–City	Mileage[a]
1 / July 6 Mon	San Francisco–Benicia, Calif.	n.a.
2 / July 7 Tue	Benicia, Calif.–Sacramento, Calif.	95
3 / July 8 Wed	Sacramento, Calif.–Placerville, Calif.	50
4 / July 9 Thu	Placerville, Calif.–Strawberry Glen, Calif.	35
5 / July 10 Fri	Strawberry Glen, Calif.–Carson City, Nev.	70
6 / July 11 Sat	Carson City, Nev.–Wadsworth, Nev.	75
7 / July 12 Sun	Wadsworth, Nev.–35 miles west of Wadsworth, Nev.[b]	35
8 / July 13 Mon	35 miles west of Wadsworth, Nev.–Lovelock, Nev.[c]	35
9 / July 14 Tue	*repair day in Lovelock, Nev.*	—
10 / July 15 Wed	Lovelock, Nev.–Dun Glen, Nev.	52
11 / July 16 Thu	Dun Glen, Nev.–Golconda, Nev.	n.a.
12 / July 17 Fri	Golconda, Nev.–Battle Mountain, Nev.	40
13 / July 18 Sat	Battle Mountain, Nev.–Dunphy, Nev.	25
14 / July 19 Sun	Dunphy, Nev.–Elko, Nev.	55
15 / July 20 Mon	*repair day in Elko, Nev.*	—
16 / July 21 Tue	*repair day in Elko, Nev.*	—
17 / July 22 Wed	Elko, Nev.–Deeth, Nev.	33
18 / July 23 Thu	Deeth, Nev.–Wells, Nev.	20
19 / July 24 Fri	Wells, Nev.–Tecoma, Nev.[d]	76
20 / July 25 Sat	Tecoma, Nev.–Kelton, Utah	75
21 / July 26 Sun	Kelton, Utah–Ogden, Utah	100
22 / July 27 Mon	*repair day in Ogden, Utah*	—
23 / July 28 Tue	*repair day in Ogden, Utah*	—
24 / July 29 Wed	Ogden, Utah–Morgan, Utah	25
25 / July 30 Thu	Morgan, Utah–Evanston, Wyo.	n.a.
26 / July 31 Fri	Evanston, Wyo.–East of Fort Bridger, Wyo.[e]	n.a.
27 / Aug. 1 Sat	East of Fort Bridger, Wyo.–Green River, Wyo.	65
28 / Aug. 2 Sun	Green River, Wyo.–Hallville, Wyo.	65
29 / Aug. 3 Mon	Hallville, Wyo.–Rawlins, Wyo.	95
30 / Aug. 4 Tue	Rawlins, Wyo.–Medicine Bow, Wyo.	62
31 / Aug. 5 Wed	Medicine Bow, Wyo.–Laramie, Wyo.	65

(cont'd)

32/ Aug. 6 Thu	Laramie, Wyo.–Fort Collins, Colo.	80
33/ Aug. 7 Fri	Fort Collins, Colo.–Denver	80
34 / Aug. 8 Sat	*repair day in Denver*	—
35 / Aug. 9 Sun	Denver–Orchard, Colo.	92
36 / Aug. 10 Mon	Orchard, Colo.–Julesburg, Colo.	141
37 / Aug. 11 Tue	Julesburg, Colo.–Paxton, Neb.	50
38 / Aug. 12 Wed	Paxton, Neb.–Brady, Neb.	35
39 / Aug. 13 Thu	Brady, Neb.–Cozad, Neb.	30
40 / Aug. 14 Fri	*rain day in Cozad, Neb.*	—
41 / Aug. 15 Sat	Cozad, Neb.–Elwood, Neb.	25
42 / Aug. 16 Sun	*rain day in Elwood, Neb.*	—
43 / Aug. 17 Mon	Elwood, Neb.–ranch near Minden, Neb.	56
44 / Aug. 18 Tue	ranch near Minden, Neb.–Minden, Neb.	10
45 / Aug. 19 Wed	*rain day in Minden, Neb.*	—
46 / Aug. 20 Thu	Minden, Neb.–Grafton, Neb.	80
47 / Aug. 21 Fri	Grafton, Neb.–Ashland, Neb.	100
48 / Aug. 22 Sat	Ashland, Neb.–Omaha, Neb.	50
49 / Aug. 23 Sun	*repair day in Omaha, Neb.*	—
50 / Aug. 24 Mon	*repair day in Omaha, Neb.*	—
51 / Aug. 25 Tue	*repair day in Omaha, Neb.*	—
52 / Aug. 26 Wed	*rain day in Omaha, Neb.*	—
53 / Aug. 27 Thu	*rain day in Omaha, Neb.*	—
54 / Aug. 28 Fri	*rain day in Omaha, Neb.*	—
55 / Aug. 29 Sat	*rain day in Omaha, Neb.*	—
56 / Aug. 30 Sun	*rain day in Omaha, Neb.*	—
57 / Aug. 31 Mon	Omaha, Neb.–Atlantic, Iowa	65
58 / Sept. 1 Tue	Atlantic, Iowa–Des Moines, Iowa	100
59 / Sept. 2 Wed	Des Moines, Iowa–Cedar Rapids, Iowa	170
60 / Sept. 3 Thu	Cedar Rapids, Iowa–Rochelle, Ill.	150
61 / Sept. 4 Fri	Rochelle, Ill.–Chicago	75
62 / Sept. 5 Sat	Chicago–Elkhart, Ind.	100
63 / Sept. 6 Sun	Elkhart, Ind.–Toledo, Ohio	150
64 / Sept. 7 Mon	Toledo, Ohio–Detroit	ca. 55
65 / Sept. 8 Tue	*repair day in Detroit*	—
66 / Sept. 9 Wed	Detroit–Wheatley, Ont.	40

67 / Sept. 10 Thu	Wheatley, Ont.–Shedden, Ont.	80
68 / Sept. 11 Fri	*repair day in Shedden, Ont.*	—
69 / Sept. 12 Sat	Shedden, Ont.–Niagara Falls, Ont.	170
70 / Sept. 13 Sun	Niagara Falls, Ont.–Palmyra, N.Y.	100
71 / Sept. 14 Mon	Palmyra, N.Y.–Little Falls, N.Y.	130
72 / Sept. 15 Tue	Little Falls, N.Y.–Poughkeepsie, N.Y.	160
73 / Sept. 16 Wed	Poughkeepsie, N.Y.–Peekskill, N.Y.	45
74 / Sept. 17 Thu	Peekskill, N.Y.–New York City	45
75 / Sept. 18 Fri	*repair day in New York City*	—
76 / Sept. 19 Sat	New York City–Hartford, Conn.	125
77 / Sept. 20 Sun	Hartford, Conn.–Waltham, Mass.	125
78 / Sept. 21 Mon	Waltham, Mass.–Boston	10
79 / Sept. 22 Tue	Boston–Kennebunk, Me.	100
80 / Sept. 23 Wed	Kennebunk, Me.–Portland, Me.	28

SOURCES: Lester L. Whitman's accounts in auto journals; Whitman's logbooks in John S. Hammond II, *From Sea to Sea in 1903 in a Curved Dash Oldsmobile*; and articles in auto journals and newspapers.

[a] There were no mileage reports on four days; these are indicated by n.a., for "not available." Because of these gaps, this list adds to 4,100 miles. The best estimate is that the Oldsmobile traveled 4,225 miles to New York City. Adding the 388 miles to Portland, Maine, gives a total trip mileage of 4,613.

[b] The car sheared a transmission pin in the desert midway between Wadsworth and Lovelock. The men walked for four hours before flagging down a freight train to ride into Lovelock.

[c] Whitman and Hammond hitched the disabled car to a wagon and towed it the 35 miles into Lovelock.

[d] The men left Tecoma at 4:30 PM but got lost in the desert and returned after dark to spend the night in Tecoma. To avoid driving through deep sand, they parked 5 miles east of town and walked in.

[e] Lost and unable to see by their flickering carriage lamps, the travelers slept in the desert east of Fort Bridger.

Mr. L. L. Whitman is starting from here at 11 o'clock this morning to make a tour across the continent from San Francisco to New York on an Oldsmobile. San Francisco sends her greetings to the great metropolis of New York.

Any courtesy that may be extended to Mr. L. L. Whitman by you will be greatly appreciated by yours very truly. —E. E. Schmitz, Mayor.[68]

That afternoon, Whitman and Hammond prepared for the last leg of their trip by installing new piston rings and grinding valves. They drove 125 miles to Hartford, Connecticut, the next day, Saturday, September 19, and put in another 125 miles over good roads on Sunday, September 20, to reach Waltham, Massachusetts. Early on

TABLE 9. Relative Speeds of the First Three Transcontinental Autos, 1903

Driving team (miles traveled)	Miles per day (elapsed time)	Miles per day (running time)	Avg. speed (elapsed time)
1903 Winton Dr. H. Nelson Jackson and Sewall Crocker (5,500 miles[a])	87	120	3.61 mph
1903 Packard Tom Fetch, Marius C. Krarup, and N. O. Allyn (4,000 miles)	64	77	2.68 mph
1903 Oldsmobile Lester L. Whitman and Eugene I. Hammond (4,225 miles)	58	77	2.41 mph

[a] Estimates are that Jackson and Crocker traveled between 5,000 and 6,000 miles; 5,500 miles is thus a compromise figure.

September 21, Day 78, they drove the 10 miles to Shattuck and Sons, Boston's Olds agency, where they met reporters and photographers (see Fig. 84), in addition to members of Hammond's family—his twin brother Joe, his oldest brother Jim, a sister, and their father.

Next morning, Tuesday, September 22, at City Point Beach with a photographer on hand, Whitman drove the auto's front wheels into Massachusetts Bay, thereby marking the ceremonial ending of their Pacific–Atlantic trek (see Fig. 85). Although it had been reported that Tom Fetch and Marius Krarup had intended to dip Old Pacific's wheels into the Atlantic, they had been too tired upon their arrival in New York City to do so. Whitman would later claim that he and Hammond were the first true "sea-to-sea" drivers.[69]

Puffing into Portland

Following their car's baptism in the Atlantic, the pair drove 100 miles north that day through a narrow strip of New Hampshire to reach Kennebunk, Maine, after nightfall. On Wednesday morning, September 23, they drove the final 28 miles to reach downtown Portland, Maine, at 10:00 AM. There, Whitman was met by his mother and sister Lizzie. In the commercial heart of the city, at Monument Square, site of an 1891 memorial to Portland's Civil War soldiers, the transcontinentalists posed in the

Fig. 84. Hammond, *left*, and Whitman pose beside the car in Boston (OHC).

Fig. 85. With flags flying, Whitman, *foreground*, and Hammond dip their wheels in the Atlantic Ocean at Boston's City Point Beach (FLP).

Oldsmobile as press photographers recorded the end of their trip (see Fig. 86). Wednesday's *Portland Evening Express* heralded their arrival with a lengthy article under a bold headline, "Pacific to Atlantic":

> The first automobile to make the transcontinental trip from San Francisco to Portland, came puffing over Vaughans bridge, up over the steep rise on Danforth street and through the city streets until it drew up at the automobile station on Plum street. The last mile of those between the western and the eastern ends of the journey was completed almost on the stroke of 10, and the machine settled back on the Portland pavements as if it enjoyed the prospect of a rest.
>
> The men who had driven the auto across country were Messrs. L. L. Whitman and E. I. Hammond, who started from the Pacific coast on July 6, and have just completed the most remarkable tour in the history of the American automobile. News had arrived in the city that the machine was on the way, and several parties went out to the Saco road to meet the tourists. But evidently they missed the travelers, for the auto came into the city with all flags flying but without escort. . . .
>
> Leaving Kennebunk this morning at 8 o'clock they followed the telegraph poles into Portland and drew up as described above at their eastern terminus at 10 o'clock. The machine bore some of the dust of fifteen odd states and the hundreds of towns through which it had passed, and some of a good coating of the mud of the Mississippi lowlands, but on top of all the good old dust of York county sat triumphant. The travelers were

tanned and grimed with the long travel over the roads but none the worse for their experiences. . . .

After stopping before the post office where photographs were taken, the tired engine responded to the lever and brought the machine up to Monument square where it became the center of another interested group. The questions that the two transcontinental travelers have answered have probably been the same from the Pacific to the Atlantic; so they laughed when someone asked, "Come far?" and another, "How do you like traveling that way?"[70]

"The Most Wonderful Journey"

The men journeyed from San Francisco to Portland in an elapsed time of 78 days, 16 hours (adjusted for the three-hour time difference between coasts). The eighty calendar days of the journey included sixty days of driving plus twenty idle days—twelve for repairs and eight for muddy roads.

The coast-to-coast Oldsmobile may have been slower than Jackson's Winton and Fetch's Packard, but the Olds Motor Works' ads (see Fig. 87) indicate that the automaker was still overjoyed by the record:

> The Oldsmobile trans-continental trip is the most wonderful automobile journey ever made. From San Francisco to New York, over mountains, across deserts, through sand and mud, the Oldsmobile won its way, surmounting every difficulty and proving to the world it is "built to run *and does it*."
>
> By this remarkable trip, the Oldsmobile demonstrates its equality with the high priced touring car. Twenty-three years' experience in the manufacture of gasoline engines enables us to make a perfect motor. Simplicity is the key-note of the entire mechanism, and it is this perfect mechanical construction which leaves "Nothing to Watch but the Road" and which made possible this runabout's wonderful trip from the Atlantic to the Pacific.[71]

In driving from San Francisco to Maine, the Oldsmobile drivers traversed more distant points than either of the first two transcontinental cars. Whitman's logbook recorded 388 additional miles from New York City to Portland, on top of the approximately 4,225 miles between San Francisco and New York City, for a total of 4,613 miles. In a celebratory mood afterward, Whitman was emboldened to state: "The experts divine that we traveled about 5,000 hard, honest miles[,] though our oft replaced cyclometers didn't stay on the Olds long enough to refute the claim."[72]

The runabout burned 239.5 gallons of gasoline to average slightly more than 19 miles per gallon for 4,613 miles. Including stops, Whitman and Hammond spent an average of 9 hours, 37 minutes on the road during each of the thirty-six days for which

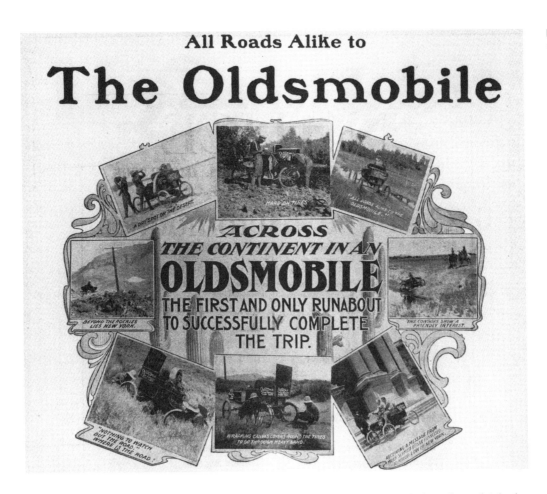

Fig. 87. Part of a Sept. 3, 1903, *Motor Age* ad.

they logged their exact travel time. During the thirty-one travel days for which the men recorded both their travel time and distance, the car averaged 7.8 miles per hour. In interviews, Whitman consistently asserted that the car needed just four new tires to complete the trip. But his logbook entries record that the car received twice that number: one new tire on the car and one spare in Omaha; two new Diamond tires in Chicago; and four new Diamond tires for the four new wheels received in Detroit.

Whitman Rides Again

"I will return to my home in Pasadena, Cal., in a few days," Whitman told *Motor Age*, "and as I look from the [railroad] car window at the dreary sage brush deserts I shall have no thought of 'gas, spark or combustion.'"[73] His resolve softened. Whitman agreed to drive the Olds transcontinental car in an eight-day, 793-mile endurance run from New York City to Pittsburgh via Cleveland, which ended on October 15, 1903.

In the same contest, Tom Fetch was at the wheel of his transcontinental Old Pacific. Heavy rains and flooding early in the run created the worst driving conditions Whitman had yet seen. The weather halted or delayed trains for thirty-six hours, knocked out telegraph lines, and literally washed away or obliterated many records kept by official observers.

"I might cross the continent a dozen times and never meet with such an experience," Whitman said after the Day 2 drive from Pine Hill to Fredonia, New York. "I prefer the discomforts of the desert to the discomforts of such a trip as that of to-day right in New York State." A "Fredonia" car driven by F. L. Thomas "bent its radiator by running into Whitman's Oldsmobile" at Newburgh, New York, on Day 1. There were thirty-four starters in the contest. Whitman won a first-class certificate for the Olds Motor Works as one of twenty-five drivers who overcame the weather and other obstacles to complete the run. He also finished fourth in his class—cars selling for $1,000 or less.[74]

Whitman made three more record-setting transcontinental trips. He drove air-cooled Franklin autos on transcontinental trips in 1904 and 1906, both with co-driver C. S. Carris (see Chapters 5 and 6). Whitman and Hammond joined forces for a second and final transcontinental run together in 1910, when they drove a Reo auto across the country in 10 days, 18 hours, 12 minutes. That record stood until 1916.

During several weeks spent at the factory and at Olds agencies in the East after the long drive in 1903, Hammond lectured mechanics, salesmen, and even engineers on the car's strengths and weaknesses. He eventually returned to the garage business in Pasadena. Later, he taught poultry husbandry and judged poultry shows. For a time, he took charge of breeding birds at San Simeon, the sprawling California ranch owned by publisher William Randolph Hearst.[75]

Car Gone, Not Forgotten

What became of the curved dash Olds runabout remains a mystery. During the 1970s, Hammond's son, John S. Hammond II, speculated that Whitman's 1903 runabout was later updated at the factory to become "Old Scout," the winner of the Olds factory's 1905 race from New York City to Seattle:

> Mr. Olds told my dad and me that he had Whitman drive the same car in the New York to Pittsburg Endurance Run; then it was shipped back to the factory where it was "modernized" as a 1904 model, replacing the wire wheels with wooden-spoked ones, etc. It was

then christened "Old Scout" and was one of the two cars driven from New York to Portland, Oregon, in the "race" to the Lewis and Clark Exposition.[76]

Hammond's further research evidently failed to support his theory, for his 1985 book fails to mention the notion that the 1903 transcontinental car became Old Scout. The Whitman–Hammond car was displayed at the St. Louis World's Fair, according to *Automobile*.[77] Hammond reported that Ransom E. Olds then bought it, before leaving the company to set up Reo Motor Car Company in 1904. A prominent Reo investor was Reuben Shettler, the Los Angeles Oldsmobile agent who had employed both Whitman and Hammond as mechanics.[78] What happened next is lost to history. "There is no record of what became of the little record breaker in later years nor has its serial number ever become known to auto historians," the younger Hammond wrote.[79]

If the car is gone, its accomplishments are not forgotten. Three contemporary owners of early curved-dash Oldsmobiles—Gary Hoonsbeen (1902), Roy Bernick (1903), and Joseph Merli (1904)—re-created the 1903 trip on the eighty-fifth anniversary of the first Olds curved-dash runabout. Their 1985 trek followed approximately the same route that Whitman and Hammond took. The Oldsmobile company commemorated this latter-day outing by publishing a thirty-two-page booklet that also traced the history of its early autos.[80]

Such a Small Machine

No one can take away the glory that belongs to the men who piloted the first two autos across North America. Whitman and Hammond, however, will go down in history for achieving a transcontinental crossing in the car of the future—a lightweight, simple, and cheap machine of the masses. The curved-dash Olds was much like the Model T, the Ford automobile that revolutionized transportation and life itself by putting America on wheels.

Americans love to cheer for the underdog. Winton and Packard executives were undoubtedly horrified to see how the comparatively small Oldsmobile runabout was attracting more attention, seemingly, than their own transcontinental cars. Because of the Oldsmobile's low weight, low power, and low price, Whitman and Hammond's transcontinental trip was said to be, "in some respects the most remarkable of the three."[81]

"Their feat is of more than passing value and even a greater one than accomplished by their two predecessors," asserted Denver's *Rocky Mountain News*, "in that they have traveled in what might be called a 'pony rig.'" The *Chicago Inter Ocean* concurred: "When the fact that the Oldsmobile tourists came across the country in such a small machine, and the size, weight, and power of the cars are taken into consideration, it must be acknowledged that their trip was indeed a bold one, and should be considered one of the big feats in the automobile world." Added *Cycle and Automobile Trade Journal*: "When one considers the hardship of this journey as described by previous transcontinental tourists who used heavy cars, the glory of the accomplishment of the Oldsmobile seems greater than when viewed alone."[82]

The trip, in fact, proved what the Olds company frequently argued in its advertising: small cars could perform as well as their heavier, more powerful, and more expensive counterparts—and they could do it more cheaply, as well. Gas consumption is a case in point. Jackson's Winton averaged about 7 miles per gallon. Total figures are unavailable for Fetch's Packard, but it averaged 12 mpg from San Francisco to Salt Lake City. The light Olds runabout averaged more than 19 mpg for its coast-to-coast trip.

The Oldsmobile trip also reinforced the lessons of the earlier Winton and Packard crossings: cars break down easily and often, travelers are at the mercy of the weather, and it is easy to stray from unmarked primitive trails. As for the breakdowns, the Oldsmobile's experiences emphasized that long-distance automobiles needed tending by seasoned mechanics.

Whitman and Hammond epitomized the ever-resourceful motorist. They used hand tools to laboriously drill out and pin a broken crankshaft in Nevada; found gasoline where there appeared to be none available in parts of Nevada and Utah; filled a broken tire casing with cracked corn when they ran out of spares in Nebraska; and repaired a collapsed wire wheel in Canada. By acting coolly in emergencies, they demonstrated, as did the Winton and Packard crewmen, that it was not enough to simply handle an auto skillfully. A transcontinentalist also had to be ingenious, adaptable, patient, and persevering.

In retrospect, the 1903 Olds trip is significant for one other reason. Of all the cars that set the coast-to-coast records detailed in this book, only the Oldsmobile is still in production.

As a driver and strategist, Whitman gained something that neither he nor any of the others aboard the three 1903 transcontinental cars had—experience. The Olds trip gave him an edge over his imitators because he learned the route and the probable weather conditions along it. On later journeys, he would prepare, equip, and drive his cars accordingly. In driving, as in other endeavors, practice makes perfect, as Whitman was to prove when he smashed the coast-to-coast speed record in 1904, and then again in 1906 and 1910. He would make his 1904 trip in a car that, while lightweight, differed in two respects from the Oldsmobile: it was air-cooled and it had 4 cylinders instead of 1.

A FASTER RUN IN AN
AIR-COOLED AUTO

5

"I struck the ground about twenty feet directly in front of the car, and Carris at the wheel was thrown out at the side."

—Lester L. Whitman, describing the effects of hitting a
stump in Wyoming

FAVORED BY MUCH BETTER WEATHER than a year earlier, Lester L. Whitman in 1904 halved the existing record by driving a Franklin from San Francisco to New York City in 32 days, 17 hours, 20 minutes. He shared the wheel with C. S. Carris, an employee of the H. H. Franklin Manufacturing Company of Syracuse, New York. Their stunning performance over a 4,500-mile route "came as a surprise to all automobilists," *Scientific American* exclaimed.[1]

The record stood for two years. Much of the credit for the 1904 record-setting run goes to good weather and a good car—a 10-horsepower Franklin runabout, the first

4-cylinder and first air-cooled auto to travel between coasts. In contrast to his 1903 Oldsmobile trip, Whitman reported a remarkably small number of breakdowns, though neither he nor the automaker were entirely forthcoming about the auto's repair record.

The Franklin's drive chain broke once and the tires suffered just two punctures between San Francisco and New York State, Whitman said. On the last day of the run, a rear spring broke when the car hit a ditch near Peekskill, New York. There were no other breakages, said Whitman.

The first person to make two transcontinental trips, Whitman had followed nearly the same route a year earlier in a 1-cylinder Olds runabout. Between the Oldsmobile's frequent breakdowns and unusually heavy rains, however, the 1903 trip had taken 72 days, 21 hours, 30 minutes. Because of his earlier trip, however, Whitman "has the advantage of his former experience."[2]

Franklin a Design, Style Leader

The H. H. Franklin Manufacturing Company sponsored the transcontinental test primarily to advertise the overhead-valve engine it had been making since producing its first autos in 1902. Whitman wrote: "The engine is a four-cylinder air-cooled motor, this being the first air-cooled car to tackle the heat and sand of that hard part of the desert route from Reno to Ogden (600 miles) and from Ogden to Cheyenne (400 miles)." Foreseeing a sales boost from a successful cross-country run, Franklin was willing to pay Whitman well for his services. How well? "It had been supposed by many of the San Francisco automobilists that the journey could not be made with an air cooled motor," reported the *New York Tribune*. "Whitman had a different opinion, however, and is said to have won $3,000 by proving it could."[3]

Herbert H. Franklin incorporated the H. H. Franklin Manufacturing Company in 1895 to make metal castings in Syracuse, New York. In 1901, the firm amended its articles of incorporation to include automobile manufacturing; midway through 1902 the company began turning out an automobile designed by a young Cornell University engineering graduate, John Wilkinson. First-year production totaled thirteen Franklin autos. By 1921, when the company produced 8,536 automobiles, the Franklin factory had 34 acres of floor space and 4,300 employees.[4]

Never among the largest U.S. automakers, Franklin's annual production nonetheless topped 10,000 three times during the 1920s: 10,552 in 1920, 10,130 in 1923, and

Fig. 88. Goggles at the ready, Whitman, *left*, and Carris pose in the transcontinental Franklin (HHFC).

14,432 in 1929. Guided by Wilkinson's engineering, however, the firm was a style and design leader, particularly in the use of weight-saving aluminum. The Franklin's 4-cylinder, overhead-valve engine was revolutionary by 1902 standards. The company was among the first to introduce a 6-cylinder engine (1906); a pressure-fed, recirculating oiling system (1912); a closed car (1913); aluminum in place of cast-iron pistons (1915); and connecting rods of aluminum alloy (1922).

During the Great Depression, Franklin held on longer than many independents—the non-independents being Chrysler, Ford, and General Motors. But Franklin production dropped steadily between 1930 and 1933—from 6,000 to 3,000 to 2,000 to 1,000 automobiles, in round numbers. With liabilities of $2.54 million far outweighing assets of $543,999, Franklin filed for bankruptcy on May 22, 1934. A reconstituted company, Aircooled Motors Incorporated, made Franklin engines in Syracuse for years afterward, primarily for aviation. The approximately fifty rear-engine autos that the Tucker Corporation of Chicago began producing in 1948 used modified Franklin helicopter engines.

The Men and the Machine

Clayton S. Carris, 27, a trim Michigan native who "had never been in the far West before," would act as mechanic and Whitman as driver on the trip, according to one source (see Fig. 88). More believable, given Carris's driving experience, is the *New York Herald*'s assertion that "the pair alternated in driving the car." Whitman later confirmed that was the case, in a 1905 promotional booklet that he wrote and Franklin published (see Fig. 89): "Carris and myself took turns in running the car, 25 to 50 miles or so, each at the wheel."[5] In later years, Carris became one of the most respected endurance drivers of the era. By the start of his 1904 Franklin journey, Whitman, 43, who lived just outside Los Angeles in Pasadena, had regained the 20 pounds he lost during his 1903 transcontinental trip in an Oldsmobile.

By August 1904, some U.S. automakers were introducing their 1905 cars. But Whitman's two-passenger, 10-horsepower Franklin runabout was clearly a 1904 model. The smallest of Franklin's 4-cylinder engines was rated at 10 horsepower in 1904 but 12 horsepower in 1905.[6] Franklin's 1904 Model A "light runabout" was a small car. With an aluminum body on a wooden frame, a wheelbase measuring 78 inches and tires of 28 × 3¼ inches, the car weighed 1,100 pounds. It sold for $1,600 with a top, or $1,400 without. Dark red was the standard finish, according to a 1904 automobile journal, "but blue or Brewster green can also be had."[7]

Until well after 1910, the typical U.S. auto had its transmission in one of three places: amidships, between the engine and rear axle but mounted independently; on the rear axle; or integral with the engine—the design that prevails today. The 1904 Franklin 2-speed planetary transmission "is in an oil-tight case attached directly to the engine base, so that the transmission cannot get out of alignment."[8]

Equipped with an engine transversely mounted under the hood, and having a bore and stroke of 3¼ inches, the 1904 chain-driven light runabout could achieve a top speed of 30 miles per hour. Whitman and Carris proved it when they "let out the vehicle at a

Fig. 89. Cover of Whitman's account, published as a Franklin promotional booklet (HHFC).

30-mile clip on some of the alkali lakes" west of Ogden, Utah. A larger, 24-horsepower, shaft-driven Franklin could attain 40 mph. In contrast to its bigger brother, the 10-horsepower model had no engine cooling fan. Whitman's model normally carried 7.5 gallons of gas.[9]

Loading Up and Heading Out

Loaded with the travelers' equipment, the red 10-horsepower 1904 Franklin runabout weighed 1,400 pounds. The men—Whitman at 176 pounds, and Carris at 156[10]— added 332 pounds more, for a total weight approaching 1,750 pounds. Whitman said the car weighed about 1,200 pounds, or 100 pounds more than the factory's official figure. Judicious but light packing was an issue of great import for the cross-country drivers:

> We have some 200 pounds of baggage, and even then we have tried to economize as much as possible. This baggage consists of one extra tire, three inner tubes, a camera, tools, extra spark plugs, some small extra parts for replacement, some chain, clothing, and last but not least, a canteen for water and an axe. You will find that you will need them in your business when you get out into the wilderness. We have a large hamper on the rear deck, and it is jammed full.[11]

Whitman also talked of packing a shovel, as he had in 1903. The extra parts included six batteries. The men also packed "ropes to wind round the tires" and a can of engine oil. At Wadsworth, Nevada, the pair bought "desert helmet-hats"—pith helmets—to shield them from the sun.[12]

Whitman did not mention bringing along the cotton-stuffed fabric "sand tires" that he lashed onto his rear pneumatic tires to help cross the Nevada desert in 1903 and none are visible in surviving trip photos. The car, however, appears to have carried a roll of canvas in the western United States (see Fig. 90), which the men may have spread on the sand for traction, as Tom Fetch and Marius C. Krarup did in 1903.

The 200 pounds of parts and equipment represented 100 fewer pounds than what Whitman and Eugene I. Hammond had piled onto their 800-pound Olds runabout the previous year. In reporting on the start of the 1904 run, the *San Francisco Chronicle* explained: "They will not run nights and carry very little equipment."[13] As it later developed, the men did do some night traveling east of Toledo, Ohio.

Whitman and Carris slightly modified their car by doubling its gas capacity to 15 gallons and installing "double-tube" Diamond tires, which were the standard size. As with the 1903 Olds crossing, Whitman lined up gasoline for the route ahead. "No difficulty was found in obtaining gasolene when wanted, though for safety's sake supplies had been shipped ahead by Mr. Whitman to many places in the West," wrote the *New York Herald*.[14]

Still trying to find the best route, Whitman planned to deviate somewhat from his 1903 itinerary. In 1904, he traveled north ("the shorter, even if more difficult route") instead of south around Lake Tahoe on the California–Nevada border. Generally, Whitman planned to follow the Southern Pacific Railroad from San Francisco to Ogden, the Union Pacific to Omaha, Nebraska, and, at Clinton, Iowa, cross the Mississippi River, "thence to Chicago and eastward through South Bend, Toledo, Cleveland, Erie, Buffalo, Albany and down the east bank of the Hudson to New York City."[15]

Fig. 90. The 1904 Franklin appears to carry a roll of canvas strapped atop the tarp covering the men's supplies. Whitman snapped this photo at an unidentified location, evidently in Nevada (HHFC).

By early in 1908, with three coast-to-coast runs to his credit, Whitman knew the way so well that he described it in detail for the New York–Paris racers, who would drive from east to west. The entire road from New York to Chicago "is pretty free from difficulty," the veteran driver said in 1908. "Illinois, after a rain, produces some sticky black mud. So does Iowa, especially along the Skunk River flats." Likewise, the Platte River in Nebraska could determine a motorist's speed and route through that state, he said. "This river varies in depth and width according to the amount of rain or melted snow that is being carried down from the Wyoming and Montana mountains. Sometimes for weeks it overflows its banks, washing out bridges and flooding the low lands for miles. In this case it would be necessary to take to the sand hills, where traveling would be slow and more or less road building necessary."

Every six or eight miles along the Union Pacific tracks—"they always have been [followed] by transcontinental automobilists to date"—motorists will encounter railroad section houses, "generally figured on as a sort of hotel," Whitman said. "If you happen to run in just before meal time the wife of the section boss will set an extra place for you, and the charge for a meal is generally two-bits (25 cents) or at most 35 cents."

Rough mountain trails and long runs between gas supplies were the norm in Wyoming. On a 150-mile stretch between Laramie and Rawlins, "gasoline can be purchased but once, at Hanna," he wrote. "From Rawlins to Rock Springs is another 150-mile stretch without gasoline, town, hotel, horse, trail. The section houses of the Union Pacific will have to be used for meals and lodging, but the occupants along this desert are as poor as Job's turkey, and ham and eggs and coffee without milk will comprise the lay-out." Another option was to stop for food or lodging at a ranch house, he said. "Part of this country is occupied by sheepmen and part by cattlemen. There is always a bitter warfare being waged between the two, and for the sake of peace if not actually safety, contestants [in the New York–Paris race] stopping at ranch houses will do well not to talk politics."

"Automobilists can be found among the inhabitants of both Rawlins and Rock Springs, who will give the travelers every possible aid within their power, while the blacksmith at Rawlins has straightened out so many sprung axles and respoked so many wheels belonging to transcontinental cars that he is almost ready to start in manufacturing complete machines." For that matter, the Union Pacific maintained machine shops at Laramie, Hanna, Rawlins, Rock Springs, and Green River, "where skilled machinists with powerful lathes can turn out complete automobiles if necessary," Whitman advised.[16]

Where in the City?

In 1903, Fetch and Krarup drove their Packard from San Francisco to New York City in a record 62 days, 2 hours, 25 minutes. Whitman was hesitant to predict that he could travel faster:

> Whether we shall beat the Packard time of sixty-one [*sic*] days I cannot say. If we should have many accidents it means much delay. If we meet much heavy rain in the East it means delay or slower traveling. Then it is a question how the air-cooled car will take to the hot desert sands. All of which makes calculation out of the question.[17]

The hardest part of his first trip came on the deserts of Nevada and Utah. "Here sand and sagebrush and poor roads make you want a balloon. In fact, a balloon would be the proper thing, and I will give you the advice to fly high at that. Here for 600 miles it is one great island plateau, burned and baked by the scorching sun."[18]

Whitman started from San Francisco on Monday, August 1, 1904, but the exact starting place and time is open to speculation. In the booklet he later wrote for the Franklin company, Whitman said he started at 5:00 PM from Golden Gate Park, and one surviving photo seems to support this contention (see Fig. 91). A different photo in the factory booklet, however, pictures "The start in front of the Cliff House, San Francisco, Cal."—the oceanside landmark north of Golden Gate Park where Whitman began his 1903 Oldsmobile trek.[19]

Fig. 91. A San Francisco pose taken before starting east shows Whitman at the wheel (HHFC).

The *San Francisco Chronicle* reported that Whitman and Carris started at 4:00 PM from the Pioneer Automobile Company garage, where Whitman had also stored his 1903 Oldsmobile. But the paper's accompanying photo depicts "L. L. Whitman and C. S. Carris leaving Jefferson Square," a park bounded by Golden Gate Avenue on the south, Eddy (north), Gough (east) and Laguna (west).[20] Regardless of their exact starting point, the autoists, undoubtedly eager to be off, did nothing more on Monday than cross the bay to Oakland, where they spent the night.

On Tuesday morning, August 2, Whitman and Carris drove to Sacramento:

> Leaving Sacramento after lunch, with the Sierra Nevada range dimly showing on the horizon, the Franklin, with full tanks of gasoline, headed for the mountain pass known as Emigrant Gap. In a few hours we reached the foot hills and began an easy ascent. On those western slopes the celebrated California peaches, pears and other fruits are raised in great quantities. . . . We made frequent stops to sample these tempting fruits, presented to us with true California liberality. If we had taken all that was offered, we would have stuck the Franklin on the first day's run.[21]

Ever Up We Climbed

Stopping at Colfax for the night, the men continued their eastward trek on Wednesday, August 3:

> When we left early in the morning, the summit was over fifty miles away, and as we neared that point, the road gradually grew worse. Large boulders had rolled into the road and streams trickling across the trail had cut deep ruts. Snow-capped peaks were occasionally seen. The scenery in places was magnificent. . . .
>
> Ever up we climbed on the low-speed gear for hours. Snow appeared at the roadside, although it was August. By Dutch Flat, Gold Run and other old-time mining centers we climbed. The streams, the banks, the hills themselves show the fierce onslaught of hydraulic mining of early days.
>
> At 5 p.m. the last grade was mounted and the Franklin stood 7,256 feet above sea level, surrounded by almost perpetual snow.
>
> We stopped to take a picture and look far away to the east where the dreaded deserts lay spread out like a panorama at our feet. We drank from the cold snow-fed stream and wished we could take it along to those waterless scorching sands ahead. I knew from experience how the remembrance of these snowy heights would rise up before us in the scorching days to come.
>
> Beautiful Donner Lake lay at our feet. The snow sheds of the Southern Pacific Railroad stretched away around the mountain sides like a huge serpent.
>
> We looked over the brakes and tightened the reverse, and then down over ledges and a rock-strewn trail, from which all dirt had seemingly been washed away into the valley

below, we cautiously descended. Again we wound along dizzy heights, ever downward; in one mile making a descent of 1,200 feet.

In a few minutes, although it seemed much longer, we were at the shore of the lake. After a six-mile spin along its shores through the sweet pine forests, we pulled up for the night at Truckee. . . . They hardly believed at the hotel that we left Colfax in the morning and came over the mountains.[22]

"Put Out Those Lights!"

On Thursday morning, August 4, the men started from Truckee, stopped for lunch in Reno, Nevada, and that afternoon set off into the desert of northwestern Nevada, hoping to cover the approximately 40 miles to Wadsworth. During the transcontinental trip, Whitman wrote letters to inform various auto journals of his progress. Though Whitman did not mention it in an August 7 letter to *MoTor*, other sources later reported that the men survived a holdup attempt on Thursday night, August 4: "Near Wadsworth, Nev., which they approached in the evening, the tourists were warned by a station agent not to stop in that vicinity because of many recent murders of travellers. Soon after the warning they were ordered to stop and put out their lights, but, paying no attention to the order, threw on high speed and raced into Wadsworth."[23]

According to a retrospective account differing in details: "Outside Wadsworth, Nevada[,] the two were held up after dark by three armed bandits. Lacking firearms, they jumped out with an axe and a shovel and stood their ground. On arriving in town they learned that there had been 20 murders nearby in the previous two weeks" —an improbably high number even by Wild West standards.[24]

Later, in the Franklin factory booklet, Whitman reported on an August 4 incident that may, or may not, have been a holdup attempt:

We reached Clark, a desert [railroad] station six miles west of Wadsworth, a little after dark. We had found deep sand in places and the road so bad that we were rather behind our expectations, and when we reached Clark, our lamps had been lighted some time.

Stopping for information at the station, the only building there, the agent told us that we had better get out of the country mighty lively, or stop at the station with him. He said we would very likely be held up by "road agents" if we camped or tarried in that vicinity. We learned at Wadsworth next day that twenty murders had been committed within two miles of that place in the two weeks past. . . .

We were warned not to stay. We were also warned not to leave. We chose to leave. We pulled out in the open desert and were going up a stiff grade about a mile from town, with the engine on low gear almost to the limit, when a gruff voice from the darkness said:

"Put out those lights, and damned quick, too!"

Instantly stopping the car, cutting off the gas from the bright acetylene headlight and clapping our caps over the oil lamps, we jumped from the car, and in less time than it takes to tell it, I grabbed the ax from the socket, and Carris had the shovel. After a moment's suspense, three men driving a pair of horses hitched to a light wagon and leading a third, saddled, rushed by.

It looked like "one on us;" but we were mighty glad to see them go, and we wasted no time in getting away at high speed into Wadsworth.[25]

Mules Move Mired Machine

On Friday morning, August 5, while Whitman and Carris bought desert pith helmets before leaving Wadsworth at 7:00 AM, residents told them "a terrible tale of woe" that was waiting for them ahead, Whitman recalled. "They said there was a big sand hill about a mile and a half east of the town where a railroad gang were at work changing the grade, and the road was all cut to pieces by heavy supply teams so that we would never be able to get over this ugly spot without help."[26] The men sent a man with a team of mules ahead, should the hill prove to be insurmountable. It did:

> We might have got around it by taking to the railroad track, but as the team was there we had them pull us through. The sand was nearly to our axle, and the grade was very steep up over the railroad track—a distance of several hundred yards. In places the differential and sprocket dragged in the sand. We cheerfully paid the driver $2.00 for the job, and I think his mules earned it.[27]

Ahead of them was the barren 70-mile stretch to Lovelock, on which Whitman and partner Eugene I. Hammond had broken down in their Oldsmobile a year earlier. As he had in 1903, Whitman drove across the 11-mile-long dry lake bed known as the Humboldt Sink, "hard and coated with a deposit of alkali dust, which the winds take up into spiral columns fifty to a hundred feet high" (see Fig. 92). "Sometimes many of these can be seen at a time and they present a weird sight."

> The sun heats the land like a furnace, and as the hot air rises, it gives place to a current of air from the Pacific and causes a light breeze. As we were traveling with the wind on our backs, the conditions were the worst possible for our air-cooled motor. The cylinders got hot, but not hot enough to cause trouble.
>
> Over this desert to Ogden, we made almost double the distance each day that I did last year with a water-jacketed engine.

Fig. 92. Whitman and the car in an unidentified desert setting—apparently the Humboldt Sink (HHFC).

Just before dark and after an awful day of heat, dust and sand, we sighted Lovelock far across the Sink. We pushed on hopefully, but were doomed to disappointment. To get off the Sink and find a road into the town was a hard question.

We chased all the trails and wheel tracks that gave any promise of a road, and after a lot of scout-duty, on foot and otherwise, we reached the town at one-thirty in the morning, where we had supper and passed the night.[28]

"We Felt Rather Chesty"

They spent the night of Saturday, August 6, in Mill City, very close to where Alexander Winton and Charles B. Shanks had called off their 1901 transcontinental attempt. Despite Whitman's earlier worries about crossing the desert, the two men experienced little trouble reaching Battle Mountain in north-central Nevada on Sunday, August 7, Day 7 of travel. "We have hit the trail good and hard, making remarkable progress and no trouble with machine," Whitman wrote to *MoTor* in his clipped, telegraphic style:

> While she grunts and snorts and flounders around in the sand drifts, we have not been troubled with hot cylinders. . . . In the deep sand we rope the wheels, and more than once we have taken the shovel and dug out the machine. The axe, too, is used on the brush and ridges [see Fig. 93]. We are already burned black as the Indians, who look at our "Red Devil" with awe. Once we had to take the railroad tracks, and bumped over the railroad ties to get by sand hills [see Fig. 94].

Fig. 93. Carris, *right*, digs up an obstruction in the trail near Carlin, Nevada. An ax-wielding Whitman stands by to assist (HHFC).

Fig. 94. Running on the railroad tracks in Nevada. From the car's lower left side hangs an ax; strapped atop the wicker basket is a shovel (HHFC).

We spent this forenoon in 28 miles of sand near Winnemucca; this afternoon made 62 miles from there to this place [Battle Mountain]. We left Golconda at 5:10 p.m. The people at this place said we were fools to strike out for Battle Mountain at that time of night, as it was 45 miles; said we would pass the night in the sage brush somewhere between these places, as there is not a stopping place or inhabitant over this distance. There is one watertank on the railroad.

We made the run and got in here before dark. Every mile was through continuous sage brush as far as the eye could see [see Fig. 95]. In fact, we felt rather chesty as we flew into the little desert town of saloons. As it was Sunday, most of the inhabitants were celebrating by getting drunk.[29]

One of his tricks for crossing the desert, Whitman said, was "we run the chain dry, without oil, finding this best in so much sand and dust, as it keeps bright and shiny, while if oiled it would be a mass of grit and grease."[30] The men, however, evidently stayed well oiled. A year earlier, someone in Wadsworth had given twelve bot-

Fig. 95. A stretch of Nevada's deep sand and continuous sagebrush (HHFC).

Fig. 96. Whitman, *left*, and Carris pose with their trophies (HHFC).

tles of chilled beer to the Packard transcontinentalists. Whitman and Carris likewise tapped into a supply of the bottled brew (see Fig. 96).

"Deep Channels" Force Detours

The drivers were lucky to find a trail between Lovelock and Ogden, Whitman recalled:

> In many places the country is cut up by deep channels, dry when we were there; but in winter taking down the water to the lower sands.
>
> In some places the banks were steep; heavy sand filled the river bed, and crossing was difficult [see Figs. 97 and 98]. Sometimes we had to follow the banks long distances to find a possible crossing, and at times, we were obliged to get the car up on the railroad track and bump over the sleepers [ties] to get past some bad ravine.
>
> Many times a day we had to use ax and shovel. The machine would flounder in a hole; or catch on a stump or high ridge in the road between the tracks. Then again, we would come upon long stretches of good road, laid out by Nature, not by man.

Fig. 97. Carris checks the ground clearance as the Franklin straddles a steep bank (HHFC).

Fig. 98. At another spot, Carris eases the car into an arroyo (HHFC).

Five hundred miles of these desert roads were opened by a man driving his team where Nature offered the least resistance. The next team followed the tracks of the first, and so after a time, some sort of a road was made, no part being improved that was passable by a wagon.[31]

In his post-run booklet, Whitman named the night stops east of Battle Mountain as Carlin (August 8) and Wells (August 9) in Nevada; and Terrace (August 10) and Ogden (August 11) in Utah. Thus the men reached Ogden at 5:00 PM on "the tenth day"—August 11.[32] Given the change to Mountain Time—and assuming that Whitman's reference to 5:00 PM was local time—he and Carris made the run in exactly one hour more than ten days from the car's San Francisco departure time of 5:00 PM on August 1.

One troubling inconsistency is Whitman's August 11 letter to *MoTor*, in which he reported that he and Carris had arrived in Ogden "yesterday," or August 10. This is an error. Although the *Ogden Standard* of August 12 made other reporting errors, it did correctly report that the pair had arrived in Ogden on August 11:

> A dust-covered automobile, carrying two begrimed passengers, arrived in Ogden yesterday afternoon [August 11], having made the trip from San Francisco overland in ten days. The two persons mentioned are L. L. Whittman [sic] and C. S. Carris, who have been on the coast for some time in the interests of an automobile company.
>
> When they started out it was not with the intention of making a record run, but merely to test the efficiency of their machine. Their destination is New York City and the whole trip is to be made in the automobile. . . .
>
> The record for an automobile run from San Francisco to New York is held by Tom Fitch [sic], who drove a Packard machine in sixty-one [sic] days. In all probability Whittman and Carris will beat this time, as they are now eight days [sic] ahead of Fitch's time for this part of the journey.[33]

Whitman's arrival in Ogden ten days after having left San Francisco thus bested Fetch's record of fourteen days, which was set the previous year (and was considerably better than the twenty days it had taken Whitman to get there during his 1903 Oldsmobile trip) (see Table 10).

Franklin Hits Stump

Whitman and Carris drove from Terrace to Ogden in a day, Whitman wrote in his August 11 letter to *MoTor*:

TABLE 10. Relative Times of the First Four Coast-to-Coast Cars (in days)[a]

Start–Finish	Jackson–Crocker (1903)	Fetch–Krarup (1903)	Whitman–Hammond (1903)	Whitman–Carris (1904)
San Francisco–Ogden, Utah	n.a.[b]	14	20	10
San Francisco–Denver	n.a.[b]	30	32	16
San Francisco–Omaha, Neb.	50	41	47	18[c]
San Francisco–Chicago	55	51	60	25
San Francisco–New York City	63	62	73	32

[a] Times are rounded.

[b] Jackson's route bypassed Ogden and Denver.

[c] This is an approximation; Whitman's exact Omaha arrival time is unknown.

You can understand we have hit the desert good and hard when I tell you we have been just ten days from San Francisco—best that has been done on these cussed sands and sagebrush wastes. We have had to dig out the machine and back up off stumps and rocks, let her down carefully into deep washes, and rush her up steep banks, plough weary miles of sand, and let out the vehicle at a 30-mile clip on some of the alkali lakes.

The sun just bakes the whole country to a crisp. We made 137 miles from Terrace yesterday and the streak of alkali dust must be still unsettled along old Salt Lake. We looked as though we had been powdered in flour, and one inch of dust lay on the rear of our car. We shall clean up the machine, look to the bearings, and hit her up [for] Denver to-morrow.[34]

The pair drove eastward through Wyoming to Laramie, and then traveled south to Denver. Their route through southern Wyoming took them through Evanston, Spring Valley, Green River (see Fig. 99), Rock Springs, Rawlins, and Rock River. At Spring Valley, about 16 miles east of Evanston, the Franklin had a potentially serious accident. According to Whitman,

While running fifteen miles an hour, our rear axle caught on a telegraph pole that had been cut off about a foot above the ground, and was hidden by tall grass growing between the wheel tracks.

We brought up good and solid, and both of us flew out over the car in regular circus fashion. I struck the ground about twenty feet directly in front of the car, and Carris at the wheel was thrown out at the side. We rolled over on the grass and looked at each other. Finding we were uninjured, except for a few bruises, we looked over the machine, which was still hanging fast to the post; and discovered *only a bent truss rod.*

Fig. 99. A small but attentive group of children inspects Carris and his steed at the Union Pacific depot in Green River, Wyoming (HHFC).

We backed off the stump and got away with never even a hint of further trouble or damage on that score.[35]

In a letter from Denver, Whitman reported a different result—that both the men and machine had emerged unscathed: "We hit a snag in the road and were both shot out of the rig twenty feet—finest thing you ever saw, no bucking broncho could do better. The machine and ourselves were uninjured."[36]

"Thrashing the Brush" to Denver

By 1904, Wyoming had bridged most of its deeper streams and rivers, although some of the bridges were crude wooden structures (see Fig. 100). Still, the Franklin had to ford many smaller streams:

In this state we lost our road several times and had to wander about for a few miles before finding it.
Changes in the road bed of the Northern [*sic*] Pacific and wire fences built along their tracks cut out miles of good roads; and obliged us to take some very rough places. We had

to cross the railroad in many places where no crossing has been made and climb steep grades at the same time.

One shower caught us near Rawlins while we were on an alkali desert, which was soon converted into a mass of slippery mud. The car refused to go except in lurches and in every direction but the right one; sometimes standing still with the rear wheels spinning. Ropes wound around the tires improved matters, and after traveling a few miles in this fashion, we reached the edge of the desert.[37]

Another hazard was a herd of ten thousand sheep blocking the road at a Wyoming location Whitman failed to specify (see Fig. 101). The men found better trails on the Laramie Plains, a high plateau in southeastern Wyoming, "the road-bed being a natural formation which packs to a smooth hard surface. The good roads and bracing air of this high altitude made this part of the trip very pleasant."[38]

They passed Fort Collins to reach Denver at about noon on Wednesday, August 17, in an elapsed time approaching sixteen days. This halved Whitman's 1903 time of thirty-two days and beat Fetch's thirty-day time by fourteen days. Denver had not been on Jackson's 1903 route. Leaving Colorado, the Franklin would travel northeasterly through Orchard and Julesburg to cross the Nebraska border (see Fig. 102). From Denver, Whitman wrote:

Fig. 101. A herd of sheep, faintly visible in the background, halts Whitman in Wyoming (HHFC).

Fig. 102. Carris stretches his legs at an unidentified Colorado stop (HHFC).

Our machine has not delayed us any and not even broken a spring. The chain parted once, and we had two punctures. Since leaving Ogden we have been wandering around in Wyoming along the Union Pacific; sometimes we were on the trail and sometimes on none, but we kept thrashing the brush till we hit something, if it was nothing more than a rabbit trail.

Sage hens were quite thick and at one place where we stopped over night we found two men that had ninety-four hens for one day's sport. All we had time to hit was chuck holes, creeks and rocks. . . . Yesterday a fierce shower hit us in the Rock[y] Mountains near Fort Collins, Colo., and delayed us on account of slippery mud.[39]

Stuck in a Creek

Because of the rain in northern Colorado, horses rescued the Franklin for the second and final time of the trip, as Whitman related in more detail in the 1905 Franklin publicity booklet:

Near Fort Collins we got in a bad washout. A cloud-burst some time before had taken the entire road-bed out of Owl Canon, and for half a mile, we had to run in the bottom of the creek.

About twenty-five emigrant wagons were trying to get through this pass when we arrived. They were "doubling up," that is, putting two teams to a single wagon, and having a bad time at that. After a hasty survey of this situation, we plunged the Franklin into the foaming water, and down the stream we went. Rocks were piled everywhere, but a rough path had been cleared, and we managed very well until[,] dropping down over one steep ledge into deep sand and gravel[,] the car refused to budge.

A team of horses stood within ten feet, the driver waiting to help up the next team. Water was up to the floor of our car, and rather than get out into the cold water and shovel out the rear wheels which had sunk into the deep gravel, I said:

"Fifty cents for fifty feet!"

The teamster waded in, dropped a chain over the axle, said "Get up," and in five minutes we were off again. This time, and that one bad spot outside of Wadsworth are the only instances when we had a team hitched to the car, and then it was more a matter of convenience than necessity.[40]

Whitman does not mention it, but photographs reveal that he and Carris had installed fenders on the car, evidently in Denver. Many other ocean-to-ocean drivers ran fenderless across the western United States. Even heavy-gauge steel fenders could rattle to pieces on rough roads, and removing them lightened a car. Running without fenders also made it easier to repair springs and tires, dig out buried wheels, rope the wheels for extra traction, and push the vehicle by grasping the wooden wheel spokes.

A Good Day in Omaha

The autoists arrived in Lexington, Nebraska, on Monday, August 22, Day 22, and left at 9:00 AM on Tuesday, after spending the night there, Lexington's *Dawson County Pioneer* implies. The cross-country record "promises to be broken if the Franklin drivers meet with no accident," the newspaper predicted. Whitman and Carris evidently shared that belief, for the "fine automobile" that reached Grand Island, some 80 miles east of Lexington, "was manipulated by two men, who were in elegant spirits over the success of their trip" (see Fig. 103).[41]

Conflicting dates in local newspaper accounts make it difficult to chart the Franklin's progress through Nebraska. Whitman's letters offered contradictory dates and times, as well. Published months later, his account in the factory booklet is frustratingly vague: the car reached Omaha "at noon of the fourth day from Denver," he wrote. Is this four *calendar* days or four *elapsed* days, which is equal to five calendar days? He neglects to say, and it does not matter—the statement is already meaningless because Whitman was similarly unclear about when he reached Denver. What is clear is that his trip across Nebraska was extremely fast in comparison to his muddy,

Fig. 103. Whitman examines a robust cornfield, mostly likely in Nebraska or Iowa (HHFC).

Fig. 104. Automobile fever was epidemic in Omaha, as Whitman (*at the wheel*) and Carris discovered during a stop at the H. E. Fredrickson agency (HHFC).

twenty-day crawl a year earlier. "How we flew!" he exclaimed. "And so did the dust, but in a long cloud behind us like the tail of a comet."[42]

The auto "passed through" Grand Island on Wednesday, August 24, according to that city's newspaper. But Omaha's three daily newspapers, however, disagree on whether Whitman and Carris reached Omaha on Tuesday, August 23, or Wednesday, August 24.

Regardless, automobile fever had gripped Nebraska's biggest city: Barney Oldfield and Alonzo Webb were in town, smashing world's records on a half-mile dirt track at the city's Sprague Street "driving park." In that atmosphere, and despite arriving in what the *Omaha Daily News* called a "machine covered with mud and the tires nearly worn through," Whitman and Carris nonetheless "created enthusiasm among the auto people, residents and visitors," observed the *Omaha World-Herald*. As Jackson had done a year earlier, Whitman and Carris posed for photographers outside H. E. Fredrickson's automobile and buggy showroom (see Fig. 104). Whitman, who also appeared before a crowd of three thousand racing fans, "drove on the track with his Franklin and after a hearty greeting started off on his way across Iowa," according to the *Omaha Daily Bee*.[43]

All in all, it was a good day to be driving a Franklin in Omaha. Local automobile agent H. E. Fredrickson, who over the years would greet many of the transcontinental drivers who passed through the city, starred in one race for amateurs. Fredrickson drove a Franklin against a Rambler in "one of the most interesting and exciting of the day's races." Kicking up clouds of dust, the autos roared around the track within a car's length of one another for most of the three-mile race. "Amid great excitement the Franklin finally got to the front on the last lap and finished three lengths to the good."[44]

On to Chicago

"From Omaha a four hundred mile run was made to the Mississippi River without a stop, in order to get over the clay and dirt roads of Iowa before the fall of rain, which threatened," the *New York Herald* reported. "Fortunately little rain was had on any part of the trip, though as a consequence the dust was heavy throughout."[45] Whitman described driving across Iowa in a two-day spurt: from Omaha to Des Moines, Iowa, on one day, and through Cedar Rapids to at least Fulton, Illinois, on the second. (He did not specify whether he and Carris stayed overnight in Des Moines or drove the two days without stopping to rest.)[46]

Chicago newspapers reported that the Franklin reached Chicago on Friday, August 26, after a twenty-five-day journey from San Francisco—thirty-five days ahead of Whitman's 1903 pace and twenty-six days ahead of Fetch's fifty-one-day record. "At Wheaton, twenty miles from the city, the first enthusiastic escort car met us," Whitman wrote. "From there on our ranks increased and when we got to Michigan Avenue we found a long row of cars tooting horns lined up to receive us. We were taken to the Chicago Automobile Club, 'watered,' fed and put to bed."[47] According to the *Chicago Inter Ocean*:

> The men were driving a ten horse-power Franklin and declare the light machine stood the trip in remarkable shape. The roads were good in some places, declared Mr. Whitman, poor in others, and some you couldn't discover at all.
>
> "Automobiling is having a great boom all over the far West now," declared Mr. Whitman, "and as yet there is no let up in sight. Especially on the coast is the motor car popular, and even in the vast plains you will find the rancher and well off farmer adding an auto to his stock.
>
> "In almost every Western city of any importance there is an automobile club doing everything in its power to boost the game, and many races, tests, and trips have been held during the season, and many more are scheduled. Denver will be the scene of a big race meet in the near future, and the promoters hope to secure all the best drivers of the country."[48]

Bicyclist Pedals for Petrol

From Chicago, where the car received a new set of Diamond tires, the autoists raced ahead to South Bend and Elkhart, Indiana, and on into Ohio. Whitman's stop in South Bend on Saturday, August 27, "will necessarily be short as he wants to 'keep going' and may stop only a few moments."[49]

The only time Whitman ran out of gas "was within two miles of Toledo," according to the *New York Herald*, "but, borrowing a bicycle and tin can, he rode back to the city for a supply." It was not Whitman on the bicycle, however, as he later revealed: "Once *only* did we get out of gasoline, and this was in Ohio. A boy and bicycle took [the] can and went a mile and a half for a gallon to put us into the near-by next town."[50] Except for this delay, Whitman and Carris drove steadily through northern Ohio, across the northwestern corner of Pennsylvania, and into western New York.

The transcontinentalists "were in the city five minutes Tuesday morning [August 30] on their Franklin automobile," reported the *Erie (Pa.) Dispatch*. "They left Cleveland at 3 a.m. and reached this city at 11:30, running down State street to the telegraph office so as to send a message to Buffalo and New York, the direction in which they were going. The men took dinner at a farm house 20 miles east of this city. They expect to reach New York before Saturday [September 3], which will be just two days more than a month."[51]

Since leaving Toledo, "the only sleep either Whitman or Carris got was what they could snatch while the car was whizzing through the country," the *Dispatch* reported. The men drove nearly continuously over a 325-mile stretch from Toledo to Rochester, New York, one newspaper reported. Other newspapers reported that on several days during their journey, the pair had traveled 200 miles or more, "and on other days the mileage was light to give the tourists opportunity to rest."[52]

"I don't know that anything very thrilling has happened," Whitman told reporters in Buffalo, New York. "Only had two punctures all the way and they happened west of Chicago. Of course we hurt the feelings of a few dogs but there was nothing more serious. Our air-cooled motor is working remarkably."[53] According to the *Erie Dispatch*, Franklin employee W. H. Beck, "who has been following Whitman by train, started out [from Buffalo] to meet him" in an auto. This was apparently later during the same day, August 30, that the car reached Erie. The *Dispatch* account continues:

Mr. Beck went out as far as the Fresh Air Mission's hospital at Athol Springs [New York], where he waited. There is a sharp turn in the road at that point. Beck had been waiting about 15 minutes when a noise like a sewing machine was heard and the next moment Whitman and Carris hove in sight looking [more] like mounds of dust than human beings. From Athol Springs into Buffalo Beck set the pace. The cars left the springs at exactly 4:25 o'clock and pulled up to the [Buffalo] automobile club rooms at 5.[54]

Gotham Welcome Vociferous

Another Franklin representative, C. R. Seymour, met the car at Ossining, New York, as the autoists drove toward New York City on Saturday, September 3, the last day of the trip (see Fig. 105). "The best previous time for the trip was cut almost in half, and the little four-cylinder machine dashed along Jerome avenue into New York as if its journey might have been begun only at Yonkers," the *New York Herald* reported. "San Francisco was left at five o'clock in the afternoon of August 1, and Central Bridge,

Fig. 105. Whitman, *left*, and Carris pose in their gauntlet-length driving gloves and leggings known as puttees. The escorting autos suggest that the setting is near New York City, perhaps Ossining, New York (NAHC).

COAST TO COAST BY AUTOMOBILE

New York, was reached at half past twelve o'clock" on the afternoon of September 3 (see Fig. 106). As the car drove along Jerome Avenue toward the Automobile Club of America clubhouse at 58th Street and Fifth Avenue, "a large delegation of tradespeople were out to welcome them."[55] The transcontinental auto officially ended its trip by reaching the clubhouse at 1:20 PM, according to the *New York Times*, and Whitman concurred. *Automobile* and the *New York Tribune*, however, put the arrival time at 1:40 PM.

"To say that the public was amazed is putting it mildly," Whitman later wrote. "Photographers, press agents and reporters were so vociferous in their welcome that we finally took refuge inside the Club House."[56]

Fig. 106. A group of noisy celebrants greets Whitman, *left*, and Carris at New York City's Central Bridge (AAMA).

If one assumes the car reached New York City at 1:20 instead of 1:40 PM on September 3, Whitman and Carris had crossed the continent by auto in 32 days, 17 hours, 20 minutes (subtracting three hours for the time difference between coasts). "The first and last days' runs were short ones of only 50 miles," *Scientific American* noted, "and it is probable that if the tourists had traveled a little longer on these and some of the other days when the roads were fairly good, they could have reduced the record to exactly thirty days."[57]

Regardless, Whitman and Carris had beaten Fetch's 1903 record time of 62 days, 2 hours, 25 minutes by more than twenty-nine days; they had beaten Jackson's 1903 time by nearly thirty days, and Whitman's 1903 time into New York City by forty days. Nearly all accounts put the 1904 Franklin's distance at 4,500 miles, meaning the drivers averaged nearly 138 miles per day for the elapsed time. The men rested one day in Ogden and a day or more in Denver, and possibly elsewhere, but conflicting accounts make it difficult to calculate the car's running time. The Franklin averaged about 20 miles per gallon of gasoline on the trip, press accounts indicate.

"The worst roads encountered were those over the mountains," *Motor World* wrote, "though Mr. Whitman says that east of Denver he found few stretches as bad as that from Utica to Albany." Whitman and Carris traveled 325 miles on their best day—between Cleveland and Rochester—and 75 miles "in the Nevada desert" on their worst.[58]

"No Break-downs of Consequence"

The Franklin company radiated praise for its automobile (see Fig. 107), claiming in one ad that the run to Ogden "across the blazing sands of the Great American Desert, throughout the broiling, sizzling days in the fierce middle of August, without stop, break or hitch . . . has settled the air-cooling question forever."[59] Whitman—who purposely deceived the press about his Oldsmobile's breakdowns and repairs in 1903—breezily summarized the Franklin's repair record:

> At Ogden, Denver, Omaha, Chicago and Toledo we opened the engine base, drew off the old oil, tightened the connecting rods when necessary, and put in [a] new supply of oil. . . . During the entire journey there were no break-downs of any consequence, nothing except of the most trivial nature, which was easily and quickly set right.[60]

Whitman had expressed similar sentiments about the Oldsmobile, though in reality that car had required some fifty new parts or sets of parts to complete the coast-to-

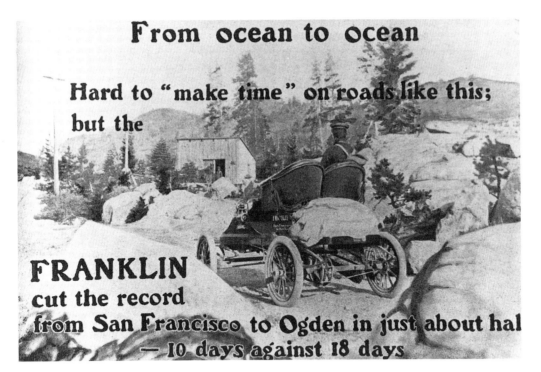

coast trek. Whitman revealed slightly more to the *New York Herald*: "Except for a chain that parted while in the West and a rear spring that was broken by the wheels dropping into a ditch near Peekskill there were no breakages at all, according to Mr. Whitman. These were quickly repaired and the delays were slight."[61] His Franklin undoubtedly had more mechanical problems than Whitman allowed, but must have performed better than the Oldsmobile to have lowered the transcontinental speed record so convincingly.

Good Weather; Few Mishaps

Fair weather helped, too. At the finish, Whitman credited good weather for making the fast trip possible. As *Scientific American* put it, "Very little rain was met with, and although the roads were extremely dusty, there were no muddy stretches to impede the progress of the little car." Generally dry roads meant "there were no serious accidents and few mishaps of any kind," the *New York Times* added. "There was also very little night riding done."[62] The travelers avoided making many long stops, either for repairs or for rest. Aside from overnight stays (see Table 11), the only stops of a half-day or more were made in Omaha, Chicago, Toledo and Syracuse,

TABLE 11. Probable Overnight Stops on the 1904 Franklin Trek

San Francisco start:
5:00 PM, Aug. 1, 1904

California
1. Oakland
2. Colfax
3. Truckee

Nevada
4. Wadsworth
5. Lovelock
6. Mill City
7. Battle Mountain[a]
8. Wells

Utah
9. Terrace
10. Ogden[b]
11. Morgan

Wyoming
12. Fort Bridger
13. Rock Springs
14. Rawlins
15. Rock River

Colorado
16. Fort Collins
17. Denver
18. Orchard

Nebraska
19. Big Springs
20. Lexington
21. Grand Island[c]
22. Omaha

Iowa[d]

Illinois
23. Fulton
24. Chicago

Indiana
25. Elkhart

Ohio
26. Bryan
27. Toledo
28. Cleveland

Pennsylvania
(no overnight stops)

New York
29. Buffalo
30. Syracuse
31. Utica
32. Peekskill

New York City finish:
1:20 PM, Sept. 3, 1904

SOURCE: *New York Herald*, Sept. 4, 1904; no dates given.

[a] In *From Coast to Coast in a Motor-Car*, Whitman lists Carlin as a night stop between Battle Mountain and Wells.

[b] Evidence suggests the car arrived in Ogden on August 11.

[c] The Franklin "passed through" Grand Island on Wednesday, August 24. The *Grand Island (Neb.) Daily Independent*'s account says nothing about the autoists staying the night.

[d] Whitman's *From Coast to Coast in a Motor-Car* account implies that the men stayed overnight in Des Moines.

according to the *New York Herald*, neglecting to mention the time spent in Ogden and Denver.[63]

As he did in 1903, Whitman in 1904 carried a single letter cross-country by auto. According to the *New York Herald* article published one day after the finish,

> Messrs. Whitman and Carris officially terminated the journey at the rooms of the Automobile Club of America, where Mr. Whitman delivered to W. E. Scarritt, president of that club, a letter intrusted to him by R. P. Schwerin, president of the Automobile Club of California. Mr. Scarritt indicated the widespread effect of the record ride when he mailed an answer to Mr. Schwerin last night, in which he said in part:
> "... The questions of speed, of economy, of comfort, of utility, have long since been threshed out in automobiling. The question of reliability is the one remaining factor that disturbs us all. Such a triumphal journey as that just completed by Mr. Whitman goes a long way toward the solution of this last vexed problem.
> "Such trips as that completed to-day by L. L. Whitman and C. S. Carris are high water marks, which indicate the possibilities ahead of us."[64]

Automobile and *Scientific American*, among other journals, lauded the Franklin's performance: "The air-cooled car has certainly proved itself equal to a long, arduous journey, though many doubts were expressed before and during the journey as to its capability of accomplishing the distance," wrote *Automobile*. "That this particular make of air-cooled motor car was speedy and had endurance, was demonstrated on the track and in the New York–Pittsburg test of last October," *Scientific American* noted. "But that it could so successfully break all records in a long transcontinental trip over roads, trails, mountains, and across trackless wastes of alkali and sage brush, was something that came as a surprise to all automobilists. . . . No motor could be submitted to a more severe test than the little four-cylinder air-cooled one on the transcontinental Franklin car underwent, and this test has again proven the entire practicability of the small multi-cylinder air-cooled motor, even when a fan is not used to cool it."[65]

Whitman himself was on hand when the H. H. Franklin Manufacturing Company displayed the 1904 transcontinental car in January 1905 at New York City's Madison Square Garden auto show.[66] Later in 1905, Whitman used the car again to try to set a new speed record between Los Angeles and San Francisco. He was accompanied by Ralph C. Hamlin, the Los Angeles Franklin agent. The two men set off at 12:01 AM on June 15, 1905, in hopes of cutting 10 hours from the record of 53 hours, held by a Packard. The Franklin arrived at Third and Market Streets in San Francisco at 1:54 PM on June 16, setting a record of 37 hours, 53 minutes.[67] Later still, Whitman used the now-famous car to assist victims of the April 18, 1906, San Francisco earthquake.[68]

Car's Authenticity in Doubt

Ralph C. Hamlin eventually acquired the 1904 Franklin and kept it in Los Angeles, "where its activities are confined to occasional jaunts about town for exhibition purposes or an appearance in the movies. It still wears upon its side the inscription, 'San Francisco to New York.'"[69] Later, the Natural History Museum of Los Angeles County acquired and displayed Hamlin's car. The car then became part of the independent Petersen Automotive Museum in Los Angeles, which the county operates. In recent years, though, the car's authenticity has been called into question.

In 1976, automotive researcher Ralph Dunwoodie, then a buyer for Harrah's Automobile Collection in Reno, Nevada, traveled to Los Angeles to inspect the Franklin, armed with many original photos taken of the car during its transcontinental trip. He concluded that the Hamlin car was not Whitman's 1904 Franklin, primarily because it was missing screw holes in the dashboard and frame where photos indicated accessories had been fastened to the transcontinental car. In a letter to the author dated August 29, 1994, Dunwoodie explained, "I would have purchased the Hamlin '04 if it had been the authentic car."[70]

One add-on item was a large plate, centered at the back of the transcontinental car's wooden frame. That plate is missing on the Hamlin car, according to both Dunwoodie and James Zordich, who in 1976 was associate curator of the Natural History Museum's transportation collection. But, according to Zordich, there are "many other screw holes . . . which display no obvious purpose" surrounding the factory's serial-number tag on the rear frame member. Zordich wrote to Dunwoodie:

> Another event occurred which could have substantiated the car's validity, but even in this case the result is not conclusive. Whitman recorded that a partially cut-off telegraph pole had been intercepted by the rear axle of the Franklin causing the truss rod to be bent. The truss rod on our vehicle shows no sign of ever having been damaged, although, it could have been replaced at a later time. . . . I, too, have some suspicions, but cannot develop a statement at this time which would be conclusive.[71]

Leslie Kendall, curator of the Petersen Automotive Museum, said he had no definite evidence to confirm that the Hamlin car is the transcontinental record-setting vehicle.[72] Even in the absence of definite evidence, the Natural History Museum of Los Angeles County continues to maintain that Hamlin's 1904 Franklin is the one in which Carris and Whitman set the coast-to-coast speed record.[73]

Trek an Investment in Advertising

By completing the fourth auto trip across America and simultaneously halving the speed record, Whitman and Carris convincingly proved that the automobile was a force to be reckoned with. Thanks to them, a stunt that had been nearly unthinkable early in 1903 was well on the way to becoming routine in 1904. And, as the car's manufacturer had surmised, the cross-country adventures of Whitman and Carris made exciting reading.

With the successful crossing, the automaker was able to silence its critics, real or imagined, by proving that a 4-cylinder, air-cooled engine performed as well as a 1-cylinder engine cooled by water, and it won a tonneau-load of free publicity in the process. Alternative designs—such as electric or steam-powered autos, or those with air-cooled, 2-cycle, rotating, sleeve-valve or rotary engines—never caught on with American motorists. The air-cooled Franklin proved the advantage of this particular design. Twice during Whitman's earlier 1903 Oldsmobile trip through the desert, sagebrush branches had knocked open a petcock, drained the cooling system, and allowed the engine to overheat. In 1904, driving the Franklin, he had no such problems.

For his part, Whitman learned how he could make more money in one month ($3,000) than he could working for years as a mechanic. Money and reputations were on the line. In a single year, the transcontinental tour had evolved from an experiment designed to test the capabilities of the automobile—with results generally reported openly and honestly to anyone interested in them—to a promotional and advertising stunt, where any weaknesses of the machine were deemphasized or masked.

W. E. Scarritt, president of the Automobile Club of America, perhaps overstated the case when he said in 1904, "The questions of speed, of economy, of comfort, of utility, have long since been threshed out in automobiling. The question of reliability is the one remaining factor that disturbs us all."[74] True, automobiles were relatively expensive in 1904 and production low. But the number of horses, carriages, and wagons still in use at the time suggests that many Americans still questioned the economy and utility of automobiling. Others questioned the very reality of such an invention; for years to come, transcontinental drivers would relate that many people were still frightened of a machine they had never seen before.

Whitman and Carris's achievement did little to answer Scarritt's disturbing question of reliability. For the Franklin's fast trip only *implied* reliability: the automaker made no attempt to detail the auto's breakdowns and repairs, as the Packard Motor Car Company did after Tom Fetch's 1903 trek. The Franklin company, by contrast, remained silent on this subject. And Whitman himself, though neglecting to reveal the auto's repair record, acknowledged that good weather had much to do with the car's fast time.

In fact, it was 1915 before observers learned from an impartial source that even the best-built automobiles took a tremendous beating while setting transcontinental speed records. Immediately after Cannon Ball Baker's transcontinental Stutz Bearcat reached New York City on May 18, 1915, automaker Harry C. Stutz sent the car to the Automobile Club of America's testing lab. Roads, metallurgy, and automobile design had all improved between 1904 and 1915. ACA engineers nonetheless pinpointed some serious wear in the Stutz's engine, wheel bearings, and transmission. The car had even broken a spring.

In its post-run advertisements, the Franklin company played up the hardships that its 1904 runabout had faced. The same ads gave the car a glowing, yet unsubstantiated, clean bill of health. Where is the proof? There is none. In the years and trips that followed, other makers willingly and profitably copied Franklin's strategy. No one seemed to mind: automakers will be automakers, after all, given to occasional excesses. The auto journals issued no calls for more accountability.

Unchecked by the public or the trade press, some drivers and backers of transcontinental record-breaking autos began circulating accounts that were more fictional than factual. Not long after the Stutz emerged from its laboratory tests, the *New York Times* in 1916 began questioning the extravagant claims made by others who were less eager for public scrutiny. Its investigation effectively overturned a 1916 record claimed by former Indianapolis taxi driver Bobby Hammond, who drove an Empire automobile. Hammond contended that he checked in at hotel desks and other places in cities along his route. But when the *New York Times* checked with Hammond's supposed witnesses, many could not corroborate Hammond's stops, thus throwing his entire speed record into doubt.[75]

Despite such attempts to shade the truth, American autos and the roads they followed were clearly improving, as later transcontinental trips would further demonstrate. New challenges awaited. After sitting out a year, Whitman and Carris would return with a vengeance in 1906, becoming the first transcontinentalists to use relay drivers and to attempt a day-and-night trip between coasts.

COAST TO COAST IN
FIFTEEN DAYS

6

"On the trip from Carroll they killed no less than twenty chickens, mortally wounded a pig and had some narrow escapes."
—*Marshalltown (Iowa) Evening Times-Republican*, on the
Franklin's fast run across central Iowa

IN AUGUST 1906, three relay drivers helped cross-country veterans Lester L. Whitman and C. S. Carris cut the transcontinental record in half, to 15 days, 2 hours, 12 minutes. The makers of the Franklin automobile sponsored the trip "to demonstrate the practicability of the high-powered, air-cooled car, and also of the six-cylinder type of engine."[1]

The car proved to have "an ability, reliability, and endurance not hitherto believed possible in any motor-car," the H. H. Franklin Manufacturing Company of Syracuse, New York, would later claim.[2] The automaker spent at least $8,000 for the right to

225

make such a statement. Nearly half that amount went to Whitman and Carris in salaries. Drivers Melvin S. Bates, James Daley, and Clayton B. Harris received much smaller amounts of both money and credit for their contributions. Though the weather interfered, Whitman organized the trek as a ten-day run in which drivers would spend twelve-hour shifts at the wheel of the slightly modified, 30-horsepower, 1906 Franklin, and then go ahead by train to meet the car later.

"We run day and night by taking relays, or shifts," he explained. "While two or three are running the machine, the others are on the railroad train sleeping and preparing to take their relay at some point ahead."[3] The car, however, had seats for just two men; the third man sat atop a steamer trunk behind the seats. Many future cross-country record-setters would emulate Whitman's innovation as used on this run, the first transcontinental trip in a 6-cylinder auto, and the first to use relay drivers to facilitate a day-and-night schedule. Whitman envisioned a nearly nonstop trip, but an accident and other delays idled the car an average of one hour for every two spent in motion.

Following the railroad also ensured that repair parts were never far away—except in Ohio, when the car crashed on a bad curve at night, injuring two relay drivers and a local guide, smashing the automobile's front end, and forcing a thirty-six-hour pit stop. It was the longest single delay of a trip in which the car spent a cumulative total of more than five days of its supposed day-and-night run immobile. It took 6½ hours to lift the car from the Humboldt Sink in Nevada. Rains in Wyoming and the Midwest slowed the car further.

Bad weather hampered the autoists from the start, as flooding near San Francisco forced Whitman to ship the car by ferry to Stockton, where it began the trip under its own power some 90 miles inland. Thus, Whitman's was not a "true" coast-to-coast record in a car under its own power. Nevertheless, the trip's time of just over fifteen days from San Francisco to New York City included the delay in ferrying the car to Stockton, so observers have accepted the transcontinental record as genuine.

Mechanically, the Franklin auto performed well, though not flawlessly. It broke a spring, sprung a leak in its gas tank, and experienced other problems. Standing by in Cleveland, three mechanics jumped at the car and hurriedly replaced its steering column. Whitman reported just two punctures; the car received new tires in Chicago and several spark plugs, but otherwise needed little engine work.

The crew ran afoul of the law in Iowa, in a dispute over damage to a wagon. "We tried to run away, but Winchesters in the hands of irate farmers dissuaded us," Whitman recounted.[4] Rocketing down Iowa's dirt roads at speeds of 60 miles per hour, the Franklin killed an average of one chicken every six minutes during a two-hour dash between Carroll and Marshalltown, the car's local guide reported.

A speeding ticket in Buffalo, New York, cost the drivers a hefty fine and detained them 1½ hours, the same amount of time lost when the auto spooked a horse that jumped into the Erie Canal. After lowering the transcontinental record, Carris and the rest of the crew, minus Whitman, returned to Chicago with the Franklin. They then sped from Chicago to New York City to set a speed record between those cities.

The 1906 run from San Francisco to New York City had its nightmarish elements, as Whitman tells it:

> We climbed, coasted, slid, drove and bumped 4,000 miles twice as fast as it was ever done over the same route before. We roasted, shivered, fasted, thirsted most mightily. We plunged in, dug out, pushed along, came in under the wire and chalked up some figures that beat the multiplication table. We covered nearly 600 miles through deep desert with the mercury at 120 degrees at an average of eleven miles an hour, and most of the way not a drop of water was obtainable.
>
> We traveled thirty miles over railroad ties with four passengers in four hours, because bumping over the ties was better than trying to get through by way of the road. . . . You hear a lot about gentle Mother Earth and her kindness toward man; but when you've traveled a few thousand miles through floods, mud, sand, alkali, and gumbo you come to think this maternal benevolence is altogether too strenuous and sticky and that a good man-made road beats nature all to pieces.[5]

The Franklin Six

For 1906, the Franklin company added a 6-cylinder to its line of engines, which were air-cooled until the company produced its last auto in 1934. For its second transcontinental run, the automaker chose a 1906 Model H, priced at $4,000. Instead of water for cooling, blades in the flywheel and a fan in front of the engine pulled air over the finned cylinders. The 2,500-pound transcontinental car weighed between 3,000 and 3,200 pounds loaded, according to various estimates. This included 400 pounds of parts and equipment and extra gasoline and oil. The car had a 20-gallon gas tank and 1-gallon oil tank.[6]

The transcontinental car used tires measuring 36 × 3½ inches front, and 36 × 4 inches rear. With 4-×-4 inch cylinders and a compression pressure of 62 pounds per square inch, the engine developed 30 horsepower at 1,500 rpm, giving the 3-speed car a top speed of 50 miles per hour or more. Auxiliary exhaust valves, a Franklin 1905 innovation, "open when the pistons reach their lowest points and allow the greater part of the burned gases to escape immediately. The remaining gases are expelled from the main exhaust valves in the ordinary manner."

Suggesting modifications to the stock design, *Scientific American Supplement* called the car a "special touring runabout," which the *New York Times* further defined as a Franklin "with touring equipment on a runabout frame." But the *Cleveland Plain Dealer*'s assertion that it was "made up as a runabout" implies that the body was on a touring car frame.[7]

Photos reveal three obvious modifications. First, there was a snorkel-tube extension on the front of the car, "for the purpose of increasing the draft of air to the motor cylinders." Second, as he had in 1904, Whitman attached a large hamper—not wicker this time, but a solid wooden box built in behind the seats—on the car for carrying baggage and supplies. He took along a steamer trunk, as well. Third, the car carried a large, dash-mounted "searchlight" for night driving (see Fig. 108).

San Francisco's great earthquake and fire four months earlier had caused "a blockade of freight cars for miles around," Whitman explained. "The car . . . was shipped from New York to San Francisco by express, the expense being 27 cents a

Fig. 108. This photo, snapped at Cheyenne, Wyoming, clearly shows the Franklin's front-end snorkel tube, wooden box, and searchlight. A cigarette dangling from his lips, Harris drives and Carris assists (HHFC).

COAST TO COAST BY AUTOMOBILE

pound, and as the car weighs 3,000 pounds, the shipping bill alone amounts to $810. . . . We wanted to make this record run now because it is the best part of the year for such a test."[8]

"Clean Score" Carris

Clayton S. Carris, who at the time of the 1904 crossing with Whitman was described as a 27-year-old from Syracuse, New York, spent much of his time behind the wheel (see Fig. 109). As a Franklin representative, the sturdy Carris (in 1912 he would stand 5 feet, 9½ inches tall and weigh 185 pounds) would put 10,000 miles on a 6-cylinder Franklin by May 1907, visiting "nearly all of the principal cities east of Chicago."[9] He always scored well in the Glidden Tours, the annual reliability runs sponsored by the American Automobile Association, as well as in various regional endurance runs.

In one contest on December 12, 1908, Carris was described as "a careful and experienced driver," who "made no attempt to 'burn up' the country roads, satisfying himself with getting into controls comfortably according to schedule." He consequently beat the thirteen other cars entered in the 210-mile Massachusetts endurance event. Two-thirds of the entrants finished with perfect road scores, "but the Franklin was

the only one surviving a searching examination of two hours on the part of the technical committee, which was finally forced to give up the task without even finding a screw or nut loose that would call for the slightest of penalties."[10]

Carris secured "perfect Franklin scores" in five endurance runs—including the Glidden Tour—during the previous season, *Automobile* said in late 1908. "Mel" Bates and "Jimmie" Daley, as they were known, also drove in the 1908 Glidden Tour; like Carris, Bates turned in a perfect score, according to an H. H. Franklin Club publication (see Fig. 110).[11] One of Carris's five perfect scores in 1908 came near Boston as he ran up 1,607 miles and survived a three-way runoff among winners in the Bay State Endurance Run. He started off 1909 by placing second in the Quaker City Motor Club's New Year's run near Philadelphia.[12]

Carris turned in a perfect score during a one-day, 243-mile run from New York City to Boston in March 1909. In June 1909, "the veteran Franklin-Carris combination [was] a long-margin winner" of its class (touring cars $2,000 and up) in Pennsylvania's 750-mile State Highway Endurance Contest. In fact, it was news when "Clean Score" Carris was penalized during a spring 1909 Pittsburgh endurance run. Because heavy rains had turned the contest into a "mud plug," however, thirteen of the twenty-four starters dropped out and every finisher earned penalties.[13]

Whitman: Record-Setter and Rescuer

Though taking a year off following his 1903 Oldsmobile and 1904 Franklin transcontinental crossings, Whitman was far from idle. "Mr. Whitman has been representing the Franklin car on the Coast during the past year," the August 2, 1906, *Automobile* reported.[14] He and co-driver Ralph C. Hamlin, the Los Angeles Franklin agent, helped publicize the Franklin during a mid-1905 long-distance run. Hamlin and Whitman left Los Angeles at 12:01 AM on June 15, 1905, in the Franklin that Whitman had driven during his 1904 crossing. Whitman hoped to cut ten hours from the fifty-three-hour Los Angeles–San Francisco record that four men in a Packard had set a year earlier.[15]

Automobile wrote: "The car, which is a regular stock model, is provided with powerful searchlights, and the men are fairly well acquainted with the roads." Though the trip was slightly under 500 miles, "the course is a very hilly one. The Coast Range of mountains is crossed no less than five times and there are several stretches intersected by a series of deep gulches where the driving is especially trying." Whitman and Hamlin also forded several streams, including the Ventura River.[16]

"They had had no trouble with the car, but experienced a good deal of difficulty in keeping warm at night, owing to the dense fogs. At one time during the night the two men stopped by the roadside and built a fire of hay from a neighboring ranch in order to warm themselves." Nevertheless, the car pulled up to Third and Market Streets in San Francisco at 1:54 PM on June 16 in a record time of 37 hours, 53 minutes.[17]

Whitman and his wife were in San Francisco on April 18, 1906, when an earthquake and the fires it spawned nearly leveled the city. "I got out the old, faithful transcontinental car, threw away the hamper, and carried fleeing people to Golden Gate Park, where thousands slept in the open and watched the destruction by fire after the earthquake had shaken the city," Whitman wrote. "The panic of the people was terrible. Martial law was enforced and the soldiers from the Presidio held the city. Many [citizens] were shot for not obeying orders. I had a rifle shoved in my face by a soldier while I was after people in my Franklin."[18]

In New York, during the hours following the 5:13 AM San Francisco earthquake, the Merchants' Association filled fourteen freight cars with canned food and later dispatched a boxcar containing $60,000 in medicine. Thus, on his 1906 transcontinental run, one of the three letters Whitman carried was from San Francisco Mayor Eugene

E. Schmitz, who "deemed it a particularly opportune way by which to send his greetings to a people and state that responded so quickly and nobly at the moment of San Francisco's great distress; appropriate because the automobile was the one means of travel and communication that survived the fire and earthquake and made relief work possible and effective."[19]

Attention to Minute Detail

Whitman's planning of the 1906 relay run, which meant coordinating the car with train schedules, was "a deal of minute detail, carefully studied and worked out beforehand, of which the mere driving was but small part," according to the *New York Times*. The Franklin company or its local agents assisted by lining up guides to ride with the car over difficult or unfamiliar stretches. "Over the rails, too, was sent a complete outfit for the repair of the car in case of accident. This included an entire set of four wheels ready to be affixed should accident cripple the regular wheels in use. A complete extra running gear with duplicates of every part was shipped with these wheels from point to point" so that the car and its repair parts were always within 200 miles of one another.[20]

According to *Automobile*, Whitman packed the car with these supplies:

In the hamper are carried half a dozen extra inner tubes, extra cans of gasoline and oil, together with a few small parts which might be required in making repairs on the car. A steamer trunk intended for the men's clothing, blankets to protect them from the cold at night, rubber ponchos to ward off rain and wet, is strapped back of the seats on top of the hamper.

The car is fitted with a dash searchlight in addition to the regular lamp equipment, and is also provided with two stout hickory sticks, which, crossing the deserts, are often necessary in prying the car out of the sand. There is also furnished an ax with which to cut away obstructions on the mountain roads; a large-sized revolver, and a compass. Each man has been provided with a khaki suit, a helmet as protection from the severe heat of the desert sun, and a canteen in which to carry drinking water sufficient for several days.[21]

The car also carried a block and tackle, and "was fitted with ordinary pneumatic tires having no special devices for use in crossing the sandy deserts," according to press accounts.[22] Whitman thus apparently traveled without the sand tires that he used with much lighter cars during his 1903 and 1904 runs. At 3,000 pounds or more, the 1906 car was evidently too heavy to benefit from strapping on the wider, cotton-stuffed sand tires. Whitman did, however, carry tire chains, as photos reveal. Photos also show two spare tires strapped to the right running board.

In the factory's account of the trek, *Across America in a Franklin*, Whitman also reported that the car carried an extra gasoline tank, a spare set of batteries, a bag of tools, a brake band, an unspecified number of spark plugs, "a sack of bolts, nuts and small parts . . . and 150 feet of rope."[23]

Five men helped with the car, all Franklin employees. Whitman and Carris "conducted the record-breaking run of the Franklin" auto, but it was M. S. Bates, James Daley, and C. B. Harris "who held her wheel much of the 15 days and 2 hours she occupied in her journey," the *New York Times* reported.[24]

Other press accounts differed on the men's duties. The *Chicago Daily News*, for instance, said Carris, Harris, and Whitman were the drivers, Bates and Daley the mechanics. But Daley "was head tester [test driver] in the factory for a number of years," according to a 1921 house organ, *The Franklin News*.[25] Bates and Daley also drove Franklins for the automaker in various endurance contests, and Whitman's rigorous schedule suggests that every man would be expected to drive. His planned ten-day trip called for ten relay points, at which the car would meet a train to exchange drivers, each of whom would drive a twelve-hour shift. If just two men took the car for a twenty-four-hour stint, as was often the case, each man had to drive half that time. As the trip stretched to more than fifteen days, the autoists added seven relay points for a total of seventeen, according to Whitman.

Was Whitman foolish for traveling without a mechanic in the car? Probably not. The car carried only a few spare parts. Whitman was a former Oldsmobile mechanic; for all their driving experience, Carris and the other drivers, too, undoubtedly could turn a wrench. It may have been Whitman's plan that, in a serious breakdown, the two or three men in the car could remove the broken piece while the other crewmen hurried back by train with the parts cache to help complete the repairs.

A Brave Start

A *San Francisco Call* reporter covered the Franklin's start (see Fig. 111) on Thursday, August 2, 1906:

> Whirling over the roads between this city and the summit of the Sierras in an automobile L. L. Whitman and his intrepid assistants have made a brave start in their record-breaking trip to New York.

There was no demonstration at the start, which was made from the Franklin automobile establishment, beyond the hearty handshakes and the well wishes of the friends of the drivers. The machine was gone over repeatedly during the afternoon in an effort to adjust every part of the car to its highest point of efficiency. The delicate engine was given especial care, as it will be the first with six cylinders to be used under such trying conditions.

Whitman held a levee for an hour before the appointed time to start. He was dressed in ordinary street attire and would not be picked out by the casual spectator as the hero of the occasion.

He glanced carelessly at his watch and announced: "Five minutes more!" He called off the minutes and climbed into his machine as the hands pointed to 5 o'clock. There was a whirr of machinery and the big car, which was headed toward the west, was backed down on the Golden Gate avenue sidewalk to Larkin street, where its frowning front was soon turned toward its goal in the East.

Down Market street to the ferry was its route and then the trying journey was taken up in earnest. Whitman hopes to cut his old record in half and will endeavor to cover the distance in fifteen days.

Although Whitman will do only a share of the driving, he will receive most of the credit, as he planned the trip and its success depends chiefly upon his organization of the record trial.

When the car started on its big trip, W. H. [*sic*] Bates was at the wheel, with Whitman at his side.[26]

Most other newspapers and auto journals chose to emphasize Whitman's ten-day schedule. Curiously, the *Call*'s headline over its story of the start came close to predicting the actual record time: "Whitman Expects to Drive Car to New York Cutting Former Mark to Fifteen Days." The *San Francisco Examiner* explained why the Franklin started its coast-to-coast trip in reverse gear: "Owing to a blockade in the street the motorists covered the first fifty yards of their journey by running the machine backwards on the sidewalk."[27]

The *Examiner* coverage included a three-column photo—too fuzzy to reproduce here—showing Bates at the wheel and Whitman in the car alongside him, parked beside the newspaper offices under a large sign, "The S. F. Examiner." The article makes no mention of the start from the Franklin agency:

> When the veteran tourists drove away from "The Examiner" building at 5:15 p.m., their machine was running perfectly, and jumped ahead at the touch of the throttle as if it was anxious to begin its long journey. Owing to the high waters in the San Joaquin valley, the tourists traveled to Stockton by boat.
>
> Whitman and W. H. [*sic*] Bates made the first relay, and will drive from Stockton to the summit of the Sierra Nevadas, where they will be relieved by Carris and Harris. . . . In answer to a question as to what part of the route would be found the best traveling, Whitman replied that he would enjoy the twenty-mile stretch of boulevard from Yonkers in to New York City the best of all.[28]

The Franklin company and nearly all press accounts—except those in the *Examiner* and *Call*—use 6:00 PM as the official starting time. This was perhaps when the car left San Francisco on the ferry to Stockton. The 6:00 PM departure time is the most likely one, for after leaving the Franklin agency at 5:00 PM and the *Examiner* office at 5:15 PM, Bates made one other stop. "Rolling down Market Street at the start," according to Whitman, "we met Mayor Schmitz, who shook hands with us and gave us 'Good-bye and good luck.' "[29]

Floods Delay Auto

Flooding between San Francisco and Sacramento had forced Whitman to postpone his noon start and change his route (see Fig. 112). "They will go to Stockton by boat, arriving there at 8 a.m. to-morrow," wrote Thursday's *San Francisco Chronicle*. "This will be a handicap of ten hours." The predicted fourteen-hour boat trip actually stretched to fifteen hours, recounted Whitman, who put the handicap at twelve hours: "We lost twelve hours on the second day on account of the swollen rivers of the San

Joaquin Valley, requiring fifteen hours to ferry across and make a run that should take three hours ordinarily. We covered 245 miles the first day and 175 miles the second, although the first day included a 7,000-foot climb."[30]

"We started from west to east because the ascent of the mountains is easier coming that way," Whitman explained. By crossing the country in little more than fifteen days, Whitman and Carris would handily beat their 1904 crossing time of 32 days, 17 hours, 20 minutes, "and but for a series of untoward accidents would have made the run in close to eleven days," the *New York Times* would later report. Rushing through the Sierra Nevada, the Franklin's time "nearly equaled that required by the Overland Limited, the Union Pacific's fastest train."[31] The car traveled through the sandy, mountainous northern half of Nevada, via Reno, Lovelock, Mill City, Winnemucca, Elko, and Wells, reaching Ogden, Utah, in less than four days—six days ahead of the 1904 record pace. The car was eleven days ahead at Chicago.

Later, Whitman gave the *New York Times* a list showing the car's location at 6:00 PM daily (see Table 12), though times in local news stories reveal errors in the list. According to Whitman's list in the *New York Times*, the Franklin reached Summit, California—where Charles B. Shanks and Alexander Winton got stuck in the snow in 1901—at 6:00 PM on Friday, August 3, or just twenty-four hours after their San Francisco start. (The same trip had taken Winton and Shanks five days.) But Whitman told an Ogden newspaper that the car's Summit arrival time was actually 7:40 PM on Friday.

TABLE 12. Franklin's Location at 6:00 PM Daily, 1906

Day / date	Location
1 / Aug. 2	San Francisco (start: 6:00 PM)
2 / Aug. 3	Summit, Calif.
3 / Aug. 4	Lovelock, Nev.
4 / Aug. 5	Wells, Nev.
5 / Aug. 6	Ogden, Utah
6 / Aug. 7	Rock Springs, Wyo.
7 / Aug. 8	Red Desert, Wyo.
8 / Aug. 9	Laramie, Wyo.
9 / Aug. 10	Kimball, Neb.
10 / Aug. 11	Kearney, Neb.
11 / Aug. 12	Cedar Rapids, Iowa
12 / Aug. 13	Chicago
13 / Aug. 14	Cleveland
14 / Aug. 15	Conneaut, Ohio
15 / Aug. 16	Buffalo, N.Y.
16 / Aug. 17	Poughkeepsie, N.Y. (finish: New York City, 11:12 PM)

SOURCE: "A Record Auto Run and What It Means," *New York Times*, Aug. 19, 1906 (quoting Lester Whitman). Times vary somewhat from those given in local newspapers along the route.

"The Best of Luck"

Whitman and Bates had driven the car Friday on the first relay from Stockton to Summit, "where they were relieved by Carris and Harris," according to the *Daily Nevada State Journal* in Reno, where the car arrived at midnight that same day. In his later account, Whitman says Carris and *Daley* drove from Summit, through Reno, to Lovelock. Reno's *State Journal* reported that Whitman took the train from Summit and planned to meet the car again north of Lovelock in Mill City, Nevada. The Franklin had arrived in Reno with Bates, Carris, Daley, and Harris aboard, the newspaper said—a suspect report, because the car could scarcely accommodate three men, much less four. At either Mill City or Lovelock, Whitman evidently planned to begin another twelve-hour stint at the wheel of the car, which on Saturday and Sunday would traverse the sandy and rocky roads across northern Nevada and into Utah.[32]

"Unless something unforeseen happens," Harris predicted in Reno, "we will surely make a wonderful cut in the transcontinental record. So far we have had the best of luck, not a breakdown or delay of any consequence occurring between San Francisco and Reno" (see Fig. 113). The travelers left Reno "after dining at the Golden hotel and procuring necessary supplies. . . . Bates is the only one of the party who will try to find amusement along the road. He carries a Winchester rifle on the rear of the car, and during the second relay in the mountains he intends to go gunning for bear."[33]

The *Reno Evening Gazette*, like other newspapers across the country, played up the drivers' nonstop schedule: "They will sleep and eat on the machine and the auto will be kept in motion at all times."[34] The men contradicted the *Gazette* on both counts, however, by stopping to eat at Reno's Golden Hotel and, later, by parking the car for as long as six hours to sleep in a hotel at Laramie, Wyoming. Traveling at night had its share of dangers, as Whitman well knew:

> All through Nebraska and Wyoming barb wire fences and barb wire gates will be encountered across the trail. If running at night the greatest precautions will be necessary, for no matter how powerful the searchlight it fails to pick up a wire fence until too late to apply the brakes, and somebody gets badly cut by the flying wires as the auto crashes through.[35]

In general, the crewmen followed a daytime driving schedule until they reached Chicago. As *Automobile* wrote: "Up to the time of arrival at Chicago the car had been run only during the day—though some of the days were rather elastic—but there a night and day schedule was laid out," as the autoists tried to beat the Chicago–New York City speed record.[36]

Stuck in Old Humboldt

The Franklin had covered the difficult 100 miles from Reno to Lovelock—still in western Nevada—by 6:00 PM, Saturday, August 4, or forty-eight hours after the start. Later that evening, Whitman sent the *San Francisco Chronicle* a telegram from Mill City: "Making the dust fly; reached Mill City at 10 to-night. Stuck in the mud on the Old Humboldt sink six hours this P.M. We were five days reaching this place on my last run, two days this time" (see Fig. 114).[37]

"We had no serious trouble after leaving Summit until we reached the Humboldt

Fig. 113. The confident Harris at Battle Mountain, Nevada. For unexplained reasons, the Franklin traveled as far as Ogden with its right rear fender bent skyward (HHFC).

Fig. 114. A crewman inspects the Franklin on a smooth stretch of Nevada sand, most likely on or near the Humboldt Sink (HHFC).

river," a watercourse northeast of Reno, Whitman would later tell the *Ogden Morning Examiner*. "There we ran into a sink where the mud was so soft that the bed of the car dragged on the ground. We lost fully six hours in getting out of this sink."[38] In a later *New York Times* interview, Whitman fixed the time loss at 6½ hours.

In a 1909 feature, *Motor Age* described the vestiges of Nevada's prehistoric seas and lakes:

> The ancient shore lines of these lakes are plainly visible in places. The transcontinentalist skirts the shores of Humboldt lake and crosses the Humboldt sink. This 100 miles calls for an 8-hour trip and is the hardest part of the whole 4,100 miles on the driver and passengers. . . .
>
> The majority of this sink has a 2-inch surface crust beneath which is a black muck or quicksand, and if the car breaks through the crust it sinks to the hubs and a block and tackle has to be used to extricate the machine. . . .
>
> Owing to the excess of salt and alkali it is necessary to wear a handkerchief over the mouth and nose in this territory and good goggles to protect the eyes. Whitman in the transcontinental trip made but 17 miles in 7 hours over this sink; he lost a canteen and all hands had to go 10 hours in the burning sand and sun without a drop of water.[39]

Despite voluminous coverage of the trip, only *Motor Age* and *Motor Way* reported the story of the lost canteen: Quoting Whitman, *Motor Way* wrote: "'The driver[s] suffered much during that time because the new canteen, which was carried, happened to leak and, as the other water supply was exhausted, the hard working drivers had nothing to drink during all this time, during which the thermometer had reached 110 to 120 degrees.'"[40]

Over the Sleepers to Winnemucca

Freed from the mud of the Humboldt Sink, the car continued through Lovelock to Mill City. From Mill City to Winnemucca, the crew "bumped for thirty miles over the railway sleepers," Whitman wrote. "If you want to know why, go out there and take a look at the situation—we took the easiest way."[41] Alexander Winton and Charles B. Shanks would have agreed with Whitman's assessment, for it was in deep sand 2 miles east of Mill City that their transcontinental aspirations had ground to a halt in 1901.

The Franklin reached Wells in northeastern Nevada at about 6:00 PM on Sunday, August 5. Shortly thereafter, the car crossed into Utah to begin the drive north around the Great Salt Lake to Ogden. Whitman and Harris traveled ahead by train, reaching Ogden at 7:10 AM on Monday, August 6, several hours before the 2:00 PM arrival of

Bates, Carris, and Daley in the Franklin. "The big machine and its drivers were literally covered with alkali dust," the Ogden newspaper reported.[42]

From Ogden, Bates, Carris, and Daley would take the train to Granger, Wyoming, according to Whitman. He and Harris would drive east to Granger "after a few repairs have been made on the machine by L. H. Becraft" (see Fig. 115).[43] A publicity-conscious automobile agent, Becraft had previously acquired and displayed Whitman and Hammond's worn-out shoes and clothing from their 1903 coast-to-coast trip in an Oldsmobile.

Becraft discharged the Franklin after installing new tires and making unspecified repairs, according to the *Salt Lake Tribune*. But neither of two other papers covering the Franklin's Ogden stop said anything about new tires; Whitman afterward claimed that the car received new tires just once—in Chicago. By reaching Ogden in less than four days, the Franklin had beaten Whitman's 1904 record time of ten days to that point. So fast was the Franklin that "in several instances the big machine got ahead of the schedule time of the trains between San Francisco and Ogden."[44]

"Give Us a Good Horse"

Three Utah newspapers disagree on exactly when the Franklin was in Ogden on Monday. The *Salt Lake Telegram* reported that the Franklin arrived "shortly before noon" and left at 2:00 PM. The *Salt Lake Tribune* put the times at 1:15 and 4:05 PM. The *Ogden Morning Examiner* gave only an arrival time, of 2:00 PM. The confused *Salt Lake Telegram* writer believed the trek involved a second car: "The relay will be taken up somewhere in Wyoming, by men and a machine that is traveling on the Southern Pacific and Union Pacific train. The men and machine which arrived in Ogden this morning will then be taken aboard the train and will take up the relay at some point further east."[45]

At Evanston, Wyoming, Harris and Whitman crossed paths with a milling throng of revelers, the *Wyoming Press* reported in its "Local Gossip" column.

> The touring car reached here on Monday night during the excitement attendant upon the departure of Mr. and Mrs. Chas. Blyth [a front-page story announced their marriage] and as it had been reported that they would make the trip to Salt Lake in an automobile, the car was soon surrounded by the anxious rice throwers.
>
> The machine was in charge of L. L. Whitman who left Ogden as No. 8 pulled out and beat the time of the Los Angeles limited into Evanston. They left as soon as they had refilled their reservoir and were followed for some distance by the more skeptical of the charivariers until it was made certain that they would not pick up the bride and groom.
>
> From here they make the run to Granger where the two men in charge will be relieved by two others following by train, and will themselves take the train to a point farther ahead where they will again take charge of the machine.
>
> The car is a thirty horse power Franklin car, the trip is being made to prove that such a trip can be made with the cooling appliance peculiar to this make of machine. Four relays were made between San Francisco and Ogden and eight more will be made between that point and New York. For ourselves, give us a good horse.[46]

Approaching the Green River east of Granger, Whitman reported, the car "lost three and one-half hours in fording across a tributary." To cross the Green River itself, Carris and Bates "had to wade the whole time waist high in ice-cold water and shove the machine across, driven constantly down stream by the swift current." More specifically, the two men "got out their hickory sticks and pried their craft ashore inch by inch."[47]

Axle Breaks Near Laramie

Speeding on across southern Wyoming (see Fig. 116), the Franklin reached Rock Springs on Tuesday, August 7, Day 6, as the *Rock Springs Miner* recorded:

> Whitman, the Franklin Automobile expert, driving a fine, six cylinder 30 horse power machine, passed through Rock Springs Tuesday afternoon on a trans-continental run.

Fig. 116. The Franklin on
a road through shaggy
sagebrush, typical of
Wyoming (HHFC).

Whitman is attempting to cover the distance between San Francisco and New York in
ten days and will come near doing it.

He has so far, more than kept up his schedule of 350 miles a day and his car was in first
class shape, having stood the road much better than any machine that has passed through
here on a trans-continental run.[48]

Traveling east across the Red Desert in south-central Wyoming, the Franklin
reached the settlement of Red Desert at about 6:00 PM on Wednesday, and continued
on through Rawlins and Fort Steele (see Fig. 117), to finally reach Laramie at about
6:00 PM on Thursday, August 9, Day 8 of the trip, according to the schedule Whitman
later gave to the *New York Times*. As often happened with newspapers along the
Franklin's route, Friday's *Laramie Republican* differed on the time:

The Franklin automobile, being driven from San Francisco to New York in an effort to
cover the transcontinental trip, reached here from the west last night, after midnight, and
left for the east this morning at 6 o'clock, six [*sic*] days from San Francisco. . . .

A delay of thirty-six hours occurred on Red desert on account of running into a mud-
hole and breaking the rear axle. The party then had to walk about three miles, where
they got coal oil, as their gasoline was all used. In spite of the delays it is believed they will
make the record over the continent.[49]

Fig. 117. Daley
approaches a plank
bridge over the North
Platte River at Fort
Steele, Wyoming
(HHFC).

Adding credence to the *Laramie Republican*'s account, Friday's *Wyoming Tribune* of Cheyenne also mentioned that an unspecified breakdown west of Laramie had delayed the car on Thursday. Whether the breakdown may have occurred earlier than Thursday, thereby delaying the crew a full thirty-six hours, is open to speculation. Whitman later told reporters that the crewmen burned 1.5 gallons of kerosene—the common name for coal oil—during an emergency, but he did not explain the circumstances. He likewise said nothing about damaging the rear axle, in Wyoming or anywhere else.[50]

Whitman did, however, speak later about the car getting stuck in eastern Wyoming as it had in Nevada's Humboldt Sink, resulting in "a similar loss in time"—that is, 6½ hours. *Automobile* credited the delay as "another quicksand mishap," and reported that it had occurred between Rawlins and Cheyenne (Laramie is about midway between those two cites) and that it had delayed the travelers eight hours.

In his summary of the trip, Whitman finally spelled out exactly what had happened in Wyoming. Between Elko and Ogden, he said, the auto was "terribly wracked" by washouts ranging from 2 to 6 feet deep. "This continuous severe punishment must have gradually weakened the rear driving-axle; for within twenty-four hours [after leaving Ogden] it suddenly gave way, from no apparent cause. This held us up twenty-eight solid hours while we sent to Cheyenne for a new rear axle. When it came, we took about ten minutes putting it in." Whitman did not say exactly where in Wyoming the axle broke, but the *Laramie Republican* may have been correct in saying west of Laramie. Between Red Desert and Rawlins, Whitman continued,

> we tried to cross the bed of a creek on a slippery clay bottom; but, although we put sagebrush down to make a track, our wheels would not take hold. We went to a [railroad] station two and one-half miles away for help; and about fifty men came and pulled us out.
>
> But after getting out, there was only gasoline enough to run two and one-half miles. Then we bought some kerosene and ran seventeen miles on kerosene to Rawlins—which speaks volumes for the Franklin carburetor. I don't believe there's another carburetor that would run that distance on kerosene.[51]

Fig. 118. Daley rounds a curve in a scene that one account identified as "near the summit of the Rocky Mountains in Wyoming"—that is, Sherman Hill (HHFC).

Lost in the Hills

Throughout Wyoming, Whitman and his crew encountered rain and mud, swollen streams that had to be forded, and irrigation ditches. According to *Automobile*, "The block and tackle was often in requisition to haul the car from the soft, sticky beds of the streams." According to the Laramie newspaper, Whitman and Daley checked into the Kuster Hotel, most likely to clean up and perhaps catch a few hours' sleep.[52] But during the next day's run into Cheyenne, Whitman and Daley encountered trouble in an area later known as the Fort Warren Maneuver Reserve:

> The big motor car was expected to reach the city yesterday afternoon but was delayed by a breakdown west of Laramie and still further time was lost this morning on Sherman hill [see Fig. 118] when the chauffeurs lost their way in the mountains and for two hours ran their machine around steep hills and up canyons trying to find the road to Cheyenne.
>
> They left Laramie at an early hour but soon missed their way and finally ran into the picket line around the Crow creek maneuver reserve. Here they were halted by the soldiers who refused to permit them to enter the reserve. They asked for directions regarding the road to Cheyenne, but the soldiers, from distant army posts, could tell nothing regarding the roads and for a long time the motorists drove their car along the reserve

line, losing much valuable time but finally discovering a road and coming on to Cheyenne.

The car remained about an hour here and was taken on east by the second relay of chauffeurs, composed of C. S. [C]arris and C. B. Harris, who will take the car to North Platte.[53]

"Well Coated with Mud"

Forty miles east of Cheyenne, the Franklin crossed into Nebraska, where it would travel the Platte River Valley through Kimball, North Platte, Kearney, Grand Island, and Omaha (see Fig. 119). Just after noon on Saturday, August 11, Bates and Whitman "stopped to 'coal up' with gasoline at Bolte's shop" in Kearney. Dr. H. Nelson Jackson had also stopped at Bolte's garage, in 1903, during the first transcontinental trip.[54] The local paper reported that the Franklin drivers "are headed for New York city and report losing thirteen hours between Oakland and Sacramento, Cal., on account of flooded roads. The gentlemen themselves and their machine, a powerful six cylinder type, were all well coated with mud and the outfit proved an attractive object to those of the small crowd who had their kodaks."[55]

According to a wire story that appeared in the *San Francisco Call*, the car reached Omaha on Saturday evening, "making the run to that point in nine days, cutting the record in half."[56] In fact, the 9½ days to Omaha had cut nearly two weeks off the record-setting time of the 1904 Franklin. The *Chicago Daily Tribune* reported that the car had raced through Omaha at 3:00 AM on Sunday, not Saturday.[57] This seems more likely, since it tends to explain why the Omaha newspapers failed to cover the auto's arrival.

As in Wyoming, muddy roads east of Omaha slowed the Franklin. "In Iowa the car was preceded by a furious rainstorm which made the roads almost impassable," wrote *Scientific American Supplement*, which also showed two photos of the Franklin splashing through a 100-mile stretch of Nebraska mud.[58] Surviving photos (see Fig. 120) show two horses pulling the car out of a muddy ditch at one unspecified location.

Already fifty-four hours behind their ten-day schedule because of "rains and washouts in Nebraska and elsewhere," the autoists finally found dry roads in Iowa on Sunday, August 12. Accordingly, they drove fast and hard through western and central Iowa. According to the *Marshalltown Evening Times-Republican*, C. E. Eldridge of Marshalltown climbed aboard the Franklin to guide the car over the 110-mile stretch from Carroll to Marshalltown. The car reached Marshalltown "in a little more than two hours," at 4:00 PM. "Eldridge states that at times it made a speed of sixty miles an hour. On the trip from Carroll they killed no less than twenty chickens, mortally wounded a pig and had some narrow escapes."[59]

Fig. 120. Bates waits in the car as a farmer prepares to pull the Franklin from a ditch (HHFC).

The "Merry Ha Ha"

But a run-in with the law following an accident east of Marshalltown delayed the drivers—later identified as Carris and Harris—4½ hours, according to a *Times-Republican* article under a Montour, Iowa, dateline:

> On reaching what is known as Indian town, near here [Montour], the car which was being driven at a speed of forty miles an hour, struck a buggy being driven by Frank Lewis, a well known farmer. The buggy was broken to pieces and one of the horses badly crippled. Luckily Lewis escaped without serious injury. Lewis telephoned to Justice Millard here, but that official was given the merry ha ha when he attempted to hale the men as they sped the big machine thru the streets of this place.
>
> Millard determined to see that justice was meted out to the reckless drivers and telephoned to Tama to have the men arrested. But the Tama authorities only got a fleeting glance at the law breakers and Millard got busy with the phone again. He got Cedar Rapids police headquarters, then Belle Plaine, and Chelsea. The constable at Chelsea is an energetic officer and got busy at once. With two other men they got a team and started out to head off the offenders. They didn't have long to wait.
>
> Planting themselves across the right of way they brought the auto to a standstill and informed the drivers they were under arrest. They submitted after some parleying and were escorted back to Tama where they were met by Justice Millard and taken back to Montour, where they settled for the damage to Lewis' outfit and the cost of prosecution and headed for Clinton, shortly before midnight.[60]

With Carris at the wheel and Harris as his passenger, the men reached Chicago at 5:10 PM on Monday, August 13. Whitman had already arrived in Chicago by train to drive the car to Toledo. The drivers stopped in Chicago "long enough . . . to change tires on their car, lay in a good meal, be checked in by Charlie Toot, then resume the flight, leaving Carris to go by train with the two mechanics," according to the *Chicago Daily News*.[61]

The newspaper did not explain it, but Charlie Toot was probably the local auto-club official charged with recording the Franklin's arrival and departure times. The Franklin's eleven-day dash to Chicago had "shattered beyond recognition" the 25-day record set by Whitman and Carris in 1904.[62] As Whitman commented:

> You may think that although we came here in less than half the time Mr. Carris and myself required on our previous Franklin cross-country run, that everything went without a hitch, but such was not the case. People generally have no idea what such a long run means, and when a motorist makes good time, they are generally under the impression that it is because the car is fast and the roads excellent.

While the car has, of course, very much to do in such an enterprise, the roads and the men who drive are as important a factor as the car. We came over some roads which were excellent, but we also went through paths and highways which were almost impassable, and sometimes it required several hours to cover only a few miles.[63]

"A Bunch of Angry Farmers"

Whitman gave the *Chicago Daily News* his version of Sunday's accident in Iowa, which he said involved a wagon, not a buggy, and delayed the drivers nearly twice as long as the Marshalltown paper asserted:

We lost eight golden hours—eight hours, that's one-third of a day, a good night's sleep— all through a little mishap out in Iowa. . . . A farmer's horse took fright at the long bonnet on the Franklin, plunged around and broke the pole to the wagon. Carris did not stop as he ought to have done, so thirty-five miles farther on he was confronted by a bunch of angry farmers armed with shotguns. Then he stopped and the Hawkeyes made him drive back those thirty-five miles and satisfy the owner of the runaway. . . .

Another mishap was at Clinton, Iowa, where we lost two hours to-day changing a gasoline tank, the old one having sprung a leak. But now we ought to be able to hike along at a lively gait, for while it has been raining some in the east the roads ought to be drying out now.[64]

In a *Motor Way* interview, however, Whitman said Bates and Daley were the drivers involved in the Marshalltown incident, which he described as a "collision with a farmer's wagon, whose horse became scared and ran away." He also told *Motor Way* that the gas tank was repaired in Sterling, Illinois, about 30 miles east of Clinton.[65] Paraphrasing Whitman, the *Erie (Pa.) Dispatch* further described the incident involving what it called a farm wagon pulled by two horses:

The pair became frightened at the large machine, and started to rear. In some manner the pole on the wagon was broken, and this excited the farmer. He stormed at the speeders and threatened all sorts of things.

The autoists thought but little of the affair at the time, but when they reached the next town, an attempt was made by the villagers to stop the car. However, the machine was going at such a rapid rate of speed that they were unable to capture them, and the record breakers believed it was a closed incident until they reached a bad spot on the road thirty-six miles from where the accident happened.

Here they found a line of natives strung along the road, several of whom were armed with Winchester rifles. Upon seeing the car approaching the men with the guns raised them to their shoulders and told the driver to slow up the car or they would send him and his party to "Kingdom Come." It is needless to say that the machine stopped and the entire party returned to Cedar Rapids [*sic*], where the automobilists paid their fine and started on their way, after being delayed eight hours.[66]

This story continued to grow in the telling. In his account written after the fact, Whitman related that Daley, the driver, had been confronted by "three deputies with guns, and a hundred blood-thirsty natives demanding unconditional surrender. . . . The farmer declared that Daley smashed his buggy-pole, although Daley never knew it; and has his doubts to this day."[67]

A year and a half later, Whitman doubled his estimate of the size of the crowd, for a *New York Times* article on auto racing. "Mr. Whitman discovered that even in distant Iowa, local constables were on the watch for strange automobiles," the *Times* wrote about the 1906 incident. Quoting Whitman, the *Times* continued:

An old farmer caught sight of the dust when we were going fast. He evidently thought it a good time to lay in a new buggy pole, and telegraphed ahead to the next town to stop us long enough to collect, but we didn't stop.

At the second village, about twenty-eight miles from where we passed the farmer, three men with rifles and a crowd of 200 natives blocked the roadway. Quickly turning around, we tried to take a side street around the town. But, alas, the road ended in a barnyard, and the three armed men rapidly pursing, effectually cornered us and it was a case of surrender.

"Goll darn you, don't point that gun at me," yelled one of our mechanics. The men jumped aboard and made us go back the twenty-eight miles, and squeezed out $25.[68]

"Fastest Bit of Work"

Between Chicago and New York City, the Franklin relay team planned to drive the car day and night in hopes of beating Bert Holcomb's Chicago–New York speed record. Holcomb, a tester with the Electric Vehicle Company of Hartford, Connecticut, had set records over the route beginning as early as September 1903. Interestingly, during that 1903 Chicago–New York run in one of Electric Vehicle's Columbia gasoline autos, relay drivers boarded a train to rest between stints at the wheel. Thus, while Whitman was the first to use relays for a transcontinental speed run, he did not originate the idea. Press accounts said the distance between Chicago and New York ranged from slightly more than 1,000 miles to about 1,250 miles, depending on the route. In his most recent record, set on October 6, 1904, Holcomb, assisted by other drivers, had covered the distance in 58 hours, 53 minutes.[69]

A *Cleveland Plain Dealer* reporter interviewed the drivers as the Franklin "flashed into Cleveland," Carris at the wheel, behind a pilot, on Tuesday, August 14, Day 13. The car was "travel stained and mud spattered, covered from bonnet to tail lamp with dust, but with everything running as smoothly and easily as a finely balanced Waterbury watch."

> The people on the West Side who happened to see two autos tearing like mad through the streets yesterday evening about 6 o'clock evidently figured that someone was trying to test the new orders of Chief Kohler regarding auto speeding. They were wrong in their calculations, however, for it was the big Franklin and the pilot car, which had picked them up a mile the other side of Rocky river and which were endeavoring to make up some of the time lost between Toledo and Cleveland. The speed limit was possibly exceeded, but it was in a good [cause] and no complaints were registered.[70]

During the dash into Cleveland, Carris boasted: "We have had excellent luck so far, and we hope to keep it up all the way. We have been unusually lucky with our tires, neither a puncture nor blow out all the way. At Chicago we thought it best to change tires, as the ones we had were beginning to wear badly." Whitman contradicted Carris about the tires by describing two puncture incidents. As a photo from Ogden reveals, one of these punctures evidently occurred in Utah.[71]

In Cleveland, three mechanics—"men who had been selected by the Franklin company especially for the work"—were anxiously awaiting the transcontinental car at the local Franklin garage on Vincent Street. The Syracuse factory had forwarded to Cleveland a new steering post, "for the one in use had been worn somewhat in the long run," the *Plain Dealer* explained.

> Here it was that what is probably a new record for auto repairs was established. Almost before the car had stopped, two mechanics were under the machine, one in the body, and in the remarkably quick time of twelve minutes the old steering post had been removed, a new one substituted and the flyer was ready to continue her run against time. So quickly were the repairs made that the crew had not yet finished their hasty meal, when word was sent them that the car was ready.
>
> A hasty overhauling of the most exposed parts . . . a few drops of oil here and there and in twenty minutes from the time she rolled into the garage, the flyer was on her way east, lamps and searchlight lit and engine running smoothly. . . . Auto men throughout town last night were of the opinion that the changing of the steering post was the fastest bit of work of that kind ever done.[72]

Crackup Near Conneaut

E. L. Springsteen of the Cleveland Franklin agency rode east with the car to act as guide. It was just northeast of Cleveland that the good luck Carris had spoken of earlier ran out. One dozen accounts of the car's accident on the Ohio–Pennsylvania border differ markedly on nearly every detail.[73] The consensus appears to be that, while driving in a heavy fog along the south edge of Lake Erie near Conneaut, Ohio, late Tuesday night, Carris crashed the car off a sharp, dangerous curve. Most accounts said he hit a deep ditch; some said a stone wall.

The car—conflicting accounts say it was traveling at 25, 35, even 45 miles per hour—may have overturned. Thrown from the auto, Carris apparently sprained an ankle and Harris sprained or fractured a knee. Springsteen escaped, like the others, "with slight bruises."[74] The crash badly bent the car's front axle. It also damaged the steering and transmission gears, bent the front wheels, tore off the fenders, and smashed the seats. Repairs took thirty-six hours, thus ending the autoists' assault on the Chicago–New York City speed record.[75]

Physically closest to the scene, the *Erie Dispatch* reported that on Tuesday night, August 14, "a short distance west" of East Springfield, Pennsylvania, Carris and Harris were making

> rapid time until they struck the macadamized road just this side of the Ohio state line. This road is one of the finest in the country, but seems to be fatal for automobilists. When they reached the exact spot where the Cleveland party met such a tragic end a few months ago, the car made a certain turn, and before the driver was aware what had happened, it was in the ditch and its machinery damaged. Luckily none of the occupants were hurt, though a wild-eyed young man did spread the report around the city about midnight that one of the men was nearly killed.[76]

More believable were other reports describing the bruises, sprains, and fractures the autoists sustained after being thrown 15 to 25 feet from the car. Abandoning the disabled auto, the men traveled by rail to meet Whitman in Erie, where his train had arrived earlier that evening, the *Dispatch* said. Along with "a couple of expert repairmen" and their tools, everyone then piled into an auto to return to the crash site. According to the *Erie Dispatch*, the plan was to work all night by the roadside in hopes of coaxing the car into Erie on Wednesday morning. The *New York Herald* would blame this "primitive roadside machine shop, hastily set up," for delays in making repairs. Other reports indicated that the car was towed back the few miles to Conneaut and repaired there. Indeed, two surviving photos show the damaged car being repaired at the W. H. Webb & Son Auto Garage in Conneaut (see Fig. 121).[77]

By most accounts, the accident happened between 10:00 PM and midnight on Tuesday, at a curve both Cleveland newspapers identified as 3 miles east of Conneaut—still on the Ohio side of the state line. They joined the *Erie Dispatch* in asserting that a fatal auto crash had occurred weeks or months earlier at the same "sharp Van Slyke curve." The Franklin "went headlong into a deep ditch, escaping by two feet the telegraph pole which caused the death of two Clevelanders in the recent smashup there." The Franklin apparently continued straight ahead when it ran into the sharp curve, plunging over a low embankment into a creek.[78]

Whitman's Accounts of Crash

Most reports said Carris was driving and Harris was with him. Assuming that *Motor Way* quoted him correctly, Whitman, as often happened, gave a different version in a speech he delivered soon after reaching New York City:

> Bates and Harris were in the machine when this happened. They had with them a guide, who said the road was straight and good ahead, so Bates let her out to about 40 miles an hour. It was not only dark, but a little foggy.
>
> They came to a turn without knowing it, and didn't turn, so they went over an embankment—then stopped. Bates got up and lay in the road, feeling pretty badly. Harris

Fig. 121. Harris, his arm draped casually over the steering wheel, and two unidentified helpers show off the wrecked auto at Conneaut, Ohio (HHFC).

crawled out, not feeling any injuries; but later his leg began to hurt. His knee hurts him now, though he is able to walk about.

They walked back to the town [Conneaut]—four miles—got a team, hauled the machine out of the ditch and took it back with them. There it required all next day to get the car in shape at the blacksmith's shop, and 36 hours' time was lost.[79]

A surviving photo taken in New York City lends credence to Whitman's account: it shows Bates wearing a roughly fashioned splint and bandage on his right hand (see Fig. 122).

Because he was not in the car, Whitman had to piece together his own version of the crash after the fact, just as the auto journals and local newspapers did. Consequently, his accounts, in all their variations, are not automatically the most authoritative ones. In what was perhaps Whitman's final word on the subject, however, he described the crash yet again for the factory's post-run publicity booklet. In this version, he failed entirely to mention Bates's involvement:

Fig. 122. At the wheel, Bates, his right hand bandaged, poses with Whitman in New York City. The glass is gone from the dash-mounted searchlight (HHFC).

COAST TO COAST BY AUTOMOBILE

About eleven o'clock at night nearly up to the Pennsylvania line, thirty-two miles west of Erie, while sailing along at almost forty miles an hour on a fine stretch of road, they swung around a curve too short to hold; missed an iron bridge by twenty feet; plunged down a steep bank into the creek; crashed into a stone abutment on the opposite bank— and the car stopped.

Harris and Carris, however, kept right on after the record. In order to have the proper "light and leading" toward New York, Harris took the searchlight with him—clutched to his breast—and Carris tried to carry away the steering-wheel; and thought better of it and left it bent up over the dash.

The guide on the steamer-trunk pointed the way over the tree-tops in a graceful arc for fifty feet or so, into a friendly mud-puddle.

He was the first to show up uninjured. Carris sprained his ankle and bumped the front of his intellect; Harris wrenched his knee. Otherwise they were all right. . . .

When 3,150 pounds of automobile running like a fast express jumps into a bank of rock there are apt to be some proceedings to report. Front-axle, springs, steering post, lamp and front mud-guards did not look exactly wealthy; but they were certainly better off.

The engine was in perfect running order. The wood-sills were all whole; except the tip of one, where the lamps bolt on; rear axle all right, but one wheel had its spokes slightly sprung. The hamper hung out over one wheel, and the gasoline tank was aleak.

We towed the wreck back to Conneaut, Ohio, and took thirty-six hours getting machine and invalids patched up and on the road again.[80]

Repair Parts Are Missing

Ironically, the repair parts that Whitman had so carefully sent along by train were at that moment out of reach:

When the accident happened at Conneaut the gear had been shipped on to Buffalo. It was impossible to recover it, and before it was gotten new material to make repairs was secured from the factory at Syracuse. The very object for which it had been carried all the way across the country was defeated by this unavailability at the crucial time, but its transmission was a necessary safeguard, nevertheless.

The repairs at Conneaut that cost $600 and thirty-six hours' delay were the replacing of the steering gear, which had been twisted beyond possibility of future use, and the straightening of the forward wheels and the placing of new axle and springs.[81]

Whitman spoke with a *Cleveland Leader* reporter while the car was being repaired: "Providing we find no more ditches we will blow into New York in two days," he predicted. When he described the accident a few days later, at the end of the run, however, he never mentioned a ditch. "We hit a stone fence in the darkness and were thrown over it, while going at a forty-five-mile-an-hour pace," Whitman is quoted as saying, even though he had not been in the car. "It is a wonder the machine was not smashed beyond repair there and the men killed."[82]

Helping with the repairs were "superintendent F. J. Haynes, of the Franklin motor car works, with five men from the factory," the *Cleveland Leader* reported. Bates, Carris, Daley, Harris, and Whitman—all Franklin employees—could well have been those five men from the factory. Three of the five could have been the hand-picked mechanics who replaced the steering column in Cleveland, as well.

Whoever they were, the factory men worked on the car in Conneaut until 11:00 PM on Wednesday, August 15, Day 14, "when a start was made," according to the *Leader* version. "The only new part which had been added after the smashup was a front axle. Upon starting it was found that there was a slight defect in the transmission gear, so the car was returned to the garage and this gear taken apart."[83]

Twelve hours later, "shortly after" 11:00 AM on Thursday, August 16 (or about thirty-six hours after the crash), the car finally got back under way. The *New York Herald* found a silver lining to the crackup: "The fact that the record smashing machine had been delayed by plunging into a ditch in Ohio, rather than detracting from the merits of the performance, served to focus public attention upon the outcome."[84]

The two surviving photos show the aftermath of the nighttime accident. The car is missing its hood and front-end sheet metal, three fenders, seats, searchlight, carriage lamps, right headlamp, and hamper. Photos of the car taken east of Conneaut show that the mechanics who rebuilt the Franklin left off its barrel-shaped extension and rear fenders and replaced the smashed headlamps with a different style—fitted with bales, or handles. The glass is broken out of the car's dash-mounted searchlight, and its left-side carriage lamp is dented (see Fig. 123).

After a 90-minute delay to pay a speeding fine, the Franklin departed Buffalo at 1:00 AM on Friday, August 17. Later, along the Erie Canal towpath, Whitman would recall, "We lost a similar length of time through scaring a canal horse into the Erie Canal and having a lock held open until he was fished out."[85]

Showered with Congratulations

Various, sometimes contradictory, press accounts say the car reached Syracuse at about 7:00 AM on Friday; Albany at 3:00 or 3:30 PM; Hudson at 4:30 PM; Poughkeepsie at 6:00 PM; and Ossining, just north of New York City, at 9:00 or 9:15 PM. The car

Fig. 123. All five men pose with the repaired car at an unidentified stop east of the accident scene. Harris, *left*, and Carris are standing beside the right front fender. Daley is driving, Bates is holding the searchlight lever, and Whitman is standing at attention behind the pair (HHFC).

rolled to a stop at Kingsbridge, "on the upper extremity of Manhattan Island, where the run ended officially," reported *Automobile*. There, concurred the *New York Times*, the crew "was met and officially timed by the Technical Committee of the New York Motor Club."[86] Most accounts say Whitman was driving; photos taken later that night outside the New York Herald building show all five of the drivers posing with the car (see Fig. 124).

Conflicting accounts make it hard to say exactly when Whitman reached Kingsbridge. His arrival time in "New York" was 11:00 PM, Whitman told a Hotel Astor banquet crowd immediately following the run, but he perhaps rounded off the figure. Among the next day's newspapers, the *New York Tribune* gave the Kingsbridge arrival time as 11:02 PM. The *New York Times* said 11:10 PM, as did the August 25, 1906, *Scientific American*. In a subsequent article about the cost of the transcontinental trip, the *New York Times*, without explanation, changed the arrival time to 11:12 PM. The September 1906 issue of *MoTor* and the September 8, 1906, *Scientific American Supplement* also used a "New York" arrival time of 11:12 PM.

Fig. 124. Dirty and battered, the Franklin pulls up to the curbside "Evening Telegram" bulletin board outside the New York Herald building. *Left to right*: Whitman (standing by searchlight), Carris (at wheel), Daley (passenger seat), Harris (partly obscured behind Daley), and Bates (standing on left running board). The men in the center foreground and in front of the car are unidentified (AAMA).

Some reports at least suggested that Kingsbridge was not the official end of the trip. In his "travel stained machine," the *New York Herald* reported, Whitman had pulled up in front of the Herald building at Broadway and 35th Street at 11:55 PM on Friday (see Fig. 125): "Cars were drawn up in welcoming line at Ossining, Tarrytown, and Yonkers, while at Kingsbridge fifteen Franklin machines, loaded with passengers, waited to escort the transcontinental riders into Herald Square. From the latter point Whitman and Carrus [*sic*] were taken to the Hotel Astor, where a supper awaited them."[87]

Cycle and Automobile Trade Journal, however, reported the car's Herald Square arrival time as 11:30 PM. A wire report datelined New York City that appeared in the *Cleveland Plain Dealer* said the run had concluded when the car pulled up to the Hotel Astor at 11:55 PM.

Out of all these choices, the H. H. Franklin Manufacturing Company selected 11:12 PM as the official ending time, establishing a coast-to-coast record of 15 days, 2 hours, 12 minutes (subtracting three hours for the time change). This mark would stand until Whitman and Eugene I. Hammond, driving a Reo, broke it in 1910.

"They were taken to the Hotel Astor and showered with congratulations," a New York paper gushed. "Whitman said that, beyond feeling somewhat tired, he was none the worse after his long trip." After the celebrations at the hotel, however, Whitman allowed that "the fifteen days of broken sleep were beginning to show." He went on: "One of the boys was so foolish as to attempt a bath before retiring; the consequence was that he fell asleep in the bath-tub, soaked five hours, and when he woke up the water was cold and the sun shining in the window."[88]

Fig. 125. Another view of the record-breaker, *far left*, in Herald Square with two escorting cars. *Left to right*: Carris (gripping steering wheel), Whitman (behind wheel), Harris (behind Whitman), Daley (with cigarette in hand), and Bates (AAMA).

The Man of Untiring Will

At the Astor, "Encomiums were showered on the men who had achieved the wonderful performance, and then the men in turn were asked to relate their experiences." Addressing the crowd was Whitman, a man with dark eyes, that pierced and snapped with the vigor of the consciousness behind them; with slight dark mustache and brown hair, where hair remained; of light, but lithe, build that bespoke endurance and power, and such a carriage as might be expected in a man to do things.

It was the scientist, the skilled mechanician clearly, but most of all the man of obdurate, untiring will, the man to meet obstacles. The others were clearly men of force and skilled in their calling, but it is not to be wondered at, after seeing the man, that Whitman has gotten all the credit of the transcontinental journey.[89]

Only after he had traversed the rough trail from San Francisco to Ogden in less than four days did he begin to believe it was possible to reach New York City in ten days, Whitman said. Delays beyond Ogden prevented it, however. The car's running time—"allowing for all delays and stops at stations en route," as the *New York Times* put it—was 11 days, 8 hours, according to Whitman.

In figuring such a record as we have made in our car, nothing but the actual performance —the elapsed time from start to finish—should be considered. The delays are to be expected, must be counted on; they make the performance difficult and give it half its value. If it were a question of plain driving[,] many hours would long ago have been clipped from this time.

Actually our delays amounted to 73 hours and our hourly stops at the 17 relay points made the time we lost just 6 hours short of 4 days. . . . The distance by rail from point to point over the route was 3,400 miles. The actual road distance was between 4,100 and 4,200 miles. . . .

Our daily runs marked out were, of course, laid off with due consideration of the character of the roads and the topography of the country traversed. We had a stretch of 500 miles, from Cheyenne to Omaha, laid off for one day; another of 492 miles, from Omaha to Chicago, and we figured on two days for the 900 miles [*sic*] from Chicago to New York.

On the other hand, we laid off a day of 125 miles in Nevada, and considered ourselves lucky if we made it. On that stretch we bettered the time, and so over other difficult stretches. What we considered easy we failed on.[90]

Down Time

Whitman did not explain the reason for the hour-long stops at the various railroad relay points. Perhaps they represented an average amount of time for the crew to add gasoline and oil, or inspect and adjust the car. Engine adjustments were minor, however, as "the engine operated throughout the trip with scarcely any trouble and not more than two or three hours were consumed in making adjustments."[91]

According to the *New York Times*, Whitman itemized the 73 hours in actual delays: 36 hours for repairs at Conneaut; 12 hours for flooding in the San Joaquin Valley; 8 hours for scaring an Iowa farmer's horse; 6½ hours stranded in the Humboldt Sink; 6½ hours stuck in Wyoming's "mudholes and quicksand"; 3½ hours crossing a Green River tributary; 3½ hours fording rivers in Iowa; 1½ hours for speeding in Buffalo; and "a similar length of time"—1½ hours—for scaring a horse along the Erie Canal.[92]

This, however, adds up to 79 hours, however, and fails to account for the 28 hours that Whitman claims was lost when the rear axle broke in Wyoming; or the 2 hours lost replacing the leaky gas tank at Clinton, Iowa, as Whitman described for the *Chicago Daily News*. Actual delays, then, according to Whitman's own figures, thereby totaled 109 hours. Add to that the 17 hours spent at relay points and the Franklin's total down time for mishaps, maintenance, or repairs was at least 126 hours.

Whitman's *New York Times* accounting evidently excluded the car's nearly 6-hour overnight stay in Laramie, as reported by the *Laramie Republican*; the stop of at least three hours in Chicago; and the 20-minute repair stop in Cleveland. Added to 126 hours in other delays, these 9⅓ additional lost hours increase the Franklin's non-running time to at least 135⅓ hours—or 5 days, 15 hours, 20 minutes—and there were undoubtedly other undocumented stops en route. Thus, the car's running time was something less than 9 days, 10 hours, 52 minutes—or well below the figure of 11 days, 8 hours that the *New York Times* attributed to Whitman. This lends credence to the lower running time given in the *New York Herald*. "Mr. Whitman avers that he can make the trip within ten days in a Franklin car," the *Herald* said, "and his running schedule shows that his machine was in operation not more than that time."[93]

Parts and Pieces

Between San Francisco and New York City, the car needed very few new parts, according to various press accounts and to Whitman. "On the whole run, we changed tires at Chicago because we wanted new tires to make a record run to New York, we replaced four spark plugs, and had two punctures. This was absolutely the only damage sustained, except that done when we collided with the fence at Conneaut," Whitman said in his address to the Hotel Astor revelers. In his speech as the *New York Times* reported it, Whitman neglected to mention the installation of two new parts: a gas tank at Clinton, Iowa, and a steering column at Cleveland.[94]

In his own summary account, however, Whitman said the car also used four sets of batteries. And at Cheyenne, "We replaced a spring, one of whose leaves had slipped out." *Motor World* also reported that, until the accident near Conneaut, "the only mechanical mishap had been a broken spring, although three spark plugs had been replaced and the carburetter cleaned several times."[95]

"We used 263 gallons of gasolene, one and a half gallons of kerosene, twenty-one gallons of cylinder oil, three gallons of gear and transmission oil," Whitman recounted.[96]

Press accounts generally say the Franklin traveled between 3,500 and 4,200 miles. But "there is no very accurate way of determining the actual distance covered, because all the speed registers they had on starting had to be abandoned for one reason or another."[97] Averaging Whitman's range of between 4,100 and 4,200 miles yields 4,150 miles. Assuming this distance, the car's average fuel mileage was 15.7 miles per gallon; average engine-oil consumption was 197.6 mpg, or 49.4 miles per quart; average speed was 11.46 miles per hour for the elapsed time (compared to Dr. H. Nelson Jackson's average of 3.61 mph during the first transcontinental trek in 1903); and average progress per day was a fraction less than 275 miles.

When a reporter asked if he would ever attempt another coast-to-coast auto trip, Whitman answered "emphatically that he would not," *Motor Way* reported. "'No one

Fig. 126. Whitman, *foreground*, poses in the Franklin after announcing his retirement from coast-to-coast speed dashes. Carris is the passenger (HHFC).

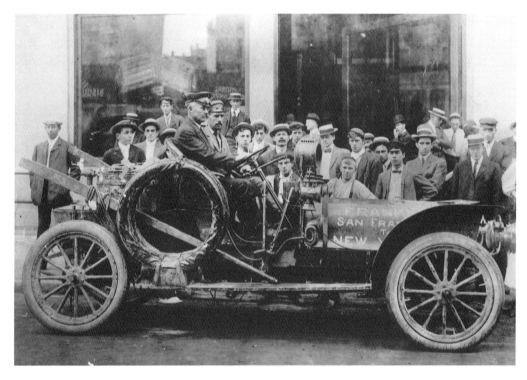

knows what it means unless he has been through it. Looping the loop in a motor car is more sensational, but I don't think the man who does it takes quite as many chances as a man who goes out after a trans-continental record. However, I speak only from a one-sided experience'" (see Fig. 126).[98]

"The Most Severe Test"

The fastest transcontinental run to date left many observers agog: "His [Whitman's] feat at once establishes the high perfection to which the construction of the American automobile has attained," the *New York Herald* said. "After the first flurry of wonder over the whirlwind dash of the Franklin car from ocean to ocean the feature of the trip that seemed to awake the most impression was the splendid demonstration of the efficiency of the six cylinder motor. Up to Mr. Whitman's record ride gasoline engines of more than four cylinders were considered largely as of an experimental nature." Noted *Scientific American Supplement*: "The new record is one of which the manufacturers of the Franklin car may well be proud. The transcontinental journey is certainly the most severe test to which a motor car can be put."[99]

After a rest, Whitman started the Franklin on the following Saturday and headed out for an anti-climactic drive to City Hall, "where he delivered a letter carried by him from the Mayor of San Francisco to the Mayor of New York," according to the *New York Herald*:

> In the absence of both Mayor and Acting Mayor the letter was left with the Mayor's secretary. He also delivered a letter from Major General [Adolphus W.] Greely, at San Francisco, to Major General Wade, at Governor's Island. Mr. Whitman bears a letter from the president of the Automobile Club of San Francisco to the president of the Automobile Club of America.[100]

The H. H. Franklin Manufacturing Company spent more than $8,000 for the transcontinental trip, it was reported: $2,500 went to Whitman ("a part of which is dependent on success"); "a little over half that sum" went to Carris; more than $200 went to "mechanics," which apparently referred to the other drivers; and more than $4,000 had been spent to equip the car and pay for such en route expenses as railroad freight and passenger charges, $600 in repair bills at Conneaut, Ohio, and more than $100 in fines. The cost of the trip rose to nearly $10,000 after Carris and others returned with the car to Chicago for a second crack at setting a Chicago–New York City speed record.[101]

Chicago to New York: Take Two

Joining Carris in the Chicago–New York record attempt were Harris, Bates, and Daley, who variously rode in the car or went ahead by train. Whitman did not participate, according to the most authoritative accounts. Hoping to cut ten hours from the record, the crew left Chicago at 2:00 AM on Tuesday, September 4, 1906, and reached Kingsbridge, New York, at 11:58 AM on Thursday, September 6. Subtracting one hour for the time difference, they traveled the distance in 56 hours, 58 minutes, cutting Bert Holcomb's record by 1 hour, 55 minutes. According to Carris:

> The only accident we had was in Ohio, just after we entered the State, when we struck a load of hay which carried away the hood of the machine and broke the fan. Despite this, we made a good run, although heavy rains made the roads hard going in Ohio, until we reached Syracuse Wednesday night, where a stop of one hour was made for repairs, the longest single stop on the journey. From Little Falls to Schenectady, through the Mohawk Valley, we ran through dense fog and were unable to drive faster than six or seven miles an hour.[102]

A year later, the same crew—with Charles Talbot substituting for Harris—used a 1908 Franklin to lower the record to 39 hours, 53 minutes.[103] The fate of the 1906 Franklin transcontinental car went unrecorded.

"A Far Cry from 1903"

In an elapsed time of slightly more than 15 days and a running time of 9½ days, the Franklin set a coast-to-coast speed record that would stand unbeaten—unchallenged, even—for four years. When Whitman lowered his own mark in 1910, his new record stood until Cannon Ball Baker, driving a V-8 Cadillac, beat it in 1916.

In the meantime, commentators did their best to analyze the achievement of five men and a Franklin. The completion of the transcontinental railroad in 1869 had been hailed as "the greatest step ever made in the material progress of a great nation," *Motor World* reflected in an editorial about the Franklin's speed record.

> The day of the bicycle followed next and first single riders and then relays, demonstrated that . . . something like a reasonable running time could be made even with human power.
> This was followed by a further lapse of interest until, three years ago, the automobile entered the arena. At first, its performances in this field were not greatly superior to those of the two wheeled machine, but successive trials have cut days at a time off the record, finally culminating in Whitman's marvellous dash. . . .

Although none of the previous attempts on the record were carried out with such attention to detailed preparations of a nature insuring success, still nothing demonstrates so strikingly the phenomenal development of the automobile as his reduction of the performance of three years ago by more than two thirds. It is indeed a far cry from the 64-day trip of Dr. Jackson in 1903.[104]

Whitman's experience, his attention to detail, and the railroad-relay system all made possible the 1906 record run, financed by $8,000 or more of Franklin corporate profits. Thus, in three short years, the torch had been passed from Jackson, an amateur autoist who paid his own way, to a relay team of professional racers. The 1906 Franklin trek proved that setting a speed record was now clearly out of the realm of the typical amateur motorist. But there were other records for amateurs to break. When, for instance, would ordinary people undertake to drive across the country, not for records but for pleasure, thus signaling that a transcontinental auto trip was an opportunity available to all? Just two years after Whitman set his fifteen-day record, Jacob M. Murdock would inaugurate the summer ritual of family long-distance motoring by becoming the first person to drive across the country with his wife and children on board.

AN AVERAGE MOTORIST
IN AN ORDINARY CAR

7

"We struck one of these [beaver] holes and the car slid sidewise, one front wheel overhanging the bank and the weight of the car resting on the engine pan and fly wheel. Just at that time the right rear tire went flat."

—Jacob M. Murdock, recounting a mishap in the
"Duck Pond," an Iowa swamp

Opening the floodgates for millions of motorists to follow, Jacob M. Murdock, 44, a Pennsylvania lumberman, left Los Angeles on April 24, 1908, and pointed his Packard toward New York City. Some thirty-two days later, he finished "the most remarkable and convincing demonstration of the touring practicability of the automobile that has yet been given."[1]

Many auto journals and newspapers erred by calling Murdock's trip "the first transcontinental tour ever undertaken by a private owner," as the *Chicago Daily Tri-*

bune phrased it. But Dr. H. Nelson Jackson, the first person to drive an auto across the country, in 1903, did so as a private owner without help from the Winton factory. Other accounts falsely claimed that Murdock drove only by day. The *New York Times* asserted that Murdock "had no relay or extra part[s] awaiting him at any point of the route." In fact, Murdock sent extra tires and springs ahead by rail.[2]

Murdock's actual contributions were considerable, however. Carrying six passengers, including a mechanic, Murdock organized the largest automobile touring party to cross the continent to that time. By all accounts, Murdock drove the entire distance himself; his time was the fastest yet for either a single driver or a single team of drivers. Only relay teams had driven faster. Murdock beat by 14 hours, 13 minutes the record time of 32 days, 17 hours, 20 minutes that Lester L. Whitman and C. S. Carris had set in 1904. (In 1906 Whitman and Carris lowered their own record to 15 days, 2 hours, 10 minutes—less than half Murdock's time—but they did so by alternating at the wheel with three other drivers.)

More important for the popularity of the automobile, Murdock showed that with careful preparation and alert driving, the average motorist was capable of crossing the continent relatively safely in an ordinary car.

Murdock loaded his 1908 Packard Model Thirty touring car with a week's supply of food, as much as 20 gallons of extra gas, and a tool kit worthy of the best transcontinental drivers of the day.[3] The Packard company had agreed to provide him with repair parts en route. The car performed well but was built much too low for the rutted trails of the west. Crossing the Mojave Desert—and particularly Death Valley, on the California–Nevada border—became the most dangerous part of the trip. But the entire 1,600 miles between Los Angeles and Cheyenne, Wyoming, was difficult.

For safety, Murdock tried to travel near railroad tracks through the Southwest. But even with veteran transcontinentalist Lester L. Whitman on board as a guide, the Murdocks lost their way in Death Valley. One of the crew's three female passengers wrote of her fears during a grim and disorienting day spent struggling across the desert's hot, shifting sands. Using binoculars, one crew member finally spotted railroad tracks, which the Murdocks followed to safety.

Steering by crude maps and a compass, the Murdocks reached Ogden, Utah. The "remarkably good" roads of Nevada became a "nightmare" of deep gullies and washouts in Utah.[4] A blizzard and hard rains idled the Murdock party for more than a day in Wyoming. Despite continuing muddy roads in Iowa, Illinois, and south-central Pennsylvania, the family finished the eastern half of its trip with comparative ease.

Carrying guides in the West and a hired mechanic the entire distance, the Murdocks arrived in New York City on May 26—32 days, 3 hours, 7 minutes after starting, and a month earlier than they had expected. Editors and other observers went wild, declaring that transcontinental motoring had finally come of age. Murdock summarized his experiences in a thirty-two-page booklet, *A Family Tour from Ocean to Ocean*, which the Packard company published in 1908.[5] An articulate writer who made five or more additional transcontinental tours, Murdock subsequently advised motorists on how to pack and what to expect when they, too, treated their families to a cross-country automobile trip.

Other Families Tried It

The Murdock family was not the first to set off on a transcontinental auto trip. On June 7, 1906, two families from Wenatchee, Washington—some 150 miles east of the salt water of Seattle's Puget Sound—began a 4,900-mile odyssey through ten states to New York City. The travelers were Winfield S. "Win" Gehr, 44, his wife, Emma, 35, and their dog, Snip; and William Edward "Ed" Camfield, 36, his wife, Nellie, 34, and son, William Jr., 5. The families drove Gehr's 1906 Model E Glide, a five-passenger, 4-cylinder, 36-horsepower touring car made by the Bartholomew Company of Peoria, Illinois.

When they finally reached Gotham on November 28, 1906, after 174 days of driving, camping, and fishing, the press hailed the trek as unprecedented. "While automobiles have previously crossed the continent," declared the *New York Times*, "this is the first time that the journey has been successfully accomplished by a regular touring car carrying its full complement of passengers, besides being the first time that women have ever made the journey."[6]

Emma Gehr's journals, however, revealed a different story. An entry dated November 23, 1906, reveals that Camfield and Gehr loaded the Glide onto a railcar at Linesville, Pennsylvania, to ship it to New York City in time to be displayed with the Bartholomew Company's autos at the annual Grand Central Palace show, which opened on December 1. Thus, the 1906 Glide expedition, a novel long-distance journey, had not been a transcontinental trip after all.[7]

Inspiration: Three Versions

Although he was a Johnstown, Pennsylvania, businessman, Murdock spent winters in Pasadena, California, Whitman's hometown. Whitman, whose transcontinental trips had followed a more northerly route to Utah's Great Salt Lake, agreed to accompany the Murdocks as far as Ogden: "He had never been over the southern route to Ogden, and at Mr. Murdoch's [sic] invitation gladly joined him to that place."[8]

Murdock gave at least three versions of what inspired his trip. "We had spent nearly all winter touring through California in a touring car of the stock type, and had about completed our plans to journey home on the train, but my wife evolved the idea of traveling east in the automobile," he would explain in a *San Diego Union* interview.[9] But reporters who interviewed him at the Bellevue-Stratford Hotel in Philadelphia on the day before he finished his run reported a different story. Murdock explained:

> I had occasion to make several trips between Johnstown and Pasadena this winter. I spent many hours looking out of the [railroad] car windows and dreaming dreams of making the journey home some day in my automobile. You see, I had been reading in the trade papers with great interest the tale of the Pekin[g]–Paris run and the stories of the present New York–Paris race.
>
> When I reached Pasadena in February I had no idea of attempting the journey, and had even gone so far as to buy my railroad tickets home. I would keep asking myself: "Is there a road across the United States?" My answer would always be "yes." Then I got to talking with L. L. Whitman, who lives in Pasadena, of how I could find it and of the possibilities of making the journey with my family.
>
> Finally I determined to make the attempt; at least, I resolved to go to that point when the discomforts should exceed the pleasures, and then to stop. That point, you see, was never reached.[10]

By 1911, Murdock had evidently forgotten his former doubts and wrote with more conviction about his intentions three years earlier. He also clearly stated the purpose of the trip:

> I had in mind just one thing: to successfully demonstrate that it was possible for one person to drive a touring car, with its usual equipment of a cape cart top, side curtains, glass windshield, speedometer, and such other extras as had been discarded on trips across the continent up to this time, and I wanted, in place of the usual company of all athletic male members, to substitute, in their stead, my family, which included three women, making seven persons in all. The extra baggage required for parties with a personnel such as ours greatly increased our load.[11]

Actually, Murdock's plans were so tentative that he "did not make any announcement of the big undertaking," reported the *Johnstown (Pa.) Daily Tribune* of May 4, 1908. "California newspapers, however, took note of the extensive preparations and gave out the story, making positive statements where Mr. Murdock's intentions were conditional. If everything went well on the trip, he proposed to continue it from Pasadena to New York. If there was any trouble, or members of the party seemed fatigued, it was the intention to abandon the journey at any convenient point and take the train for home in Johnstown, shipping the car."[12]

However the trip idea came about, the Murdocks decided to pursue it. "I told my family that I felt I could drive as many hours each day as they were able to ride, therefore I intended to drive all the way myself, which feat I accomplished," Murdock said.[13] He did make exceptions to his plan for driving only during daylight hours and not at all on Sundays.

The family's Packard touring car was filled to capacity. In addition to Whitman, Jacob Murdock and his wife of twenty-one years, the former Anna D. Young of Johnstown, brought along their three children: Florence Lillian, who went by her middle name, 16; Alice, 14; and Jacob Milton, Jr., 10.[14] Murdock's post-trip account contains a few, poorly identified trip photos. Likewise, the photographs that accompanied a few news reports of the Murdock trip inevitably failed to identify the passengers by name.

Shortly after Whitman departed in Ogden, Payson W. Spaulding, a lawyer from Evanston, Wyoming, joined the crew. The seventh crewman was a hapless mechanic whose name the newspapers and auto journals have rendered variously as P. E. Damay, Philip de May, Clarence Demay, Philip DeMay, and Philip de Meyard, among other variations.

From a collection of three dozen 1908 news articles, the twelve that mention his name spell it seven ways. Only one of the twelve gives the mechanic's hometown—Philadelphia. In his *Family Tour from Ocean to Ocean* booklet, Murdock referred to his mechanic by name twice, once as Phillip "De May" and once as Phillip "DeMay," but did not name his hometown. Despite the confusion, "De May" was described in the press as "a professional driver and expert mechanic who was brought from the east especially for this trip. He can rectify anything which goes amiss."[15]

Introducing Murdock

Who was Jacob Murdock? He was born September 25, 1863, in Ligonier, Pennsylvania, and as a young man, he moved with his family to the larger nearby city of Johnstown, where he worked at his father's lumber business. Murdock was secretary of the Johnstown Lumber Company from 1883 until February 1889, when he opened his own wholesale lumber company. He renamed the enterprise J. M. Murdock &

Brother when Wilbert F. Murdock joined him. By the mid-1920s, when Murdock was also vice-president of the First National Bank in Johnstown, the Murdock mills were "located throughout Pennsylvania and West Virginia."[16]

Early on, both brothers became officers of Somerset Stone Company. Long before the 1908 transcontinental trip, the Murdock brothers built the Bare Rock Railroad—an irony, because Jacob Murdock's transcontinental auto trip signaled the beginning of the end for railroad passenger service. Even before his famous trip, Murdock, a member of the Automobile Club of America, was known to the editors of *Automobile Topics*. He had often contributed articles to their magazine.[17] At the time of his transcontinental tour, *Automobile* described Murdock as

> a tourist who has been notable for his unselfish labors for fellow-tourists, the author of the standard route between Philadelphia and Pittsburg (which, through Mr. Murdock's courtesy, forms one of [the] *Automobile Topics* tours), and a much traveled man who spends much of his time motoring in California. Readers of *Automobile Topics* will recall the photos taken during these trips, which have embellished these pages from time to time.[18]

Murdock was an "earnest" Methodist and a Republican, "though in no sense a politician." During the mid-1920s, he chaired his county Good Roads Association. "Mr. Murdock has always been interested in hunting and has made many trips throughout Canada and the Northwest and has many trophies, including four grizzly and three brown bears."[19]

Getting Ready to Ride

Murdock's preparations for the coast-to-coast trip were designed mainly to guarantee his family's safety. He explained: "I made, two weeks before I started, a trip of 150 miles into the Mojave desert, the place I most, and almost only, feared. Then I came back and persuaded Mr. Whitman to accompany me as far as Ogden. I did not wish to lose my family in the desert. I knew I would feel safe in staying by them if he were along to go for help if needed."[20]

But the automobile, he suggested, could take care of itself. "I had but little fear that the car would carry us successfully if we were able to stay with it." He thus carried "a stock of but very few extra parts, as these are not likely to be needed." His foray into the desert also allowed him to test a homemade winch. "Before we left the coast we tried it out by putting the car into the worst sand we could find. With the machine buried to the top of the hubs, and the brakes set hard, the windlass never failed to lift the car to solid ground." On the trip, he explained, "We used ours once only, but that once saved us a 5-mile walk to the nearest town, and at least a half day's delay."[21]

The winch was "Mr. Murdock's own invention, and he has had it patented," according to the *Johnstown Daily Tribune*. The drum is much like that used by house movers, but is smaller. Two wooden arms, which fit into the drum, are being carried on the side of the car. With ropes attached to the front axle, it is expected the machine can be lifted out of a bad place and carried to solid ground without great effort. The whole apparatus weighs only a couple hundred pounds."[22] Murdock may well have invented the winch, but a search of 1900–1909 patent records reveals no such patent under his name.

The "two wooden arms" were actually "two hickory poles, eight feet long, suitable for levers for the winch or pries for lifting the car out of deep mud and sand," Murdock wrote. Strapped to the right running board, the poles were similar to those Whitman and Carris carried on their transcontinental Franklin in 1906. The winch "consisted of a steel drum, three inches in diameter and a foot long, able to revolve on a five-foot [steel] shaft which might be driven into the ground," Murdock added. "Three-foot iron bars served as stakes for guy lines to support the top of the main shaft."[23] To drive the winch shaft and stakes into the ground, Murdock also carried a sledgehammer on the floor of the tonneau.

During his busy two weeks of preparations, Murdock assembled an impressive collection of supplies and tools, some of which he expected to use only between Los Angeles and Cheyenne. East of Cheyenne, he contended, "one might make the run in perfect safety, and carry no more than on any ordinary tour through the eastern states."[24]

"My touring equipment embraced 250 feet of rope of assorted sizes, two shovels, pick, axe, sledge hammer and wrench. We used our cooking outfit quite often, as we slept not a little in unfinished shacks."[25] These "unfinished shacks" were at least located in villages, according to *Automobile*'s list of the travelers' night stops. The Murdock party "only once was obliged to camp out in the open air," said the *New York Times*.[26] The rope was an invaluable aid in the desert:

It is the only thing with which we could successfully work our way through the deep sand. We tried strips of canvas but could make no headway with them. . . . A good way to wrap the wheels is to tie one end of the rope to a spoke of the wheel, then wrap it round and round the entire rim and tire, and tie the other end to the hub of the wheel. This gives a good chance to draw it tight before fastening to the hub.[27]

In a wooden box strapped to the right running board, Murdock carried two 5-gallon gas cans, which he kept filled as far east as Chicago. He reported carrying an additional 10 gallons in cans while crossing two desolate stretches. The first was over the 414-mile route from Los Angeles to Goldfield, Nevada. The second was between Tonopah and Ely, Nevada, a distance of 212 miles by Murdock's route, "where gasoline and oil must be carried for the entire distance. I know of none to be had between these two points."

Sardines, Olives on Board

According to Murdock, "Before starting I wrote ahead to a number of places on the proposed route to arrange for [a] gasoline supply, addressing my letters in all cases to 'Any automobile garage or gasoline dealer.' I received prompt assurances of there being ample gasoline supplies at the desired points." When he stopped to buy gasoline during the trip, he routinely asked about the next available gas supply. "I never asked a dealer where I could next get supplies that he did not tell me correctly."[28]

The travelers also carried a food box and 7 gallons of water, 1 gallon per person, "distributed in four vessels, so that, had one of them sprung a leak, we would have had the others in reserve. Of all the supplies water is the most important." The car's "commissary box" had a hinged lid to keep the food dry, said Murdock. "On our trip we carried fresh bread, butter, salt, sugar, coffee, tea, bacon, eggs, crackers, canned apricots, peaches and tomatoes, sardines, flour and marmalade. These were replenished from time to time all the way to Omaha. East of Omaha we had no occasion to depend on our commissary box." The travelers had other food besides, as one passenger described "a scanty luncheon of crackers, cheese, fruit and olives. . . ." Having a dual purpose, the commissary box sat "crosswise in the tonneau in the place of the ordinary folding seats, the box itself serving as a middle seat," Murdock said.

Murdock took other precautions, according to the *Johnstown Daily Tribune*, which closely followed the adventures of the local family. "Tires and springs, practically the only important parts of the machine likely to give way, have been shipped to points along the route, and as those places are passed the supplies, if not needed, are reshipped to another point farther ahead."[29]

Though Packard would later use the trip as advertising fodder, a company official at first tried to discourage the undertaking, according to Murdock: "I wrote to the general manager of the Packard Motor Car Company. He was optimistic—in proposing that I could have more fun in other and easier kinds of touring." The Packard company assisted Murdock's endeavor, however, "to the extent of sending spare parts ahead of him."[30] These parts undoubtedly included the four tires and six inner tubes that Murdock sent ahead to Ogden.

Other equipment included binoculars; a "sheet iron camp stove" strapped to the back of the car, inside which was carried "several bundles of wire intended for any necessary quick repairs and which was mainly used for fastening minor extras"; a Winchester rifle; one 1-gallon and two 2-gallon canteens, hung from the carriage-lamp brackets; a tank of compressed air for pumping up tires; a tank of Prest-O-Lite compressed acetylene for the headlamps; and a "large water pail with close-fitting top."

Murdock started from Pasadena with three extra tires strapped to the right running board, two 1-gallon cans of oil carried under the spare tires, and nine extra inner tubes stashed beneath the rear seat. He replaced the tonneau floor mat with "folded strips of canvas, eight by twenty feet, with eyelets so that they might be laced together to form a shelter tent or be used as a cover for the car. For tent poles we used the hickory pries. We carried seven pairs of blankets, a large quilt, a woolen lap robe and two water proof lap robes."

In a *Motor Age* article advising motorists on how to pack for transcontinental travel, Murdock revealed that he also carried two dozen straps, 1¼ inches wide and in lengths ranging from 2 to 5 feet, for strapping items to the car. "Sometimes we had only a few of them in use, other times they were all in use. We carried them on the oil lamp brackets, so as to be within easy reach."[31]

"I Didn't Reinforce Anything"

In 1907 the Murdock family toured Europe in the same Packard, which began the transcontinental journey with 5,400 miles on it. "I did not reinforce anything before I started and did not even have the engine gone over," Murdock claimed.[32] Despite its heavy load—up to 5,500 pounds, including fuel, equipment and passengers—the car performed well, he later said. The carburetor did not require adjusting even in the mountains at 9,000 feet. Only once—during a Wyoming snowstorm—did the engine misfire, he said.

"The 1908 Packard car shows a continuance of the well known Packard policy of one model a year and that model a development of, rather than a departure from, the preceding model," wrote *Motor News*. The automaker introduced its Packard Thirty —sometimes referred to as the Packard 30—for the 1907 model year. It manufactured the Thirty through 1912, giving each year's model a different letter code, which for 1908 was Model UA. The 1908 Packard UA used an engine of 4 cylinders, each pair of cylinders cast separately with a T-head valve-in-block arrangement. The engine, with a bore and stroke of 5 × 5½ inches, had a radiator cooling fan and water pump. The engine developed 30 horsepower at 650 rpm under the "European rating," but as much as 60 horsepower "by the American system."[33] Murdock claimed that his car's gas mileage was normally 10 miles per gallon or higher.

The 1908 Thirty came equipped with front tires of 36 × 4 inches and slightly larger rear tires of 36 × 4½ inches. "The only change which we made in the car," Murdock said, "was to put on front wheels equipped with 36 by 4½-inch tires, so that all tires on the car would be interchangeable." The car, equipped with Continental tires, had a 123½-inch wheelbase.

The 1908 Packard had a 3-speed, sliding-gear transmission. Gasoline flowed to the engine by gravity from a 21-gallon copper tank under the car's front seat. The 1908 Thirty came with a low-tension Eisemann magneto and a storage battery, either of which could power the engine's ignition system. The 1908 Packard touring car weighed 3,300 pounds empty. Its body and frame were painted "Packard blue" and its running gear (springs, wheels, axles and other parts) were painted "cream yellow." The car sold for $4,200—or $4,350 if equipped with a top and side curtains. From its model-year introduction in May 1907, the Packard Motor Car Company made 1,303 of its 1908 Packard Thirty autos.[34]

Day 1: Lighten Load

Murdock, who described the nearly 1,600 miles from Los Angeles to Cheyenne as "dry country," preferred to cross the desert in the early spring. The crossing of Death Valley was "the only really dangerous part of the journey," he warned. If the family could reach Ogden, forecast the *Los Angeles Examiner*, "a Pasadena to New York banner will be unfurled, as from that point eastward the journey will be less difficult and its final success will be practically assured."[35]

According to Murdock's account in the post-run Packard booklet, the family started east from "our winter bungalow in Pasadena" at 8:00 AM on Friday, April 24, 1908 (see Fig. 127). In the press, however, his reported departure times ranged widely, from 2:00 AM to 8:00 PM. The *Pasadena Daily News* suggested that the travelers were planning from the outset to make it a record-setting trip: "Very little time will be taken up with stops, the party proceeding all day and so timing their journey as to spend the nights at towns along the route as much as possible."[36]

Murdock recalled:

We got up Friday morning, April 24, with the trepidation of a small boy tentatively sizing up the weather through window curtains on the dawn of Independence Day. It was a great and auspicious morning and we made a brave bluff at eating breakfast with a relish. At eight o'clock we were ready. Under an escort of friends we sailed away for the outskirts of the city, where we bid a bunch of adieus and picked up Whitman.

Our party was thus complete, consisting of Mrs. Murdock, our daughters, Lillian and Alice, Jacob Milton, Jr., L. L. Whitman, who was to accompany us to Ogden; our mechanic, Phillip DeMay, and myself. . . .

Our own 1,020 pounds of weight, plus 1,200 pounds of supplies and equipment, plus the car, made a total of 5,500 pounds. I realized that we had a heavy undertaking on our hands. In fact, we hardly had been a mile off the boulevards before we decided

Fig. 127. The Murdocks prepare to leave Pasadena in their loaded Packard. Occupying the back seat, though in an indeterminate order, are Anna Murdock and daughters Lillian, 16, and Alice, 14. Murdock is driving. Jacob Milton Jr., 10, stands to the right of his father. On the far right is mechanic Philip De May (NAHC).

to lighten our load, and consequently dropped off some of our bedding, a sleeping bag and a wall tent. At San Dimas, about 25 miles from Pasadena, we met friends who exchanged good-will for about 125 pounds of unnecessary comforts. Thereafter we did not reduce weight.[37]

By 3:30 PM on Friday, Murdock had covered the 141 miles to Daggett, California, where he stopped for gas. The roads from Los Angeles had been "good, well-defined and easily followed, but immediately upon leaving Daggett they became very poor."

At Otis, four miles farther on, we obtained directions from a liveryman as follows:
"Follow the main road clear to the foot of the ridge. About 18 miles out you will come to Coyote Lake, a dry lake, which you must cross and on the other side of which you will run into deep drift sand. Yes, it's pretty blamed bad. Most automobiles go that far and then turn back. However, if you keep on going ahead you can get through. There are only four miles of it, and these four become better the farther you go."
After we had crossed the bad roads east of Otis and reached and crossed Coyote Lake we plunged straight into our first experience in drift sand. This stuff is like quicksilver. The more you shovel the deeper it gets. It blows into your eyes and ears and, despite persistent effort by the entire crew, headway is very, very slow. First we tried shoveling; then we laid down strips of canvas on which to run the wheels and succeeded in getting well settled in the deepest part.
The sky had deepened to a dark blue, like our own spirits, but the coming night did not change the view much because there was nothing in the view to change—a vast lack of everything except sand. The whole situation was a large deficiency. As a last resort we wrapped the wheels with heavy rope, which greatly improved our traction, which, in turn, greatly improved our nerve. We forced our way ahead from three to six hundred feet per effort. Just as night fell silently and without damage on the soft sand, we managed to pull through.
We lighted our headlights and started going over fair road through a rolling desert country. We watched carefully along the way for Garlic Wells, supposed to be about sixteen miles distant and where we wished to camp for the night. We found this metropolis of the desert at nine o'clock. It proved to consist of a well, a platform and a windlass. We soon had our stove up, a fire burning and a supper cooking. We feasted and made camp. The women occupied the car and the rest of us rolled in blankets on the ground.

Thus, on his first day of driving, Murdock traveled 173 miles northeast from Pasadena to a point in the desert that he also referred to as Garlic Lake and Garlic Spring. The dry lake and the spring are about 3 miles apart, both about 30 miles northeast of Daggett, according to an H. M. Gousha Company 1935 California highway map. Because Garlic Wells does not appear on the map, it appears Murdock meant Garlic Spring. The *New York Times* maintained this was the only time the family camped out, but Murdock reports that the travelers camped again the next night.

Death Valley "A Blank Space"

"Road maps of southern California, Nevada, Utah and Wyoming, such as they are, may be had at the large book stores," Murdock wrote. "The only maps which we had at the start were small vest pocket state maps, such as are purchased at book stores, showing the latest government surveys." But, "there are practically no maps of the desert. The latest United States survey maps show a blank space in the Death Valley district. Many of the places marked were practically no settlements at all, or the mere tumbledown shacks of deserted mining camps," Murdock said. The Mojave Desert "abounded in dry lakes, some five to seven miles across, with a spongy surface that took a bit of nerve to tackle."[38]

At 6:10 AM on Saturday, April 25, Day 2, the travelers left Garlic Spring for what became an 11-hour, 67-mile drive to Resting Springs, California, where the family rested on Sunday. It was a well-deserved rest. Murdock drove the first 30 miles in just under two hours, through Crackerjack, a mining camp, to Cave Spring, California, "literally described by its name, there being a big spring within a little cave and a six-by-ten mining camp to keep it company," he recalled.

> Here is the best water in that part of the country, so we filled all our canteens and pails. Also, we filled up on road directions. Leaving, we traversed for fifteen miles the tortuous bottom of a deep canon, which suddenly spilled itself onto the edge of Death Valley desert.
>
> We soon found that our drift sand experience at Coyote Lake had been merely a kindergarten for us in the art of tractionless travel.
>
> Along the Amargosa Wash all trace of the road disappeared. The rocky bottom of the creek is covered with drift sand, with occasional traces of water. Here the Death Valley is five to ten miles wide, the higher ground being a formation of immense sand drifts.
>
> During heavy wind storms these sand drifts are shifted and blown in every direction. While we were there the heat was intense and the wind blew the fine sand so fiercely about us that we were compelled to put up the top and side curtains. We traveled part of the time in the bed of the wash and part of the time on the bank.
>
> Sometimes, after managing to get started, we would succeed in making a quarter of a mile; generally we would accomplish only a couple of hundred feet before being again stalled. Each time we shoveled away the sand, tightened the ropes on the wheels and made another start.
>
> After we had been out of the canon for a couple of hours and had left all evidence of road and direction five or six miles behind us we were, in a measure, lost. With the aid of map and compass we chose a southerly course as the most likely one. We floundered around for eight hours, eighteen miles and thirty gallons of gasoline.

"Terrible, Threatening Sand"

One of the passengers—Murdock identifies her only as "one of the female members of our party," most likely his wife, Anna—wrote this account of their harrowing journey through Death Valley:

> The only water in the valley fairly boils in the soft beds of tiny alkali streams. It was beside one of these streams, with its shallow, almost stagnant bit of water, that we stopped one day near noontime late in April. . . . We had not only left the last sign of habitation, Cave Springs Camp, 12 miles behind us, but we had lost even the faintest trace of civilization. . . .
>
> For 3 hours we bumped and shoveled our way ever so slowly, under the scorching rays of the sun; even with heavy ropes wrapped around the wheels of the car, and the engine's rushing whirring at full speed, we could not force the car forward. The two other men [apparently Whitman and the mechanic, since Murdock was driving] of the party either shoveled sand from under the wheels, trying in vain to reach more solid footing, or stretched strips of canvas over the sand, in hopes that they might afford firmer hold for the jumping wheels, but it was slow work.
>
> As noontime drew near, the sun got so hot that it almost burnt the seat covers, so we had to put up the top; of course, this hindered traveling even more, but we could not endure the withering sun, even at such a cost. . . .
>
> By this time we knew absolutely nothing of where we were. We had been pushing ahead in hopes of coming to something or some place. As to how we could get out of the terrible valley, we had no idea; but we had provisions to last us seven days, pure water in our canteens, and we had stopped beside water that could be boiled if necessity should demand. The machine would afford us shelter from severe weather. With this much in our favor, we decided that the end had not yet come, even if we were in Death valley. . . .
>
> With the aid of a compass and a brief road map, we figured out that there ought to be a little camp and, perhaps, a railroad somewhere to the left of us. But when we got out our field glasses and scanned the horizon and could find no trace of anything behind us except miles of terrible, threatening sand, which we had labored through and which it would have been folly to attack again, and which separated us from the living world, we realized our danger. . . .
>
> We determined to find some sign of a camp or a road, or even a telegraph pole, somewhere, if it was to be found. So, having again consulted the map and searched in vain for even the slightest trace of man, we decided that two of the men of our party would start out on foot to find a way, but not to lose sight of the machine and the rest of the party even for an instant. . . .
>
> After a search of some 2 hours, we were all somewhat cheered with the report that one of our party had seen what looked like a railroad, far to the northeast. So . . . we turned the Packard up the pebbly bed of the little stream. Where a stray railroad track had signaled to us, across the great hot plains of Death valley, we sought for a road to the world of man.[39]

Oasis Looms, Town Booms

Those stray tracks belonged to the Tonopah & Tidewater Railroad, which the Packard crossed once on Day 2 and several times on Day 4 to avoid sandy stretches, according to Murdock (see Fig. 128). On Saturday, Day 2, he followed the tracks to China Ranch, California, and beyond,

> where we again shoveled, groveled, plowed and floundered. Our dauntless spirit pretty nearly reached ebb-tide. Through field glasses we sighted, at the foot of a steep ridge, a clump of green trees with the green grass growing all around. We got back on the job, reached the trees, which proved to be Resting Springs, and camped over Sunday. . . .
>
> Resting Springs was indeed an oasis in a barren desert, beautiful in its green contrast to the everlasting sand. It was one of the old landmarks on the edge of Death Valley desert in the days of the forty-niners. The warm water flowing out of the large spring pours over the ground and irrigates a few acres, on which small patch of fertility rests a group of ranch buildings, comprising the home of an old settler of the Golden Era.

Leaving Resting Springs on Monday, April 27, 1908, the travelers passed through the Nevada towns of Lee, a mining camp (see Fig. 129), Gold Center, and Beatty, as they headed northeast toward Goldfield.

Fig. 128. De May plays the spotter as Murdock crosses railroad tracks at an unidentified desert location (NAHC).

Just an hour before dark we struck out in the effort to reach Goldfield [before] night. We were told there was a well-traveled automobile road between these two places, and that once on it there would be no difficulty in following it to Goldfield. Prophecy correct. We went to bed in the notorious boom town of miners, stock merchants, gamblers and prize fighters shortly after ten o'clock. The hotel here was surprisingly good, having most of the eastern conveniences except size.

The transcontinental Packard party spent the night at the Goldfield Hotel, having made 174 miles despite the bad roads. Murdock wrote:

> Cars built for Eastern use are at a great disadvantage in this district. They have too low clearance for the rocks and deep ruts, nor are they wide enough to fit the ruts. These rocks and ruts gave us great trouble. They would catch the flywheel and we were in constant fear of ripping it off. I had to stop at least ten times a day to pry the pan away from the flywheel. This question of clearance was, in fact, the most difficult of our problems in this region.[40]

At both Ogden and Cheyenne, Murdock had the engine pan removed and repaired. Because of its 56½-inch tread—the distance between its left and right wheels—the Packard was too small to fit the ruts made by wagons having a 61½-inch tread, Murdock complained. This "causes one wheel of the machine to climb along the side of one of the ruts."[41]

Pants Decamp

In Goldfield, Murdock ran across "a young man who was thoroughly familiar with the country hereabouts," and who sketched a rough but accurate map of landmarks along the 240-mile route to Ely. Following this map, the travelers left Goldfield at 10:30 AM on Tuesday, April 28. "There are quite a few automobiles around Tonopah

Fig. 129. This unidentified photo quite possibly shows the mining camp of Lee, Nevada, which Murdock described as "well up on the side of the mountain ridge" (*Automobile*, May 28, 1908).

and Goldfield," Murdock noted. "Some of them are built especially for that section of the country in order to obtain more than ordinary clearance. Both owners and chauffeurs in that district are a gay and cheerful lot. They drive with open throttles and without mufflers. To stand the abuse which the roads and drivers give them the cars ought to be good ones."

Murdock had nothing but praise for the roads from Tonopah—which he reached at 12:30 PM Tuesday—northeast through Ely. "The road was remarkably good, there being lots of long stretches admitting of 25 to 30 miles an hour going. Our only guides were rough pencil drawings and the United States maps. We steered by compass a lot. In fact, we reached Ogden, having strayed no further than five miles from the true course."[42]

Covering eighty-four miles in something less than eight hours, the voyagers stopped for the night on Tuesday at Stone Cabin, which "accommodated an hospitable family who provided us with comfortable beds in an outlying shack." Murdock recalled: "We cooked our own evening meal. It was here that a coyote or some other alien of the night came in through an open window and carried off Milton's trousers, Milton having carelessly taken them off before retiring. For the next three days, on account of the scarcity of clothing stores en route, he was forced to travel in a combination of pajamas and overalls."

Between 7:15 AM and 8:00 PM on Wednesday, April 29, Day 6, Murdock drove the 155 miles from Stone Cabin to Ely. That afternoon, "We made a wrong turn and were soon lost in a district of sage brush, where there was no road and where the brush finally became so thick that we could not proceed. Leaving the car we hunted on foot for the road and after awhile brought the car back to it." Nevada roads "are fairly good" when they follow valleys or unbroken land, Murdock concluded afterward. "As soon as they straggle into the foothills they are very badly washed out and in some places almost impassable."

Lonely Country

One further adventure awaited the Murdocks late Wednesday:

> Just before entering Ely we climbed a stiff grade and, dropping down the other side, gave the fly wheel a bad bump on a hidden rock. We did not stop to make an examination and, in fact, drove the car all the rest of the way across the continent without finding out whether or not we had knocked the clutch out of alignment.

This was one of the memorable days of our journey. At one point in the forenoon we were 120 miles distant from the nearest railway station. Bumping along the hard spots in the middle of the desert, without a single sign of habitation or civilization, it was easy to do a little incidental romancing, not to mention a little worrying should any serious accident occur in such a remote district. Perhaps we sighed in relief as we passed scattered ranches toward evening and neared Ely and its comfortable hotel. A small town is a big sight in the middle of Nevada [see Fig. 130].

The roads from Ely north to Cobre, Nevada, near the Utah border, were even better than those west of Ely, for there was "not a grade or a hill and few 'washes.' For 140 miles it is good for 75 miles an hour," Murdock said.[43]

For safety, the tourists followed the railroad tracks through Nevada where possible, meeting the Southern Pacific main line at Cobre and following it to Ogden. Still, it was lonely country, according to Murdock. "Through one stretch of 220 miles in Nevada we traveled without encountering a human being or meeting with a habitation of any kind."[44] Exactly where this stretch of road might have been is unclear, since Murdock's longest day's drive in Nevada was 167 miles and the car stopped at a town each night.

Except during a brief rainy season, Nevada's lakes and rivers are dry. "Only the wells, 20 to 75 miles apart, can be relied upon for water," Murdock reflected (see Fig. 131). "It generally costs 15 cents to water a team of horses or 50 cents a barrel for water to carry away. Contrary to the usual customs of the road, automobiles are on the free

Fig. 130. This unidentified small town is apparently one of the big sights the Murdocks viewed in Nevada (*Automobile*, May 28, 1908).

Fig. 131. According to Murdock, the wells generally consisted of a bucket and windlass, a platform, and a barrel, as does this one at an undisclosed desert stop (*Automobile*, May 28, 1908).

list. The westerner has a keen appreciation of progress and would like to see automobiles running thick and fast through the country."

Buoyed with optimism, Murdock expected to drive the 180 miles from Montello, Nevada, to Ogden on Friday, May 1, Day 8 of the trip. But, "It took us two days of the hardest work," he wrote. "From Cobre to Kelton [Utah] it is a nightmare. You have to straddle ruts a man could almost stand in." And Saturday's drive from Kelton to Ogden was through "a veritable swamp with mud two feet and water four feet deep in places," he said.[45]

The 25 miles from Kelton to Lakeside was "fairly passable." East of Lakeside, however, loomed "five miles of swamp with deep muddy fords through many streams. So we hit the railway ties to Promontory. After five miles of this we were able to leave the tracks for smoother going, but were compelled to do considerable dodging between up-and-down places that were steeper than any hills I ever heard of before." Murdock counted twenty-five or thirty steep hills "that would stop the wheels and stall the motor. We would have to throw on power and then block the wheels behind and repeat the operation." Using this process—identical to the "jumping" method Tom Fetch and Marius C. Krarup employed in their 1903 Packard crossing—the 1908 travelers spent four hours climbing one 300-foot hill, Murdock recalled.[46]

"Some Hilarious" at Ogden

Reaching Ogden at 3:00 PM on Saturday, May 2, Day 9, the tourists checked into the Reed Hotel, while the Packard checked into L. H. Becraft's garage "for inspection and general cleaning up," the *Ogden Morning Examiner* reported. During the 1,002 miles from Los Angeles to Ogden, "not a stop was made for any mechanical cause, and even the awful grind on our Continental tires caused no trouble," Murdock told his hometown newspaper.[47] As he later wrote, "We were some hilarious as we rode into that city [Ogden] on the afternoon of the ninth day, for we were so far ahead of our expectations and the record that we could not help feeling glad, very glad."

Whitman, who would leave the Murdocks at Ogden, had stopped at Becraft's auto agency and garage during his 1906 Franklin trip. "Mr. Whitman states that the worst road across the continent has been encountered by the party and he can see no reason why Mr. Murdock cannot continue the rest of the way to New York at an average rate of 150 miles a day," the *Ogden Morning Examiner* said. Becraft would accompany the car to Evanston, Wyoming, the newspaper added.[48]

The tourists rested in Ogden on Sunday, May 3, for the following day's 85-mile drive into Wyoming. "They left Ogden Monday morning, went forty miles up the Weber Canyon, through Devil's Gate, and to the town of Morgan [Utah]," the *Johnstown Daily Tribune* recounted. "From there they climbed 3,000 feet up the mountain through a heavy rain over slippery dirt roads to Evanston, where they remained until Wednesday for the roads to dry."[49] The Packard had its first tire puncture on Monday, though earlier, in Nevada, Murdock had replaced a tire "which had been a badly worn one at the start of the tour."

Because of the recent rains, the drive was more difficult than intimated in the *Johnstown Daily Tribune*. According to Murdock, Wasatch Hill near Wasatch, Utah, just west of the Wyoming state line,

> was a particularly slippery climb on account of its steepness and washed-out, deep ruts. In fact, we tried all the traction makers such as ropes, canvas, etc., that we had. Eventually we got up by short jerks, consisting of speeding up the engine, throwing in the clutch, jumping a few feet, stopping, blocking the rear wheels and doing it over again.
>
> The rest of the road to Evanston was flat, muddy, but not extremely difficult. We got in late in the afternoon, pretty well tired out from our first experience with real adobe.

New Guide Accepts Ride

At the Murdocks' invitation, Payson W. Spaulding, an Evanston lawyer, joined the party "in the capacity of companion and guide," the local *Wyoming Press* reported. "Mr. Spaulding has business requiring his presence in Washington, D.C., and if they succeed in making good time he will remain with the auto party all the way to Philadelphia."[50] Spaulding, in fact, was still with the car when it reached New York City.

Press accounts do not reveal how Murdock and Spaulding got acquainted. Whitman perhaps told Murdock of Spaulding, who was active in the Wyoming good-roads movement. In mid-March 1908, he had served as a local guide for the Thomas entry in the New York–Paris race. In September 1913, soon after the Lincoln Highway Association announced the route of America's first transcontinental highway, which traversed Wyoming and a dozen other states, Spaulding was named Wyoming's state consul for the road. He was a big reason that the Cowboy State "gave the highway an enthusiastic welcome." To help promote the Lincoln Highway within Wyoming, Spaulding "drove all the way across the state and back, a trip of nearly 900 miles."[51]

Murdock recounted only that "Spaulding appeared on the scene" to pilot the car into Evanston on Monday. On the next day, "Spaulding volunteered to accompany us and we enlisted him on the spot. It was one of the best deals in friendship I ever have made. Spaulding was real, inside and out, and knew the western country better than its mother."

Winch Works in Wicked Wash

Snow followed rain as Murdock slogged across Wyoming, perhaps regretting his springtime start from Los Angeles. Leaving Evanston on Wednesday morning, May 6, for the drive through southwestern Wyoming, the seven-person Murdock party

> ran in the mud over the Bear River Divide, the slippery condition of the roads rendering descent quite difficult on the eastern slope. Just before going into Cumberland they ran into a bad wash, the car standing almost perpendicular, but it was extricated without assistance by the use of the winch which Mr. Murdock has invented and carries with him.
>
> From Cumberland the party ran to Diamondville, on the Oregon Short Line, thence down Ham's Fork to Opal, and to Granger for the night, having traveled that day forty-five miles north in order to avoid fords that were impassable.
>
> On Thursday the party left all so-called roads and struck through the sage brush, the Packard safely carrying its seven passengers to Wamsutter, crossing the Az[u]sa and Marston washes in good shape. The latter is about thirty feet deep and fifty-five feet across the top, with sides almost straight up and a sand bottom. From there one goes through Rock Springs and up the historic Bitter Creek to Wamsutter.[52]

Transcontinental autoists regarded the Marston Wash as a fearsome obstacle. In mid-June 1909, Spaulding would act as local guide for Hugo Alois Taussig, a San

Francisco wine merchant who was making a leisurely transcontinental crossing in a chauffeur-driven Thomas auto. East of Granger, as Taussig later wrote,

> Our road took us over a series of washes (gullies), of which Marston Wash was considered the worst, and which we were told we would not be able to cross without the assistance of a team of horses. Good luck, a sixty horse power engine, or good driving, however, took us over the washes.[53]

In his post-run factory booklet, Murdock elaborated on Wednesday's mishaps, beginning with the washout near Cumberland, 35 miles northeast of Evanston:

> About the first thing we did was to get into trouble. It was down in Guild Hollow on the way to Cumberland. We dropped down a bank and slid the car nearly on end immediately in front of another impossible cliff. The descent was so steep that when the front wheels hit the bottom, the car nearly turned turtle. We yanked the car out backward with the windlass and were glad we had brought it along. Then we dug off the corners of the embankment on both sides, filled in the bottom of the washout a little and rushed it. . . .
>
> Just east of Opal, which looks like it when the sun sets, we tried to cross a deep irrigating ditch diagonally and caught the fly wheel on the corner of the bank, stopping the car. The car was so strained and twisted that the engine could not be started and·it took us nearly a half-hour to dig out below the fly wheel, thus relieving the strain [see Fig. 132].

Fig. 132. De May, *right*, has evidently just finished cutting down a steep bank, allowing Murdock to drive over it. The setting appears to be Utah or Wyoming (NAHC).

In this kind of traveling the amount of straining which is given both the machinery and the car is almost unbelievable. In many places, where the roads originally had been good, they were unavailable on account of the erection of fences around new ranches. This necessitated detours and the making of new trails through the sage brush and over the washouts.

"Overflowing with Humanity"

If rain and snow were seasonal hazards, fences presented a year-round problem, according to Murdock's description:

Most of the so-called roads west of Cheyenne are mere trails. In many places, where the roads have been clear, they are not available on account of the erection of wire fences around the ranches. These wire fences cross the road at many unexpected places. So it is a common thing to have to make new trails through the sage brush and over washouts.

None of the roads is sufficiently traveled to wear the surface down for more than two tracks where the wheels and the horses run. . . . Sage brush grows between the ruts and there are no single horse rigs to tramp it down.[54]

At 7:45 PM on Thursday, May 7, Day 14, the Murdocks drove into Wamsutter, "where we met all of the twenty-five inhabitants and remained over night, having come 135 miles that day," Murdock recalled:

Sheep shearing gangs and herders had charge of the town that night and its dozen houses were overflowing with humanity and others, so we were forced to retire to the suburbs and put up with the section boss who lived about a half-mile down the railway.

Some of the herders started to shoot up the town about daybreak, but, being sheep men instead of the real article from the cattle country, it was a comparatively mild and harmless celebration. There is not much doing in the revolver line out there now-a-days, and at no time on the road were we accorded anything less than the most courteous and kindly consideration.

On Friday, May 8, Day 15, Murdock drove the 135 miles from Wamsutter to Rock River in southeastern Wyoming, passing Fort Steele in the early afternoon. In 1906, the comparatively light transcontinental Franklin had crossed the flimsy wagon bridge over the North Platte River at Fort Steele. Just weeks before Murdock's arrival, the heavy New York–Paris racers had avoided it, the Thomas crossing the river on the ice and the Zust on the Union Pacific bridge. But Murdock's nearly 3-ton Packard "crossed the river on a rickety pole bridge at the bottom of a roughly chopped-out decline on the side of the bank."

Stormy Weather

Friday morning, the party passed through Rawlins. "Mrs. Murdock was taken sick here and compelled to remain here for a few days," the *Rawlins Republican* reported. "She will overtake her husband before he reaches his home in Johnston [*sic*]." The newspaper provided no further details about Anna Murdock's illness; other accounts fail to mention it at all. And, in fact, she was with the tourists—along with a new rider, "J. Purdy," perhaps a local guide—when the car reached snowbound Laramie, as Saturday's *Laramie Boomerang* reported.[55] In his post-run booklet, Murdock described Saturday's trip from Rock River to Laramie as "eventful":

> During the morning we got off the regular route and went about three miles out of our way, coming to a river without a bridge and too deep to ford. We were forced to wade through it to a ranch on the other side in order to obtain directions. The ranchmen escorted us to a bridge three miles down the river.
>
> It was shortly after we had re-crossed and were back on the trail that we were caught in a blizzard—a genuine western one, so full of snow that we could not even see the fences along the roadside. The wind-driven snow filled the car and covered the wind shield glass with ice a couple of inches thick.
>
> We were almost frozen when we reached Laramie at 11 o'clock in the morning, having come in over another main road than the one from which we had wandered. The blizzard continued and it was so cold we remained at Laramie for the rest of the day.

Leaving Laramie early the next morning, Sunday, May 10, the coast-to-coast Packard arrived at 2:00 PM in Cheyenne, where the Murdocks and Spaulding spent the remainder of the day resting. "A very jolly party of automobilists arrived in Cheyenne yesterday on its way from California," reported Monday's *Wyoming Tribune* of Cheyenne. "Mr. Murdock says that the only accident encountered was on Sherman hill where for a time they lost their way."[56]

Murdock dismissed the incident as trivial: "Just east of Laramie, on Sherman Hill, we traveled through snow a foot deep. We lost the main road, but found it again after some wandering." It was 573 miles over the Rocky Mountains from Ogden to Cheyenne, reported the *Johnstown Daily Tribune*, raising the Murdocks' trip mileage to 1,576.

Murdock the motorist may have cursed the roads, as did other automobile pioneers. Murdock the businessman, however, understood the reasons for their wretchedness: "People are likely to forget that, unless a state is wealthy and has a high assessed valuation liable for taxes to both build and maintain, it can neither build nor maintain roads." Nevada and Wyoming "have an assessed valuation liable to taxation for road purposes of less than $1,000 per mile, as against $100,000 per mile in New York state. Yet either of these states has more than two-thirds the number of roads that New York state has."[57]

Sunday's stormy weather cleared and the coast-to-coast Packard left Cheyenne's Inter Ocean Hotel at 8:30 AM on a bright, clear Monday, May 11, according to local news reports. Murdock used the fine weather and good roads to drive 241 miles to North Platte, Nebraska.

> A speed of thirty miles an hour was maintained during most of the day, in which we rolled up the record mileage for the trip that far. . . . The next day the traveling was also good. Crossing the Platte River, which is a mile wide and eight inches deep, we took a southeastward course along the section lines. Following these section lines in a zigzag fashion, increases mileage to a great extent over the old-fashioned diagonal trunk road.

"A District of Mud"

On Tuesday, May 12, Murdock drove 235 miles, passing the famous midway marker in Kearney (see Fig. 133), and reached Columbus in time to view one of Nebraska's natural hazards. "The automobile barely missed the tornado in Nebraska Tuesday," the *Omaha World-Herald* reported, "seeing it from a distance." Though the coast-to-coast car also missed the rain accompanying the twister, "muddy roads were encountered in the afternoon," the *Johnstown Daily Tribune* summarized.[58] "Near Grand Island," Murdock confirmed, "we ran into a district of mud. At Silver Creek, which we reached about dark, we were informed that the roads to Columbus were bad. However, we pushed on and found that we had been misinformed. Wrong information of this kind is characteristic of the west, as well as the east. At Columbus, where we stayed over night, a local automobilist warned us of sand to be encountered the following day. Then we gave him a few pointers on sand as it exists in its natural home, Nevada."

The Packard's odometer showed 2,143 miles separating Los Angeles and Omaha, where the Murdocks arrived during the noon hour Wednesday, May 13, Day 20, after a muddy drive from Columbus, according to the *Omaha World-Herald*. Mud was on the menu for Iowa and Illinois, as well. In fact, "until the arrival at Chicago it was one royal battle with the roads," according to Murdock, who clashed with the enemy shortly after crossing the Missouri River bridge into Council Bluffs, Iowa, at 3:30 PM on Wednesday.[59]

> We hadn't been in Iowa a half hour before the car was stuck in the mud—over axles and hubs. "All out," was the order of the day, and the shovels and pries were promptly put into action and the car soon on its way. The best information obtained was that it had been raining steadily in Iowa for over two weeks, and in Illinois three weeks. It rained this afternoon [Wednesday] also and during the storm a perfect double rainbow was observed.[60]

Iowa has two kinds of mud, mused Murdock, who drove his family into Denison during a "hard rainstorm" at 8:00 PM Wednesday—"black in the bottom lands and yellow clay on the hillsides. We passed through a college town and noted that the colors were yellow and black."[61]

Of Muskrats and Mire

The next day, Thursday, May 14, "was a repetition of our mud-plowing experience," Murdock reported. The family left Denison at 8:40 AM and spent ten hours covering the 118 miles to Nevada. State Center, their night stop, was just 16 miles ahead, but "this is the section of road which stuck the New York to Paris cars."[62]

At twilight, four miles west of State Center, Murdock recalled, the Packard ran into

> a swamp called the "Duck Pond," credited with having the worst bit of mud road in the United States. This stretch of road is about two miles long, it being graded up about two

feet, with the water of the Duck Pond on both sides. It is undermined in many places by beavers and muskrats.

We struck one of these holes and the car slid sidewise, one front wheel overhanging the bank and the weight of the car resting on the engine pan and fly wheel. Just at that time the right rear tire went flat.

The ladies went on foot to the nearest farm house and we dug and shoveled and pushed and maneuvered until we got the car back on the road. Then we went mutteringly about the repair of our flat tire, finally picked up the rest of the party and arrived in State Centre [*sic*] about nine o'clock.

Friday's 191-mile drive to Clinton, Iowa, represented one of the longest travel days of the trip—nearly eighteen hours. According to the *Johnstown Daily Tribune*, the run

was a hard drill, the same character of roads being met with—muddy and slippery, up and down hill. About twelve miles from Clinton the car was again stuck. All members of the party united in carrying rocks and planks for making a foundation and after several hours the car was extricated and the trip continued without assistance, Clinton being reached at 2:20 AM [on Saturday]. Mr. Murdock now says that a fly with all feet fast on sticky flypaper has a better chance than an auto in Iowa mud.[63]

Despite his problems, Murdock did well to plow through Iowa's mud in just three days. Facing the same conditions five years earlier, Tom Fetch spent nearly six days driving his Packard across the state, including an idle day in Des Moines, waiting for the rain to stop.

With Neatness and Dispatch

The 141-mile run to Chicago on Saturday and Sunday, May 16 and 17, was similarly long, according to the *Johnstown Daily Tribune*. "From Clinton to Chicago is an ordinary six hours' run, but the rains had the roads in such poor condition that eighteen hours was consumed in crossing the State. Several severe thunderstorms were run through, and during one a barn was struck by lightning and burned in full view of the party. But during these storms no one suffered any discomforts, the top, side curtains, and glass front fully protecting all of Mr. Murdock's party."[64]

The Murdocks left Clinton at 11:00 AM on Saturday, nine hours after arriving, heading for the Windy City. But it took them eleven hours to travel the 35 miles to Rochelle, Illinois, where they spent Saturday night, according to the itinerary in Murdock's post-trip booklet. It was the worst one-day mileage of the trip. From Rochelle, Murdock sent *Automobile Topics* a telegram "in which he said that several of the automobiles stored in the local garage had not been taken out for three weeks on account of the mud."[65] At 3:00 PM Sunday, the Murdock motorists reached Chicago.

Despite the mud and bad weather, Murdock drove from Cheyenne to Chicago in seven days "with neatness and dispatch," the *Chicago Inter Ocean* observed. The total mileage stood at 2,686, Murdock's logbook showed. Given the long daily grinds, the 2:20 AM arrival in Clinton, and the Sunday travel in Wyoming and Illinois, the *Chicago Daily Tribune* made three errors in asserting "the journey has been a continuous string of easy stage running, devoid of night travel, with rests on Sundays."[66] The long back-to-back drives to reach Chicago clearly reveal that Murdock's pleasure trip had become a record-setting attempt.

The tourists, however, did spend the remainder of the afternoon and evening on Sunday, May 17, resting in Chicago before Monday's 143-mile ride to Goshen, Indiana. "The macadamized Indiana roads were excellent," Murdock raved. According to a Goshen-datelined story in Tuesday's *Johnstown Daily Tribune*, the autoists

> reached here last evening [Monday], having run from the Auditorium Hotel, Chicago, since morning, through thunderstorms, rain, and mud all the way. They came through Michigan City and South Bend, and would have made splendid time in spite of the weather had it not been that a bridge west of this place [Goshen] had been washed out, necessitating delay. The roads were the best encountered on the trip, excepting the natural roads of Wyoming and Nebraska. On arrival of the party here all were pretty well drenched, but no one suffered any ill effects.[67]

The account fails to explain how the car's top, storm curtains, and windshield kept the occupants dry in Illinois but not in Indiana. Later, however, Murdock accounts for it by suggesting that the storm caught the tourists with their top down:

> While replacing a blown-out casing and tube, near South Bend, a severe rain storm set in and the entire party was drenched, although the ladies had taken refuge on the porch of a nearby farm house. The fast accumulating water washed the jack out from under the car, dropping the latter down into the mud on the rim of the wheel. It was still raining when we reached South Bend, but, the road being hard and smooth, we drove on through the rain storm to Goshen, where we stayed over night.

A "Novel Feat"

According to *Automobile*, the car on Tuesday, May 19, traveled 150 miles to Toledo, Ohio, and on Wednesday, May 20, 190 miles to Warren, Ohio, home to the Packard Motor Car Company until its 1903 move to Detroit. "Touring from Los Angeles to

New York in a large Packard automobile is the novel feat being carried out by a party who stopped at the Colonial Hotel here last night," reported Thursday's *Warren Weekly Tribune*.[68]

Besides the Murdocks and Payson W. Spaulding, the party now included a "M. Vestal of Pittsburg, and W. H. Workman of Detroit," the newspaper said, without naming Murdock's mechanic. "They have passed over all kinds of roads and been exposed to all kinds of weather, but express themselves as well pleased with their trip."[69] In his post-run booklet, Murdock explained that the new members of the party were friends from Pittsburgh who helped guide the car from Cleveland to Warren.

On Thursday, May 21, Day 28, Murdock left Warren at 5:30 AM for the 78-mile drive to Pittsburgh. He covered the 79 miles to Johnstown on Friday. In the Packard publicity booklet, Murdock said that staying the night in Pittsburgh was part of his plan, "leaving us an easy run the next day to Johnstown, where we intended to spend Friday afternoon, Saturday and Sunday, in order to give all of us a good rest in our own home and among our home friends." He makes no mention of a breakdown.

Friday's *Johnstown Daily Tribune*, however, said the Murdock party spent Thursday night at Pittsburgh, due to mechanical problems in rural Pennsylvania northwest of the steel-producing city. "The only trouble with the machine on the whole journey came yesterday, when a hot journal developed about noon near Sewickley, the car having come through from Warren, O., that morning. Had it not been for that, the party would likely have reached Johnstown last night." A "burnt connecting rod bearing [caused by] the oil running low cost five hours," *Automobile* said later, apparently referring to the trouble near Sewickley.[70] As it was, the Murdocks arrived home at 4:15 PM on Friday, May 22:

> The car, a "Packard 30," of the same type as Mr. Murdock has been running for several years, stood the journey without the slightest injury. It shows distinct signs of the weather and the mud, but runs as smoothly as if it had been only on a little jaunt out on the Valley Pike. . . . The party will rest in Johnstown over Sunday, and on Monday morning will start for Philadelphia and New York City, thus completing the ocean-to-ocean journey.[71]

In fact, Murdock's 1908 Packard "was his fifth of that make," according to the *Pasadena Daily News*.[72] Eager to finish the trip, a rested Jacob Murdock took to the road again early Monday morning, "shortly after midnight":

> For thirty miles east of Windber they found the roads in miserable condition, the mud holes being so deep that at one place they stuck for half an hour. Chains were used almost

as far as Gettysburg, through which the big machine passed at 8:30 o'clock. Thereafter the roads were good and great time was made. With Mr. Murdock are his wife, three children, Mrs. Mary F. Darling, of Johnstown, and P. W. Spaulding, of Evanston, Wyo."[73]

Familiar enough with this mountainous route to drive it at night, Murdock had passed the worst of the ridges by daybreak. "Our recent experiences in the west had made us immune to the milder shocks of the Alleghenies and I even heard Mrs. Murdock say that she would never again criticize the rocky roads of her home state."

An Easy Run Ends Trip

Passing York, Pennsylvania, late Monday morning, and Lancaster at noon, Murdock pulled into Philadelphia at 4:30 PM, ending a 244-mile day, the best one-day progress of the trip. "A party of automobilists from New York, including a small army of writers from the metropolitan daily papers, had come down to Philadelphia to meet us and we spent a delightful evening at the Bellevue-Stratford, recounting the numerous experiences of the trip now so near completion," Murdock wrote.

According to Murdock's summary of his trip for reporters in Philadelphia, "We had little rain, most of it being ahead of us and leaving us its mud. . . . The mud of Iowa was unspeakable and, in fact, was the only serious obstacle east of Cheyenne."[74]

In Philadelphia, Murdock met M. J. Budlong, president of the Packard Motor Car Company of New York. Packard's Pittsburgh representative, "Mr. Bennett," was also there, as was Jacob Murdock's brother, Wilbert, who drove one of the three Packard autos that escorted the Murdock machine on the 104-mile run into New York City the next day. The number of escort autos may have been higher, as the *Johnstown Daily Tribune* reported that Murdock reached New York heading "a large number of auto enthusiasts who had accompanied him from Philadelphia."[75]

The cars left Philadelphia's Bellevue-Stratford Hotel at 8:45 AM on Tuesday, May 26, crossed the Delaware River to Camden, New Jersey, and then made what *Automobile* called "an easy run with stops at Trenton, New Brunswick and Newark [that] brought the outfit to Weehawken ferry and landed it at the Packard Motor Car Company's garage, at Broadway and Sixty-first street, at 2:07 PM" (see Figs. 134 and 135).[76] The *Johnstown Daily Tribune* also places the arrival at 2:07 PM. Offering different arrival times were *Horseless Age* (2:00 PM), the *New York Herald* (2:05 PM), and Murdock himself, in his post-run booklet (1:55 PM) As a *New York Tribune* reporter

Fig. 134. The first family to cross America by auto arrives at Packard headquarters, 61st and Broadway, in New York City. *From left to right*: Murdock (driving); Jacob Milton, Jr., sitting on the lap of Payson W. Spaulding; mechanic Philip De May (partly obscured behind Spaulding); one of the Murdock daughters; Mrs. Mary F. Darling of Johnstown; another of the Murdock daughters; and Mrs. Anna Murdock. Notice the winch pieces in a shallow wooden box strapped to the running board (NAHC).

Fig. 135. Another view of the car in New York City. *From left to right*: Mrs. Mary F. Darling, the two Murdock daughters, Payson W. Spaulding, Philip De May (behind Spaulding), Murdock, Anna Murdock, and Jacob Milton Jr. (inside spare tire) (NAHC).

observed, "The car was covered with mud, and consequently looked the worse for wear, but it ran into New York as smoothly as it ran out of Los Angeles."[77]

Murdock's itinerary, published in the May 28, 1908, issue of *Automobile* as "taken from his notebook," showed that the car had traveled 3,674 miles, which became the official distance for Murdock's run (see Table 13). Various side trips, including those taken during the two days the family spent at home in Johnstown, advanced the odometer to the 3,693-mile figure which was given in other reports.

Murdock's booklet and most popular accounts say the trip consumed 32 days, 5 hours, 25 minutes, but the math doesn't work out. The Packard left Pasadena at 8:00 AM on April 24, by Murdock's own accounting, and arrived in New York offi-

TABLE 13. Murdock's Daily City-to-City Progress, 1908

Day / Date	City–City	Distance (daily / cumulative)[a]
1 / Apr. 24 Fri	Pasadena, Calif.–Garlic Spring, Calif.[b]	173 / 173
2 / Apr. 25 Sat	Garlic Spring, Calif.–Resting Springs, Calif.	67 / 240
3 / Apr. 26 Sun	*Sunday rest day*	— / 240
4 / Apr. 27 Mon	Resting Springs, Calif.–Goldfield, Nev.	174 / 414
5 / Apr. 28 Tue	Goldfield, Nev.–Stone Cabin, Nev.	84 / 498
6 / Apr. 29 Wed	Stone Cabin, Nev.–Ely, Nev.	155 / 653
7 / Apr. 30 Thu	Ely, Nev.–Montello, Nev.	167 / 820
8 / May 1 Fri	Montello, Nev.–Kelton, Utah	84 / 904
9 / May 2 Sat	Kelton, Utah–Ogden, Utah	96 / 1,000
10 / May 3 Sun	*Sunday rest day*	— / 1,000
11 / May 4 Mon	Ogden, Utah–Evanston, Wyo.	85 / 1,085
12 / May 5 Tue	*rain day*	— / 1,085
13 / May 6 Wed	Evanston, Wyo.–Granger, Wyo.	103 / 1,188
14 / May 7 Thu	Granger, Wyo.–Wamsutter, Wyo.	135 / 1,323
15 / May 8 Fri	Wamsutter, Wyo.–Rock River, Wyo.	135 / 1,458
16 / May 9 Sat	Rock River, Wyo.–Laramie, Wyo.	—
17 / May 10 Sun	Laramie, Wyo.–Cheyenne, Wyo.	114 / 1,572
18 / May 11 Mon	Cheyenne, Wyo.–North Platte, Neb.	241 / 1,813
19 / May 12 Tue	North Platte, Neb.–Columbus, Neb.	235 / 2,048

20 / May 13 Wed	Columbus, Neb.–Denison, Iowa	172 / 2,220
21 / May 14 Thu	Denison, Iowa–State Center, Iowa	134 / 2,354
22 / May 15 Fri	State Center, Iowa–Clinton, Iowa	191 / 2,545
23 / May 16 Sat	Clinton, Iowa–Rochelle, Ill.	—
24 / May 17 Sun	Rochelle, Ill.–Chicago	141 / 2,686
25 / May 18 Mon	Chicago–Goshen, Ind.	143 / 2,829
26 / May 19 Tue	Goshen, Ind.–Toledo, Ohio	150 / 2,979
27 / May 20 Wed	Toledo, Ohio–Warren, Ohio	190 / 3,169
28 / May 21 Thu	Warren, Ohio–Pittsburgh[c]	78 / 3,247
29 / May 22 Fri	Pittsburgh–Johnstown, Pa.	79 / 3,326
30 / May 23 Sat	*rest day*	— / 3,326
31 / May 24 Sun	*Sunday rest day*	— / 3,326
32 / May 25 Mon	Johnstown, Pa.–Philadelphia	244 / 3,570
33 / May 26 Tue	Philadelphia–New York City	104 / 3,674

SOURCE: Table of mileages, taken from and published in Murdock's notebook "One Man's Family Tour from Coast to Coast," *Automobile*, May 28, 1908, p. 735.

[a] Distances given in the *Automobile* table vary slightly from some of Murdock's figures as given in the text of this chapter. In *A Family Tour from Ocean to Ocean*, Murdock used mileages that were slightly inflated by some pleasure driving he undertook during two rest days in Johnstown.

[b] In various writings, Murdock called the first night's stop Garlic Lake, Garlic Spring, and Garlic Wells. The first two are within 3 miles of one another and about 30 miles northeast of Daggett, Calif. Garlic Wells doesn't appear on period maps. Murdock presumably meant Garlic Spring.

[c] *Automobile* lists the May 21 night stop as Pulsbey, Ohio, a city that researchers at both the Ohio Historical Society and Pennsylvania Bureau of Archives and History were unable to identify. Pulsbey is, perhaps, a corruption of Pulaski, Pa., a small town between Warren and Pittsburgh. In *A Family Tour from Ocean to Ocean*, Murdock gives the night stop as Pittsburgh, and this table follows suit.

cially at 2:07 PM on May 26, Day 33 of the trip. Subtracting three hours for the time difference between coasts, Murdock's elapsed time is thus 32 days, 3 hours, 7 minutes.

The travelers were idle for five of the thirty-three calendar days consumed on the trip—four days for rest and one day due to muddy Wyoming roads. The trek encompassed five Sundays: the family traveled on two of them, rested on three. Murdock thus averaged 114 miles per day, or 4.76 miles per hour for his elapsed time. For his twenty-eight-day running time, he averaged 131 miles per day, or 5.47 mph. He set a speed record for a single driver or single crew by narrowly beating the time of 32 days, 17 hours, 20 minutes that his guide to Ogden, Lester L. Whitman, and C. S. Carris had set in 1904.

"We reached our destination nearly a month in advance of what our highest expectations had allowed," Murdock said. "Before I had started, I had calculated on an average of 100 miles a day. Before I finished I found that steady going would give a much bigger mileage than this." Murdock later advised against setting such daily goals. "Some of our hardest days showed the smallest mileage. I know nothing more disheartening than to see the sun just about to set below the horizon, when one is many miles from the place he had hoped to make that day. It is much better to start each morning with the intention to keep going until you are ready to stop and then stop."[78]

Few "Mechanical Stoppages"

According to Murdock, it took 524 gallons of gas to propel the heavily loaded Packard across the country, meaning the car averaged 7.01 mpg. The travelers paid a minimum of 44 cents per gallon—$2.20 for a 5-gallon can—in Nevada. But "even as far off the beaten path as the little mining camp of Lee, Nevada, we paid but $2.50 a can. Through Wyoming gasoline became cheaper and the price steadily reduced all the way, to a minimum of 18 cents a gallon."

Murdock, who kept no record of the Packard's oil consumption, did not reveal the cost of his trip. The car reportedly performed well, however. "Mechanical stoppages" cost the autoists just eight hours between Los Angeles and New York City, according to *Automobile*: five hours to repair—most likely replace—the burned-out engine bearing and three hours to replace a broken front-wheel ball bearing at some unspecified point in the journey.[79]

Later, however, the same article quoted Murdock as saying, "I only had to replace two springs." *Automobile* does not say how the springs broke, where they broke, or how long it took to repair them. Automotive historian Tom Mahoney contends the Packard broke one spring west of Promontory, Utah, during the 5 miles it traveled on railroad ties. Inexplicably, Murdock "said that he had not experienced the slightest engine trouble during the long journey," the *New York Tribune* asserted. Murdock put on a new set of Continental tires during the trip and had just two punctures, according to *Automobile*.[80] After more than a month traveling by auto, Murdock and his family planned to return home from New York City by train, the Johnstown newspaper reported.

Cheyenne marked the boundary between the Wild West and tamer touring through the Midwest and East, Murdock said in summarizing his trip:

The roads in many places could be described as nearly impassable, traveling difficult, the roads very hard to find, supply stations at long intervals, garages and repair shops few and the accommodations from poor to nothing. From Cheyenne east anyone could easily make this tour, but to cover the country from the Pacific Coast to Cheyenne requires—well, it might be described by the simple use of the words—unlimited enthusiasm and determination to get through.

East of Cheyenne the hotel accommodations are frequent and good, but west of that place they are very uncertain. In many places they simply consist of sufficient shelter to keep you dry and warm, with food of the very plainest variety. In Nevada, at many places, it is necessary to supply one's provisions. We stopped at some road houses, where they were able to give us accommodations, but we had to furnish all our meals.[81]

Efforts Well Expended

The auto journals anticipated correctly that other travelers would flock to imitate Murdock. The result, among other things, would be a sales boon for the auto industry, *Motor Age* predicted:

Jacob Murdock has established a record that cannot help but attract favorable attention from the buying public. His feat of driving his Packard, carrying seven, from San Francisco [to] New York in 25½ days of actual running [*sic*], coupled with the fact that Mr. Murdock owns the car himself and is not connected with the trade in any manner, will convince others of the utility of the motor car. Mr. Murdock did not make a race of it—he simply strove to show the possibilities of the thing and he has succeeded in a most admirable manner. It is to be hoped there will be others go[ing] in for long trips of this sort.[82]

According to *Automobile*, "Mr. Murdock proved a transcontinental automobile tour to be pleasurably possible and took a journey across the continent out of the category of abnormal stunts. He demonstrated that no path on this continent presents difficulties not surmountable by the pluck and patience of a tourist."[83]

Murdock had many other adventures behind the wheel of an auto. Two years after his transcontinental trek, in 1910, Murdock and "a party of other husky men with adventurous temperaments," took a trip "over the Mojave desert and into the jaws of Death valley in his motor car." The explorers traveled to more than a dozen places where autos had never ventured, because Murdock "finds it difficult to keep away from places where motoring is harder than airshipping."[84]

Murdock apparently never tried to set another coast-to-coast record, but between 1908 and 1913 he made five additional transcontinental trips. He "went on to make a fortune in varied enterprises, including a Packard dealership," but, sadly, "suffered huge losses in the depression and killed himself," *Automobile Quarterly* reported.[85]

"I remember making the remark, on our arrival at New York, that, within a few years, similar trips would be of such frequent occurrence that they would be scarcely worthy of mention," Murdock wrote in 1911. "Just how true this prophecy was is shown by the fact that in one day last summer no fewer than six cars passed through Evanston, Wyo., all transcontinental bound."[86]

Assuming they heeded Murdock's advice, all six drivers were traveling east. "It is far better going east than west, as the winds blow generally from the west, and in these extensive desert sandy stretches it is a big benefit to have them at your back rather than in your face," Murdock advised. "There are so many striking features, so much awe-inspiring scenery, so many varied experiences, that none with whom I ever have talked who have made the trip—and in the past three years there have been many of these—will not say their efforts have been well expended."[87]

But it had been an effort for each driver. In 1911, eight years after the first coast-to-coast automobile crossing, motorists could cross the country safely, but not necessarily comfortably, as Murdock learned. "Truly, it is a long, hard grind, destined to test one's enthusiasm and endurance to its fullest limit before you reach the end," he warned. Still . . .

> If you are an enthusiast, and have the time, make your preparation and make the trip, and you will have the opportunity of seeing this big country of ours in a way in which you can never see it from a railroad train; some day when things look their worst—and that day is sure to come if you undertake to drive a motor car across the continent—when you are ready to give up in despair, and when the matter of making further headway seems entirely hopeless, open up your commissary box and eat a hearty lunch. Then lie down on the warm sand and either think or sleep a few minutes, and you will be ready to start off with renewed vigor, and you will find that no matter how hard it seemed, nothing is impossible.[88]

CONCLUSION

With a better automobile, John D. and Louise Hitchcock Davis could very possibly have driven across America in 1899. Likewise Alexander Winton, had he shown greater persistence, might have crossed the continent in 1901. Instead, both attempts failed.

Then, in 1903, within weeks of one another, three automobiles puffed and wheezed out of San Francisco, transcontinental bound. As evidence that the journeys were independently planned, the autos took vastly different routes through the West. Yet the time required for each vehicle to reach New York City was remarkably similar: a 2-cylinder Winton arrived in sixty-four days, a 1-cylinder Packard in sixty-two days, and a 1-cylinder Oldsmobile in seventy-three days.

Though they established no consensus on the best route to take, successful transcontinentalists of the Pioneer Period agreed that it was better to drive from west to east. The prevailing wind was at their backs, for one thing. Most drivers also wanted to face their worst challenges—crossing streams, mountains, and deserts—while they were as fresh as their new autos. Some transcontinentalists believed that motorists driving in the opposite direction would encounter steeper grades. Concluding a coast-to-coast trip on the heavily populated East Coast also gave these trips greater publicity value.

Why did each of the 1903 trips succeed? Certainly not because the roads had improved since 1899. Poor or nonexistent roads meant terrible toil for the Winton in Oregon and Idaho, the Oldsmobile in the Great American Desert, and the Packard in the Rocky Mountains of Colorado.

Certainly not because American automobile designers had agreed on a type of automobile best suited to long-distance trips. The Winton, Packard, and Oldsmobile differed widely from one another in power (from 4½ to 20 horsepower), weight (from 800 to 2,500 pounds), price (from $650 to $2,500 new), wheel size (from 28 to 34 inches in diameter), steering control (two used a steering wheel, one a tiller), and gas mileage (from 7 to 19 miles per gallon).

Certainly not because the three autos were mechanically reliable. Breakdowns cost the Winton nineteen days and the Oldsmobile twelve days. The Packard experienced less down time but needed almost daily adjustments and twenty-eight new parts (plus new batteries) to complete its trip.

No, the three 1903 trips succeeded despite bad roads, mechanical problems, and design differences among the three automobiles. How so? Because the men who organized and participated in each trip were meticulous planners, mechanically adept, well equipped, resourceful, and determined to succeed. These qualities were essential to the first motorists to drive across the continent. Good planners sent tires, oil, and spare parts ahead by train, and telegraphed ahead to arrange gasoline supplies. Resourceful drivers often double-checked their maps by asking directions of local residents. A well-equipped auto carried food and cooking supplies, bedding, extra tires and inner tubes, many spare parts, a large tool kit, a winch or block and tackle, perhaps "sand tires" or strips of canvas to gain traction on sandy expanses, and an extra supply of gas and oil.

Someone aboard each of the 1903 transcontinental autos wrote about the daily battles with innumerable obstacles; these accounts later guided the drivers brave enough to follow them. For the first transcontinental motor trips were forbidding undertakings, far removed from pleasure trips. Drivers and passengers alike were often hot, cold, tired, thirsty, hungry, wet, dirty, and bug-bitten, not to mention bloody and bruised. Coast-to-coast motoring meant rebuilding washed-out roads, pushing the car up steep hills, using primitive hand tools to fashion repairs, wading through ice-cold streams, and winching the car through mudholes.

The dean of the early coast-to-coast drivers, Lester L. Whitman, drew upon his firsthand experience on the 1903 Oldsmobile crossing to set coast-to-coast speed records in 1904 and 1906. To set his two later records, Whitman drove air-cooled Franklin automobiles. By all accounts, the newer Franklins represented a mechanical advance over the fickle, generally troublesome, automobiles of 1903.

Jacob M. Murdock's 1908 Packard required the least attention of all the coast-to-coast, record-setting autos to that time. Though built too low to comfortably negotiate rutted roads, the Packard's wear and tear amounted to a burned-out engine bearing and a worn wheel bearing. Repairing or replacing these parts consumed just eight hours. (Unconfirmed reports say the car also broke two springs.) The heavily loaded Packard needed just one new set of tires to complete its journey—evidence that American tires, like American cars, were improving.

Because Murdock's reliable headlamps allowed him to drive after dark, his family reached shelter every night. In contrast, in 1903 Whitman and Eugene I. Hammond drove a light Oldsmobile fitted with only weak carriage lamps instead of headlamps. When they got caught after sundown on the Wyoming desert, they were stranded until daybreak.

If autos and tires had improved from 1903 to 1908, the roads they traveled on had not. Murdock's roads were just as rough in dry weather and muddy in wet weather as those encountered by the 1903 pioneers. Agitation for a coast-to-coast highway began almost from the moment the first car traversed the continent. By 1905, the U.S. Department of Agriculture's Office of Public Road Inquiry had joined the Olds Motor Works in promoting a transcontinental race between two Oldsmobiles; the race, from New York City to the Lewis and Clark Centennial Exposition in Portland, Oregon, was undertaken "to show the crying need for good roads."[1] Unfortunately, neither the 1905 contest nor a 1909 New York–Seattle race—similarly designed to promote good roads, and, specifically, a transcontinental highway—did much beyond focusing additional attention on America's primitive highway system.

Finally, in 1913, a private, non-governmental association created the Lincoln Highway, the nation's first transcontinental motor route, to run from New York City to San Francisco. Beginning in 1913, coast-to-coast drivers, with few exceptions, gravitated toward this so-called central route, from New York City through New Jersey, Pennsylvania, Ohio, Indiana, Illinois, Iowa, Nebraska, Wyoming, Utah, Nevada, and California.

Yet without federal funding, the cost of grading and surfacing the 3,389-mile highway was prohibitive. This meant that rain and snow could still ruin an otherwise well-planned transcontinental trip. Only the heavily populated eastern states could afford to pave the route with macadam (crushed rock with an oil or bituminous binder), brick, or concrete. Farther west, the Lincoln Highway would remain a dirt road for many years to come, as Emily Post discovered near Chicago during a 1915 transcontinental motor trip with friends:

As the most important, advertised and lauded road in our country, its first appearance was not engaging. If it were called the cross continent trail you would expect little, and be philosophical about less, but the very word "highway" suggests macadam at the least. And with such titles as "Transcontinental" and "Lincoln" put before it, you dream of a wide straight road like the Route Nationale of France, or state roads in the East, and you wake rather unhappily to the actuality of a meandering dirt road that becomes mud half a foot deep after a day or two of rain![2]

Publicity surrounding various record-setting transcontinental journeys made during the Pioneer Period surveyed in this volume, and later, helped to stimulate a push for good roads. This push culminated in the 1916 passage of a federal-aid highway bill. Even then, transcontinental highways improved only slowly until well into the 1920s.

"Don't allow the car to be without food of some sort at any time west of Salt Lake City," the Lincoln Highway Association warned in 1924. "You might break down late in the day and have to wait a number of hours until the next tourist comes along." Another warning—"Don't ford water without first wading through it"—suggested that despite improvements to cars and tires, a coast-to-coast motor trip was still an adventure two decades after the first one.[3]

Yet the demands and hardships of a routine transcontinental trip did change over time, as routes became more familiar and became marked, as maps and guidebooks proliferated, and as automobiles offered greater comfort and reliability. Murdock's trip at the close of the Pioneer Period demonstrated that, aside from record-breaking speed runs, coast-to-coast driving no longer required special talents beyond careful planning, alert driving, and plenty of patience. "Mechanical genius" was no longer part of the job description. (A mechanic did accompany Murdock, but he had little to do.) Though Murdock's passengers at times were hot, cold, wet, and dusty, he and his family nevertheless drove across the continent much more comfortably than anyone had to that time.

In 1911, a group of wealthy motorists confirmed Murdock's assertion that an average motorist could make the long journey a safe and enjoyable family outing. Comfort was the byword when this group—forty men, women, and children—boarded twelve Premier autos for a sightseeing trip from Atlantic City, New Jersey, to Los Angeles. The Premier journey represented a milestone both for the automobile industry and for American society at large: "There is a general feeling that the Pacific and Atlantic coasts have been brought closer together and transcontinental touring by pleasure parties is now expected to become common since the first tour of this kind has been such an unqualified success," *Motor Age* wrote. "It has been proven that there are no unsurmountable difficulties in the way."[4]

As during the Pioneer Period, automakers in later years continued to recognize the publicity value of setting a coast-to-coast record. In 1909, for instance, the Maxwell–Briscoe Motor Company sponsored the first coast-to-coast trip by a woman, Alice Huyler Ramsey, who spent fifty-nine days driving three female companions from New York to San Francisco. The Premier Motor Manufacturing Company lent its advertising manager, a Premier baggage truck, and a driver to the aforementioned 1911 caravan of twelve Premier vehicles. In helping to establish two more driving firsts, these two auto companies also promoted the automobiles they manufactured.

From 1910 through 1916, the last full year before the United States entered World War I, the makers of Cadillac, Hudson, Oldsmobile, Reo, Saxon, and Stutz motor cars all sponsored transcontinental speed runs. In September 1916, traveling in a Hudson, renowned auto racer Ralph Mulford and two other relay drivers achieved the fastest crossing of the prewar period, dashing from San Francisco to New York City in 5 days, 3 hours, 31 minutes. Thus, in the short span of fourteen years, Dr. H. Nelson Jackson's 1903 crossing time of sixty-four days had been reduced by ninety-two percent.

By 1916, the era when an amateur like Jackson could pack an automobile with tools, food, and a tent and depart on a record-setting transcontinental trip had passed. High-speed driving and quick thinking behind the wheel had become more important traits in a driver than the ability to grind valves, read a compass, and work a block and tackle.

For safety, pioneer transcontinental drivers always traveled with at least one companion. Three people rode on the 1903 Packard throughout the West. "One man cannot run a machine for the distance," crewman Marius C. Krarup had intoned at the time, "and if we had had two more men with us we could have used them at the wheel."[5]

This remained the rule for many years to come. The first documented solo transcontinental auto trip came in 1915, when silent-film actress Anita King drove a KisselKar from San Francisco to New York City. Solo drivers—often accompanied by a reporter or other non-driving passenger—replaced relay drivers as the norm after the coast-to-coast drive time fell to one week. The early practice of sending relay drivers ahead by train no longer worked because the new 1916 autos could beat passenger trains over long distances.

Shortly before World War I halted such trips, the focus of coast-to-coast speed runs shifted. Earlier, the cars had been the stars and their drivers relatively unknown. Then, in 1915, the colorful Erwin G. "Cannon Ball" Baker set a transcontinental single-driver speed record of 11 days, 7 hours, 15 minutes, in a Stutz Bearcat roadster. After Baker's fast trip, the drivers became the luminaries who, in effect, endorsed an automobile by selecting it for a high-speed, coast-to-coast run.

Following World War I and until the mid-1930s, when interest waned in transcontinental trips, Baker and a handful of other stars—Ab Jenkins, Bob McKenzie, and Louis B. Miller among them—made virtual careers out of such trips. Though transcontinental speed runs remained numerous after World War I, an increasing number of automakers stressed gas and oil economy, rather than speed, on such trips. These postwar crossings seemed routine in comparison to their prewar counterparts, and consequently received little press coverage. (Another reason for diminishing press coverage was that local newspapers found it difficult to report anything new about cars that rocketed across the country, stopping only for gas.)

Americans in the 1960s exhibited an unquenchable curiosity about the first astronauts and the spaceships they rode into orbit. Today, a rocket launch is so commonplace that it becomes a top news story only if something goes wrong. Similarly, flying long distances in an airplane, like driving long distances in an automobile, has become an everyday occurrence. As the twenty-first century unfolds, it is the very "routineness" of coast-to-coast driving that excites our interest in the pioneering trips of the early twentieth century, when the automobile and the trails it tamed were new, primitive, and steeped in adventure.

APPENDIX: THE TRIPS AT A GLANCE

The 1899 Davis Attempt

DRIVER	John D. Davis
PASSENGER	Louise Hitchcock Davis, his wife
CAR	2-cylinder, 1899 National Duryea touring cart, 5–7 horsepower
CITY–CITY	New York City–Chicago
DATES	July 13, 1899–October 1899 (exact ending date unknown)
DISTANCE	At least 1,132 miles
FIRSTS	First recorded U.S. transcontinental attempt; first woman rider to attempt a transcontinental trip; most likely the world's longest auto trip to date, for a man or a woman.

The 1901 Winton–Shanks Attempt

DRIVER	Alexander Winton
PASSENGER	Charles B. Shanks
CAR	1-cylinder, 12-horsepower Winton
CITY–CITY	San Francisco–2 miles east of Mill City, Nevada

DATES	May 20, 1901–May 29, 1901
DISTANCE	530 miles
FIRSTS	First attempt at a west-to-east crossing; second coast-to-coast attempt on record.

The 1903 James–Crocker Trip

DRIVERS	Dr. H. Nelson Jackson and Sewall K. Crocker
CAR	1-cylinder, 20-horsepower, 1903 Winton touring car, nicknamed "Vermont"
CITY–CITY	San Francisco–New York City
DATES	1:00 PM, May 23, 1903–4:30 AM, July 26, 1903
DISTANCE	5,000–6,000 miles
ELAPSED TIME	63 days, 12 hours, 30 minutes
RUNNING TIME	46 calendar days
AVERAGE SPEED (for elapsed time)	3.61 mph (for 5,500 miles)
FIRSTS	First transcontinental crossing.

The 1903 Fetch–Krarup Trip

DRIVER	E. Thomas Fetch
PASSENGERS	Marius C. "Chris" Krarup, observer; and N. O. Allyn, mechanic (on western half of trip)
CAR	1-cylinder, 12-horsepower, 1903 Packard Model F touring car, nick-named "Old Pacific" (now on display at Henry Ford Museum, Dearborn, Michigan)
CITY–CITY	San Francisco–New York City
DATES	3:05 PM, June 20, 1903–8:30 PM, August 21, 1903
DISTANCE	4,000 miles
ELAPSED TIME	62 days, 2 hours, 25 minutes

RUNNING TIME	52 calendar days
AVERAGE SPEED (for elapsed time)	2.68 mph
FIRSTS	Broke coast-to-coast speed record by 34 hours, 5 minutes. First transcontinental car to cross Nevada on a central route that many record-breaking trips would follow. First crew to cross sand by spreading strips of canvas.

The 1903 Whitman–Hammond Trip

DRIVERS	Lester L. Whitman and Eugene I. Hammond
CAR	1-cylinder, 4½-horsepower, 1903 Oldsmobile runabout
CITY–CITY	San Francisco–New York City and Portland, Maine
DATES	*To NYC*: 3:00 PM, July 6, 1903–3:30 PM, September 17, 1903 *To Portland*: 3:00 PM, July 6, 1903–10:00 AM, September 23, 1903
DISTANCE	*To NYC*: 4,225 miles *To Portland*: 4,613 miles
ELAPSED TIME	*To NYC*: 72 days, 21 hours, 30 minutes *To Portland*: 78 days, 16 hours
RUNNING TIME	*To NYC*: 55 days *To Portland*: 60 days
AVERAGE SPEED (for elapsed time)	*To NYC*: 2.41 mph *To Portland*: 2.44 mph
FIRSTS	Lightest, cheapest, and least-powerful car to cross the continent to date; first to carry U.S. mail; first transcontinental trip using U.S. and Canadian roads; first trip between such distant cities; first crew to use wide, cotton-stuffed canvas "sand tires" to traverse sandy stretches.

The 1904 Franklin Relay

DRIVERS	Lester L. Whitman and Clayton S. Carris
CAR	4-cylinder, 10-horsepower, 1904 Franklin runabout
CITY–CITY	San Francisco–New York City

DATES	5:00 PM, August 1, 1904–1:20 PM, September 3, 1904
DISTANCE	4,500 miles
ELAPSED TIME	32 days, 17 hours, 20 minutes
RUNNING TIME	Not available
AVERAGE SPEED (for elapsed time)	5.73 mph
FIRSTS	Cuts coast-to-coast record nearly in half. First crossing in a 4-cylinder auto and with an air-cooled engine. Whitman becomes the first driver to make two crossings.

The 1906 Franklin Relay

DRIVERS	Melvin S. Bates, Clayton S. Carris, James Daley, Clayton B. Harris, Lester L. Whitman
CAR	6-cylinder, 30-horsepower, 1906 Franklin Model H runabout
CITY–CITY	San Francisco–New York City
DATES	6:00 PM, August 2, 1906–11:12 PM, August 17, 1906
DISTANCE	About 4,150 miles
ELAPSED TIME	15 days, 2 hours, 12 minutes
RUNNING TIME	9 days, 10 hours, 52 minutes or less
AVERAGE SPEED (for elapsed time)	11.46 mph
FIRSTS	Halves the record of nearly 33 days; first transcontinental run by a 6-cylinder auto and one using relay drivers; first on a partial day-and-night schedule.

The 1908 Murdock Trip

DRIVER	Jacob M. Murdock
PASSENGERS	Anna (Young) Murdock, his wife; and their children, Florence Lillian, 16, Alice, 14, Jacob Milton, Jr., 10; mechanic Phillip De May;

Lester L. Whitman (Los Angeles–Ogden, Utah); and Payson W. Spaulding (Evanston, Wyoming–New York City)

CAR	4-cylinder, 30-horsepower, 1908 Packard Thirty Model UA touring car
CITY–CITY	Pasadena, California–New York City
DATES	8:00 AM, April 24, 1908–2:07 PM, May 26, 1908
DISTANCE	3,674 miles
ELAPSED TIME	32 days, 3 hours, 7 minutes
RUNNING TIME	28 calendar days
AVERAGE SPEED (for elapsed time)	4.76 mph
FIRSTS	Largest coast-to-coast touring party (seven people) to date; best time for a single driver or single non-relay team of drivers; first females, children, and family to cross.

NOTES

Introduction

1. "A Record-Breaking Run," editorial, *Motor World*, Aug. 23, 1906, p. 537.
2. "Transcontinental Autoing," *Automobile*, May 16, 1907, p. 828.
3. Ralph C. Epstein, *The Automobile Industry: Its Economic and Commercial Development* (1928; reprint, New York: Arno Press, 1972), pp. 6–7.
4. Quoted in H. Nelson Jackson, "Honk! Honk! New York or Bust!" *American Legion Monthly*, February 1936, p. 48.
5. James J. Flink, *America Adopts the Automobile, 1895–1910* (Cambridge, Mass.: MIT Press, 1970), p. 50.
6. James J. Flink, *The Car Culture* (Cambridge, Mass.: MIT Press, 1975), p. 21.
7. John B. Rae, *The American Automobile: A Brief History* (Chicago: University of Chicago Press, 1965), p. 30.
8. "Transcontinental Racing," editorial, *Automobile*, May 25, 1916, p. 951.
9. "Dr. Jackson's Success," editorial, *Motor Age*, July 23, 1903, p. 6.
10. Flink, *Car Culture*, pp. 21–22.
11. Rae, *American Automobile*, pp. 31–32.
12. "Los Angeles–Yosemite Run to Be Held in May," *Automotive Industries*, Apr. 10, 1924, p. 844.
13. Nick Georgano, *The American Automobile: A Centenary, 1893–1993* (New York: Smithmark, 1992), pp. 37, 75.
14. Flink, *Car Culture*, p. 23.
15. "From Coast to Coast by Automobile in 33 Days," *New York Herald*, Sept. 4, 1904, p. 15, col. 4.
16. "Transcontinental Auto Trips Attracting Motorists Now," *New York Morning Telegraph*, May 22, 1910, sec. 1, pt. 2, p. 2, col. 6.
17. J. M. Murdock, "From Coast to Coast in a Motor Car," *Motor Age*, Aug. 17, 1911, p. 4.

Chapter 1

1. "Automobile to Start on Monday," *New York Herald*, July 1, 1899, p. 4, col. 6.

2. "Sharp Criticisms by the Editors/Automobile Trip across the Continent May Result in a Revolution in Travelling," editorial, *San Francisco Call*, reprinted in the *New York Herald*, July 6, 1899, p. 8, col. 6; "Four Thousand Miles by Automobile," *Leslie's Weekly*, Aug. 5, 1899, p. 114; and "Ready to Start Automobile Trip," *New York Herald*, July 13, 1899, p. 4, col. 1.

3. *San Francisco Call*, reprinted in the *New York Herald*, July 6, 1899, p. 8, col. 6.

4. "Will Serve a Good End," editorial, *Chicago Times-Herald*, reprinted in the *New York Herald*, June 30, 1899, p. 6, col. 1; and "Views of Coast Editors on the Great Automobile Race," *San Francisco Call*, July 19, 1899, p. 6, col. 4.

5. "Across the Continent in an Automobile," *San Francisco Call*, July 2, 1899, p. 19, col. 1.

6. Editorial, *Horseless Age*, Oct. 18, 1899, p. 7.

7. National Motor Carriage Company ad, *Horseless Age*, June 14, 1899, p. 25; Beverly Rae Kimes and Henry Austin Clark, Jr., *Standard Catalog of American Cars, 1805–1942*, 2d ed. (Iola, Wis.: Krause Publications, 1989), p. 485.

8. Hugh Dolnar, "American Automobile Notes," *Autocar*, Aug. 19, 1899, p. 743; and "The Davis Automobile," *Erie (Pa.) Morning Dispatch*, Aug. 7, 1899, p. 5, col. 1.

9. "Map of Through Roads to the Pacific Coast," *New York Herald*, July 16, 1899, p. 4 of color section.

10. *Leslie's Weekly*, Aug. 5, 1899, p. 114; and *New York Herald*, July 13, 1899, p. 3, col. 6.

11. *New York Herald*, July 2, 1899, p. 9, col. 3.

12. "Automobile Accidents/Mrs. John Dyre Davis Tells Why Happened—Good Luck at Last," *Albany (N.Y.) Times-Union*, July 18, 1899, p. 5, col. 4.

13. "Think Troubles Are Now Ended," *New York Herald*, Aug. 4, 1899, n.p.; *New York Herald*, July 13, 1899, p. 3, col. 6; and *Albany (N.Y.) Times-Union*, July 18, 1899, p. 5, col. 4.

14. "The Davises Have Arrived," *Cleveland Plain Dealer*, Aug. 7, 1899, p. 10, col. 5; *New York Herald*, July 13, 1899, p. 3, col. 6; and *Albany (N.Y.) Times-Union*, July 18, 1899, p. 5, col. 4.

15. Louise Hitchcock Davis, "Automobile on the Road," *Cleveland Plain Dealer*, Aug. 6, 1899, p. 14, col. 1. What became of Mrs. Davis's journal is unknown. It did not, however, find its way into the collections of either the Connecticut Historical Society or the New Haven Colony Historical Society, according to letters to the author from both societies. Apparently, nothing from her journals was ever published.

16. *New York Herald*, July 2, 1899, p. 9, col. 3; "Advised to Make the Automobile Stronger," *New York Herald*, July 3, 1899, p. 4, col. 3; and "A Trans-Continental Automobile Trip," *Scientific American*, July 8, 1899, p. 26.

17. Richard P. Scharchburg, in *Carriages Without Horses: J. Frank Duryea and the Birth of the American Automobile Industry* (Warrendale, Pa.: Society of Automotive Engineers, 1993), p. 153, says 5 horsepower. *Autocar*, July 22, 1899, said "between five and six brake horsepower" at 1,000 rpm. According to David L. Cole, "John D. Davis and the Transcontinental Auto Trip of 1899," *Automotive History Review* 28 (winter 1993–94): 13, John Davis claimed the National Duryea developed 7 horsepower. Two National Motor Carriage Company ads from mid-1899 do not mention a horsepower rating.

18. Auto specifications and descriptive details are drawn from the July 5, 1899, edition of *Horseless Age*, p. 10; see also "Automobile's Trip Begins Auspiciously," *New York Herald*, July 14, 1899, p. 3, col. 6; and *Autocar*, July 22, 1899, p. 649.

19. *New York Herald*, July 14, 1899, p. 3, col. 5.

20. Ibid., p. 3, col. 6; and *New York Herald*, July 13, 1899, p. 3, col. 6.

21. *New York Herald*, July 2, 1899, p. 9, col. 3; and "To the Pacific in an Automobile," *New York Tribune*, July 14, 1899, p. 5, col. 6.

22. Accounts of the start are from *New York Herald*, July 14, 1899, pp. 3–4; "Automobile Off for the West," *New York Times*, July 14, 1899, p. 12, col. 2; *New York Tribune*, July 14, 1899, p. 5, col. 6; and "The Herald Trans-Continental Motor Carriage Tour," *Horseless Age*, July 19, 1899, p. 19. The newspapers did not agree on the starting time. The *New York Herald* put it at 11:02 AM, but the *New York Times* and *New York Tribune* agreed on 11:01 AM. The *San Francisco Call*, which apparently had its own reporter or stringer covering the start, said 11:03 AM ("Thousands Witnessed the Start," July 14, 1899, p. 1, col. 1).

23. *San Francisco Call*, July 14, 1899, p. 1, col. 1.

24. First stanza of "Across the Continent on the Automobile," poem by H. F. Rodney, printed in *San Francisco Call*, July 4, 1899, p. 6, col. 5.

25. "New Record Made Right at Start," *New York Herald*, July 15, 1899, p. 5, col. 2.

26. Untitled article, *San Francisco Call*, Aug. 1, 1899, p. 5, col. 4; and "Here and There," *Automobile*, September 1899, p. 12.

27. "A Transcontinental Automobile Vehicle," *Scientific American*, July 29, 1899, p. 75.

28. "Transcontinental Tour," *Horseless Age*, July 26, 1899, p. 21.

29. "Automobile is Now in Syracuse," *New York Herald*, July 22, 1899, p. 9, col. 6.

30. "Automobilists Have Reached Bergen," *New York Herald*, Aug. 2, 1899, p. 6, col. 5.

31. *New York Herald*, July 22, 1899, p. 9, col. 6.

32. *Cleveland Plain Dealer*, Aug. 7, 1899, p. 10, col. 5.

33. *Autocar*, Aug. 19, 1899, pp. 743–44.

34. *Erie (Pa.) Morning Dispatch*, Aug. 7, 1899, p. 5, col. 1.

35. "Automobilists Reach Buffalo," *New York Herald*, Aug. 3, 1899, p. 4, col. 5; and "No More Delays for Automobile," *New York Herald*, Aug. 8, 1899, p. 9, col. 3.

36. *Erie (Pa.) Morning Dispatch*, Aug. 7, 1899, p. 5, col. 1.

37. *Cleveland Plain Dealer*, Aug. 6, 1899, p. 14, col. 5.

38. Ibid., Aug. 7, 1899, p. 10, col. 5.

39. *New York Herald*, Aug. 4, 1899, n.p.

40. *Cleveland Plain Dealer*, Aug. 6, 1899, p. 14, col. 1.

41. "One Armed Bicyclist to Wheel across Continent," *New York Herald*, July 19, 1899, p. 6, col. 2; "He Will Wheel across the Continent," ibid., July 24, 1899, p. 4, col. 2; "Postal Messenger Boy Making Good Time on Bicycle," ibid., July 27, 1899, p. 4, col. 6; "Roe Well on His Journey," ibid., July 27, 1899, p. 7, col. 2; "Messenger Speeding West," ibid., July 28, 1899, p. 10, col. 4; and "One-Armed Bicycle Messenger Speeding toward Erie," ibid., July 30, 1899, p. 4, col. 6.

42. *Cleveland Plain Dealer*, Aug. 6, 1899, p. 14, col. 3.

43. "The Coming Automobile," editorial, *San Francisco Call*, Aug. 14, 1899, p. 4, col. 2.

44. "Transcontinental Tour Abandoned," *Horseless Age*, Aug. 23, 1899, p. 8; and "Across the Continent," *Toledo (Ohio) Blade*, Aug. 18, 1899, p. 1, col. 8.

45. *Toledo (Ohio) Blade*, Aug. 18, 1899, p. 1, col. 8.

46. "Journey Delayed," *Toledo (Ohio) Blade*, Aug. 19, 1899, p. 7, col. 4.

47. Ibid.

48. "Continued Trouble," *Motor Vehicle Review*, Sept. 5, 1899, p. 8.

49. "Automobile News," *Scientific American*, Sept. 2, 1899, p. 153.

50. "The Davises Still Repairing," *Motor Age*, Oct. 3, 1899, p. 71.

51. Julian Pettifer and Nigel Turner, *Automania: Man and the Motor Car* (Boston: Little, Brown, 1984), p. 71.

52. For reports that the Davises did reach Chicago, "Across Continent by Automobile," *Automobile Review*, Oct. 1899, p. 37; "The Davises Still Traveling," *Motor Age*, Oct. 17, 1899, p. 113; and *Horseless Age*, Oct. 18, 1899, p. 7.

53. *Motor Age*, Oct. 17, 1899, p. 113.

54. "The Transcontinental Tourists," *Horseless Age*, Aug. 16, 1899, p. 6.

55. "Automobile News," *Scientific American*, Oct. 7, 1899, p. 231, and Nov. 4, 1899, p. 299.

56. For the *Autocar* quote, see the American automobile notes dated July 15 (pp. 743–44) in that journal's issue of Aug. 19, 1899; see also Van Tassel Sutphen, "A Transcontinental Automobilist," *Harper's Weekly*, July 22, 1899, p. 731.

57. *Scientific American*, July 8, 1899, p. 26 (for the 621-mile figure); and *Harper's Weekly*, July 22, 1899, p. 731 (for the estimate of 750–800 miles).

58. "Automobile Ends 1,050 Mile Trip," *New York Herald*, Aug. 6, 1899, p. 13, col. 1.

59. The 275-mile figure is according to distances given in the "Shortest Motor Distances Via the Transcontinental Trails" section of *Best Roads of All States: Across the Continent Motor Atlas* (Chicago: Clason Map Co., n.d.), p. 4, and the Ohio map on p. 15. Although there is no publication date, this atlas uses population figures for the year 1920, so one may infer that the travel distances given are at least as recent as the year 1920.

60. *Scientific American*, Sept. 2, 1899, p. 153; and "Mishaps Do Not Stop Automobile," *New York Herald*, July 16, 1899, sec. 1, p. 6, col. 1.

61. "Automobile Awaits the New Cylinder's Arrival," *San Francisco Call*, July 26, 1899, p. 2, col. 6; and editorial, *Chicago Times-Herald*, reprinted in the *New York Herald*, June 30, 1899, p. 6, col. 1.

62. "From Ocean to Ocean by Automobile," *Cleveland Plain Dealer*, Mar. 17, 1901, p. 1, col. 7.

63. "From Ocean to Ocean by Automobile," *Automobile Review*, April 1901, p. 70.

64. Charles B. Shanks, "Fighting Their Way through the Clouds," *Cleveland Plain Dealer*, May 25, 1901, p. 1, col. 1.

65. Kimes and Clark, *Standard Catalog of American Cars*, 2d ed., p. 1507.

66. The presumed date of Winton's arrival in America has appeared variously as 1878, 1880, and 1884. William S. McKinstry, in "Alexander Winton: An Unsung Genius," which appeared in *The Historical Society News* of the Western Reserve Historical Society (Cleveland: August 1972), says Winton arrived in 1878. When Winton died in 1932, however, two obituaries claimed he had immigrated in 1880. In the Winton biography that appears in Kimes and Clark's *Standard Catalog of American Cars*, 2d ed., he is said to have arrived in this country in 1884.

67. Kimes and Clark, *Standard Catalog of American Cars*, 2d ed., p. 1507; *Historical Society News*, August 1972, n.p.

68. *Automobile Review*, April 1901, p. 70.

69. Charles B. Shanks, *Cleveland to New York in a Motor Carriage*, 7th ed. (Cleveland: Winton Motor Carriage Co., 1899?), pp. 1, 7, 8, and 20.

70. Photo and cutline, *Automobile Trade Journal*, Dec. 1, 1924, p. 247; Walter E. Gosden, "Winton: The Man and His Motorcars," *Automobile Quarterly* 22, no. 3 (1984): 312; and "Prepare for Winton's Trip," *Motor Age*, Apr. 18, 1901, p. 8.

71. *Cleveland Plain Dealer*, Mar. 17, 1901, p. 1, col. 7.

72. Ibid.

73. Ibid.

74. Ibid., p. 1, col. 7, p. 2.

75. "Hardships for Automobilists," *Cleveland Plain Dealer*, Mar. 24, 1901, p. 5, col. 1.

76. "Winton's Trans-Continental Trip," *Motor Vehicle Review*, Mar. 28, 1901, n.p.

77. "To Cross the Mountains," *Cleveland Plain Dealer*, Mar. 31, 1901, p. 8, col. 1.

78. Ibid.

79. "Miles to Receive the Automobilists," *Cleveland Plain Dealer*, Apr. 14, 1901, p. 2, col. 2.

80. Ibid.; *Ogden (Utah) Standard*, Apr. 24, 1901, reprinted as "Papers Praise Proposed Trip," in *Cleveland Plain Dealer*, Apr. 28, 1901, p. 11, col. 1; and *Motor Age*, Apr. 18, 1901, p. 8.

81. *Cleveland Plain Dealer*, Mar. 31, 1901, p. 8, col. 1.

82. Ibid., Apr. 14, 1901, p. 1, col. 7.

83. Roger J. Spiller, ed., *Dictionary of American Military Biography* (Westport, Conn.: Greenwood Press, 1984), p. 768.

84. Unheadlined blurb, *Cycle and Automobile Trade Journal*, Oct. 1, 1903, p. 38.

85. *Cleveland Plain Dealer*, Apr. 14, 1901, p. 1, col. 7.

86. "Across Continent in an Automobile," *San Francisco Bulletin*, reprinted as "The Far West is Interested," in *Cleveland Plain Dealer*, May 12, 1901, p. 9, col. 5.

87. *Motor Age*, Apr. 18, 1901, p. 8, col. 1.

88. *Cleveland Plain Dealer*, Apr. 14, 1901, p. 2, col. 2.

89. Charles Bernard Shanks, "A Letter That Never Was Delivered," *MoTor*, January 1931, p. 114.

90. Charles B. Shanks, "From Sea to Sea by Automobile," *Cleveland Plain Dealer*, May 20, 1901, p. 1, col. 1. Shafter's background is from Spiller, *Dictionary of American Military Biography*, pp. 978–80.

91. Charles B. Shanks, "Journey to the Atlantic Begun," *Cleveland Plain Dealer*, May 21, 1901, p. 1, col. 4.

92. *Cleveland Plain Dealer*, May 20, 1901, p. 1, col. 1.

93. "To Span the Continent with a Winton Automobile," *Oakland (Calif.) Enquirer*, May 20, 1901, p. 3, col. 2.

94. Charles B. Shanks, "Automobiling in the West," *Scientific American Supplement*, Aug. 3, 1901, p. 21398.

95. Ibid.

96. Ibid.

97. Ibid.

98. Charles B. Shanks, "Were Prepared for Trouble," *Cleveland Plain Dealer*, May 23, 1901, p. 1, col. 1.

99. *Scientific American Supplement*, Aug. 3, 1901, p. 21398. A highly detailed 1995 U.S. Forest Service map of the Tahoe National Forest calls the formation "Hampshire Rocks."

100. Ibid.

101. Ibid.

102. Charles B. Shanks, "Lost a Wheel in the Mountains," *Cleveland Plain Dealer*, May 23, 1901, p. 1, col. 1. Shanks spelled "Kelley" as "Keeley" in his *Scientific American Supplement* article.

103. *Cleveland Plain Dealer*, May 23, 1901, p. 1, col. 1.

104. Ibid., May 25, 1901, p. 1, col. 1.

105. Ibid.; and "Stalled in a Snowdrift," *Reno (Nev.) Evening Gazette*, May 25, 1901, p. 1, col. 4.

106. Charles B. Shanks, "Desert Sands Before Them," *Cleveland Plain Dealer*, May 25, 1901, p. 1, col. 1.

107. *Scientific American Supplement*, Aug. 3, 1901, p. 21399; *MoTor*, January 1931, p. 270; and Charles B. Shanks, "Over the Top of the High Sierras," *Cleveland Plain Dealer*, May 26, 1901, p. 1, col. 7.

108. *Scientific American Supplement*, Aug. 3, 1901, p. 21399.

109. *MoTor*, January 1931, p. 270.

110. Charles B. Shanks, "They Put in One Comfortable Day," *Cleveland Plain Dealer*, May 27, 1901, p. 1, col. 1.

111. "Across the Continent," *Daily Nevada State Journal*, May 28, 1901, p. 3, col. 1.

112. Charles B. Shanks, "Along Shelf Roads over Deep Canyons," *Cleveland Plain Dealer*, May 28, 1901, p. 1, col. 1.

113. *Cleveland Plain Dealer*, May 28, 1901, p. 1, col. 1; and *Scientific American Supplement*, Aug. 3, 1901, p. 21399.

114. *Cleveland Plain Dealer*, May 28, 1901, p. 1, col. 1.

115. "Brief Items of Town and State," *Wadsworth (Nev.) Semi-Weekly Dispatch*, May 28, 1901, p. 1, col. 2.

116. Charles B. Shanks, "They Had to Pile Brush in the Sand," *Cleveland Plain Dealer*, May 29, 1901, p. 1, col. 4.

117. Ibid.

118. *Scientific American Supplement*, Aug. 3, 1901, p. 21399.

119. *Cleveland Plain Dealer*, May 29, 1901, p. 1, col. 4.

120. "An Automobile Trip," *Lovelock (Nev.) Argus*, June 1, 1901, p. 1, col. 4; and "Brevities," *Lovelock (Nev.) Tribune*, June 1, 1901, p. 1, col. 6.

121. *Scientific American Supplement*, Aug. 3, 1901, p. 21399.

122. Charles B. Shanks, "A Hopeless Fight with Desert Sand," *Cleveland Plain Dealer*, May 31, 1901, p. 1, col. 1.

123. *MoTor*, Jan. 1931, p. 270; and *Cleveland Plain Dealer*, May 31, 1901, p. 1, col. 1.

124. "Automobile Stops in a Desert," *San Francisco Call*, May 31, 1901, p. 8, col. 5.

125. *Scientific American Supplement*, Aug. 3, 1901, p. 21398.

126. "Winton Will Gain Advertising from His Attempt," *Motor Vehicle Review*, June 13, 1901, p. 9; and "Deep and Almost Bottomless Sand," *Cleveland Plain Dealer*, June 3, 1901, p. 8, col. 3.

127. *Cleveland Plain Dealer*, June 3, 1901, p. 8, col. 3.

128. Ibid., May 31, 1901, p. 1, col. 1.

129. "A Success as Far as It Went," editorial, *Cleveland Plain Dealer*, June 1, 1901, p. 4, col. 2.

130. "Touring in the Desert," *Horseless Age*, June 5, 1901, p. 211.

131. *Motor Vehicle Review*, June 13, 1909, p. 9; the "Kipling's sketches" quotation is from the *Pittsburgh Index*, quoted in "An American Exploration," *Auto Era*, September 1901, p. 13; and "Nevada Sand Hills Block Winton's Trip across the Continent," *Cycle and Automobile Trade Journal*, July 1, 1901, p. 2.

132. *MoTor*, January 1931, p. 270.

133. See the following articles in *Automobile*: "Shanks Leaves Winton to Take Chalmers," June 18, 1908, p. 865; "Shanks a Real Estater," June 24, 1909, p. 1054; "Shanks Joins Class Journal Co.," Oct. 2, 1913, p. 627; and "Shanks Now with W., C. & P., Inc.," June 22, 1911, p. 1407. See also "Charles B. Shanks Quits the Kelly-Springfield Motor Truck Company," *Commercial Car Journal*, Sept. 15, 1913, p. 4; and "Shanks to Direct Premier Sales Work," *Automobile*, June 11, 1914, p. 1237.

134. *Automobile Trade Journal*, Dec. 1, 1924, p. 247.

135. "Pacific to Atlantic by Automobile," *Automobile*, June 27, 1903, p. 665.

136. "Alexander Winton Dies in Cleveland," *Automobile Topics*, June 25, 1932, p. 401.

137. *Historical Society News*, August 1972, n.p. This claim may or may not be true; automotive historians still debate the assertion. Many qualify the claim by contending that other inventors—Ransom Olds, for one—had previously sold individual autos but that Winton's was the first sale of a standard auto in regular production to someone other than a company officer.

138. L. L. Whitman, "The Whitman Transcontinental Expedition," *Horseless Age*, July 29, 1903, p. 121.

139. *MoTor*, January 1931, p. 270.

140. Ibid., p. 114.

Chapter 2

1. Many contemporary and retrospective accounts of this trip misspell Crocker's first name as Sewell. Census records and his obituary confirm that the spelling is actually Sewall.

2. H. Nelson Jackson, "Honk! Honk! New York or Bust!" *American Legion Monthly*, February 1936, pp. 10–11, 47–50. *Reader's Digest* printed a condensed version of this article as "First across the Continent," April 1936, pp. 99–101.

3. "Across the Continent in an Auto," *Cleveland Leader*, July 21, 1903, p. 1, col. 7.

4. "A Curiosity for This City," *Montpelier (Idaho) Examiner*, June 19, 1903, p. 1, col. 2.

5. *American Legion Monthly*, February 1936, p. 48.

6. Ibid., pp. 48, 11.

7. H. Nelson Jackson, letter to the Winton company, July 29, 1903, reproduced in "Trip Finished," *Burlington (Vt.) Daily Free Press*, Aug. 8, 1903, p. 2.

8. "First Car across the U.S.A.," *Mechanix Illustrated*, March 1953, p. 70; Arthur F. Stone, *The Vermont of Today with its Historic Background, Attractions and People* (New York: Lewis Historical Publishing Co., 1929), p. 284; but compare with Winton ad, *Motor Age*, Aug. 6, 1903, back cover.

9. Thomas H. Wolf, "The Object at Hand," *Smithsonian*, October 1990, p. 36.

10. Col. H. Nelson Jackson, as told to William Engle, "I Made the First Cross-Country Auto Trip," *The American Weekly*, May 17, 1953, p. 12; compare with "Dr. Jackson Arrives," *Motor World*, July 30, 1903, p. 659.

11. *The American Weekly*, May 17, 1953, p. 12. Jackson's mining interests are discussed in "Col. Jackson, Legion's Father in Vt., Is Dead," *Burlington (Vt.) Free Press*, Jan. 15, 1955, p. 1.

12. "Automobile Trip Ends in Triumph," *New York Herald*, July 27, 1903, p. 10, col. 2; *Motor World*, July 30, 1903, p. 659; and *Cleveland Leader*, July 21, 1903, p. 1, col. 7.

13. *American Legion Monthly*, February 1936, p. 10; and "Crossing the Continent in Heavy Automobile," *Omaha (Neb.) World-Herald*, July 13, 1903, p. 2, col. 1.

14. *American Legion Monthly*, February 1936, p. 10.

15. Sewall K. Crocker, the youngest son of Benjamin David and Catherine Crocker, was born in April 1884, according to the 1900 census, conducted while the family was living in Walla Walla, Washington, before moving to Tacoma. According to this birth date, Crocker would have been 19 at the time of the transcontinental run. But if he was 30 at his death on April 22, 1913, as the April 24, 1913, *Tacoma Daily Ledger* indicates, Crocker would have actually been 20 or 21 during the run. During Jackson and Crocker's transcontinental trip, however, most press accounts gave Crocker's age as 22.

16. Walter E. Gosden, "Winton: The Man and His Motorcars," *Automobile Quarterly* 22, no. 3 (1984): 315.

17. *New York Herald*, July 27, 1903, p. 10, col. 2; and "Covered with Dust and Mud," *Cleveland Plain Dealer*, July 21, 1903, p. 7, col. 1.

18. Jackson letter in *Burlington (Vt.) Daily Free Press*, Aug. 8, 1903, p. 1, col. 6; and "First Automobilists to Reach Chicago from San Francisco," *Automobile*, July 25, 1903, p. 84.

19. *Burlington (Vt.) Daily Free Press*, Aug. 8, 1903, p. 1, col. 6.

20. *Cleveland Leader*, July 21, 1903, p. 1, col. 7; *Mechanix Illustrated*, March 1953, p. 181; and *Smithsonian*, October 1990, p. 35.

21. Martin Sheridan, "The First Automobile Coast to Coast," *True's Yearbook*, 1952, p. 24; and *Mechanix Illustrated*, March 1953, p. 70.

22. *Burlington (Vt.) Daily Free Press*, Aug. 8, 1903, p. 1, col. 6.

23. Ralph Nading Hill, *The Mad Doctor's Drive* (Brattleboro, Vt.: Stephen Greene Press, 1964), p. 7. But compare with p. 23, "Dr. Jackson's Cross-Country Progress," *Automobile*, July 4, 1903, p. 23, which reported "the car and equipment was bought from the Pioneer Automobile Company of San Francisco."

24. *American Legion Monthly*, February 1936, p. 10; and *New York Herald*, July 27, 1903, p. 10, col. 3.

25. Smith Hempstone Oliver, "Technical Notes," originally written for a catalog of the Smithsonian's automobile and motorcycle collection, but reprinted in Hill, *The Mad Doctor's Drive*, pp. 34–39.

26. "A Statement by Dr. Jackson," *Automobile*, Aug. 29, 1903, p. 217.

27. For calculations of the car's gross weight, see *New York Herald*, July 27, 1903, p. 10, col. 3. Other information in this paragraph is from "To New York in an Automobile," *San Francisco Chronicle*, May 23, 1903, p. 9, col. 5; "Doctor Jackson's Transcontinental Trip," *Horseless Age*, July 29, 1903, p. 126; and *Motor World*, July 30, 1903, p. 659.

28. *The American Weekly*, May 17, 1953, p. 12.

29. "A Real Live Automobile," *Lake County Examiner* (Lakeview, Ore.), June 4, 1903, p. 1, col. 5.

30. *Burlington (Vt.) Daily Free Press*, Aug. 8, 1903, p. 1, col. 6.

31. Unidentified *New York American* article, reprinted as "Won a Record/Dr. Jackson's Automobile Trip of 6,000 Miles," *Burlington (Vt.) Daily Free Press*, July 28, 1903, p. 6, col. 3; and "S. K. Crocker Ambitious to Tour Around the World," *Automobile*, Aug. 15, 1903, p. 175.

32. *American Legion Monthly*, February 1936, p. 11.

33. *Automobile*, July 25, 1903, p. 84.

34. *American Legion Monthly*, February 1936, p. 11.

35. Ibid.

36. *Horseless Age*, July 29, 1903, p. 126; and *New York Herald*, July 27, 1903.

37. *The American Weekly*, May 17, 1953, p. 13.

38. *Burlington (Vt.) Daily Free Press*, Aug. 8, 1903, p. 1, col. 6. "Swanton Falls" probably refers to Swan Falls, Idaho.

39. From an unidentified Rawlins newspaper quoted in "Trans-Continental Automobile Stalled at Rawlins," *Kemmerer (Wyo.) Camera*, July 4, 1903, p. 1, col. 5.

40. *American Legion Monthly*, February 1936, p. 11.

41. B. F. Goodrich Co. ad in *Motor Age*, Aug. 6, 1903, p. 28.

42. *Burlington (Vt.) Daily Free Press*, Aug. 8, 1903, p. 1, col. 6.

43. *Motor World*, July 30, 1903, p. 668. The magazine did not say where Jackson received the new tires, but other accounts said Ontario, Ore.

44. *Automobile*, July 4, 1903, p. 23.

45. "The Winton's Trip across the Continent," *Cycle and Automobile Trade Journal*, September 1903, p. 30.

46. [Title not given], *Lakeview (Ore.) Herald*, quoted in *American Legion Monthly*, February 1936, pp. 47–48.

47. *Lake County Examiner* (Lakeview, Ore.), June 4, 1903, p. 1, col. 5.

48. Ibid., p. 1, col. 5.

49. "Additional Local," *Lake County Examiner* (Lakeview, Ore.), June 11, 1903, p. 5, col. 3.

50. *Automobile*, Aug. 29, 1903, p. 217.

51. "Local and General," *Harney Valley Items* (Burns, Ore.), June 13, 1903, p. 3, col. 4; and "From San Francisco to New York in a Winton," *Motor Age*, July 23, 1903, p. 3.

52. *Harney Valley Items* (Burns, Ore.), June 13, 1903, p. 3, col. 4.

53. *Burlington (Vt.) Daily Free Press*, Aug. 8, 1903, p. 1, col. 8; and *American Legion Monthly*, February 1936, p. 49.

54. *Cleveland Plain Dealer*, July 21, 1903, p. 7, col. 1.

55. "Automobilists Visit Vale," *Malheur Gazette* (Vale, Ore.), June 11, 1903, p. 5, col. 2.

56. Jackson actually gives the date as Saturday, June 13, but this is evidently an error, for the Nampa-based *Idaho Leader* of June 13 reported that the autoists arrived in Nampa, southeast of Caldwell, on June 12.

57. *American Legion Monthly*, February 1936, pp. 10, 48.

58. *The American Weekly*, May 17, 1953, p. 13; and a *New York American* article, reprinted in the *Burlington (Vt.) Daily Free Press*, July 28, 1903, p. 6, col. 3.

59. *Motor World*, July 30, 1903, p. 668; and *Cleveland Plain Dealer*, July 21, 1903, p. 7, col. 1.

60. *Burlington (Vt.) Daily Free Press*, Aug. 8, 1903, p. 1, col. 6.

61. *Automobile*, Aug. 15, 1903, p. 175.

62. "They Smelled the Gasoline," *Bulletin* (Mountain Home, Idaho) article, reprinted in *Automobile*, July 25, 1903, p. 80.

63. *American Legion Monthly*, February 1936, p. 48.

64. *Montpelier (Idaho) Examiner*, June 19, 1903, p. 1, col. 2.

65. *Burlington (Vt.) Daily Free Press*, Aug. 8, 1903, p. 1, col. 7.

66. *New York American* article, reprinted in the *Burlington (Vt.) Daily Free Press*, July 28, 1903, p. 6, col. 3; and *The American Weekly*, May 17, 1953, p. 13.

67. *American Legion Monthly*, February 1936, p. 48; and *Burlington (Vt.) Daily Free Press*, Aug. 8, 1903, p. 1, col. 7.

68. *Automobile*, July 25, 1903, p. 84.

69. "He Tells of Parafine Troubles," *Motor Age*, July 23, 1903, p. 11, col. 2.

70. *Motor World*, July 30, 1903, p. 668.

71. *Burlington (Vt.) Daily Free Press*, Aug. 8, 1903, p. 1, col. 7; and *American Legion Monthly*, February 1936, p. 49.

72. *Burlington (Vt.) Daily Free Press*, Aug. 8, 1903, p. 1, col. 7; and *Motor World*, July 30, 1903, p. 668.

73. "Ocean to Ocean in a Winton," *Auto Era*, July–August 1903, p. 28.

74. *Burlington (Vt.) Daily Free Press*, Aug. 8, 1903, p. 1, col. 8.

75. "Dr. Jackson Recounts Few Vehicle and Tire Troubles on Long Trip," *Automobile*, Aug. 8, 1903, p. 150.

76. *Automobile*, Aug. 29, 1903, p. 217.

77. *Cleveland Leader*, July 21, 1903, p. 1, col. 7.

78. *American Legion Monthly*, February 1936, p. 50.

79. *Omaha (Neb.) World-Herald*, July 13, 1903, p. 2, col. 1.

80. *Burlington (Vt.) Daily Free Press*, Aug. 8, 1903, p. 2; and *Motor World*, July 30, 1903, p. 659.

81. *Burlington (Vt.) Daily Free Press*, Aug. 8, 1903, p. 2.

82. "San Francisco to New York," *Kearney (Neb.) Daily Hub*, July 11, 1903, p. 2, col. 3. Bolte had been Kearney's recognized automobile expert since building his own runabout in 1900 (see Beverly Rae Kimes and Henry Austin Clark, Jr., *Standard Catalog of American Cars, 1805–1942*, 2d ed. [Iola, Wis.: Krause Publications, 1989], p. 127).

83. *Burlington (Vt.) Daily Free Press*, Aug. 8, 1903, p. 2.

84. *Motor World*, July 23, 1903, p. 633.

85. "Across Continent on an Automobile," *Omaha (Neb.) Daily News*, July 13, 1903, p. 5, col. 4. While the *Daily News* described the Winton's condition as perfect, the *Omaha World-Herald* said that before leaving Omaha on Monday morning, July 13, Jackson's car "will have a thorough overhauling and be put into condition for fast running."

86. *Omaha (Neb.) World-Herald*, July 13, 1903, p. 2, col. 1; and *Motor Age*, July 23, 1903, p. 1.

87. *Omaha (Neb.) World-Herald*, July 13, 1903, p. 2, col. 1.

88. *Motor World*, July 30, 1903, p. 668.

89. *Automobile*, July 25, 1903, p. 84.

90. *American Legion Monthly*, February 1936, p. 50; and *Automobile*, Aug. 8, 1903, p. 150.

91. *Automobile*, July 4, 1903, p. 23.

92. "Welcomed at Cleveland," *Motor Age*, July 23, 1903, p. 3.

93. *Automobile*, Aug. 8, 1903, p. 150.

94. Winton ad, *Motor World*, Aug. 6, 1903, p. 703.

95. *Cleveland Leader*, July 21, 1903, p. 1, col. 7, p. 3, col. 2.

96. *Omaha (Neb.) Daily News*, July 13, 1903, p. 5, col. 4.

97. *Cleveland Leader*, July 21, 1903, p. 1, col. 7; and *Cleveland Plain Dealer*, July 21, 1903, p. 7, col. 2.

98. *American Legion Monthly*, February 1936, p. 50.

99. *New York Herald*, July 27, 1903, p. 10, col. 2.

100. *Cycle and Automobile Trade Journal*, September 1903, p. 29; and *New York Herald*, July 27, 1903, p. 10, col. 2.

101. *American Legion Monthly*, February 1936, p. 50; and *New York American* article, reprinted in the *Burlington (Vt.) Daily Free Press*, July 28, 1903, p. 6, col. 4.

102. *American Legion Monthly*, February 1936, p. 47. For the forty-six calendar days on which the car traveled, its average daily mileage would have been about 109 miles for a 5,000-mile trip, 122 miles for a 5,600-mile trip, or 130 miles for a 6,000-mile trip.

103. *Burlington (Vt.) Daily Free Press*, Aug. 8, 1903, p. 2. But Hill, in *The Mad Doctor's Drive* (p. 32), and the author of "Suggests Great Race from Ocean to Ocean," *Motor Age*, Aug. 6, 1903 (p. 2, col. 1), both indicate that Crocker rode to Burlington in the automobile.

104. *Burlington (Vt.) Daily Free Press*, Aug. 8, 1903, p. 2.

105. *Smithsonian*, October 1990, p. 42; and *Automobile*, Aug. 29, 1903, p. 217.

106. "Rumors Arouse Winton Company," *Automobile*, Aug. 22, 1903, p. 200; and *American Legion Monthly*, February 1936, p. 50.

107. An undated *Auto Era* article, "Transcontinental Echo," in Special Collections, University of Vermont Library, Burlington.

108. Unidentified article in *Automobile Topics*, reprinted in *American Legion Monthly*, February 1936, p. 50.

109. "The Transcontinental Tours," *Horseless Age*, July 22, 1903, p. 86; and *Horseless Age*, July 29, 1903, p. 126.

110. *Motor Age*, Aug. 6, 1903, p. 2.

111. *Automobile*, Aug. 15, 1903, p. 175.

112. "Colonel Crocker Dies Suddenly at Family Residence," *Tacoma (Wash.) Daily Tribune*, May 16, 1910, p. 1. His father's estate was worth at least $250,000, the newspaper estimated.

113. "Sewall King Crocker," *Tacoma (Wash.) Daily Ledger*, April 24, 1913, p. 8.

114. "A Transcontinental Race," *Automobile*, Aug. 22, 1903, p. 197. *Motor Age*, Aug. 6, 1903, p. 2, also describes Jackson's race idea.

115. *Burlington (Vt.) Free Press*, Jan. 15, 1955, p. 1.

116. *New York American* article, reprinted in the *Burlington (Vt.) Daily Free Press*, July 28, 1903, p. 6, col. 3; and untitled editorial, *Horseless Age*, Oct. 18, 1899, p. 7.

117. "Dr. Jackson's Success," *Motor Age*, July 23, 1903, p. 6.

118. Kimes and Clark, *Standard Catalog of American Cars*, 2d ed., p. 1508.

119. Details on Winton engine production come from *Automobile Quarterly* 22, no. 3 (1984): 318, 319; and Gerald Perschbacher, "Winton Owners Kept Happy," *Old Cars Weekly News & Marketplace*, July 7, 1994, p. 46, col. 4.

Chapter 3

1. M. C. Krarup, "From Coast to Coast in an Automobile," *World's Work*, May 1904, p. 4742.

2. The car's empty weight is from "Entries for the N.A.A.M. Endurance Run from New York to Cleveland and Pittsburg, October 7 to 15, with Official Data," *Automobile*, Oct. 3, 1903, p. 350. Various press estimates put the car's empty weight as high as 2,600 pounds, however.

3. *World's Work*, May 1904, p. 4742.

4. "Pacific to Atlantic by Automobile," *Automobile*, June 27, 1903, p. 665; and "The Packard Trans-Continental Trip," *Cycle and Automobile Trade Journal*, Aug. 1, 1903, p. 38.

5. Packard ad, *Motor Age*, Sept. 3, 1903, p. 22.

6. Marius C. Krarup, "Overland Trip from the Pacific Ocean—San Francisco to Sacramento," *Automobile*, July 4, 1903, p. 12.

7. The estimate of 750 photos is from Beverly Rae Kimes, ed., *Packard: A History of the Motor Car and the Company* (Princeton, N.J.: Princeton Publishing Co., 1978), p. 78.

8. Lincoln Highway Association, *The Lincoln Highway: The Story of a Crusade That Made Transportation History* (New York: Dodd, Mead & Co., 1935), p. 7.

9. *Automobile*, July 4, 1903, p. 12; and Kimes, *Packard*, p. 78.

10. Quotations in this paragraph were drawn from the following sources: *Automobile*, July 4, 1903, p. 12; "Ocean to Ocean in Auto," *New York Times*, Aug. 22, 1903, p. 1, col. 1; "Gasoline-Driven Auto Bridges the Continent," *San Francisco Chronicle*, Sept. 10, 1950, p. 1L, col. 1; "Transcontinental Automobilists Welcomed by Denver Chauffeurs," *Denver Post*, July 21, 1903, p. 8, col. 1; "Packard Tourists Arrive in Chicago," *Chicago Inter Ocean*, Aug. 11, 1903, p. 1, col. 7 of sports section; "Transcontinental Auto Tourists Are in Denver," *Rocky Mountain News* (Denver), July 21, 1903, p. 8, col. 2; and *Motor Age*, Sept. 3, 1903, p. 22.

11. *Denver Post*, July 21, 1903, p. 8, col. 1; and "Through Nevada," *Horseless Age*, July 29, 1903, pp. 132–33. Contrary to the *Horseless Age* article, local newspaper accounts indicated that Allyn was still in the car as far east as Council Bluffs, Iowa. See, for example, the *Omaha (Neb.) World-Herald* and *Council Bluffs (Iowa) Sunday Nonpareil*.

12. Packard ad, *Motor Age*, July 16, 1903, p. 31.

13. Specifications are from *Automobile*, Oct. 3, 1903, p. 350; and Ron Santucci, "Resurrecting a Legend: Terry Martin and the Packard Old Pacific," *Automobile Quarterly*, 20, no. 3 (1982): 329. The car's new price is from Beverly Rae Kimes and Henry Austin Clark, Jr., *Standard Catalog of American Cars, 1805–1942*, 2d ed. (Iola, Wis.: Krause Publications, 1989), p. 1066.

14. M. C. Krarup, "Over the Old Forty-Nine Trail in an American Automobile," *Automobile*, Aug. 1, 1903, p. 102.

15. Krarup says 20 feet in ibid., p. 103, but 24 feet in *World's Work*, May 1904, p. 4745.

16. "Motorneers Would Cross Continent," *San Francisco Chronicle*, June 21, 1903, p. 37, col. 4. Kimes, *Packard*, p. 78, refers to an extra axle strapped to the rear deck.

17. *Automobile*, July 4, 1903, p. 12.

18. M. C. Krarup, "Through the Humboldt River Valley on the Overland Car," *Automobile*, Aug. 15, 1903, p. 157.

19. *Chicago Inter Ocean*, Aug. 11, 1903, p. 1, col. 7 of sports section.

20. "Start of Long Journey," San Francisco wire story in *Wyoming Tribune* (Cheyenne), June 21, 1903, p. 5, col. 4.

21. *World's Work*, May 1904, p. 4742.

22. *Colorado Springs Gazette*, July 20, 1903, reprinted as "Old Pacific is Coming" in *Warren (Ohio) Weekly Tribune*, July 30, 1903, p. 7, col. 1.

23. Marius C. Krarup, "Overland Trip from the Pacific Ocean—Placerville to Slippery Ford," *Automobile*, July 18, 1903, p. 51.

24. Marius C. Krarup, "Across America in an American Automobile," *Automobile*, July 25, 1903, p. 74.

25. *Automobile*, July 4, 1903, p. 12.

26. Ibid.; and *San Francisco Chronicle*, June 21, 1903, p. 37, col. 4. Two weeks later, before starting on their own transcontinental trip, Lester L. Whitman and Eugene I. Hammond would also photograph their Oldsmobile runabout beside Cliff House.

27. *Rocky Mountain News* (Denver), July 21, 1903, p. 8, col. 2.

28. "From Pacific to Denver in an Auto," *Denver Times*, July 21, 1903, p. 6, col. 2.

29. *World's Work*, May 1904, p. 4740; compare with "Across the Sierra Nevada," *Horseless Age*, July 15, 1903, p. 76, an account of the start furnished to the auto journal by the Packard Motor Car Co.

30. *Automobile*, July 4, 1903, p. 12.

31. "Dr. Jackson Reaches Pocatello," *Automobile*, June 27, 1903, p. 665.

32. *Cleveland Plain Dealer*, "Covered with Dust and Mud," July 21, 1903, p. 7, col. 1; and "From Pacific to Cleveland," Aug. 15, 1903, p. 10, col. 1.

33. *Automobile*, July 4, 1903, p. 13.

34. Ibid.; and *Horseless Age*, July 15, 1903, p. 76.

35. *Automobile*, July 4, 1903, p. 14.

36. Ibid., July 18, 1903, pp. 53–54.

37. Ibid., p. 54.

38. *Automobile*, July 25, 1903, p. 74; and *World's Work*, May 1904, p. 4744.

39. *Automobile*, Aug. 1, 1903, p. 102.

40. Ibid.

41. *World's Work*, May 1904, p. 4746.

42. *Automobile*, Aug. 1, 1903, p. 103.

43. *Horseless Age*, July 29, 1903, p. 132; and *Automobile*, Aug. 1, 1903, p. 103.

44. *Automobile*, Aug. 1, 1903, pp. 103–4.

45. Ibid., p. 104.

46. *Automobile*, Aug. 15, 1903, p. 156.

47. *World's Work*, May 1904, p. 4747; and *Automobile*, Aug. 15, 1903, p. 157.

48. *Automobile*, Aug. 15, 1903, p. 156.

49. *Horseless Age*, July 29, 1903, p. 134; and *Automobile*, Aug. 15, 1903, p. 156.

50. *Automobile*, Aug. 15, 1903, p. 158.

51. Ibid.

52. "This, That and T'Other," *Free Press* (Elko, Nev.), July 4, 1903, p. 3, col. 3.

53. *Automobile*, Aug. 15, 1903, p. 158.

54. Ibid., p. 159.

55. Ibid., p. 160.

56. *Cycle and Automobile Trade Journal*, Aug. 1, 1903, p. 41.

57. "Story of a Transcontinental Journey," *Automobile*, Sept. 19, 1903, p. 287.

58. Ibid., p. 287.

59. Ibid., p. 288.

60. Packard ad, *Horseless Age*, Sept. 16, 1903, p. viii.

61. *World's Work*, May 1904, p. 4749.

62. *Automobile*, Sept. 19, 1903, p. 289.

63. "Crossing the Nation," *Salt Lake (City) Tribune*, July 5, 1903, p. 6, col. 1.

64. "Paper Checks an Auto Ride," *Salt Lake (City) Herald*, July 5, 1903, p. 5, col. 5.

65. "Crossing States Aboard an Auto," *Ogden (Utah) Standard*, July 6, 1903, p. 5, col. 3.

66. Ibid., and *Salt Lake (City) Herald*, July 5, 1903, p. 5, col. 5; both newspapers printed Krarup's statement. Though not quoted directly here, "Suit Stops Auto Trip," *Salt Lake (City) Telegram*, July 5, 1903, p. 3, col. 3, contributed details to this section.

67. *Salt Lake (City) Herald*, July 5, 1903, p. 5, col. 5; and *Automobile*, Sept. 19, 1903, p. 289.

68. *Automobile*, Sept. 19, 1903, p. 289.

69. *World's Work*, May 1904, p. 4749.

70. "With the Overland Car through Utah into Colorado," *Horseless Age*, Sept. 30, 1903, pp. 357–58.

71. Ibid., p. 358.

72. Ibid.

73. *Horseless Age*, Sept. 30, 1903, pp. 358–59.

74. Ibid., p. 359.

75. *Cycle and Automobile Trade Journal*, Aug. 1, 1903, p. 41.

76. *Horseless Age*, Sept. 30, 1903, p. 359.

77. *World's Work*, May 1904, p. 4750. Krarup used the older "Grand River" designation for a stretch now typically known as part of the Colorado River.

78. "Thrilling Incidents of E. Tom Fetch's Trip in the Packard Motor Car Pacific," reprint of a July 13, 1903, *Daily Sun* (Grand Junction, Colo.) article in the *Warren (Ohio) Weekly Tribune*, July 23, 1903, p. 7.

79. *Denver Post*, July 21, 1903, p. 8, col. 4. The "steep and slippery hill" description is a caption typed along the top of a photo that is part of the "Packard Collection" at the Detroit Public Library's National Automotive History Collection.

80. But the *New York Times*, Aug. 22, 1903, p. 1, col. 1, quotes Fetch as saying "the shortest day's run we made was twenty-four miles, in Iowa." Similarly, Packard's *Motor Age* ad of Aug. 13, 1903 (p. 23), says the auto traveled from Gypsum through Edwards to Redcliff on July 16—about 45 miles.

81. *World's Work*, May 1904, p. 4752.

82. Ibid.

83. *Denver Post*, July 21, 1903, p. 8, col. 1; and *Denver Times*, July 21, 1903, p. 6, col. 2.

84. The July 29, 1903, issue of *Horseless Age*, printing a Packard press release, also says Allyn left the car at Colorado Springs. If so, he perhaps rejoined the crew for a short distance in Nebraska and Iowa. Just two men were in the auto when it passed through Columbus, Neb., according to an untitled

blurb in the July 31, 1903 *Columbus Telegram*. But Allyn was in the car when it arrived in Omaha on July 31 ("Auto Is Going Overland," *Omaha (Neb.) World-Herald*, Aug. 1, 1903, p. 12, col. 5). And Allyn was apparently still with the car at Council Bluffs, Iowa ("Mobilists from Frisco," *Council Bluffs (Iowa) Sunday Nonpareil*, Aug. 1, 1903, p. 5, col. 4). Fetch and Krarup were the only occupants, however, when the car finally arrived in Chicago on August 10.

85. *Denver Post*, July 21, 1903, p. 8, col. 1.

86. "'Across Continent' Auto in Denver," *Denver Republican*, July 21, 1903, p. 8, col. 1.

87. "Fetch and Krarup Reach Denver from San Francisco," *Automobile*, Aug. 1, 1903, p. 124; and *Rocky Mountain News* (Denver), July 21, 1903, p. 8, col. 2.

88. *Salt Lake (City) Tribune*, July 5, 1903, p. 6, col. 1; Packard ad, *Horseless Age*, July 22, 1903, p. ix; and "May Come to Warren," *Warren (Ohio) Weekly Tribune*, July 23, 1903, p. 1, col. 6.

89. *Denver Post*, July 21, 1903, p. 8, col. 4.

90. *Denver Times*, July 21, 1903, p. 6, col. 2.

91. "Crossing the Continent by Automobile," *Scientific American*, Jan. 13, 1906, p. 24; reprint of a July 20, 1903, *Colorado Springs Gazette* article in *Warren (Ohio) Weekly Tribune*, July 30, 1903, p. 7, col. 1; and Thomas R. [*sic*] Fetch, "Journeys from Ocean to Ocean: The Story of One Trip," *MoTor*, October 1903, p. 19.

92. *World's Work*, May 1904, p. 4753.

93. Ibid., pp. 4753–54.

94. Packard ad, *Motor World*, Aug. 27, 1903, p. 805; and *New York Times*, Aug. 22, 1903, p. 1, col. 1.

95. "Fetch Finds Bad Roads," *Warren (Ohio) Weekly Tribune*, July 30, 1903, p. 5, col. 4; and *MoTor*, October 1903, p. 19.

96. *Columbus (Neb.) Telegram*, July 31, 1903, p. 1, col. 1.

97. *Omaha (Neb.) World-Herald*, Aug. 1, 1903, p. 12, col. 5.

98. *World's Work*, May 1904, p. 4754; and "Fetch and Krarup Met at Chicago by Club Members," *Automobile*, Aug. 15, 1903, p. 160.

99. *Automobile*, Aug. 15, 1903, p. 160.

100. "Packard Tourists Commence Last Lap," *Motor Age*, Aug. 13, 1903, p. 8.

101. *World's Work*, May 1904, p. 4754; and "Auto Party Arrives Here from the Pacific Coast," *Chicago Daily Tribune*, Aug. 11, 1903, p. 3, col. 4.

102. *Chicago Inter Ocean*, Aug. 11, 1903, p. 1, col. 7 of sports section.

103. *World's Work*, May 1904, p. 4754.

104. Unidentified *Conneaut (Ohio) News* article, reprinted as "Fetch Broke Speed Limit," *Warren (Ohio) Weekly Tribune*, Aug. 20, 1903, p. 8, col. 4.

105. "Auto Tourists Here Yesterday," *Erie (Pa.) Dispatch*, Aug. 17, 1903, p. 3, col. 4.

106. *World's Work*, May 1904, p. 4754.

107. *New York Times*, Aug. 22, 1903, p. 1, col. 1.

108. "Arrival of Overlanders in New York," *Automobile*, Aug. 29, 1903, pp. 205–6.

109. *New York Times*, Aug. 22, 1903, p. 1, col. 1.

110. *Automobile*, Aug. 29, 1903, p. 206. Winslow was now listed as an unspecified representative of the Cadillac company.

111. *New York Times*, Aug. 22, 1903, p. 1, col. 1.

112. "Record Journey by Automobile," *New York Herald*, Aug. 22, 1903, p. 5, col. 1. The reader will recall that the *Herald* had been one of the sponsors for the abortive 1899 Davis attempt.

113. *Automobile*, Aug. 29, 1903, p. 206.

114. *New York Times*, Aug. 22, 1903, p. 1, col. 1.

115. Packard ad, *Horseless Age*, Sept. 30, 1903, p. iii.

116. The back of the retouched photo indicates that the Packard Motor Car Company copied it from Krarup's original and assigned it Packard negative number 948-A. The factory photo was among those donated to the Detroit Public Library's National Automotive History Collection when the Packard company closed in 1958. It is now part of the NAHC's "Packard Collection."

117. *Chicago Inter Ocean*, Aug. 11, 1903, p. 1, col. 7 of sports section.

118. Quoted in Kimes, *Packard*, p. 81.

119. "Anxious Waiting in Binghamton," Oct. 17, 1903, p. 392; "Last Runs of Endurance Contest N.Y. to Pittsburg," Oct. 17, 1903, p. 415; and "Endurance Run Gold Medals Awarded," Dec. 5, 1903, p. 600, all in *Automobile*.

120. "Why He Didn't Drive in Chicago," *Automobile*, July 18, 1907, p. 88.

121. "Famed Driver, Tom Fetch, Dies," *Automotive News*, April 3, 1944, p. 44.

122. "Two Interesting Relics of Famous Runs," *Automobile*, Dec. 6, 1906, p. 828.

123. *Automobile Quarterly* 20, no. 3 (1982): 328–33.

124. Terry Martin wrote a two-part account of his trip for *Packard Cormorant*, which is published by Packard Automobile Classics, an international Packard club. See "The 'Transcontinental' Old Pacific 2," *Cormorant*, Autumn 1984, pp. 18–33, and Winter 1984–85, pp. 14–29.

125. Charles B. Shanks, "Automobiling in the West," *Scientific American Supplement*, Aug. 3, 1901, p. 21399.

126. *Chicago Inter Ocean*, Aug. 11, 1903, p. 1, col. 7 of sports section.

127. Packard ad, *Horseless Age*, Sept. 2, 1903, p. xxviii.

Chapter 4

1. Oldsmobile ad, *Scientific American*, April 9, 1904, p. 303.

2. They apparently followed this practice only in the West. In Chicago, "a change of clothes was resurrected from the luggage box" ("Olds Transcontinentalists Reach Chicago in Heavy Rain," *Motor Age*, Sept. 10, 1903, p. 12).

3. Using these logbooks, Hammond's son, John S. Hammond II, wrote *From Sea to Sea in 1903 in a Curved Dash Oldsmobile* (Egg Harbor City, N.J.: Laureate Press, 1985).

4. Hammond, *From Sea to Sea in 1903*, pp. 10, 11.

5. Ibid., p. 12.

6. "Origins of Old Scout," *Car Classics*, April 1972, n.p., an article written "through the efforts of John S. Hammond II, son of Eugene I. Hammond"; and John S. Hammond II, "The Whitman-Hammond Curved Dash Olds 1903 San Francisco to Boston Expedition," *Bulb Horn*, May–June 1978, p. 19.

7. From among the 180 newspaper and journal articles used as sources for the Jackson–Crocker, Fetch–Krarup, and Whitman–Hammond crossings, just one article treated the ventures as a three-way race: "The party at present in the lead, apparently, was last heard of from Omaha, Neb. He [Jackson] is reported to be a private automobilist and to be making the trip solely for pleasure" ("The Transcontinental Tours," *Horseless Age*, July 22, 1903, p. 86).

8. "Ocean to Ocean Runabout Tour Ended," *Automobile*, Sept. 26, 1903, p. 303; and L. L. Whitman, "A Trio of Overland Automobile Trips," *Motor Age*, July 23, 1903, p. 3.

9. Hammond, *From Sea to Sea in 1903*, p. 12.

10. *Automobile*, Sept. 26, 1903, p. 303.

11. John S. Hammond II, Eugene Hammond's son, wrote several articles about the trip, in addition to his 1985 book. Unfortunately, he contradicts himself—first saying that Whitman was born in South Paris, but later changing that to Turner, Maine.

12. Biographical information on Whitman is drawn from Hammond, *From Sea to Sea in 1903*, pp. 9–11, and *Automobile*, Sept. 26, 1903, p. 303.

13. Oldsmobile company, booklet, *Curved Dashing across America: San Francisco to New York, June 30–August 5, 1985* (Lansing, Mich.: Oldsmobile Public Relations, 1985?), pp. 5–7; and Beverly Rae Kimes and Henry Austin Clark, Jr., *Standard Catalog of American Cars, 1805–1942*, 2d ed. (Iola, Wis.: Krause Publications, 1989), p. 1017.

14. Specifications are from *Automobile*, "News and Trade Miscellany," July 18, 1903, p. 72, and "Proposes to Try in a Runabout," June 27, 1903, p. 665; see also Hammond, *From Sea to Sea in 1903*, pp. 13, 163–66; and Kimes and Clark, *Standard Catalog of American Cars*, 2d ed., p. 1018.

15. Hammond, *From Sea to Sea in 1903*, p. 15. All subsequent unattributed narration represents the author's summary of letters and articles that appeared in *Automobile*, *Horseless Age*, *Motor Age*, and other auto journals, plus various daily newspapers; in addition, summaries make use of Whitman and Hammond's logbook entries, as recorded in *From Sea to Sea in 1903*; as well as L. L. Whitman's eleven-page account of the trip, "From Sea to Sea or Golden Gate to Hell Gate." Whitman's account later appeared as the first chapter in a factory booklet titled *From Sea to Sea and Above the Clouds in an Oldsmobile* (Boston: Oldsmobile Company of New England, 1903 or 1904).

16. Hammond, *From Sea to Sea in 1903*, p. 19.

17. "Will Travel in Auto to New York," *San Francisco Bulletin*, July 6, 1903, p. 2, col. 1.

18. Whitman, *From Sea to Sea and Above the Clouds*, pp. 4–5.

19. Hammond, *From Sea to Sea in 1903*, p. 83.

20. *Motor Age*, Sept. 10, 1903, p. 13; and Hammond, *From Sea to Sea in 1903*, p. 146.

21. Whitman, *From Sea to Sea and Above the Clouds*, p. 13.

22. Hammond, *From Sea to Sea in 1903*, p. 30.

23. Ibid., p. 47.

24. Whitman, *From Sea to Sea and Above the Clouds*, p. 6; and "After a Coast Record," *Automobile*, June 22, 1905, p. 761.

25. "Crossing the Continent," *Daily Nevada State Journal* (Reno), July 12, 1903, p. 2, col. 3.

26. Hammond, *From Sea to Sea in 1903*, p. 48.

27. Ibid.; and L. L. Whitman, "Runabout Transcontinentalists Hail Ogden, Utah, with Joy," *Automobile*, Aug. 8, 1903, p. 141.

28. Hammond, *From Sea to Sea in 1903*, p. 48; and *Rocky Mountain News* (Denver), Aug. 8, 1903, p. 8, col. 4.

29. L. L. Whitman, "The Whitman Transcontinental Expedition," *Horseless Age*, July 29, 1903, p. 121.

30. Whitman's logbook entries for July 11, 12, and 13, 1903, in Hammond, *From Sea to Sea in 1903*, pp. 48–53, put the breakdown point, variously, at 25, 27, and 35 miles west of Lovelock. Whitman's descriptions suggest that the 35-mile figure is most reliable.

31. Whitman, *From Sea to Sea and Above the Clouds*, p. 8.

32. Hammond, *From Sea to Sea in 1903*, pp. 64, 89; compare with Whitman, *From Sea to Sea and Above the Clouds*, p. 7.

33. "News Items Collected About Town During the Week," *Lovelock (Nev.) Argus*, July 18, 1903, p. 3, col. 1.

34. Hammond, *From Sea to Sea in 1903*, p. 69.

35. Hammond, *From Sea to Sea in 1903*, p. 71.

36. L. L. Whitman, "The Whitman Cross-Continental Tour," *Horseless Age*, Aug. 5, 1903, p. 151; and *Automobile*, Aug. 8, 1903, p. 141.

37. "Evanston in Brief," *Wyoming Press* (Evanston, Wyo.), Aug. 1, 1903, p. 1, col. 3.

38. L. L. Whitman, "The Whitman Transcontinental Tour," *Horseless Age*, Aug. 19, 1903, p. 199; and Hammond, *From Sea to Sea in 1903*, p. 90.

39. "The Overland Oldsmobile Reaches Denver," *Motor Age*, Aug. 13, 1903, p. 5.

40. *Bulb Horn*, May–June 1978, p. 22.

41. Whitman, *From Sea to Sea and Above the Clouds*, p. 9.

42. Hammond, *From Sea to Sea in 1903*, p. 91.

43. "Crossing the Continent," *Laramie (Wyo.) Boomerang*, Aug. 6, 1903, p. 4, col. 4; but compare with photo in Hammond, *From Sea to Sea in 1903*, p. 60.

44. Hammond, *From Sea to Sea in 1903*, p. 95.

45. Ibid.; but compare with *Horseless Age*, Aug. 19, 1903, p. 199.

46. "Reach Denver on Overland Trip," *Denver Republican*, Aug. 8, 1903, p. 8, col. 1.

47. "Local Happenings," *Keith County News* (Ogallala, Neb.), Aug. 14, 1903, p. 1, col. 4.

48. "Cross Country Automobiling," *Motor Age*, Aug. 27, 1903, p. 5.

49. Whitman, *From Sea to Sea and Above the Clouds*, p. 10.

50. *Motor Age*, Aug. 27, 1903, p. 5; and L. L. Whitman, "Whitman's Transcontinental Tour," *Horseless Age*, Sept. 2, 1903, p. 270.

51. "Auto Tourists Arrive in Omaha," *Omaha (Neb.) World-Herald*, Aug. 24, 1903, p. 2, col. 4.

52. Whitman, *From Sea to Sea and Above the Clouds*, pp. 9–10.

53. Unidentified article, reproduced in Hammond, *From Sea to Sea in 1903*, p. 118.

54. Hammond, *From Sea to Sea in 1903*, p. 120.

55. *Motor Age*, Sept. 10, 1903, p. 12.

56. "Surprises Develop at Detroit Races," *Automobile*, Sept. 12, 1903, p. 263.

57. Hammond, *From Sea to Sea in 1903*, p. 135; and *Automobile*, Sept. 26, 1903, p. 304.

58. Hammond, *From Sea to Sea in 1903*, p. 138.

59. *Automobile*, Sept. 26, 1903, p. 304.

60. Ibid.

61. Hammond, *From Sea to Sea in 1903*, p. 140.

62. Most accounts are vague about the Oldsmobile's exact finishing time. The magazine *Automobile*, in "Ocean to Ocean Runabout Tour Ended," put the finish "at about the same hour" as the start, or about 3:00 PM. Whitman neglected to mention the concluding time in *From Sea to Sea and Above the Clouds*. The original logbook entries, assembled in John S. Hammond II's *From Sea to Sea in 1903* (p. 145), describe the finish only as "late afternoon." An unidentified New York City news account reproduced on page 150 of the Hammond book said it was "about 5 o'clock." According to "Across Continent in an Automobile," *New York Herald*, Sept. 18, 1903, p. 12, col. 4: "Central Bridge was crossed at half-past three o'clock yesterday afternoon, the tourists then going over to Riverdale Drive and ending the day's run just before the storm broke at a garage in West Sixtieth street." What detracts from the *Herald*'s otherwise authoritative-sounding account is that nearly every other source—including Whitman's logbooks—says Whitman and Hammond pulled up *during* the rainstorm. But I will nonetheless accept 3:30 PM as the approximate ending time.

63. *New York Herald*, Sept. 18, 1903, p. 12, col. 5.

64. "Oldsmobile Crosses Continent in 50 Days' [*sic*] Actual Running," *Cycle and Automobile Trade Journal*, Oct. 1, 1903, p. 34.

65. *Automobile*, Sept. 26, 1903, p. 303.

66. Hammond, *From Sea to Sea in 1903*, p. 155.

67. Whitman, *From Sea to Sea and Above the Clouds*, p. 8.

68. "Third Transcontinental Party Reaches Destination," *Motor Age*, Sept. 24, 1903, p. 7.

69. Hammond, *From Sea to Sea in 1903*, p. 153.

70. "Pacific to Atlantic," *Portland (Maine) Evening Express*, Sept. 23, 1903, n.p.

71. Oldsmobile ad, *Motor Age*, Sept. 3, 1903, p. 27.

72. Hammond, *From Sea to Sea in 1903*, p. 158.

73. "Whitman Reaches Portland," *Motor Age*, Oct. 1, 1903, p. 11.

74. See the following articles, all in the Oct. 17, 1903 issue of *Automobile*, for a running commentary of the race: "Notes of Second Day's Run," p. 393; "Second Day—Pine Hill to Binghamton," p. 388; and "Some Statistic Data of the Run," p. 422.

75. "E. I. Hammond Dies; Set Mark in Auto," *New York Times*, Nov. 21, 1948, p. 88, col. 7.

76. John S. Hammond II expounded his theory about the fate of the transcontinental 1903 runabout in the April 1972 *Car Classics* and the May–June 1978 *Bulb Horn*.

77. Photo and cutline, *Automobile*, Sept. 17, 1904, p. 315.

78. Nick Baldwin, G. N. Georgano, Michael Sedgwick, and Brian Labin, *The World Guide to Automobile Manufacturers* (New York: Facts on File Publications, 1987), p. 407.

79. Hammond, *From Sea to Sea in 1903*, p. 159.

80. Oldsmobile company booklet, *Curved Dashing across America*.

81. *New York Herald*, Sept. 18, 1903, p. 12, col. 4.

82. *Rocky Mountain News* (Denver), Aug. 8, 1903, p. 8, col. 4; "News and Views of the Automobilists," *Chicago Inter Ocean*, Sept. 6, 1903, p. 3, col. 7 of sports section; and *Cycle and Automobile Trade Journal*, Oct. 1, 1903, p. 34.

Chapter 5

1. "A Record Transcontinental Automobile Trip," *Scientific American*, Sept. 17, 1904, p. 192.

2. "Whitman Starts East," *Automobile*, Aug. 13, 1904, p. 168.

3. L. L. Whitman, "Another Transcontinental Trip," *Automobile*, Aug. 13, 1904, p. 186; and "Auto across Continent," *New York Tribune*, Sept. 4, 1904, p. 6, col. 6.

4. In this and the following paragraphs, production, factory size, and employment figures come from John Sherman Proter, ed., *Moody's Manual of Investments, American and Foreign: Industrial Securities* (New York: Moody's Investors Service, 1934), pp. 1788–89, and from earlier and later editions. *Moody's* does not specify whether its production figures are for model years or calendar years. Details on the automaker's technical innovations are drawn from Thomas H. Hubbard, "The Case for Franklin," *Automobile Quarterly* 5, no. 3 (1967): 235; and Beverly Rae Kimes and Henry Austin Clark, Jr., *Standard Catalog of American Cars, 1805–1942*, 2d ed. (Iola, Wis.: Krause Publications, 1989), p. 578.

5. "From Coast to Coast by Automobile in 33 Days," *New York Herald*, Sept. 4, 1904, p. 15, col. 3; L. L. Whitman, *From Coast to Coast in a Motor-Car* (Syracuse, N.Y.: H. H. Franklin Manufacturing Co., 1905), pp. 6, 30.

6. Telephone conversation between Peter Kunan of the H. H. Franklin Club and the author, March 27, 1996.

7. ALAM, *Hand Book of Gasoline Automobiles* (New York: Association of Licensed Automobile

Manufacturers, 1904), p. 26; and "Franklin Air-Cooled Cars," *Cycle and Automobile Trade Journal*, January 1904, pp. 102–6.

8. *Cycle and Automobile Trade Journal*, January 1904, pp. 102–6.

9. ALAM, *Hand Book of Gasoline Automobiles*, pp. 26; for quote, see L. L. Whitman, "From Golden Gate to Hell Gate," *MoTor*, September 1904, p. 12.

10. The men's weights are from H. A. French, "To Make Second Trip across the Continent," *San Francisco Chronicle*, July 31, 1904, p. 34, col. 2.

11. *MoTor*, September 1904, p. 12.

12. *Automobile*, Aug. 13, 1904, p. 168; and Whitman, *From Coast to Coast in a Motor-Car*, p. 14.

13. "Whitman is Off on his New York Trip," *San Francisco Chronicle*, Aug. 2, 1904, p. 5, col. 1.

14. *Automobile*, Aug. 13, 1904, p. 186; and *New York Herald*, Sept. 4, 1904, p. 15, col. 5.

15. Whitman, *From Coast to Coast in a Motor-Car*, p. 9; and *Automobile*, Aug. 13, 1904, p. 168.

16. "The Road in America/What an Experienced Automobilist Says of the Cross-Country Route," *New York Times*, Jan. 19, 1908, sec. 4, p. 4, col. 2.

17. *San Francisco Chronicle*, July 31, 1904, p. 34, col. 2.

18. Ibid.

19. Whitman, *From Coast to Coast in a Motor-Car*, p. 6.

20. *San Francisco Chronicle*, Aug. 2, 1904, p. 5, col. 1. The boundaries of Jefferson Square are given in Work Projects Administration, *San Francisco: The Bay and Its Cities* (New York: Hastings House, 1947), pp. 289–90.

21. Whitman, *From Coast to Coast in a Motor-Car*, p. 8.

22. Ibid., pp. 9–11. Whitman reverses the order: Gold Run is west of Dutch Flat.

23. *New York Herald*, Sept. 4, 1904, p. 15, col. 5.

24. "Wadsworth, Nevada," *Horseless Carriage Gazette*, Sept.–Oct. 1992, p. 37.

25. Whitman, *From Coast to Coast in a Motor-Car*, pp. 12–14.

26. Ibid., p. 14.

27. Ibid., p. 15.

28. Ibid., pp. 17–18.

29. *MoTor*, September 1904, p. 12.

30. L. L. Whitman, "Through the Desert Sands," *Automobile*, Aug. 20, 1904, p. 217.

31. Whitman, *From Coast to Coast in a Motor-Car*, pp. 18–20.

32. Ibid., p. 20.

33. "Eight Days Ahead of Record," *Ogden (Utah) Standard*, Aug. 12, 1904, p. 7. The *Standard* misstated the existing transcontinental speed record (it was 62 days, not 61) and the relative San Francisco to Ogden times of the 1903 Fetch-Krarup and 1904 Whitman-Carris treks (the Franklin was four days faster, not eight). This misinformation likely came from Whitman himself. On its own, however, the newspaper managed to misspell both Whitman's and Fetch's names.

34. *MoTor*, September 1904, p. 12.

35. Whitman, *From Coast to Coast in a Motor-Car*, pp. 23–24. In this account, Whitman mistakenly placed Spring Valley between Rock Springs and Rawlins. The small town—not shown on modern highway maps—is farther west, between Evanston and Rock Springs.

36. L. L. Whitman, "Hitting the Sage-Brush Trail," *Automobile*, Aug. 27, 1904, p. 238.

37. Whitman, *From Coast to Coast in a Motor-Car*, pp. 22–23. The Northern Pacific ran through Montana, not Wyoming. Whitman meant to say Union Pacific, and he uses the correct name in other references.

38. Ibid., p. 24.

39. *Automobile*, Aug. 27, 1904, p. 238.

40. Whitman, *From Coast to Coast in a Motor-Car*, pp. 25–26.

41. Unheadlined blurb, *Dawson County Pioneer* (Lexington, Neb.), Aug. 27, 1904, p. 8, col. 1; and "Local and Personal," *Grand Island (Neb.) Daily Independent*, Aug. 25, 1904, p. 4, col. 1.

42. Whitman, *From Coast to Coast in a Motor-Car*, p. 27.

43. "Auto Tourists," *Omaha (Neb.) Daily News*, Aug. 24, 1904, p. 2, col. 2; and "Whitman Reaches City," *Omaha (Neb.) World-Herald*, Aug. 24, 1904, p. 3, col. 6; and "Oldfield Breaks Records," *Omaha (Neb.) Daily Bee*, Aug. 24, 1904, p. 2, col. 3.

44. *Omaha (Neb.) Daily Bee*, Aug. 24, 1904, p. 2, col. 3.

45. *New York Herald*, Sept. 4, 1904, p. 15, col. 5.

46. Whitman, *From Coast to Coast in a Motor-Car*, p. 27.

47. Ibid.

48. Untitled blurb, *Chicago Inter Ocean*, Aug. 28, 1904, p. 4, col. 2 of sports section.

49. "Autos and Autoists," *South Bend (Ind.) Tribune*, Aug. 27, 1904, p. 15, col. 2.

50. *New York Herald*, Sept. 4, 1904, p. 15, col. 5; but compare with Whitman, *From Coast to Coast in a Motor-Car*, p. 31.

51. "Across America in One Month," *Erie (Pa.) Dispatch*, Sept. 2, 1904, p. 3, col. 3.

52. Ibid.; and *New York Herald*, Sept. 4, 1904, p. 15, col. 3.

53. *Erie (Pa.) Dispatch*, Sept. 2, 1904, p. 3, col. 3.

54. Ibid.

55. *New York Herald*, Sept. 4, 1904, p. 15, col. 3.

56. Whitman, *From Coast to Coast in a Motor-Car*, p. 30.

57. *Scientific American*, Sept. 17, 1904, p. 192.

58. "New Coast to Coast Record," *Motor World*, Sept. 8, 1904, p. 871.

59. Franklin ad, *Automobile*, Sept. 17, 1904, p. 63.

60. Whitman, *From Coast to Coast in a Motor-Car*, pp. 30–31.

61. *New York Herald*, Sept. 4, 1904, p. 15, col. 5.

62. *Scientific American*, Sept. 17, 1904, p. 192; and "Automobile Record Across the Continent," *New York Times*, Sept. 4, 1904, p. 10, col. 4.

63. *New York Herald*, Sept. 4, 1904, p. 15, col. 4.

64. Ibid., p. 15, col. 3.

65. "Transcontinental Record," *Automobile*, Sept. 10, 1904, p. 299; and *Scientific American*, Sept. 17, 1904, p. 192.

66. Photo of 1904 Franklin, p. 113; "H. H. Franklin Mfg. Co.," p. 120; and "In Attendance at Complete Vehicle Stands," p. 146, all in *Automobile*, Jan. 21, 1905.

67. "After a Coast Record," *Automobile*, June 22, 1905, p. 761; and "New Coast Record," *Automobile*, June 29, 1905, p. 792.

68. "How the Automobile Helped in San Francisco. Whitman, the Transcontinentalist, Was in the Thick of It," *Automobile*, May 3, 1906, p. 747.

69. "Thirty-Three Days from California to New York City," *Denver Post*, Aug. 22, 1926, n.p.

70. Dunwoodie's letter to the author, Aug. 29, 1994.

71. James Zordich, letter to Ralph Dunwoodie, April 13, 1976, copy in author's possession.

72. Leslie Kendall, telephone interview with author, Aug. 31, 1994. According to Kendall, the 1904 Franklin in the museum's collection carries a serial number of 790 and an engine number of 794. Of the thirty contemporary articles—including those Whitman wrote himself—used in preparing this chapter, none mentions the serial or engine numbers of the transcontinental Franklin, however. That

avenue is thus unavailable for documenting the car's history. Kendall graciously provided photocopies of all the information the Petersen Automotive Museum has in its file on the car—primarily copies of 1976 letters between Zordich and automotive historian Arthur Hammond Amick, regarding questions about the car's authenticity. Nothing bin the material conclusively documents the car's origin, however.

73. Gina Ward, manager of media relations for the Natural History Museum of Los Angeles County, telephone interview with the author, March 29, 1996.

74. *New York Herald*, Sept. 4, 1904, p. 15, col. 4.

75. "Hammond Insists on His Auto Record," *New York Times*, May 26, 1916, p. 22, col. 4.

Chapter 6

1. "Transcontinentalist Whitman: He Starts on Another Across-the-Country Trip, This Time in a 30-Horsepower Six-Cylinder Franklin," *Automobile*, Aug. 9, 1906, p. 185.

2. Franklin ad, *Scientific American*, Nov. 10, 1906, p. 353.

3. "Automobile on a Long Journey," *Ogden (Utah) Morning Examiner*, Aug. 7, 1906, p. 5, col. 5.

4. "A Record Auto Run and What It Means," *New York Times*, Aug. 19, 1906, p. 7, col. 3.

5. "An Automobile Race Nearly around the World," *New York Times*, Dec. 1, 1907, sec. 5, p. 2, col. 2.

6. Technical details in this and the following paragraphs come primarily from "Mechanical Briefs of 1906 Models: The New Franklins," *MoTor*, November 1905, p. 59; and "A New Transcontinental Automobile Record," *Scientific American Supplement*, Sept. 8, 1906, pp. front cover–25647. The historical background on the Franklin company is from Beverly Rae Kimes and Henry Austin Clark, Jr., *Standard Catalog of American Cars, 1805–1942*, 2d ed. (Iola, Wis.: Krause Publications, 1989), pp. 578–79.

7. "Auto's Record Run across the Continent," *New York Times*, Aug. 18, 1906, p. 5, col. 1; and "Across Country in Twelve Days," *Cleveland Plain Dealer*, Aug. 15, 1906, p. 7, col. 1.

8. "Franklin's Cross-Country Trip," *Motor Way*, Aug. 16, 1906, p. 10.

9. Untitled blurb, *Automobile*, May 23, 1907, p. 878. Carris's height and weight—up from a trim 156 pounds in 1904—is according to the New York State chauffeur's registration issued to him on February 1, 1912, as reproduced on the cover of the December 1963 issue of *Air Cooled News*.

10. "A New England Reliability Run," *Automobile*, Dec. 17, 1908, p. 843.

11. Ibid.; "Franklinites Will Miss James Daley, Old Time Cross Country Driver," *Franklin News*, May 16, 1921, p. 3; and "5th Annual AAA Reliability Tour," *Air Cooled News*, December 1963, pp. 2–7.

12. "Bay State Endurance Tie Finally Called a Draw," *Automobile*, Oct. 8, 1908, p. 496; and "Matheson Gets Three Out of Four in Quaker Club Run," *Automobile*, Jan. 7, 1909, p. 49.

13. "Over Muddy Roads from the Metropolis to the Hub," *Automobile*, March 18, 1909, n.p.; "State Highway Run an Endurance Test," *Motor Age*, June 24, 1909, p. 26; and "'Andy' Auble, Oldsmobiler, wins Pittsburgh Endurance Race," *Automobile*, May 6, 1909, p. 733.

14. "News and Trade Miscellany," *Automobile*, Aug. 2, 1906, p. 159.

15. Information on the Los Angeles–San Francisco speed run is from *Automobile*: "After a Coast Record," June 22, 1905, p. 761; and "New Coast Record," June 29, 1905, p. 792.

16. Ibid.

17. Ibid.

18. "How the Automobile Helped in San Francisco./Whitman, the Transcontinentalist, Was in the Thick of It," *Automobile*, May 3, 1906, p. 747.

19. Gordon Thomas and Max Morgan Witts, *The San Francisco Earthquake* (New York: Dell, 1972), p. 155; and *Automobile*, Aug. 9, 1906, p. 185.

20. *New York Times*, Aug. 19, 1906, p. 7, col. 3; and "Cost of Auto Records across the Continent," *New York Times*, Aug. 26, 1906, p. 5, col. 5.

21. *Automobile*, Aug. 9, 1906, p. 185.

22. *Scientific American Supplement*, Sept. 8, 1906, p. 25646.

23. L. L. Whitman, *Across America in a Franklin* (New York: H. H. Franklin Co., 1907?); reprinted in *Air Cooled News*, December 1956, pp. 19. The author is indebted to Carey S. Bliss, *Autos Across America*, 2d ed. (Austin, Texas: Jenkins & Reese Cos., 1982), p. 6, whose book provides the original publisher's name, the original (although speculative) publishing date, and the original length (30 pages) of Whitman's booklet, information that was not reproduced in the 1956 *Air Cooled News* reprint.

24. *New York Times*, Aug. 19, 1906, p. 7, col. 3.

25. *Franklin News*, May 16, 1921, p. 3.

26. "Whitman Expects to Drive Car to New York Cutting Former Mark to Fifteen Days," *San Francisco Call*, Aug. 3, 1906, p. 7, col. 3.

27. Stuart Gayness, "Whitman Confident of Breaking His Own Record to New York," *San Francisco Examiner*, Aug. 3, 1906, p. 9, col. 2.

28. Ibid., p. 9, col. 1.

29. *Air Cooled News*, December 1956, p. 19.

30. "Will Attempt to Lower His Record," *San Francisco Chronicle*, Aug. 2, 1906, p. 8, col. 4; and *New York Times*, Aug. 19, 1906, p. 7, col. 3.

31. *New York Times*, Aug. 19, 1906, p. 7, col. 3; *New York Times*, Aug. 18, 1906, p. 5, col. 1; and "Making Auto Records across the Continent," *New York Times*, Aug. 15, 1906, p. 4, col. 4.

32. "Trying to Break Automobile Record," *Daily Nevada State Journal* (Reno), Aug. 4, 1906, p. 3, col. 3; and *Air Cooled News*, December 1956, p. 19.

33. *Daily Nevada State Journal* (Reno), Aug. 4, 1906, p. 3, col. 3.

34. "Trying for Auto Record," *Reno (Nev.) Evening Gazette*, Aug. 3, 1906, p. 1, col. 7.

35. "The Road in America/What an Experienced Automobilist Says of the Cross-Country Route," *New York Times*, Jan. 19, 1908, sec. 4, p. 4, col. 3.

36. "Whitman's Record-Breaking Trip," *Automobile*, Aug. 23, 1906, p. 254.

37. "Whitman is Ahead of His Former Record," *San Francisco Chronicle*, Aug. 5, 1906, p. 30, col. 4.

38. *Ogden (Utah) Morning Examiner*, Aug. 7, 1906, p. 5, col. 5.

39. "Traveling By Motor from Coast to Coast," *Motor Age*, Sept. 2, 1909, p. 4.

40. *Motor Way*, Aug. 16, 1906, p. 10.

41. *Air Cooled News*, December 1956, p. 20.

42. *Ogden (Utah) Morning Examiner*, Aug. 7, 1906, p. 5, col. 5.

43. Ibid.

44. "Making Record Run across the Country," *Salt Lake (City) Tribune*, Aug. 7, 1906, p. 10, col. 2.

45. "Relay in Automobile Race Reaches Ogden," *Salt Lake (City) Telegram*, Aug. 6, 1906, p. 8, col. 5.

46. "Local Gossip," *Wyoming Press* (Evanston), Aug. 11, 1906, p. 8, col. 4.

47. *New York Times*, Aug. 19, 1906, p. 7, col. 3; and *Air Cooled News*, December 1956, p. 20.

48. "Local Mention," *Rock Springs (Wyo.) Miner*, Aug. 11, 1906, p. 3, col. 3.

49. "Franklin Car Comes to City from West," *Laramie (Wyo.) Republican*, Aug. 10, 1906, p. 3, col. 6.

50. "Lost in Hills," *Wyoming Tribune* (Cheyenne), Aug. 10, 1906, p. 1, col. 5.

51. *Air Cooled News*, December 1956, p. 20.

52. "Whitman Far Ahead of Record," *Automobile*, Aug. 16, 1906, p. 199; and "Hotel Arrivals," *Laramie (Wyo.) Republican*, Aug. 10, 1906, p. 3, col. 2.

53. *Wyoming Tribune* (Cheyenne), Aug. 10, 1906, p. 1, col. 5.

54. Thirteen months earlier, Theodore H. Bolte of Kearney had registered the 213th auto in Nebraska—a homemade "Bolte Runabout" ("Nebraska Secretary of State Motor Vehicles Register," 1905–1907, microfilm roll RG2, Nebraska State Historical Society, Lincoln).

55. "Overland in a Motor Car," *Kearney (Neb.) Daily Hub*, Aug. 11, 1906, p. 3, col. 3.

56. "Whitman Reaches Ogden [*sic*] in Nine Day Run," *San Francisco Call*, Aug. 12, 1906, p. 39, col. 2.

57. "Autoists Set New Mark," *Chicago Daily Tribune*, Aug. 14, 1906, p. 6, col. 4.

58. *Scientific American Supplement*, Sept. 8, 1906, p. 25646.

59. "Auto Hits Farmer," *Marshalltown (Iowa) Evening Times-Republican*, Aug. 13, 1906, p. 1, col. 6.

60. Ibid.

61. "Sees a New Auto Mark," *Chicago Daily News*, Aug. 14, 1906, p. 6, col. 7.

62. *Chicago Daily Tribune*, Aug. 14, 1906, p. 6, col. 4.

63. *Motor Way*, Aug. 16, 1906, p. 10.

64. *Chicago Daily News*, Aug. 14, 1906, p. 6, col. 7.

65. *Motor Way*, Aug. 16, 1906, p. 10.

66. "Transcontinental Autoists in an Accident Near Erie," *Erie (Pa.) Dispatch*, Aug. 15, 1906, p. 1, col. 5.

67. *Air Cooled News*, December 1956, p. 21.

68. "American End of New York to Paris Race," *New York Times*, Dec. 22, 1907, p. 3, col. 4. The *Times* was a sponsor of the upcoming 1908 New York–Paris race and was interviewing Whitman about what the racers should expect in America.

69. For Holcomb, see the following articles in *Automobile*: "Chicago–New York Relay Record Run," Oct. 3, 1903, p. 357; "One Car 1,100 Miles Continuously," Oct. 10, 1903, pp. 361–62; and "Chicago–New York Record Holder Dead," Nov. 7, 1907, p. 716; see also "New Automobile Record/Bert Holcomb Beats Best Previous Time from Chicago to New York," *New York Times*, Oct. 7, 1904, p. 7, col. 6. There is no consensus on Holcomb's 1904 time. Some accounts say 58 hours, 43 minutes; others, 58 hours, 45 minutes. I have used the *New York Times*'s figure of 58 hours, 53 minutes.

70. *Cleveland Plain Dealer*, Aug. 15, 1906, p. 7, col. 1.

71. "Predicts Ten Days to Cross Continent," *New York Herald*, Aug. 19, 1906, p. 16, col. 3, quotes Whitman on punctures; but compare with photo (Fig. 115) in this volume.

72. *Cleveland Plain Dealer*, Aug. 15, 1906, p. 7, col. 1.

73. Accounts of the accident were published in various auto journals, as well as the Cleveland, New York City, and Erie, Pa., newspapers.

74. "Record Breakers Meet an Accident," *Cleveland Leader*, Aug. 16, 1906, p. 8, col. 4.

75. "Transcontinental Autoists in an Accident Near Erie," *Erie (Pa.) Dispatch*, Aug. 15, 1906, p. 1, col. 3; "Record Breakers Meet an Accident," *Cleveland Leader*, Aug. 16, 1906, p. 8, col. 4; "Auto Leaps Into Creek," *Cleveland Plain Dealer*, Aug. 16, 1906, p. 1, col. 7; "Whitman Has Accident," *Motor Way*, Aug. 16, 1906, p. 11; "Whitman's Whirlwind Drive," *Motor World*, Aug. 16, 1906, p. 498; "Autoists Resume Race After 36 Hours' Delay," *Cleveland Leader*, Aug. 17, 1906, p. 8, col. 6; "More Delay for Whitman in Run," *New York Herald*, Aug. 17, 1906, p. 12, col. 2; "Cuts Down Auto Time," *Chicago Daily News*, Aug. 18, 1906, p. 1, col. 3 and p. 2, col. 6; "Coast to Coast in 15 Days 6 Hours," *New York Herald*, Aug. 18, 1906, p. 5, col. 2; "Auto's Record Run across the Continent," *New York Times*, Aug. 18, 1906, p. 5, col. 1; "Whitman's New Record," *New York Tribune*, Aug. 18, 1906, p. 2, col. 5; "A Record

Auto Run and What It Means," *New York Times*, Aug. 19, 1906, p. 7, col. 3; "Completion of Whitman's Transcontinental Run," *Horseless Age*, Aug. 22, 1906, p. 247; "Whitman's Record-Breaking Trip," *Automobile*, Aug. 23, 1906, p. 254; "Whitman Lowers Record," *Motor Way*, Aug. 23, 1906, p. 8; and "Cut the Transcontinental," *Motor World*, Aug. 23, 1906, pp. 547–48.

76. *Erie (Pa.) Dispatch*, Aug. 15, 1906, p. 1, col. 4.

77. Ibid.; and "More Delay for Whitman in Run," *New York Herald*, Aug. 17, 1906, p. 12, col. 2.

78. *Cleveland Leader*, Aug. 16, 1906, p. 8, col. 4; and *Cleveland Plain Dealer*, Aug. 16, 1906, p. 1, col. 7.

79. *Motor Way*, Aug. 23, 1906, p. 8.

80. *Air Cooled News*, December 1956, p. 21.

81. *New York Times*, Aug. 26, 1906, p. 5, col. 6.

82. *Cleveland Leader*, Aug. 16, 1906, p. 8, col. 4; and *New York Times*, Aug. 19, 1906, p. 7, col. 3.

83. *Cleveland Leader*, Aug. 17, 1906, p. 8, col. 6.

84. *New York Herald*, Aug. 18, 1906, p. 5, col. 2.

85. *New York Herald*, Aug. 19, 1906, p. 16, col. 3; and *New York Times*, Aug. 19, 1906, p. 7, col. 3.

86. *Automobile*, Aug. 23, 1906, p. 254; and *New York Times*, Aug. 18, 1906, p. 5, col. 1.

87. *New York Herald*, Aug. 18, 1906, p. 5, col. 2.

88. "Whitman's New Record," *New York Tribune*, Aug. 18, 1906, p. 2, col. 5; and *Air Cooled News*, December 1956, p. 22.

89. *New York Times*, Aug. 19, 1906, p. 7, col. 3.

90. Ibid. The Chicago–New York distance was about 1,000 miles, not 900 miles.

91. *Scientific American Supplement*, Sept. 8, 1906, p. 25646.

92. *New York Times*, Aug. 19, 1906, p. 7, col. 3.

93. *New York Herald*, Aug. 19, 1906, p. 16, col. 3.

94. *New York Times*, Aug. 19, 1906, p. 7, col. 3.

95. *Air Cooled News*, December 1956, p. 21; and "Whitman's Whirlwind Drive," *Motor World*, Aug. 16, 1906, p. 498.

96. *New York Times*, Dec. 1, 1907, sec. 5, p. 2, col. 2.

97. "Men and Motor Who Broke the Cross Country Record," *Toledo (Ohio) Blade*, Aug. 21, 1906, p. 10, col. 5.

98. *Motor Way*, Aug. 23, 1906, p. 8.

99. *New York Herald*, Aug. 18, 1906, p. 5, col. 2; *New York Herald*, Aug. 19, 1906, p. 16, col. 3; and *Scientific American Supplement*, Sept. 8, 1906, p. 25646.

100. *New York Herald*, Aug. 19, 1906, p. 16, col. 3.

101. *New York Times*, Aug. 26, 1906, p. 5, col. 5.

102. "New Time from Chicago by Record-Making Auto," *New York Times*, Sept. 7, 1906, p. 10, col. 7.

103. "Franklin Lowers Chicago–New York Mark," *Automobile*, Aug. 29, 1907, p. 296; and "Chicago–New York Record Broken," *Motor Age*, Aug. 29, 1907, p. 4.

104. "A Record-Breaking Run," editorial, *Motor World*, Aug. 23, 1906, p. 537.

Chapter 7

1. "One Man's Family Tour from Coast to Coast," *Automobile*, May 28, 1908, p. 733.

2. "Crossing Continent in Auto," *Chicago Daily Tribune*, May 18, 1908, p. 11, col. 7; and "Murdoch [*sic*] Tourists at Philadelphia," *New York Times*, May 26, 1908, p. 8, col. 5.

3. In several 1908 news articles, Murdock refers to a five-day food supply. In an account he wrote for *Motor Age* years later (see J. M. Murdock, "From Coast to Coast in a Motor Car," Aug. 17, 1911, p. 5), however, he calls it a seven-day supply.

4. "From Pacific to Atlantic in a Big Touring Auto," *San Diego Union*, June 7, 1908, p. 12, col. 1; and *Automobile*, May 28, 1908, p. 735.

5. J. M. Murdock, *A Family Tour from Ocean to Ocean* (Detroit: Packard Motor Car Co., 1908).

6. "Across the Continent in Big Touring Car," *New York Times*, Dec. 30, 1906, p. 8, col. 3.

7. Gary Bragg of the Wheels O' Time Museum in Dunlap, Illinois, near Peoria, generously provided me with copies of the two Emma Gehr journals in his possession. Florence Chadbourne and Lorene Dodd of the Genealogical Society of North Central Washington in Wenatchee sent me a wealth of biographical information on the two families. Other trip information is from two dozen articles that appeared in the *Wenatchee (Wash.) Daily World*, the *Wenatchee (Wash.) Republic*, and the *Peoria (Ill.) Herald-Transcript* between May 31, 1906 and March 28, 1907, and from *Automobile* and *Motor Way*.

8. *New York Times*, May 26, 1908, p. 8, col. 5.

9. *San Diego Union*, June 7, 1908, p. 12, col. 1.

10. *Automobile*, May 28, 1908, p. 733. The *New York Times*, May 26, 1908, p. 8, col. 5, gives a similar version.

11. *Motor Age*, Aug. 17, 1911, p. 3.

12. "Johnstown Family Crossing Continent in a Touring Car," *Johnstown (Pa.) Daily Tribune*, May 4, 1908, p. 1.

13. *Motor Age*, Aug. 17, 1911, p. 3.

14. For biographical details of the Murdock family, see Southwest Pennsylvania Genealogical Services, *Biographical and Portrait Cyclopedia of Cambria County, Pennsylvania* (Laughlintown, Pa.: SPGS, n.d.), pp. 240–41; and John E. Gable, *History of Cambria County, Pennsylvania* (Topeka, Kan.: Historical Publishing Co., 1926), pp. 1109–10. Press accounts generally agreed on the children's ages, but see *Automobile*, May 28, 1908, p. 733, which gives Jacob Jr.'s age as 8 instead of 10.

15. "Family Starts for New York," *Pasadena (Calif.) Daily News*, April 24, 1908, p. 10, col. 1.

16. In this and the following paragraph, information on Murdock's background is from Southwest Pennsylvania Genealogical Services, *Biographical and Portrait Cyclopedia*, pp. 240–41; and Gable, *History of Cambria County, Pennsylvania*, pp. 1109–10.

17. A. L. Westgard, "Long Distance Touring in America," *Club Journal*, May 1, 1909, p. 84, mentions Murdock's club membership.

18. "A Family Tour across the Continent," *Automobile Topics*, May 30, 1908, p. 508.

19. Gable, *History of Cambria County, Pennsylvania*, p. 1110.

20. *Automobile*, May 28, 1908, pp. 733–34.

21. *Motor Age*, Aug. 17, 1911, pp. 3, 7.

22. *Johnstown (Pa.) Daily Tribune*, May 4, 1908, p. 9. Murdock (in *Motor Age*, Aug. 17, 1911, p. 7) says the winch weighed 100 pounds, half the weight claimed by the *Johnstown Daily Tribune*.

23. Murdock, *A Family Tour from Ocean to Ocean*, p. 7. From this point on, unattributed quotations are from Murdock's *A Family Tour from Ocean to Ocean* booklet, and will not be cited individually.

24. *Motor Age*, Aug. 17, 1911, p. 7.

25. *Automobile*, May 28, 1908, p. 735. The article here quotes Murdock as saying he carried 250 feet of rope, but elsewhere (p. 734) reports that he said 150 feet. In *A Family Tour from Ocean to Ocean* (p. 7), Murdock says he strapped on the rear luggage carrier a box "containing two hundred feet of ¼-inch rope, which was never used; one hundred feet of ⅞-inch, 50 feet of ⅜-inch and 50 feet of 1¼-inch Manilla rope for general emergency use"—400 feet in all.

26. *New York Times*, May 26, 1908, p. 8, col. 5.

27. *Motor Age*, Aug. 17, 1911, p. 7.

28. Ibid.

29. *Johnstown (Pa.) Daily Tribune*, May 4, 1908, p. 1.

30. Beverly Rae Kimes, ed., *Packard: A History of the Motor Car and the Company* (Princeton, N.J.: Princeton Publishing Co., 1978), p. 117.

31. *Motor Age*, Aug. 17, 1911, pp. 7–8.

32. *Automobile*, May 28, 1908, p. 735.

33. "Packard 'Thirty' for 1908," *Motor News*, July 1907, p. 2.

34. Specifications are from *Motor News*, July 1907, pp. 2–4; "Packard Gasoline Cars," *Cycle and Automobile Trade Journal*, March 1908, p. 82; ALAM, *Hand Book of Gasoline Automobiles* (New York: Association of Licensed Automobile Manufacturers, 1908), p. 51; *Packard "Thirty," 1908*, a factory catalog; and Kimes, *Packard*, pp. 110, 777, 803.

35. *Motor Age*, Aug. 17, 1911, pp. 7, 4; and "Start on Trip to New York by Auto," *Los Angeles Examiner*, April 25, 1908, p. 7, col. 1.

36. *Pasadena (Calif.) Daily News*, April 24, 1908, p. 10, col. 1.

37. When the travelers later loaded the car with extra gas, water, and supplies for the trip across Nevada, the Packard's total weight once again approached 5,500 pounds. At Egbert, Wyoming, east of Cheyenne, Murdock ran the car onto a scale. Even minus the extra supplies they had carried in Nevada, the transcontinental Packard weighed 5,300 pounds, he said.

38. *Motor Age*, Aug. 17, 1911, p. 6; and *Automobile*, May 28, 1908, p. 734.

39. *Motor Age*, Aug. 17, 1911, pp. 4–6.

40. *Automobile*, May 28, 1908, p. 734.

41. *Motor Age*, Aug. 17, 1911, p. 6.

42. *Automobile*, May 28, 1908, p. 734.

43. Ibid.

44. *San Diego Union*, June 7, 1908, p. 12, col. 1.

45. *Automobile*, May 28, 1908, pp. 734–35.

46. Ibid.

47. "Traveling in Family Motor," *Ogden (Utah) Morning Examiner*, May 3, 1908, p. 8, col. 6; and *Johnstown (Pa.) Daily Tribune*, May 4, 1908, p. 1.

48. *Ogden (Utah) Morning Examiner*, May 3, 1908, p. 8, col. 6.

49. "Murdock Car in Wild Wyoming," *Johnstown (Pa.) Daily Tribune*, May 11, 1908, p. 1, col. 2.

50. "Local Gossip," *Wyoming Press* (Evanston), May 9, 1908, p. 8, col. 3.

51. George Schuster, mechanic and a driver of the Thomas racer, recalled Spaulding's assistance in George N. Schuster and John T. Mahoney, *The Longest Auto Race* (New York: John Day Co., 1966), p. 142. For Spaulding's good-roads efforts, see Lincoln Highway Association, *The Lincoln Highway: The Story of a Crusade That Made Transportation History* (New York: Dodd, Mead & Co., 1935), pp. 70, 140.

52. *Johnstown (Pa.) Daily Tribune*, May 11, 1908, p. 3.

53. Hugo Alois Taussig, *Retracing the Pioneers: From West to East in an Automobile* (San Francisco: privately published, 1910), p. 41. For the make of Taussig's auto and his occupation, see "Auto Here Making Trip from Frisco to New York," *Wyoming Tribune* (Cheyenne), June 22, 1909, p. 1, col. 4.

54. *Motor Age*, Aug. 17, 1911, p. 6.

55. "Short Stories about People and Things Here and Hereabouts," *Rawlins (Wyo.) Republican*, May 9, 1908, p. 4, col. 3; and "From Coast to Coast in Big Touring Car," *Laramie (Wyo.) Boomerang*, May 9, 1908, p. 1, col. 1.

56. "In an Auto," *Wyoming Tribune* (Cheyenne), May 11, 1908, p. 5, col. 3.

57. *Motor Age*, Aug. 17, 1911, pp. 1–2.

58. "Automobiling from Los Angeles to Pennsylvania with Family," *Omaha (Neb.) World-Herald*, May 14, 1908, p. 3, col. 7; and "Iowa Mud the Toughest Ever," *Johnstown (Pa.) Daily Tribune*, May 19, 1908, p. 1, col. 5.

59. *Omaha (Neb.) World-Herald*, May 14, 1908, p. 3, col. 7; and *Johnstown (Pa.) Daily Tribune*, May 19, 1908, p. 1, col. 5.

60. *Johnstown (Pa.) Daily Tribune*, May 19, 1908, p. 1, col. 5.

61. Though his route Thursday took him through Ames, home to Iowa State University (then called Iowa State College), Murdock fails to identify the "college town" to which he alluded. Regardless, ISU's colors—once black, silver, and white and now yellow and red—have never been yellow and black, according to a special-collections archivist at the ISU library. These *are* University of Iowa colors, but Murdock passed well to the north of Iowa City. He was perhaps referring to a small, private college no longer in existence.

62. *Johnstown (Pa.) Daily Tribune*, May 19, 1908, p. 1, col. 6.

63. Ibid.

64. Ibid.

65. *Automobile Topics*, May 30, 1908, p. 509.

66. "Fast Packard Trip," *Chicago Inter Ocean*, May 17, 1908, p. 6, col. 3 of classified section; and *Chicago Daily Tribune*, May 18, 1908, p. 11, col. 7.

67. *Johnstown (Pa.) Daily Tribune*, May 19, 1908, p. 1, col. 6.

68. "Locals," *Warren (Ohio) Weekly Tribune*, May 21, 1908, p. 5, col. 4.

69. Ibid.

70. "Murdock Party Reaches City," *Johnstown (Pa.) Daily Tribune*, May 22, 1908, p. 1, col. 5; and *Automobile*, May 28, 1908, p. 733.

71. *Johnstown (Pa.) Daily Tribune*, May 22, 1908, p. 1, col. 5.

72. *Pasadena (Calif.) Daily News*, April 24, 1908, p. 10, col. 1.

73. "Murdock Party on the Home Stretch," *Johnstown (Pa.) Daily Tribune*, May 25, 1908, p. 1, col. 5.

74. *Automobile*, May 28, 1908, p. 735.

75. "Coast to Coast in Only 25 Days," *Johnstown (Pa.) Daily Tribune*, May 27, 1908, p. 1, col. 6. In *A Family Tour from Ocean to Ocean* (p. 25), Murdock claimed four autos escorted him from Philadelphia to New York City.

76. *Automobile*, May 28, 1908, p. 735.

77. "Long Auto Trip Over," *New York Tribune*, May 27, 1908, p. 10, col. 4.

78. *Automobile*, May 28, 1908, p. 735; and *Motor Age*, Aug. 17, 1911, pp. 3, 8.

79. Ibid., p. 733.

80. Ibid., p. 735; Tom Mahoney, "Coast to Coast in 32 Days," *American Petroleum Institute Quarterly* (autumn 1957): 15; and *New York Tribune*, May 27, 1908, p. 10, col. 4.

81. *Club Journal*, May 1, 1909, p. 85.

82. "Current Comment," editorial, *Motor Age* May 28, 1908, p. 9.

83. *Automobile*, May 28, 1908, p. 733.

84. "Over the Mojave Desert into the Jaws of Death Valley," *Motor Age*, July 7, 1910, pp. 24–25; and "Through Death Valley in an Automobile," *Automobile*, July 14, 1910, pp. 46–47.

85. Lincoln Highway Association, *The Lincoln Highway*, p. 6; and Tom Mahoney, "Packard—A Great Name Passes On," *Automobile Quarterly* 1, no. 3 (fall 1962): 227.

86. *Motor Age*, Aug. 17, 1911, p. 4.

87. *New York Times*, May 26, 1908, p. 8, col. 5; and *Motor Age*, Aug. 17, 1911, p. 1.

88. *Motor Age*, Aug. 17, 1911, p. 8.

Conclusion

1. "Ocean to Ocean Race," *New York Tribune*, May 9, 1905, p. 5, col. 6.

2. Emily Post, *By Motor to the Golden Gate* (New York: D. Appleton and Co., 1916), p. 67.

3. Lincoln Highway Association, *A Complete Official Road Guide of the Lincoln Highway*, 5th ed. (Detroit: Lincoln Highway Association, 1924), pp. 41–43.

4. "Long Ocean to Ocean Trail Is Blazed," *Motor Age*, Aug. 17, 1911, p. 8.

5. "Packard Tourists Arrive in Chicago," *Chicago Inter Ocean*, Aug. 11, 1903, p. 1, col. 7 of sports section.

ILLUSTRATION CREDITS

AAMA	Reprinted with permission of the American Automobile Manufacturers Association, Detroit
FLP	Automobile Reference Collection, Free Library of Philadelphia
HHFC	H. H. Franklin Club
JSH	John S. Hammond
JW	Jim Winton
MHS	Mattapoisett (Mass.) Historical Society
MOT	Reproduced from *Motor Magazine* © 1931 by permission of the Hearst Corporation
MSU	Michigan State University Archives and Historical Collections, East Lansing
NAHC	National Automotive History Collection, Detroit Public Library
NAM	Courtesy of the William F. Harrah Foundation National Automobile Museum, Reno, Nevada
OHC	Oldsmobile History Center, Lansing, Michigan
UVSC	Special Collections, University of Vermont Library, Burlington

343

INDEX